D0147327

# A Contemporary Reader for Creative Writing

# Books by Robert DeMaria

## NOVELS

*Carnival of Angels*
*Clodia*
*Don Juan in Lourdes*
*The Satyr*
*The Decline and Fall of America*
*To Be a King*
*Outbreak*
*The Empress*
*Blowout*
*Secret Places*
*A Passion for Power*
*Sons and Brothers*
*Stone of Destiny*

## NON-FICTION

*A Theme-Correction Guide*
*Subjects and Sources*
(with Raymond Short)
*The Language of Grammar*
*The College Handbook of Creative Writing*
*A Contemporary Reader for Creative Writing*
(with Ellen Hope Meyer)

# A Contemporary Reader for Creative Writing

**Robert DeMaria**     **Ellen Hope Meyer**

Dowling College

**Harcourt Brace College Publishers**

Fort Worth  Philadelphia  San Diego  New York  Orlando  Austin  San Antonio
Toronto  Montreal  London  Sydney  Tokyo

| Publisher | Ted Buchholz |
| Acquisitions Editor | Stephen T. Jordan |
| Senior Project Editor | Cliff Crouch |
| Production Manager | J. Montgomery Shaw |
| Senior Art Director | Serena Barnett Manning |
| Permissions Editor | Julia C. Stewart |

**Library of Congress Cataloging-in-Publication Data**

DeMaria, Robert.
    A contemporary reader for creative writing / Robert DeMaria, Ellen
Hope Meyer.
        p.   cm.
    Includes bibliographical references (p.) and index.
    ISBN 0-15-500727-0
    1. Creative writing.   2. College readers.   I. Meyer, Ellen Hope.
II. Title.
PN3355.D32   1993                       93–3647
808'.02—dc20                          CIP

**International Standard Book Number:** 0-15-500727-0

Copyright © 1994 by Harcourt Brace & Company

All rights reserved. No part of this publication may be reproduced or
transmitted in any form or by any means, electronic or mechanical,
including photocopy, recording, or any information storage or retrieval
system, without permission in writing from the publisher.

Requests for permission to make copies of any part of the work should
be mailed to: Permissions Department, Harcourt Brace & Company,
8th floor, Orlando, Florida 32887.

Special acknowledgments of copyright ownership and of permission
to reproduce works included in this volume precede the index and
constitute an extension of this page.

*Address for editorial correspondence:*
                  Harcourt Brace College Publishers
                  301 Commerce Street, Suite 3700
                  Fort Worth, Texas 76102

*Address for orders:*   Harcourt Brace, Inc.
                  6277 Sea Harbor Drive
                  Orlando, Florida 32887

*Phone:*             800 / 782-4479, or
                  (*in Florida only*) 800 / 433-0001

Cover illustration by Zita Asbaghi, New York

Printed in the United States of America

3 4 5 6 7 8 9 0 1 2 3    016    9 8 7 6 5 4 3 2 1

# *Preface*

The purpose of this book is to provide readings for Creative Writing workshops. The short stories, poems, and plays included have been chosen because they illustrate certain specific aspects of the writer's craft. Mostly our choices represent current writing, reaching back, with one or two exceptions, no further than twenty years.

Each selection has been assigned to an appropriate chapter, but most of the choices can illustrate a number of points. A story with a strong plot, for instance, might also have good characters or a significant setting. A poem with startling metaphors might also have an uncommon theme.

We have chosen contemporary works on the assumption that a current frame of reference will be more useful to student writers than historical examples of literary technique. The latter are commonly read in literature courses, where the aim is to help the reader to understand and appreciate them. In writing workshops we are interested in the nuts and bolts of literature, the craft of writing. Giving some preference here to contemporary work does not mean that the classics cannot provide us with adequate illustrations, but, rather, that the use of illustrations from recent work has an added advantage: It gives apprentice writers a chance to find out what is going on right now in their field, what ideas are being explored, and what techniques are being used.

Each of our eleven chapters deals with a specific aspect of the writer's craft. The readings that illustrate each aspect are preceded by a brief introduction, designed to encourage class discussion. At the end of each chapter are suggested writing assignments.

Some instructors will enjoy taking a systematic approach to the techniques of craft, but others may feel that a workshop should be an unstructured forum in which manuscripts can be read and discussed. Either way, it is useful to have a few good illustrations available. Furthermore, it is useful to have those illustrations arranged in such a way as to be readily accessible.

This reader can be used independently or in conjunction with Robert DeMaria's *College Handbook of Creative Writing* (Harcourt, 1991; second edition in press), which follows basically the same organization.

It is our hope that this book will enrich the writing workshop experience. If it succeeds, then some of the credit must go to those people who were kind enough to assist us in this project. We thank Claire Dudley of *Choice* magazine for reading the first draft and making invaluable suggestions. Especially helpful were all those wonderful editors of literary magazines and quarterlies who made copies of their publications available to us, and who, in some cases, screened their issues for the best work they had published. The very heart of any reader or anthology is, of course, the material itself: We thank the contributing authors for their generosity in allowing us to use their work. Finally, we thank our editors at Harcourt Brace for understanding what we wanted to do in this book and helping us to do it.

*Robert DeMaria*
*Ellen Hope Meyer*

# CONTENTS

### Poetry

## 3 Character 91

### Fiction

### Drama

### Poetry

## 4 Plot 135

### Fiction

### Drama

# 9  Thoughts    321

# 10  Time    359

# 11  Images and Sounds    389

# CONTENTS BY GENRE

## FICTION

# POETRY

# DRAMA

# Introduction

Creative Writing as an academic field of study has become increasingly popular in recent years at both the graduate and undergraduate levels. It is a performance field involving workshops in which students produce original works of fiction, poetry, and drama. Some programs include dramas for film and television as well as for the live stage.

Fiction, poetry, and drama are linked together because they spring from the human imagination. A logical Martian visiting our planet might find it totally absurd for such an intelligent form of life to devote so much of its time to dreams and fantasies, to things that do not actually exist. We ourselves are sometimes amazed to discover that certain companies are willing to pay millions of dollars for the right to publish one of these fictions or to make it into a film.

Not only are works of the imagination in demand as entertainments, they are highly regarded as serious avenues to wisdom and the mystical experience of beauty. Along the path to modern civilization there are not only monuments to statesmen, philosophers, and scientists, but to great artists, including writers. All the evidence points to the simple conclusion that acts of the imagination are important to the human psyche. Some writers talk about *inspiration,* as though their works are secret messages from distant places. Others talk about tapping the unconscious mind, a journey inward that is sometimes as mysterious as the journey outward. Imaginative writing seems to be related to the dream process, which studies have revealed to be essential to human sanity. Such observations are the subjects of continuing research and speculation. The temptation to pursue these matters is great, but that pursuit would take us away from the business at hand, which is to find good contemporary examples of the writer's craft.

## The Craft of Writing

Once we get away from the quest for the ultimate truth about writing, about why it exists and how it functions, we can turn our attention to the refreshingly mundane subject of the writer's craft. In Creative Writing workshops it is more important to examine techniques than it is to indulge in philosophical combat. Writers are not really philosophers. They are more *doers* than *thinkers*. Their dominant urge is to construct a great mirror of human experience, and possibly to create a thing of beauty. When they succeed, we see our world—and perhaps ourselves—more clearly.

A writer is as much a craftsman as a carpenter or silversmith or sculptor is. Like them, he (or she) must learn the fundamentals of the job. While craft is hardly a substitute for talent, it is just as essential, providing the writer with certain tools and techniques that are useful in making an artifact. Writers can be brilliant and innovative, but they can't really reinvent the wheel of art.

When we study the craft of writing we usually begin by identifying four basic elements: *theme, plot, setting,* and *characters*—the writer's job, after all, is to tell a story or recite a poem or prepare a script for a drama. These four basics deal more with content than methods. Every literary work has a *theme,* some idea or dramatic focus. Almost always something happens (*plot*) no matter how trivial it might seem, and if something happens, then it has to happen somewhere (*setting*), and it has to happen to someone (*characters*).

Writers have always faced the difficult problem of how to deal with these basic elements. Although narration involves certain fundamental techniques, there have been changes and developments over the years. Now, more than ever before, there are many approaches to telling a story. In earlier times, fairly rigid literary conventions were the norm. Today there is greater freedom, and we have the advantage of both traditional techniques and innovations.

*Technique* does not refer to content; it is a *way* of doing something. Some teachers refer to techniques as *strategies*. Writers are faced with numerous technical problems. It is necessary, for instance, to *describe* characters and locations. Every narrative has to be told from a certain *point of view*. The *tone* and *style* have to be appropriate to the content. When characters speak, their *dialogue* must be presented effectively. If their *thoughts* are to be revealed to the reader, a way must be found to accomplish this, and since all action takes place in *time*, the writer must deal with such things as period, sequence, duration, and transition.

This is the stuff of which the writer's craft is made. Good writers over the years have met these challenges successfully, and new writers can learn from them.

## Learning to Write

Ever since Creative Writing workshops were first offered to college students, there have been critics who maintain that writing cannot be taught, that workshops are a waste of time. Some go even further: They claim that the workshop has a dampening effect on the writer's imagination and imparts a deadly similarity to the works that are produced in such settings. The implication is that workshops are no better than factories.

Not too long ago the *Mississippi Review* devoted an entire special issue to workshops. It included fiction and poetry that was produced in writing workshops and a collection of brief statements by thirty-eight writing teachers. This excellent project (vol. 19, nos. 1 and 2) sheds considerable light on the kind of writing produced by workshop students and the techniques and attitudes of the teachers. The editors came to an interesting conclusion: "The work we saw was as complex and interesting and difficult and diverse as writing gets."

We are persuaded by this project and other evidence that workshop writing is no different than non-workshop writing. The quality of the work that comes out of workshops suggests that the experience is beneficial. The variety in style suggests that student writers do not conform to any rigid rules of structure or point of view. Moreover, the variety in content suggests that students have lives and backgrounds that are not significantly different from the lives of writers in general. Attending a writing workshop does not disqualify anyone from all the usual intensities and passions of life. Nor does avoiding workshops guarantee a life of high adventure. The British poet Philip Larkin was a librarian. The American poet Wallace Stevens was an insurance executive. Thom Gunn, on the other hand, whose poems sometimes reek of motorcycle fumes, studied with academic masters and was later a teacher.

Though there are still unresolved controversies in the field, most teachers of Creative Writing would probably agree with what Paul Ruffin (editor of *The Texas Review*) had to say in the *Mississippi Review* symposium: "Whereas I would be among the first to agree that an instructor cannot teach just any person to write publishable poetry and prose, I do believe that anyone with a trace of innate talent in the direction of creative literature can be taught to improve on his craft." Further on he says: "The study of the techniques of accomplished writers (the masters, if you will) is essential, as is the mastery of basic theory and terminology . . . ."

That is why we have put together *A Contemporary Reader for Creative Writing.*

# Theme

## Introduction

## Fiction

Lynne Sharon Schwartz     *Killing the Bees*
Daniel Meltzer     *People*

## Drama

Max Apple     *Trotsky's Bar Mitzvah*

## Poetry

Alan Dugan     *Against the Text "Art is Immortal"*
David Ignatow     *Witness*
Mary B. Campbell     *Warning: Nuclear Waste Dump*
A. R. Ammons     *The History of Motion*
Claire Nicolas White     *Home-Coming*

## Writing Assignments

A literary work can be about almost anything, but it must be about *something*. When Virginia Woolf discussed "the proper stuff of fiction" and concluded that there were no limits to what one could write about, she was trying to open a door that James Joyce had already broken down. By now we all know that anything goes, at least as far as subject matter is concerned.

The *subject* of a literary work, however, is not the same as its *theme*. Nor should theme be confused with *situation* or *plot*. All of these terms are meaningful and useful, but they need careful definition.

A *subject* is a broad category such as love, war, madness, good, or evil. We can say that *Hamlet* is about revenge, but, obviously, that does not really tell us what the play is all about. We can go on to describe the *situation*. We can say that the ghost of Hamlet's father visits him to reveal that he has been murdered and to insist that it is Hamlet's duty to avenge that death. Still, we will not know what the play is all about. We can add a detailed description of the *plot*, which is a summary of the action. We will feel more fully informed but not entirely enlightened. Finally, we can summarize the *theme*. We can say that self-doubt and indecision can cripple one's ability to act and can lead to tragedy.

*The subject* is a broad classification of materials.

*The situation* is a set of circumstances with which the work begins.

*The plot* is a summary of the action.

*The theme* is the central message of the work or its central dramatic impact.

These four aspects of a literary work may help to describe it, but no description of a literary work can take the place of the whole thing. The main point of an essay is fairly easy to capture in a statement. In imaginative literature, however, we are not dealing merely with statements; we are dealing with the re-creation of experience.

Naturally, all themes are not profound or "literary." Light entertainments, even comic-book sorts of adventures, have some kind of simple theme such as the struggle between the good guys and the bad guys. In serious writing, the theme is very important. It is central to the whole work. It informs and unifies the work. It reflects the writer's values and ideas and particular view of the world.

Some themes are universal, of course, but changing times give rise to new themes. Literary works that reach us from the remote past seem to deal with epics of war, with grand passions, with high tragedies and eternal love. There are no ordinary people in the dramas of ancient Greece, and if there was a Willy Loman peddling his wares in London, Shakespeare was not moved to write about him, unless one can argue that Lear was his Loman.

Matters of morality loom large in earlier literature. There was always an interest in characters, though often they were larger than life. But with the industrial revolution and the electronic age there came new concerns: the plight of the poor, social injustice, alienation, loneliness. The structure of the traditional family is threatened. Coming of age in the modern world is horribly confusing. The relationship between the sexes is in a state of chronic overhaul. Sex has become an obsession, money a devil and a god, crime an epidemic and an entertainment. We are haunted by natural and man-made disasters. We live in a world of philosophical and political chaos. The themes of contemporary writing, as in all periods, reflect both the spirit of the age and the insights of the individual writer.

The Western world has been haunted by the Holocaust since World War II, when Hitler ordered the extermination of the Jews and other groups, establishing the perfect Aryan type— golden-haired and powerful—as the goal of this "purification." Ilse, the central character in Lynne Sharon Schwartz' "Killing the Bees," is haunted by events of her childhood in Germany. Her parents were Jews; her father (it is implied) was killed in a gas chamber, while she and her mother escaped. She was stung by a bee during the escape.

As the story opens, she is living comfortably with her American husband and daughter when they discover a large hive of bees in the walls of their house. They try several times to eliminate the bees, but only succeed in minor massacres. Finally, they are forced to call in an exterminator, a wonderfully tall, muscular, golden-haired young man, to spray the bees in their chamber within the walls. The parallels are fairly clear.

Ilse can't understand herself. She can't sleep. She listens all night to the sound of the bees. She identifies with the bees (the Jews, allegorically speaking), but she wants them killed. She is a person who has learned to behave "as she perceived other normal girls to behave, a tactic which worked so well that she adopted it for the rest of her life." She has assimilated into her new culture. Killing the bees is the accepted thing to do, the normal thing, but her father was killed that way when exterminating Jews was the accepted thing. The parallels haunt her. The conflict exhausts her. She feels guilty. After the Aryan exterminator has done his job, Ilse washes her hands (like Lady Macbeth).

Her family does not know what is going on in her mind. When her daughter suggests that they use the dead bees as fertilizer (the same proposal was made during WW II with reference to the Jews), Ilse almost hits her. The story conveys the gap between a repressed inner life and the ordinary decorums of the outer life.

As is usual in a well-developed story, it is difficult to reduce the theme or themes to a simple statement. Could they be summed up by saying, "Thou shalt not kill?" Hardly. Nevertheless, the complex theme is the heart of the story, just as the complex symbol of the bee community is at the center of Ilse's consciousness.

In "People," Daniel Meltzer gives us a witty account of the debasement of language in our high-tech world. He uses an exaggerated contemporary lingo that is drawn largely from the world of business and the yuppie culture of New York. The ingenious wordplay has a satirical purpose: It reflects the coldness and depersonalization of the midtown marketplace, and perhaps of the world at large. Country music lingo is represented here as well. The reader is left with the uneasy feeling that an impoverished language may lead to a loss of reality in personal relations.

*Trotsky's Bar Mitzvah,* by Max Apple, deals with several themes familiar to Americans, including the conflict between immigrant tradition and the New World, and what that does to family relationships. In this play, plot and theme are well married, as the boy is forced to choose between his grandfather's ideas and a New-World Bar Mitzvah. Another thematic strand is expressed by the black assistant baker, who finds it ridiculous that the grandfather cannot give up his intellectual abstractions for simple humanity.

Several of the poets challenge the famous adage *vita brevis, ars longa* (life is short but art endures), a favorite subject for poetry. Here they question whether or not writing and the arts in general can have any kind of lasting value in a world that increasingly appears to be doomed. Alan Dugan, for instance, ends his discussion of the erosion of works of art with a reference to modern techniques of destruction. "This time," he says, "we can really blast the beast of man to bits." And in "Witness," David Ignatow declares that "We cannot write ourselves into eternal life." In spite of that, he says, writers continue to write, and he advances a reason for that. Mary B. Campbell writes with force and humor about environmental perils. She challenges poetry to outlast the thousands of years which may be only the half-life of plutonium. A.R. Ammons compares the process of life with the formation of art in "The History of Motion."

Racial and family relationships, the Holocaust, alienation, art, environment, and poverty: Such is the subject matter of modern life, or at least some of it. It is the author's point of view which illuminates these issues, gives them meaning and artistic shape. Another major source of thematic material these days is the endlessly fascinating subject of interior exploration and revelation. In Claire Nicolas White's "Home-Coming," images of interiors give way to a sense of self, a psychic interior. Many selections in this reader will serve as further examples of the current interest in individual consciousness, including Jennifer Egan's "Sacred Heart," Margaret Atwood's "Variations on the Word Sleep," and Josephine Jacobsen's "The Woods." A conflict between individual needs and the pressures to be active in improving the world is presented in Carol Ascher's "In Sight of Josephine." In this story everything is played out in the arena of one person's consciousness.

*Lynne Sharon Schwartz*

# Killing the Bees

1    After Ilse and Mitch had both been stung twice, Mitch sprayed
insecticide around the flower beds at the side of the house,
where the bees seemed to congregate. But the very next day
Cathy, their youngest child, got stung on the back of the neck.
It was a bright May afternoon, the three of them out on the
lawn with the Sunday papers, Cathy plugged into her Walkman. Quiet Ilse made a great fuss, jumped up and grabbed a
handful of damp soil from the flower bed to slap on the bite,
then crooned soothing words—as if, Cathy said with a brave
10    patronizing smile, she were an infant and not almost fifteen.
       "But doesn't it hurt a lot?"
       "It hurts, Mom, but I'll live."
       "What's the matter?" Mitch must have been dozing be-
hind the travel section. He rearranged his body in the lawn
chair and blinked, trying to look alert. He was a graying man
of fifty-three, handsome in a ruddy, solid, ex-athlete's way,
with strikingly pale blue eyes. He owned a chain of hardware
stores. A safe man, Ilse thought each evening when he returned
from work. And decent, competent, sexy: mornings, watching
20    him dress—the ritual bending, reaching, zipping, and buttoning—she felt a reflexive pleasure, compounded with satisfaction, like the interest on capital, at how durable this pleasure
had proved. If that was love, then she loved him well enough.
       "It's those bees again. We really must do something
about them. Poor baby. Come, let me wash it and put on some
ointment."
       "God, what would you do if I had rabies?"
       Ilse knew why she was making a fuss: the one time she
herself had been stung as a child—at four years old—her
30    usually attentive mother hardly seemed to care. That baffling
lapse, the utter failure to respond properly, even more than the
throng at the airport or the loudspeaker barking, the pinched,
scared faces and the forest of gleaming tall boots, told Ilse
something portentous was happening. Her father had already
kissed them goodbye and disappeared, leaving her mother
teary, and she was close to tears again five minutes later,

showing some papers to a mustached, uniformed man at a desk, who waved his clipboard in the air and called them to a halt in a gritty voice. Soon, like a little firecracker fizzling out,
40   he spat a bad name at them and sent them on. Her mother was tugging her by the hand, rushing towards the stairs at the plane, when Ilse let out a howl.

"Shh! Don't make noise. What is it?"

"Something is in my dress! In back!"

Her mother yanked at the dress and slapped her back hard—to kill the bee, she said later—but that only made the sting worse.

"Be still now, Ilse!" she ordered. "I'll take care of it afterwards."
50   But Ilse wailed running up the stairs, and as they entered the plane people looked up disapprovingly. Her mother kept her head bowed. Only when they were above the clouds did she become herself again, rubbing spit on the sting till Ilse calmed down.

"When we meet our cousins," she said, belatedly kissing the sore spot, "can you say 'How do you do,' in English? How do you do?" She exaggerated the shape of the words on her lips and Ilse repeated. How do you do. But for long after, she felt betrayed in her moment of need.
60   In England, when she asked for her father, her mother said "He's coming. He'll come as soon as he can." In time she understood there was a war going on: the children at school wouldn't let her play and made fun of the way she spoke. Her mother couldn't get a job and often they were hungry. Just as the hunger was becoming unbearable, food would appear, Ilse never knew how. If she complained, her mother said cryptically, "Still we're lucky. Lucky." She stopped asking about her father and eventually the war was over. When they went looking for a flat in London she heard her mother tell the landla-
70   dies he was killed in the war. Then her mother would murmur some words very low, as if she were embarrassed, and the landladies' granite faces would loosen a bit, and a Mrs. Soloway finally let them have a room.

In bed with Mitch that night, Ilse heard a humming noise, muffled, but rhythmic and relentless like the plangent moan of an infirmary.

"Listen. Do you hear anything?" she whispered.

"Only you breathing." Mitch lay with his head on her stomach, his arms locked around her hips. Always, after they
80   made love, his voice was heavy and sweet with a childlike

contentment. "You sound sensational, Ilse. Do it a little harder." He began kissing her belly again.

She smiled even though the noise agitated her. "Not that, silly. Listen. It sounds like something in the wall."

He groaned and sat up, businesslike, turning on the lamp as if that could make the noise clearer. They stared at each other, concentrating, and indeed enlightenment came. "I bet it's those fucking bees. They've managed to get into the wall now. Jesus Christ!" He turned away to roll himself in the

90   sheets.

"Hey, I didn't put them there," Ilse said softly. "Come on back."

"You know what I'll have to do now? Make a hole in the goddamn wall and spray inside. Just what we needed. A bee colony."

"My sweet baby," she said, stroking him. "My prince to the rescue. My Saint George killing the dragon."

"It's going to stink to high heaven," he said.

Mitch slept, but hours later Ilse was still trapped in

100  wakefulness by the humming noise. She pictured a gigantic swarm of bees fluttering their wings together in the dark, a shuddering jellylike mass. It was an unbearable sound, ominous, droning. Of course, she thought. Drones.

The next two evenings Mitch forgot to bring the extra-strength spray home from the store. On the third day Ilse phoned to remind him. "Look, I hate to keep nagging, but I've hardly slept."

"They can't come out, Ilse."

"I know. I'm not afraid of bees anyway. It's the noise.

110  Just bring it, will you please?"

After dinner he listened with his ear to the wall for the place where the noise was loudest, then chipped with a screwdriver until a tiny hole appeared. Quickly he shoved a small rectangle of shirt cardboard over the hole, and using that as a shield, made the hole bigger. When it was about a half inch in diameter, he told Ilse to go out of the room and close the door. She closed the door but stayed, standing back. It didn't seem fair to protect herself while he was in danger. Besides, she felt an eerie fascination. Mitch moved the cardboard aside and

120  inserted the nozzle of the spray can. The smell was nasty and stinging, but not as bad as she had imagined. Then he covered the hole again and they fixed the cardboard to the wall with thumbtacks. Ilse heard a sharp crackling like the sound of damp twigs catching a flame.

"What's that?"

"It's them. That's what you wanted, isn't it? Let's just hope it gets them all."

A wave of nausea and dizziness assaulted her, and she lay down till it passed. That night she slept well, in blissful silence.

The following morning, one of her days off—she worked as a part-time secretary at a law firm in town—she was outside, kneeling to put in the marigolds, when she noticed a patch a few feet off that looked like speckled black velvet. She crawled closer. The corpses of bees, hundreds, thousands, the obscene remains of a massacre. She had never thought about where they would go, never thought further than getting rid of them. Why hadn't they simply rotted in the wall unseen? Peering up, she spied a dark mass the size of a cantaloupe, attached like a tumor to the outside wall not far from their bedroom window, and almost hidden by the thick leaves of the maple. Somehow they had never thought to look for a hive, but now it seemed obvious.

Ilse was not squeamish. She had disposed of dead ants and flies and even mice, but the sight of the slaughtered bees paralyzed her. She knelt in the garden for a long time, then dragged herself inside and phoned Mitch, but when he answered she found she couldn't tell him right away.

"This must be our lucky day," she said instead. "Both wanderers heard from." There had been a postcard from their son, Brian, who was working on a cattle ranch in Wyoming, and another from Melissa, who had just completed her second year of law school and, with three girlfriends, was recuperating for a week in Jamaica before starting her summer job.

"That's great." He sounded distracted.

Stammering a bit, Ilse mentioned the dead bees and the hive near the bedroom window.

"A hive eh? I should have known. Well, just sweep them up, Ilse, okay? I'll have a look when I get home."

"Yes, well—you can't imagine how hideous... These are enormous bees. It's like a battlefield.... What should I do with them?"

"Do with them? Put them in the garbage, sweetheart. Unless you want to hold a mass funeral."

"I see I shouldn't have bothered you."

"Ilse, it's just that I've got a store full of customers. Leave it if you can't do it. Or have Cathy do it. It's not worth bickering over."

170 　　　She tried sweeping them into a dustpan, but as she
watched the bodies roll and tumble, the wings and feelers lacing
and tangling, she felt faint. Finally she abandoned the task and
left the marigolds, too, for another day. When Cathy came
home from school she asked her to do it and Cathy obliged, with
pungent expressions of disgust but no apparent difficulty.

　　　Mitch got on a ladder and sprayed the hive. There was
silence for several nights and they thought it was over. Then
Ilse woke before dawn and heard the humming in the wall,
fainter, but still insistent. She began to weep, very quietly, so as
not to wake Mitch.

180 　　　After the war her mother got a clerical job at the National Gallery in London, where she met an American tour
guide and married him.

　　　"We're going to have a new life, darling," she told Ilse
excitedly. Mostly they spoke German when they were alone,
but her mother said this in English. "We're going to America
with Robbie. Denver. You'll love it, I know." Ilse nodded. She
was a silent child, the kind who seems full of secrets. At school
she had few friends, was politely enigmatic, and did her work
adequately, but the teachers nonetheless accused her of dream-
190 ing. In America she changed. Robbie was all right; he looked
like a cowboy and sounded like Gary Cooper, and Ilse treated
him as a casual friend of the family. But she did love America.
No one shunned her. They liked her British accent and were
eager to hear stories of life in London. I can be a normal girl,
she whispered to herself one morning in the mirror. From now
on. And she behaved as she perceived other normal girls to
behave, a tactic which worked so well that she adopted it for
the rest of her life. Meanwhile, when she was old enough to
understand, around Cathy's age, she went on a binge of read-
200 ing books about the war, till she was satisfied that she compre-
hended what had happened to her father, what his final years
or months had been like, and had lived them in her bones up to
the point where his own bones lay in a ditch, indistinguishable
from the millions of others.

　　　"You never talk about him." She expected her mother
would hedge and say, About who? but she was mistaken.

　　　"What can I say? He died in the war."

　　　"But I mean, about how."

　　　"Do you know how?" her mother asked.

210 　　　"Yes."

"Well, so do I. So ..."

She was craving a significant scene, tears and embraces, or lies and shouting, culminating in cloak-and-dagger truths, secret horrors not included in any books, and above all in profundities vast enough to connect the past to the present, but her mother offered nothing.

"Did you cry?"

"What a question, Ilse. I cried plenty, yes."

But she was not about to cry anew for Ilse. They were
220 lucky, her mother repeated with lips stiff and quaking. "Remember all your life what a lucky person you are."

Ilse fled from the room. Now she had long forgiven her mother. At the time they boarded the plane for London, she realized, the day she got stung, her mother was twenty-four years old. A girl the age of Melissa, who was swimming and dancing in the Caribbean moonlight and about to earn extravagant sums of money. And at the time of their talk, her mother had known Robbie for as long as she had known Ilse's father. Her mother was truly lucky. In compassion, Ilse
230 stopped pestering her and let her live her lucky life.

Twice more Mitch moved aside the cardboard and sprayed into the hole. Twice more the bees crackled, the room smelled, and the nights were silent, then the noise returned.

"It's no use. We need an exterminator." And he sighed a husbandly sigh of overwork.

"I'll take care of that." Ilse was expert at arranging for services and dealing with repairmen. In the yellow pages she found just what was needed: Ban-the-Bug, which promised to rid your home of pests for good. Ban-the-Bug's logo was a
240 familiar black-bordered circle with a black line running diagonally through the center. Three times a week Ilse saw that same symbol, but in red, on the door of Ban-the-Bomb, a local group with a small office opposite her own. Except instead of the mushroom cloud in the center, Ban-the-Bug's circle displayed a repulsive insect suggesting a cross between a winged cockroach and a centipede. The black line was firm and categorical: it meant, Ilse knew, No More, Get Rid Of, *Verboten.*

On the telephone, she did not even have to supply details. Ban-the-Bug understood all about the problem and
250 would send a man over late that afternoon.

"Don't worry, you'll never have to hear that sound again," a reassuring, motherly voice told Ilse.

Never again. She would sleep in peace. The soothing promise echoed as she shopped and chatted in the market and set out on the kitchen counter all the ingredients for a Chinese dinner. With another secretary from the law firm she was taking a course in Chinese cooking, and Mitch and Cathy had been teasing her for a demonstration. Cathy had brought a friend home from school, and both girls volunteered to help.

260 As Ilse sautéed garlic and ginger, the kitchen filled with a luxurious, tangy odor. She chopped the pork and set the girls to work on the peppers and scallions and cabbage.

The smell made her hungry, and as usual, hunger made her think of being hungry in London, such a different kind of hunger, long-lasting and tedious, like a sickness, and panicky, with no hope of ever being fully eased.

That was far away now, though. Her present hunger is the good kind, the hunger of anticipation.

The girls are jabbering across the large kitchen. Having

270 raised two children to adulthood, Ilse is not passionately interested in the jabbering of teen-agers. But this conversation is special. It snares her. Evidently they are learning about World War II in history class, and Mary Beth, a thin, still flat-chested girl with straight blonde hair, is a Quaker, Ilse gathers. She is explaining to Cathy the principles of nonviolence.

"But there must be limits," Cathy says. "Like supposing it was during the war and you saw Hitler lying in the road, half dead and begging for water. You wouldn't have to actually kill him, just . . . sort of leave him there."

280 "If a dying person asks me for water I would have to give it," says Mary Beth.

"Even Hitler?"

Mary Beth doesn't hesitate. "He's a human being." Ilse chops pork steadily with her cleaver. She rarely mixes in.

"But my God! Well, supposing he asks you to take him to a hospital?"

"I guess I would. If it was to save his life."

"You'd probably nurse him and help him get back to work, right?" Cathy is irate, Ilse notes with a keen stab of

290 pleasure in her gut.

"No, you don't understand. I'd never help him make war. But see, if I let him die it would be basically the same as killing him, and then I would become like him, a killer."

"So big deal. You'd also be saving a lot of people."

"I'd rather try to save them by talking to him, explaining what—"

"Oh, come on, Mary Beth. What horseshit."

Ilse accidentally grazes her finger with the cleaver and bleeds onto the pork. She sucks, tasting the warm blood with surprising glee. It has just left her heart, which strains toward her daughter with a weight of love.

"Look, Cathy," replies Mary Beth, "the real issue is what do I want to be? Do I want to be a truly good person or do I want to spend the next fifty years knowing I could have saved a life and didn't? How could I face myself in the mirror? I'd be, like, tainted."

This Mary Beth is a lunatic, that much is clear, thinks Ilse. Get rid of her this instant. Out, out of the house! But of course she cannot do that. The girl is Cathy's blameless little friend, invited for a Chinese dinner.

"Who gives a damn about your one soul!" exclaims Cathy. "What about all the other souls who'll die?"

Enough already, please! moans Ilse silently, watching her blood ooze through a paper napkin. What kind of people could teach their children such purity? They should teach her instead about the generous concealments of mirrors. Taste every impurity, she would like to tell Mary Beth, swallow them and assimilate them and carry them inside. When you're starving you'll eat anything. Ilse has. And none of it shows in any mirror.

"I'm sorry for those people. I mean it. I'd try to help them too. But I can't become a killer for them."

"That's the most selfish, dumbest thing I ever heard."

It begins to appear the friends will have a real falling-out. Not worth it, in the scheme of things. "How're you girls doing with the chopping?" Ilse breaks in. "Oh, that looks fine. Mary Beth, do the cabbage a little bit smaller, okay? Cathy, would you get me a Band-Aid? I cut my finger."

As soon as she gets the Band-Aid on, she hears a van pull into the driveway. Ban-the-Bug. The symbol with the grotesque insect is painted on the van. In her torment she has forgotten the appointment. She greets the smiling young man at the kitchen door and takes him around to the side of the house where the hive is. Behind her she can hear the girls tittering over how good-looking he is. Well, fine, that will reunite them. And indeed he is, a dazzling Hollywood specimen, tall, narrow-hipped, and rangy, with golden hair and tanned skin. Blue eyes, but duller than Mitch's. Wonderful golden-haired wrists and big hands. He is holding a clipboard with some papers, like a functionary, and *Ban-the-Bug* is written in red script just above the pocket of his sky blue shirt, whose sleeves are rolled up to the shoulders, revealing noteworthy muscles. Ilse points out the hive and he nods, unamazed.

"I would judge from the size," he says, "you've got about forty thousand bees in there."

Ilse gasps.

"Yup, that's right." His tone is cheerfully sympathetic. Really a charming young man. Perhaps attended the local
350 community college for two years, like Brian, Ilse thinks, found he was not academically inclined, though bright enough and looked for any old job till he could decide what he wanted. He would make a nice tennis instructor. "They're honeybees. There's most likely a lot of honey in the wall."

"Oh, can we get it out?" Ilse loves honey.

"Well, once we spray, it won't be good anymore." He sounds genuinely regretful. "You see, the bees take turns fanning the honey with their wings to keep it at sixty-five degrees. But now with the warm weather it'll melt pretty fast. You
360 might even have to break through the wall and get rid of it. It could smell or stain, it's hard to say."

She envisions forty thousand bees frantically fanning, protecting their product and livelihood, their treasure and birthright. That is the terrifying, demented noise she hears at night.

"Will you get them all?"

"Oh sure." He laughs. "No problem. We guarantee. Any that don't die just fly away—with the hive gone, you won't be seeing them around. Except if you have holes in the wall some might try to get back in and start all over."
370     "I don't think there are any holes."

"Could you just sign this paper, please?" He holds out the clipboard.

Ilse is always careful about what she signs. Robbie taught her that when she first came to America. "What is it?"

"Just routine. That we're not responsible for any damage to property, the terms of payment, the guarantee, and so on. Go ahead, read it. Take your time."

Feeling rather foolish, she scans the document. It is merely what he said, as far as she can see, and seems excessively
380 formal for so simple a transaction. The undersigned is to pay half now and half on completion of the service, but since this case will probably require only one visit, the young man says, she can pay all at once. A hundred dollars for forty thousand

bees. A quarter of a cent per bee, Ilse rapidly calculates, though it is a meaningless statistic. She signs and hands the document back.

"How long will it take?"

"Ten, fifteen minutes at the most."

"No, I mean before they're all gone."

390 "Oh." He chuckles at his little error. "The stuff works gradually, like, in stages. You might still hear something this evening, but then, during the night"—and he grins so ingenuously that she realizes he is just a boy, after all—"*baaad* things will happen to them."

He pauses, but Ilse has no ready response.

"Okay, I'll do the inside first." He fetches several cans and a small toolbox from the van and follows her up to the bedroom, where she shows him the makeshift cardboard patch. He nods as if he has seen it all before, and asks her to

400 leave the room and close the door. Although she again has a secret hankering to stay and watch, Ilse obeys. So she never gets to see exactly what is done, but sits at the kitchen table, writes out a check, and waits. The girls have vanished for the moment, leaving their assigned vegetables ably chopped. In a few minutes the Ban-the-Bug man reappears and goes outside to do the hive. After she thanks him and watches him drive away, Ilse scrubs her hands at the sink before returning to the food—why, she does not know, for she has touched, nothing alien except his pen and paper.

410 Mitch, when he comes home, is pleased at what she has accomplished, and listens respectfully as she relates all the pertinent facts. The dinner is excellent and lavishly praised, and the girls seem to be reconciled. Mary Beth is not such a thoroughgoing prig, as it turns out—she can be highly amusing on the subject of her family's foibles and idiosyncrasies. Later, in bed, Mitch wants to make love, but Ilse cannot summon the spirit to do it. He is disappointed, even a trifle irked, but it will pass. There will be other nights. She lies awake listening. The sound is feebler, and intermittent. She trusts it

420 will stop for good very soon, as she was promised.

The next day, after work, she returns home and finds Cathy stretched out on a lawn chair, Walkman on, eyes closed. She calls to get her attention and Cathy unplugs. Ilse asks her to gather up and dispose of the corpses, which are so numerous they look like a thick, lush black and gold carpet. Shaking her head morosely at her fate, Cathy fetches a broom and dustpan. Ilse remains there as if turned to a salt block, watching her daughter work.

"Do we really need to go to all this trouble?" Cathy
430  grumbles. "I mean, maybe you could use them for fertilizer or something."

She darts two giant steps to Cathy, grabs her shoulder, and shakes her hard. "How dare you say such a thing!" Her other hand is lifted, in a fist, as if to deliver a killing blow. "How dare you!"

Cathy, pale, shrinks back from her mother. "What did I say? Just tell me, what on God's green earth did I say?"

*Daniel Meltzer*

# *People*

1 What did he think of my idea, I wanted to know.

He'd be talking with his people, he said. He wanted to run it by his people. He would want to run some numbers.

I could touch base in a week or so, or one of my people.

He himself would be out of pocket for a while, but I could check in with his girl, or one of my people could check in with his girl or my girl could check in with his girl.

At some point down the road I should meet with his people directly, he said, even bring some of my people in to sit 10 down with some of his people as we get further along in the process.

My other line beeped. I excused myself. It was my girl. It's my girl. I said.

He said he'd be meeting with his people that day, on a number of matters, my idea being one of them. It was definitely something he wanted them to look at. He thanked me for bringing him my idea and said we'd be talking further once his people had had a chance to look at it. I thanked him and went back to my girl.

20 She was calling from a photo studio downtown where she was posing for another underwear spread. The photographer was in the darkroom, she was on a break and she wanted to know what he said.

He's going to talk to his people, I said.

He likes it, she said.

He didn't say that, I said. It could mean he doesn't understand it, or that he doesn't like it and he doesn't want to commit himself. Plus he's out of pocket for a while and there would be no word.

30 She sighed and said it was a good idea and not to be negative. She was cold out of the lights, she said, and was going to get some tea. We could have dinner, she'd make some pasta and salad. I'd bring the wine and dessert, as always.

We've known each other less than a year. I hadn't really thought of her as my girl, or my woman or whatever we're supposed to call them, but we see a lot of each other when she's around. She makes good money modeling bras and panties or bathing suits sometimes and travels a lot, posing in front of the Acropolis or Buckingham Palace or the Berlin Wall or the Pyramids or with kangaroos or llamas or lions or even polar bears.

I don't have a girl of the kind he would have assumed I meant. I have Linda and she's my girl in a different way. But she's not really my girl.

Actually, I do have a girl. Her name is Fanny and she's seven and lives with her mother in Chattanooga, of all places. But she's my little girl. When she was born she was our baby. But not *my* baby. My wife Jill was my baby then. First she was my girl, then she was my baby. First Fanny was our baby and now she's my girl. My little girl.

Jill hasn't been my baby since after Fanny was born and certainly not since she discovered Country and Bill. Bill is a good old boy, but he's not Jill's boy. She calls him her man.

Bill plays acoustic guitar with the Mississippi Misfits. He was an up-and-coming when he and Jill met at Yoga at the Y. Now he and the Misfits are hot, Jill says.

Jill and Bill are in Chattanooga with Fanny and Jill is working as a disc jockey on a local station. She's helping her man, plugging his records and personal appearances and the like. Fanny's taking up fiddle.

The last time we spoke Jill was experimenting with a Southern accent. Jill likes to experiment. I never did, she said. It was what was wrong with me.

At her urging, I tried loosening up, opening up, being more open to change. I let my hair grow. I did various drugs. I got in touch with my feelings. I got an earring.

Jill was very shy when I first met her. She was inexperienced with sex. She said later that she should have had lovers before she met me, that she should have experimented before me, that she should have gotten certain things out of her system.

I had gotten it all out. I thought I had. Girls, when we used to be able to call them that. Pot, rock-and-roll. I was getting back to basics at a time when she needed to test her limits.

We had Fanny right away. I had a good job and we got day care and so on and Jill didn't have to give up her job. But

she got tired of it after a while, anyway. She missed Fanny all day, she said. So she quit. I was doing all right, so I said go ahead. Then she got bored at home doing the domestic stuff.
80 She took up painting, classes at the Art Students' League, photography, then photo-journalism. She turned the bathroom into a darkroom. I got shaving cream on an important negative once. It could have won a prize, she said. It was an accident, but she was very upset.

Yoga relaxed her, she said. I went along, but I couldn't sit in that position because of my back.

Some people sit still to relax. I prefer to be in motion, get around. I like to travel, look out a train window or just walk the city. Or a hike in the country once in a while.

90 She met Bill at Yoga, had an affair with him and took off with him and Fanny in a van. I got Fanny back for a while, but she cried. I see her one weekend a month now. She comes here, sleeps in her old room, and looks more and more like me. But she talks with an accent now, says things like y'all and gree-its. She calls me her Daddy Jim.

I'm out of work. I got laid off after the crash. They gave me a good severance and the first thing I did was take a long vacation. Eight weeks. I went all over Europe and even into Russia. I met Linda in Berlin. She was standing in front of the
100 Wall in white lace bra and panties, drinking a beer. I didn't know what to make of her. I offered her my jacket. She smiled. The photographer and her assistant came back with some sausages and thought I was molesting their model. Linda explained. I was embarrassed but I laughed along with them. I ran into them the next day at the airport. They were flying back to the States. I was on my way to Venice. I looked her up when I got back home and called her. She was very sweet, not what you would expect from someone who appears half-undressed in every newspaper in the country just about every
110 week.

She looks deep into my eyes when I speak. You're an idea man, she said to me on our second or third date, you're out front.

Linda is from upstate. She lives in a large loft on a top floor downtown in the flower district. It's not much of a neighborhood, but the loft is enormous under its tent-like skylight, and of course it always smells like a garden. It's very sparely furnished with just a few very modern pieces, painted brick walls, high-tech lighting, and a king-sized bed.

120       The first time we made love I thought I was dreaming. She is even more impressive in the flesh than in the papers. Plus, she's a very romantic lover, completely uninhibited and very responsive.

After we make love, we lie awake and talk. She is very bright and a good listener. She has seen quite a bit of the world and she has learned much from her travels. She's encouraged me to be more confident and to get my ideas out. She says they have global possibilities.

Being an idea man has required a completely different
130  way of thinking. But change is good. And knowing Linda has been good. In more ways than one, obviously. There is a great deal of commerce in ideas these days, a lot going on that most people are not aware of.

I sold short the summer before the crash. I did all right in the market, plus the severance. I told them the crash was coming, but they wouldn't sell when I knew we'd peaked. As a result, the company lost a lot. They unloaded me along with some others when the sales started to fall off. I can spot a trend before it hits, but I was low on the pole and they resented that I had taken my
140  profits before the crash when they hadn't. With my severance and my profits I don't have to rush into anything. I'm in a good position, Linda says. Linda knows a lot about positions.

After my troubles with Jill, I thought I had lost interest in sex for good. Linda brought me back to life. She says I turn her on with my seriousness, with my ideas. None of them are earth-shattering. I just step back, get a little wider view, see things from a slightly different angle.

So I have these ideas which Linda says have global potential and I'm out there networking; poised, as Linda says, to
150  happen. But it occurred to me that something was missing, something wasn't in place. I couldn't make it happen by myself. I didn't have any people.

That night, after the phone call, after dinner and after we had made love under the stars in her king-sized bed on the satin sheets, with a quadrophonic playing Tristan, I told her I was concerned because I don't have any people. It seems important, I said, to have people. He had indicated an expectation that I would have people.

Linda stretched her long white body and squeezed her
160  eyes shut. Wagner was killing us with the love-death and the
morning's roses downstairs were filling the room through the
vents.

People, Linda said. She got serious, got up and got us
some mineral water, her young skin glowing in the moonlight
as she slid across the floor to the kitchen island and back.

I think my talent is that I can see just a little bit ahead of
most people. But this time Linda was even ahead of me.

You don't need any people, she said as she handed me
the glass of water. You're beyond that.
170  But he said down the road his people would want to
meet with my people, I said as she slipped beside me and
dropped her wet hand to my thigh. I called you my girl.

Your what? She lifted her hand.

I explained it to her. I could have said my woman, I said.

They don't talk that way, she said. And I didn't have to
impress him. Do you think of me as your girl?

I don't know, I said.

Roses, she said, inhaling the delivery downstairs.

He said his people would be running the numbers on my
180  idea.

And?

The numbers'll be fine, I said.

And you didn't need any people to know that, did you?

No, I said.

My ex talked that way, she said. He was always just in
on the red-eye from the coast to log in with his people on some
property, taking meetings, doing a deal. They think it makes
them sound hip. It's just intimidation, exclusionary, but they
can't intimidate you, baby. They need you. Travel light.
190  You're the idea man. Word's getting around.

She was right. Just the week before, she had introduced
me to someone at a party and he said he had heard of me.

The following week, Linda set me up with an attorney,
and I incorporated. During our brief meeting, I wondered
whether the lawyer, an athletic-looking, middle-aged man
with an office across from City Hall, had ever slept with her.
He probably had, I concluded, but he was very cordial and
businesslike. They shook hands when we left. I shook his hand
too.

200         We went down to a stationery shop and ordered a
letterhead.
            I made her Vice President.
            This makes you my people, I said.
            Your what?
            My people. I can touch base with you now, run things by
you, bring you into the process.
            Wait a minute, she said.
            You're my vice president, I said.
            That's just on paper. It's your show, baby.
210         She had begun calling me baby.

            But Linda looked worried. Her face had taken on a
serious expression. Not like the face of an underwear model.
            The following month in the *Times* magazine, she looked
different, older. Still sexy, maybe even more so, but older.
Thirtyish.
            We ordered billing forms, took a post office box.

            The man called me back the following month. Not the
man, actually. His girl. My machine now answers with the
company name. It's Linda's voice now and she's got a sexy
220  voice, much sexier than mine. His girl left a message. I called
back.
            His people thought the idea was interesting, he said, but
they had a problem with the numbers. They didn't see how it
could possibly be made to work, given the numbers.
            I asked him to be more specific and they were obviously
talking low concept.
            They're right, I said, if you approach it that way. But if
that is what they're thinking, if that's the way they want to go,
then you should probably pass on it. We could show them very
230  simply how it works high concept, I said, which is the only way
I would want to see it approached anyway. But if they think
that's out of their reach, then...
            I'll talk to my people, he said. I'll get back to you.
            I'll be out of pocket for a few days, I said. You can set it
up with my office.
            That's how I avoided calling Linda my girl.
            A couple of days later he called and Linda got back to
him. She booked us for an hour with his people the following
Monday, informing him of our fee, which was twice what she
240  gets for posing for the underwear ads, then sent a note to
confirm. She put off a shoot for the Victoria's Secret Christmas
catalog to be there and bought herself a suit and a briefcase.

Give them only the bare essentials, Linda said. They want more, let 'em book another hour. We want to arouse their interest, not completely satisfy their curiosity. You give them everything, what the hell do they need you for after that? Let 'em take an option. How much should we ask for an option? First refusal? You got another prospect lined up?

250    I didn't, but it wasn't hard to come up with half a dozen other firms who conceivably would be interested.

We put together a proposal, threw in some graphics and looked up three recent surveys that backed up our premise. We gave them just enough to show that it would fly, but not enough for them to run with.

On Monday, we showed up at 11:00 A.M. at his office, which was about half the size of Linda's loft. White carpeting, Bauhaus, tiny track lights hitting Warhol lithos along the white walls, a pencil-thin black desk with no drawers. He ushered us through a doorway into the conference room and introduced us
260    to his people: six men and one woman, all wearing dark suits and glasses, in chrome and leather swivel chairs around a mahogany table. Each had a lined legal pad and two sharpened pencils and a glass of water before them. Two carafes center table. They were all named Henderson or Mitchell or Davis or something like that. Linda's suit was from Chanel. Just low enough at the neck, high enough at the hem and trim enough inbetween. The men looked impressed. So did the woman.

We gave them an hour. I did most of the talking, since it was my idea, for about forty minutes. I talked very high con-
270    cept all the way. Throughout my presentation they bobbed their heads up and down through their bifocals or little half-moons as they balanced the figures and charts on the page with the verbal picture I was giving them of the global possibilities Linda and I had worked out. When I was done, Linda went into licensing, rights, and our role in development.

There were a few questions, mostly having to do with renewals and other matters indicating a generally positive reaction, but Linda cut them off at the hour, telling them we had another appointment.

280    Excuse me, one of them asked Linda as she rose and smoothed her suit. Haven't I seen you before?

Linda took off her horn-rimmed glasses with the windowpane lenses and shot him with her deep blues, smiling just slightly as she snapped the gold-plated locks on her case.

I don't know, she said. Have you?

We took a cab back to the loft, made love with the sounds of trucks coming and going outside and a fresh updraft of peonies all around us, had lunch at a French restaurant, took in a movie, came back to the loft and made love again.

290 We lay in silence for a while afterward. The perfume from the peonies had faded. The next morning's flowers had not yet arrived.

I wanted to stay, but Linda had to be up early for the Victoria's Secret shoot. I dressed, let myself out. You were good, she called to me in the half-light as I reached the door. You too, I said.

The sun had set when I got back to my place. There was a message on the machine. It was Jill, asking if it was all right if Fanny kind of skipped next weekend, sugar, on account of her 300 man Bill had invited them all over to Macon to meet his people.

I went for a walk.

It was warm and everyone was out; walking their dogs, licking their ice cream, shouting over the traffic, sipping wine from plastic glasses outside theaters or from paper bags in doorways, playing their music, courting, snorting, sporting their labels, dealing, stealing, feeling, ranting at their demons, seeking, fleeing, hiding, making their night.

I walked the length of the island, passed through many 310 different neighborhoods, sections, districts, down canyons of immeasurable sleeping wealth, took a rail in my hand and pressed my face against a wall of fog.

Water lapped beneath my feet. A ferry horn sounded in the distance. I could hear voices, but could not make out what they were saying. Finding a phone, I gave the eleven-digit number.

Hullo? a husky baritone with a mouth full of food drawled. In the background, what might have been a reel was being scraped from a fiddle. Hullo? he demanded again. 320 Hullo? Who the goddamn hell is it?

I replaced the receiver. Someone on the ferry laughed. Once more the horn. And then all was silent. Except for the lapping of the water at my feet. I breathed the mist, held it, let it go, turned and walked back uptown.

*Max Apple*

# TROTSKY'S BAR MITZVAH

1 ## CHARACTERS

**LARRY**  *A thirteen-year-old boy. He is dressed in a blue suit, wears a prayer shawl, and carries a prayer book. It is his Bar Mitzvah day.*
**GRANDPA**  *A very old man dressed in baker's whites.*
**ASSISTANT BAKER**  *A middle-aged black man also dressed in a baker's outfit. He wears Walkman earphones as he works.*
**VOICE OF LAVERNE**  *The cashier in the store section of the bakery.*
**VOICE OF LARRY'S FATHER**

## SETTING

10 *The rear of a bakery—there is an oven, several long tables, and large racks for bread and rolls.*

| | |
|---|---|
| LARRY | Well, it's the big day, finally. |
| GRANDPA | To me it's like every other day. They earn their bread by the sweat of my brow. |
| LARRY | C'mon, Grandpa, you don't have to work today, just this once, can't you stop being a communist and come to my Bar Mitzvah? |
| GRANDPA | *(Gives LARRY a very angry look.)* We've been over this a hundred times. When you decided to go for superstition and capitalism, you got my answer. |
| LARRY | But it's just for a couple of hours, and just today. What harm can it do? |
| GRANDPA | *(Gives LARRY angry stare and continues to knead dough.)* Everything I taught you, you've forgotten already. Instead of me, you listened to your father. I could have taken you to Cuba—with him you'll end up in Miami Beach. |
| LARRY | But Grandpa, Stalin was an anti-Semite. In Russia they'd torture you. Daddy says they're not even |

30                          communists there. He says you're the last
                         communist in the world.

GRANDPA    I'm not talking Russia, I'm talking revolution. I'm
                         talking the worldwide brotherhood of workers.

ASSISTANT BAKER    *(Near the oven and wearing headphones.)* Hold
                         it down, comrade, you're louder than punk—

GRANDPA    I'm talking right and wrong and distribution of
                         goods and ownership of production. I'm not
                         talking Russia. I'm talking about the world to
                         come, the one you should be leading. And instead
40                          you stand here with a prayer book and you go out
                         to beg bourgeoisie presents. *(Spits—wipes his
                         mouth with the back of his hand—goes back to
                         the dough-kneading.)*

*(From the front of the shop we hear the cash register ringing up sales.)*

LARRY    All right, forget the Bar Mitzvah, pretend it's a
                         birthday party. I'm your only grandson. I want
                         you to come to my party.

GRANDPA    I don't go to parties.

LARRY    But I want to celebrate this.

50 GRANDPA    I'll celebrate when the workers are victorious.

LARRY    Grandpa *(becoming angry now)*, I don't care
                         about workers or revolutions or even about
                         religions. I just want you to be there with me when
                         all this stuff about being a man happens.

GRANDPA    You'll become a man when you throw off the yoke
                         of capitalism.

LARRY    I don't even know what that means.

GRANDPA    Of course you don't, because you live in the midst
                         of stockbrokers and insurance salesmen. You go
60                          to the synagogue of good manners. Your God says
                         "Have a nice day" and turns away from the Third
                         World to watch a ball game on color TV. For this
                         kind of celebration you've got your parents; you
                         don't need me.

LARRY    You came to my grammar-school graduation.

GRANDPA    Because education is a weapon.

LARRY    You always come to my Little League games.

GRANDPA    Because the revolution needs strong bodies.

ASSISTANT BAKER    So do I need some strong bodies. C'mere and
70                          give this poor *shvartzer* a hand.

*(Grandpa and Larry go over to help him lift a hundred-pound sack
and pour some flour into a huge bowl.)*

| | |
|---|---|
| Assistant Baker | You can't tell this old man nothin'. I been tryin'…it's no use. But if you want, I'll come as a representative oppressed black man so long as I won't have to do no Yid talk. All I can say is "no-good *shvartzer*" and "a *shvartz jahr*" and "*shvartzer chazar*." They only use black words around me. |
| 80  Grandpa | All words are black words. |
| Larry | My father said I'd be wasting my time. |
| Grandpa | Your father is the one who wastes time: a stockbroker—a manipulator of capital, a bloodsucker. |
| Larry | He works hard, Grandpa. |
| Grandpa | Sure he does—it's not easy to rob and pillage. |
| Larry | He says you're a crazy and bitter man. |
| Grandpa | And I say he should choke on his Gucci loafers. |
| Larry | I knew you'd never come to the party at the house, but I thought you'd come to the synagogue. |
| 90 | |
| Grandpa | Why? Do I like God's house any more than your father's? They're both in the same business. |
| Larry | *(Trying another approach.)* Grandpa, I wrote a socialist speech, only the rabbi said I had to put it in religious words. |
| Grandpa | *(Sarcastically.)* Oh, your rabbi says. Every time the cat farts they make a new rabbinic law. |
| Larry | I said the time was coming when there would be liberty and justice for all. |
| 100  Voice of LaVerne | *(Offstage.)* Any more white bread? I could use some sliced whites. And a few dozen biscuits, too, they're all gone. |
| Assistant Baker | *(Singing.)* No more biscuits! You hear dat? The revolution done ate up the biscuits. Mammy's little baby loves de revolution, but they's eatin' up his biscuits. |
| Grandpa | They suck the blood and minerals out of Africa and this man laughs. In Chicago and Oakland they eat black babies, and this wise man laughs. |
| 110  Larry | They really eat children? |
| Grandpa | They suck on the knucklebones of the poor and they make soup out of our feet. |

LARRY      *(Laughing nervously.)* I don't believe that. Mom
           says you exaggerate. She says you told her she'd
           give birth to monsters if she married Dad. Do you
           think Sheryl and I are monsters?

GRANDPA    About your sister I'll be silent. You, my
           sweetheart, are no monster.

LARRY      Then why can't you come to my Bar Mitzvah?

120 GRANDPA    Because your religion is a monster and your party
           will be monstrous and your father is a beast. Now
           leave me alone. I've got to work.

*(ASSISTANT BAKER calls LARRY over to him.)*

ASSISTANT BAKER    Don't let him get away with that shit, Larry. He
           loves to have folks beggin' at him to go to stuff. If
           there was no communists, he'd do that anyways.
           You just got one mean old grandpa.

LARRY      But you know he's not mean to me. Ever since I
           can remember he brings me donuts and cookies,

130        he takes me to the movies. I know he hates Dad,
           but still he walks through our house to get me.
           He's never been mean to me.

ASSISTANT BAKER    He's all talk, that old man. If it ain't commie
           talk, he's hating' sports or music. When I started
           bringin' my stereo to work, you shoulda seen him
           go at rock 'n' roll. He carried on so much that I
           finally had to lay it on him, that when it comes to
           the real thing, no white, not even commie Yids,
           is gonna tell us *shvartzers* how to blow the lid. But

140        until then, I'm gonna play my music, and when
           the trumpets of justice sound, they're gonna be
           right on key. That shut him up.

VOICE OF LAVERNE    Bring up those rolls, okay, fellas? They're
           waitin' on the rolls.

LARRY      *(Volunteering.)* I'll carry them out. *(He exits with a
           large basket of rolls.)*

ASSISTANT BAKER    *(To GRANDPA.)* Why don't you just go with the
           kid? What kind of a fuck-face are you anyway?
           Look how lucky you are to have a kid like him.

150        He could be sucking up to the rich ones. Instead,
           he's hanging around here—always comin' back
           here to you. Your daughter don't care about you,
           neither do the communists; nobody does but this
           kid. That boy, he's the only revolution you ever
           gonna see.

*(GRANDPA seems to think about this.)*
*(LARRY returns with the empty steel bin.)*

LARRY    They need more rolls, also gingerbread cookies.
160                    LaVerne says they're as busy as Christmas Eve up
                       front.

*(ASSISTANT BAKER loads up more baked goods.)*

LARRY    I'm gonna talk about Noah and the flood, Grandpa.
                       You wanna hear?

*(GRANDPA says nothing.)*

ASSISTANT BAKER    Lay it on me brother, my ancestors was
                       there—Old Black Joe and Aunt Jemima and Noah
                       himself, black as anything.

LARRY    Noah was the only good man during bad times. In
                       those days nobody knew how to do the right thing
170                    so God made a flood to destroy the whole world.
                       But he didn't destroy Noah and Noah's family
                       because they were good. And he didn't destroy all
                       the animals because they were just animals and
                       didn't understand about being good.

GRANDPA    You believe there was a flood?

LARRY    *(Shrugs.)* I guess.

GRANDPA    You believe in the Ten Commandments, too?

LARRY    Yes.

ASSISTANT BAKER    *(Boogies a little.)* I looked over Jordan and
180                    what'd I see … ? All them Bar Mitzvahs comin'
                       after me.

*(ASSISTANT BAKER does a tap-dance number on one of the baking*
*tables. He takes LARRY's tallis and uses it as a veil in a parody of a*
*female veil dance.)*

GRANDPA    *(Aside.)* For him we need a revolution.

LARRY    So God sent the flood to destroy the world, since if
                       everyone in it was bad, the world was already
                       destroyed. But that left all those innocent animals
                       who hadn't done anything bad at all.

190  ASSISTANT BAKER    And all of them animals they lined up to get on
                       the ark and Noah said, "Not you, Mr. Pig, Ah'm
                       fixin' to hate you another ten thousand years."

VOICE OF LAVERNE    Where in the hell are the rye breads?

LARRY    *(Continuing despite the interruptions.)* And then
                       God promised that He'd never destroy the world

|  |  |
|---|---|
|  | again no matter how bad people got. So we don't have to worry anymore like they did in the old days. |
| GRANDPA | This is what you're going to say? |
| LARRY | Yes. |
| 200 GRANDPA | That since the world won't be destroyed, we don't have to worry? |
| LARRY | We don't have to worry about that, we can worry about other things. |
| GRANDPA | *(Slaps his head in disbelief.)* About bombs and war and nuclear destruction, about the Holocaust and Cambodia and Vietnam, about Hiroshima and Nagasaki—about all this we don't have to worry? |
| VOICE OF LAVERNE | I wish to hell there were six dozen rye breads out here. Sliced. |
| 210 LARRY | *(Getting flustered.)* All I know is I want you to come to my Bar Mitzvah, and I don't care about the whole world. |
| GRANDPA | And I want you to care about the whole world, at least about all the workers. |
| LARRY | I'm only thirteen. I can't care about everybody yet. |
| ASSISTANT BAKER | You got a girlfriend? |
| LARRY | *(Shakes his head.)* No. |
| 220 ASSISTANT BAKER | He don't even care about girls, you expect him to care about workers? |
| LARRY | I'm waiting Grandpa, we've got to go now. I have to be there by nine-thirty or they'll just go ahead without me, and this part doesn't come up again for a whole year. |
| VOICE OF LAVERNE | Just forget it, boys. I told the customers to eat cake. |
|  |  |
|  | *(ASSISTANT BAKER rushes out with the loaves.)* |
| LARRY | Grandpa, I won't ever bug you like this again ... I |
| 230 | promise—not for confirmation, graduation, not even for a wedding. |
| GRANDPA | *(Softening.)* Larry, my *boychik,* you know I love you. *(GRANDPA hugs boy.)* |
| LARRY | *(Crying.)* Of course I know that. |
| GRANDPA | Then love me, too, and don't ask me to come there among everyone and everything I hate. Don't ask |

me to lie about the world even for a few hours. To me that would be the Flood—all those stockbrokers and lawyers and the rabbi and everything I turned my back on fifty years ago. Even for you I can't pretend.

LARRY       Do you hate my father that much?

GRANDPA     I don't hate that harmless *shmuck.* I hate the system.

LARRY       Is my Bar Mitzvah part of the system?

GRANDPA     Yes.

VOICE OF FATHER     *(Out front.)* Larry, we can't wait any longer—please hurry.

LARRY       I'm coming, Daddy. *(To GRANDPA.)* You mean the words are wrong, or just going and doing it there with everyone?

GRANDPA     Not the words, in the words there is nobility.

ASSISTANT BAKER     Damn right—they got all them words for "*shvartzer.*" Who knows how many words they must have for God?

LARRY       Then I'm going to do it here.


*(LARRY begins to chant his Bar Mitzvah portion in Hebrew. After a few sentences there is clapping from the front.)*

VOICE OF LAVERNE     Wonderful, sweetheart, but your daddy's out here going nuts, he says it's now or never. Your choice if you want to stay with Grandpa or have your Bar Mitzvah.


*(LARRY hugs GRANDPA and leaves, crying).*
*(GRANDPA goes back to making dough.)*

GRANDPA     *(To ASSISTANT BAKER.)* C'mon, then. The revolution needs gingerbread men. It's already got enough jazz.

ASSISTANT BAKER     Screw the revolution, old man. I like the boy's singing. He sung a lotta words and I didn't hear no "*shvartzers.*" I didn't know you folks could sing like that.


*(LARRY comes running back in. He now has no prayer shawl on, and his suit jacket is also removed. He has been crying.)*

LARRY       *(Hugs GRANDPA, getting flour on his face.)* I'm not gonna have a Bar Mitzvah. I'd rather have a revolution.

VOICE OF FATHER    *(Angry, offstage.)* I hope you're satisfied,
old man—I hope you've got what you want now.
*(Door slams.)*

*(GRANDPA hugs LARRY, and slowly takes off his apron.)*
280  GRANDPA    The revolution will take a while, maybe until
you're in college. C'mon George. *(He nods to
ASSISTANT BAKER.)* We're gonna take my Trotsky
to his Bar Mitzvah.
ASSISTANT BAKER    I ain't dressed for no party.
GRANDPA    Yes you are—for this boy it's going to be a workers'
Bar Mitzvah.

*(LARRY lights up.)*
Assistant Baker    Lemme hear that song again.

*(The three hustle offstage, with LARRY once more chanting his Hebrew*
290  *song.)*

## *Alan Dugan*

# *Against the Text*
# *"Art Is Immortal"*

from AGNI

1  All art is temporal. All art is lost.
Go to Egypt. Go look at the Sphinx.
It's falling apart. He sits
on water in the desert and the water table shifts.
He has lost his toes to the sand-
blasts of the Saharan winds
of a mere few thousand years.
The Mamelukes shot up his face
because they were Iconoclasts,
10  because they were musketeers.
The British stole his beard
because they were imperialist thieves.
It's in the cellar of the British Museum
where the Athenians lost their marbles.

And that City of Ideas
that Socrates once had in mind
has faded too, like the Parthenon
from car exhaust, and from
the filthiness of the Turks
20  who used it as a dump.

If that city ever was
for Real in public works
and not just words he said:

No things but in ideas.
No ideas but in things
I say as William Carlos Williams said,
things as the Sphinx is our thing,
a beast of a man made god
stoned into art to guard the dead
30 from nothing, nothing and vanishing
toes first in the desert,
sand-blasted off into nothing
by a few thousand years of air,
sand, take your pick, picker,

go to Egypt, go look
at the Sphinx while it lasts.
Art is not immortal.
Art is not mortal.
All art is ideas in things.
40 All art is temporal. All art is lost.
The imperial desert is moving in
with water, sand and wind
to wear the godly native beast of man apart
back to the nothing which sculpted him.

And remember the Mamelukes, remember the Brits.
They were the iconoclasts of their own times,
primitive musketeers, primitive chiselers. This time
we can really blast the beast of man to bits.

*David Ignatow*

# Witness

1 We can't write ourselves into eternal life
and that is the sorrow and waste of writing,
but those who would write in this knowledge
have found a subterfuge by which to let
themselves be prompted, in heady confidence
of meaning: the wealth of self
spread among the readers who themselves
will read for reasons of earth:
that they have been witness
10 to their birth, growth and death
and shared the earth with earth.

*Mary B. Campbell*

# *Warning: Nuclear Waste Dump*

1 This poem has to last
Ten thousand years
And be translated
Into every language
In the world.

Whoever conquers New Jersey
Must come equipped
With this poem, or die.

The poem must not depend
10 On music for its beauty
Since it must be equally beautiful
In every language
There will ever be.

It has to be so beautiful
That people will say it
For five hundred generations.
It must be universal
And timeless.

Millions of lives depend
20 On the beauty of this poem
But it cannot change
From ear to ear:

The critic who discovers
Its figurative sense
Must be silenced,
For the poem means
Exactly what it says.

We must find a way
To teach the birds
30 And the animals
To say it too,
And the trees, and water.

# A. R. Ammons

# The History of Motion

1 Frost the papercutter
snips the killed
page from the finished text

and nature's book gives up
a sheet of crickets
to oblivion, a blankness

chirping can fill again next
year, freshness no more
than the gap of repeating

10 interval: this is not

boring for crickets, say,
round the round once only:
for those whose round

rewinds many times, a groove
would deepen blank black
except that time, rounding

& rounding, enscribes the
center forward so the spiralling
tip enters consequence, a story.

*Claire Nicolas White*

# HOME-COMING

1　After falling asleep
in ten different rooms
in mountains, in plains,
facing East, facing West,

I wake in the dark
and grope for a light.
I stumble and fall
in the most foreign place

of all. Where is this
10　tall room of serene
whiteness, these floors
painted red, this smell
of clean sheets and wood-smoke?

Beyond, in a hall
with mysterious closed doors
and burnished oak chests
stairs descend to a house

filled with objects that creak
and glow in the dark.
20　This must be the ultimate
inn, where I landed

my mission fulfilled,
where the perfect decor
awaits me, reinventing
the life I inhabited
　　all along.

# WRITING ASSIGNMENTS

1.  Write a one-act play or short story on one of the following situations:
    a)  A young man and woman who are career-oriented and very interested in success try to negotiate the terms of their personal relationship.
    b)  A parent is at odds with a child who gets understanding and affection from a grandparent. Be specific about the values and issues. Make something happen.
    c)  Someone is haunted by an early childhood experience that helps to explain something that he or she does as an adult.

2.  Write a poem on one of the following subjects:
    a)  the swift passage of time.
    b)  "Art alone is eternal" (Théophile Gautier).
    c)  Literature has no influence on human nature or history.
    d)  technology versus nature.
    e)  "nature, red in tooth and claw" (Tennyson).
    f)  "This is the way the world ends..." (T.S. Eliot).

# *Chapter 2*

# *Setting*

## Introduction

## Fiction

Paul Bowles    *The Eye*
Tim McCarthy    *The Windmill Man*

## Drama

Joyce Carol Oates    *Under/Ground*

## Poetry

Philip Appleman    *Gathering at the River*
Mark Doty    *Noir*
Bruce Bond    *Gallery of Rivers*
Jay Parini    *Working the Face*
Al Young    *New Autumn, New York*

## Writing Assignments

Anything that happens has to happen somewhere. In fiction and drama this is fairly obvious. Even in most poetry there is a setting of sorts, although the events may be minimal. In some poetry, however, all we have is an observation, a commentary, or a striking image, and often there is no particular setting involved. On the other hand, one might stretch a point and insist that there is such a thing as the landscape of the poet's mind. In that case, the speaker (or persona) of the poem is our character, and the poet's thoughts are "events."

In a literary work the setting can be anywhere, even a place called Nowhere, as in the novel *News From Nowhere,* by William Morris. His "Nowhere" is, of course, somewhere, a fictional society.

Settings can range from the familiar to the highly imaginative, from the realistic geography that is part of our common experience to the far reaches of outer and inner space. Some well-known works have been set in places as ordinary as a farm in Nebraska or as bizarre as a planet in another galaxy or an unfamiliar dimension inhabited by ghosts and spirits.

Some settings are real and specific: Manhattan, Mississippi, the Colosseum in Rome. Some are generic: a living room, a bar, a boat. And some are only dreams or fantasies: Dante's vision of Hell, Alice's Wonderland, Coleridge's Xanadu.

Since most literary works deal with experiences with which most of us can identify, they tend to have realistic settings. They do not have to be places that the reader has actually seen. There are common denominators in human experience that allow us to appreciate the things that happen to characters in almost any realistic setting in the world, whether it be Joyce's Dublin, Tolstoy's Russia, or Flaubert's France, or even the more exotic places of which Conrad was so fond.

Some realistic settings are, of course, real places with real names, and most writers do not hesitate to use those names, especially if the places are large cities such as New York, London, or Paris. They are more reluctant to use the real names of smaller places, perhaps because the people who live there may well know that the events described did not happen. Faulkner gave his fictitious region the name of Yoknapatawpha County, and Hardy called his location Wessex instead of the actual Dorset. Writers who do not have a specific location in mind simply invent a fictitious place.

The amount of time that a writer devotes to his setting depends, to some extent, on the significance of the place in relation to the whole work. Some settings are purely incidental and do not require much attention. Many one-set plays, for instance, take place in a generic living room, leaving the details to the director or designer. In *The Glass Menagerie,* on the other hand, Tennessee Williams lavishes considerable poetic description on the setting, since it has such a major effect on the lives of his characters. A setting might even be the central focus of the work—strife-torn Belfast, for instance, or the Balkans. If the place actually exists, it should be described accurately and in detail. In historical novels considerable research is often necessary.

Even some generic settings can be significant. Sometimes that significance is symbolic, as in Virginia Woolf's *To the Lighthouse* or Samuel Beckett's *Waiting for Godot.* Real places can also be used symbolically, as in Conrad's *Heart of Darkness* or E.M. Forster's *Passage to India.*

It is worth remembering, however, that whatever the setting is, a *sense of place* can be important and even exciting. For readers, it creates a shock of recognition, the sense of almost being there themselves. For writers, it is a most valuable tool in their illusionist bag of tricks. It projects a framework of reality in which their fictions can take place.

"The Windmill Man," by Tim McCarthy, is a good example of this. The remoteness and hostility of the Royal Don area in New Mexico plays a major role in the story, but the reader would not believe in its savagery were not the sense of place so strongly conveyed: "...there was nothing up there but rocks and hills, rugged arroyo-slashed rangeland, flood-heaved, wind-dried, and sun-cracked ... A long, lonely landscape that could tumble your heart and in the next breath ache low in your belly with the spirit of a half-forgotten place...." This setting, so vividly delineated, is essential to the plot, theme, and character development in this story.

A wide variety of settings figure in the selections chosen to illustrate this chapter, and they all have some bearing on the whole work.

"The Eye," by Paul Bowles, is set in Tangier, Morocco. In the opening paragraph we are told that this is a significant setting, one that has influenced the events dealt with in the story. We are told that the residents have certain primitive reactions and that the central character "would have done better to stay away." The customs and social climate of Morocco contribute to the story in such great measure that the "setting" here becomes comparable to another full character. It is unique and individual, yet it has such elemental characteristics that it touches on human experience anywhere. Certainly fear, corruption, superstition, and ignorance exist in the most civilized places.

In Joyce Carol Oates' play *Under/Ground,* the setting is at the very heart of the matter. It is a bomb shelter in the "capital city of an unnamed European country." We are not abandoned to sheer conjecture about the significance of this setting. In her opening stage directions Oates tells us: "The shelter need not be represented realistically but should be suggestive in its labyrinthine, gloomy, sinister, surreal complexity." After the three main characters are introduced she says, "As these three descend into the bomb shelter, their personalities gradually shift— from their 'daylight' or 'social' personae to deeper, more primitive personalities."

Through descriptions of riverside settings (the Jordan and the Styx), Philip Appleman projects the heaven and hell of different religions. Are they meaningful? he asks, and takes us back to the "silky Muck" of ordinary earthbound rivers. Through the use of these settings, Appleman conveys his rejection of religious solutions to the quest for meaning in favor of "honest earth-to-earth," an organic vision of life as an end in itself.

In "Noir," Mark Doty creates a dreamlike and suggestive rundown factory town, a place "in tatters, dead/since the trains stopped mattering." The setting entrances him, and spurs him to imagine a movie or narrative taking place there.

In "Gallery of Rivers," Bruce Bond calls up specific memories of Texas in descriptions that suggest how such places become part of personal and aesthetic consciousness.

A coal mine is the generic setting for Jay Parini's "Working the Face." The miner down there is envisioned as both toiler and adventurer—a "prince of darkness" who has been to the "end of it, /core and pith/ of the world's rock belly."

Al Young chooses a specific setting, Gramercy Park (New York) in the autumn, and turns it into a metaphor for the

"inward adventure" of his personal autumn. One might speculate that Oates has done a similar thing with the setting of
*Under/Ground* which surely suggests an inward voyage
into levels of consciousness, a swoop from superego, through
ego, to id.

The real setting of Morocco is as invaluable to "The Eye"
as the imaginary bomb shelter is to *Under/Ground,* or the generic one to "Working the Face."

*Paul Bowles*

# The Eye

1 Ten or twelve years ago there came to live in Tangier a man who would have done better to stay away. What happened to him was in no way his fault, notwithstanding the whispered innuendos of the English-speaking residents. These people often have reactions similar to those of certain primitive groups: when misfortune overtakes one of their number, the others by mutual consent refrain from offering him aid, and merely sit back to watch, certain that he has called his suffering down upon himself. He has become taboo, and is incapa-
10 ble of receiving help. In the case of this particular man, I suppose no one could have been of much comfort; still, the tacit disapproval called forth by his bad luck must have made the last months of his life harder to bear.

His name was Duncan Marsh, and he was said to have come from Vancouver. I never saw him, nor do I know anyone who claims to have seen him. By the time his story reached the cocktail-party circuit he was dead, and the more irresponsible residents felt at liberty to indulge their taste for mythmaking.

He came alone to Tangier, rented a furnished house on
20 the slopes of Djamaa el Mokra—they were easy enough to find in those days, and correspondingly inexpensive—and presently installed a teenage Moroccan on the premises to act as night watchman. The house provided a resident cook and gardener, but both of these where discharged from their duties, the cook being replaced by a woman brought in at the suggestion of the watchman. It was not long after this that Marsh felt the first symptoms of a digestive illness which over the months grew steadily worse. The doctors in Tangier advised him to go to London. Two months in hospital there helped him somewhat. No clear diagnosis was made, however,
30 and he returned here only to become bedridden. Eventually he was flown back to Canada on a stretcher, and succumbed there shortly after his arrival.

In all this there was nothing extraordinary; it was assumed that Marsh had been one more victim of slow poisoning by native employees. There have been several such cases during my five decades in Tangier. On each occasion it has been said that the European victim had only himself (or herself) to blame, having encouraged familiarity on the part of a servant.

40  What strikes the outsider as strange is that no one ever takes the matter in hand and inaugurates a search for the culprit, but in the total absence of proof there is no point in attempting an investigation.

Two details complete the story. At some point during his illness Marsh told an acquaintance of the arrangements he had made to provide financial aid for his night watchman in the event that he himself should be obliged to leave Morocco; he had given him a notarized letter to that effect, but apparently the boy never tried to press his claim. The other report came

50  from Dr. Halsey, the physician who arranged for Marsh's removal from the house to the airport. It was this last bit of information which, for me, at least, made the story take on life. According to the doctor, the soles of Marsh's feet had been systematically marked with deep incisions in the form of crude patterns; the cuts were recent, but there was some infection. Dr. Halsey called in the cook and the watchman: they showed astonishment and dismay at the sight of their employer's feet, but were unable to account for the mutilations. Within a few days after Marsh's departure, the original cook

60  and gardener returned to take up residence, the other two having already left the house.

The slow poisoning was classical enough, particularly in the light of Marsh's remark about his provision for the boy's well-being, but the knife-drawn designs on the feet somehow got in the way of whatever combinations of motive one could invent. I thought about it. There could be little doubt that the boy was guilty. He had persuaded Marsh to get rid of the cook that came with the house, even though her wages had to continue to be paid, and to hire another woman (very likely from

70  his own family) to do the cooking. The poisoning process lasts many months if it is to be undetectable, and no one is in a better position to take charge of it than the cook herself. Clearly she knew about the financial arrangement that had been made for the boy, and expected to share in it. At the same time the crosses and circles slashed in the feet were inexplicable. The slow poisoner is patient, careful, methodical; his principal concerns are to keep the dosage effective and to avoid leaving any visible marks. Bravado is unknown to him.

The time came when people no longer told the story of

80  Duncan Marsh. I myself thought of it less often, having no more feasible hypotheses to supply. One evening perhaps five

years ago, an American resident here came to me with the news
that he had discovered a Moroccan who claimed to have been
Marsh's night watchman. The man's name was Larbi; he was a
waiter at Le Fin Bec, a small back-street restaurant. Apparently
he spoke poor English, but understood it without difficulty.
This information was handed me for what it was worth, said the
American, in the event that I felt inclined to make use of it.

90 I turned it over in my mind, and one night a few weeks
later I went down to the restaurant to see Larbi for myself. The
place was dimly lit and full of Europeans. I studied the three
waiters. They were interchangeable, with wide black mus-
taches, blue jeans and sport shirts. A menu was handed me; I
could scarcely read it, even directly under the glow of the little
table lamp. When the man who had brought it returned, I
asked for Larbi.

He pulled the menu from my hand and left the table. A
moment later another of the triumvirate came up beside me
and handed me the menu he carried under his arm. I ordered in
100 Spanish. When he brought the soup I murmured that I was
surprised to find him working there. This brought him up
short; I could see him trying to remember me.

"Why wouldn't I be working here?" His voice was level,
without inflection.

"Of course! Why not? It was just that I thought by now
you'd have a bazaar or some sort of shop."

His laugh was a snort. "Bazaar!"

When he arrived with the next course, I begged his par-
don for meddling in his affairs. But I was interested, I said,
110 because for several years I had been under the impression that
he had received a legacy from an English gentleman.

"You mean Señor Marsh?" His eyes were at last wide
open.

"Yes, that was his name. Didn't he give you a letter? He
told his friends he had."

He looked over my head as he said: "He gave me a
letter."

"Have you ever showed it to anyone?" This was tactless,
but sometimes it is better to drive straight at the target.

120 "Why? What good is it? Señor Marsh is dead." He
shook his head with an air of finality, and moved off to another table. By the time I had finished my crème caramel, most
of the diners had left, and the place seemed even darker. He
came over to the table to see if I wanted coffee. I asked for the

check. When he brought it I told him I should like very much
to see the letter if he still had it.

"You can come tomorrow night or any night, and I'll
show it to you. I have it at home."

I thanked him and promised to return in two or three
130 days. I was confused as I left the restaurant. It seemed clear
that the waiter did not consider himself to be incriminated in
Duncan Marsh's troubles. When, a few nights later, I saw the
document, I no longer understood anything.

It was not a letter; it was a *papier timbré* of the kind on
sale at tobacconists. It read, simply: *To Whom It May Concern: I, Duncan Whitelow Marsh, do hereby agree to deposit
the sum of One Hundred Pounds to the account of Larbi
Lairini, on the first of each month, for as long as I live.* It was
signed and notarized in the presence of two Moroccan wit-
140 nesses, and bore the date June 11, 1966. As I handed it back to
him I said: "And it never did you any good."

He shrugged and slipped the paper in his wallet. "How
was it going to? The man died."

"It's too bad."

"*Suerte.*" In the Moroccan usage of the word, it means
"fate," rather than simple luck.

At that moment I could have pressed on, and asked him
if he had any idea as to the cause of Marsh's illness, but I
wanted time for considering what I had just learned. As I rose
150 to leave I said: "I'm sorry it turned out that way. I'll be back in
a few days." He held out his hand and I shook it. I had no
intentions then. I might return soon or I might never go back.

*For as long as I live.* The phrase echoed in my mind for
several weeks. Possibly Marsh had worded it that way so it
would be readily understandable to the *adoul* of Tangier who
had affixed their florid signatures to the sheet; yet I could not
help interpreting the words in a more melodramatic fashion.
To me the document represented the officializing of a covenant
already in existence between master and servant: Marsh
160 wanted the watchman's help, and the watchman had agreed to
give it. There was nothing upon which to base such an assumption, nevertheless I thought I was on the right track.
Slowly I came to believe that if only I could talk to the watchman, in Arabic, and inside the house itself, I might be in a
position to see things more clearly.

One evening I walked to Le Fin Bec and without taking a
seat motioned to Larbi to step outside for a moment. There I

asked him if he could find out whether the house Señor Marsh had lived in was occupied at the moment or not.

170      "There's nobody living there now." He paused and added: "It's empty. I know the guardian."

I had decided, in spite of my deficient Arabic, to speak to him in his own language, so I said: "Look, I'd like to go with you to the house and see where everything happened. I'll give you fifteen thousand francs for your trouble."

He was startled to hear the Arabic; then his expression shifted to one of satisfaction. "He's not supposed to let anyone in," he said.

I handed him three thousand francs. "You arrange that
180 with him. And fifteen for you when we leave the house. Could we do it Thursday?"

The house had been built, I should say, in the fifties, when good construction was still possible. It was solidly embedded in the hillside, with the forest towering behind it. We had to climb three flights of stairs through the garden to get to the entrance. The guardian, a squinting Djibli in a brown djellaba, followed close on our footsteps, eyeing me with mistrust.

There was a wide terrace above, with a view to the
190 southeast over the town and the mountains. Behind the terrace a shadowed lawn ended where the forest began. The living room was large and bright, with French doors giving onto the lawn. Odors of damp walls and mildew weighted the air. The absurd conviction that I was about to understand everything had taken possession of me; I noticed that I was breathing more quickly. We wandered into the dining room. There was a corridor beyond, and the room where Marsh had slept, shuttered and dark. A wide curving stairway led down to a level where there were two more bedrooms, and continued its spiral
200 to the kitchen and servants' rooms below. The kitchen door opened onto a small flagstoned patio where high philodendrons covered the walls.

Larbi looked out and shook his head. "That's the place where all the trouble began," he said glumly.

I pushed through the doorway and sat down on a wrought-iron bench in the sun. "It's damp inside. Why don't we stay out here?"

The guardian left us and locked up the house. Larbi squatted comfortably on his heels near the bench.

210      There would have been no trouble at all, he said, if only Marsh had been satisfied with Yasmina, the cook whose

wages were included in the rent. But she was a careless worker and the food was bad. He asked Larbi to find him another cook.

"I told him ahead of time that this woman Meriam had a little girl, and some days she could leave her with friends and some days she would have to bring her with her when she came to work. He said it didn't matter, but he wanted her to be quiet."

220      The woman was hired. Two or three days a week she came accompanied by the child, who would play in the patio where she could watch her. From the beginning Marsh complained that she was noisy. Repeatedly he sent messages down to Meriam, asking her to make the child be still. And one day he went quietly around the outside of the house and down to the patio. He got on all fours, put his face close to the little girl's face, and frowned at her so fiercely that she began to scream. When Meriam rushed out of the kitchen he stood up smiling and walked off. The little girl continued to scream and

230  wail in a corner of the kitchen until Meriam took her home. That night, still sobbing, she came down with a high fever. For several weeks she hovered between life and death, and when she was finally out of danger she could no longer walk.

Meriam, who was earning relatively high wages, consulted one *fqih* after another. They agreed that "the eye" had been put on the child; it was equally clear that the Nazarene for whom she worked had done it. What they told her she must do, Larbi explained, was to administer certain substances to Marsh which eventually would make it possible to counter-

240  act the spell. This was absolutely necessary, he said, staring at me gravely. Even if the señor had agreed to remove it (and of course she never would have mentioned it to him) he would not have been able to. What she gave him could not harm him; it was merely medicine to relax him so that when the time came to undo the spell he would not make any objections.

At some point Marsh confided to Larbi that he suspected Meriam of slipping soporifics into his food, and begged him to be vigilant. The provision for Larbi's well-being was signed as an inducement to enlisting his active support. Since to Larbi

250  the mixtures Meriam was feeding her master were relatively harmless, he reassured him and let her continue to dose him with her concoctions.

Tired of squatting, Larbi suddenly stood up and began to walk back and forth, stepping carefully in the center of each flagstone. "When he had to go to the hospital in London, I told her: 'Now you've made him sick. Suppose he doesn't come back? You'll never break it.' She was worried about it. 'I've done what I could,' she said. 'It's in the hands of Allah.'"

When Marsh did return to Tangier, Larbi urged her to
260 be quick about bringing things to a head, now that she had been fortunate enough to get him back. He was thinking, he said, that it might be better for the señor's health if her treatment were not continued for too long a time.

I asked no questions while he talked; I made a point of keeping my face entirely expressionless, thinking that if he noticed the least flicker of disapproval he might stop. The sun had gone behind the trees and the patio was chilly. I had a strong desire to get up and walk back and forth as he was doing, but I thought even that might interrupt him. Once
270 stopped, the flow might not resume.

Soon Marsh was worse than ever, with racking pains in his abdomen and kidneys. He remained in bed then, and Larbi brought him his food. When Meriam saw that he was no longer able to leave the bed, even to go into the bathroom, she decided that the time had come to get rid of the spell. On the same night that a *fqih* held a ceremony at her house in the presence of the crippled child, four men from Meriam's family came up to Djamaa el Mokra.

"When I saw them coming, I got onto my motorcycle
280 and went into the city. I didn't want to be here when they did it. It had nothing to do with me."

He stood still and rubbed his hands together. I heard the southwest wind beginning to sound in the trees; it was that time of afternoon. "Come. I'll show you something," he said.

We climbed steps around the back of the house and came out onto a terrace with a pergola over it. Beyond this lay the lawn and the wall of trees.

"He was very sick for the next two days. He kept asking me to telephone the English doctor."
290        "Didn't you do it?"

Larbi stopped walking and looked at me. "I had to clean everything up first. Meriam wouldn't touch him. It was during the rains. He had mud and blood all over him when I got back here and found him. The next day I gave him a bath and changed the sheets and blankets. And I cleaned the house, because they got mud everywhere when they brought him back in. Come on. You'll see where they had to take him."

We had crossed the lawn and were walking in the long grass that skirted the edge of the woods. A path led off to the

300  right through the tangle of undergrowth, and we followed it, climbing across boulders and fallen tree trunks until we came to an old stone well. I leaned over the wall of rocks around it and saw the small circle of sky far below.

"They had to drag him all the way here, you see, and hold him steady right over the well while they made the signs on his feet, so the blood would fall into the water. It's no good if it falls on the side of the well. And they had to make the same signs the *fqih* drew on paper for the little girl. That's hard to do in the dark and in the rain. But they did it. I saw the cuts
310  when I bathed him."

Cautiously I asked him if he saw any connection between all this and Marsh's death. He ceased staring into the well and turned around. We started to walk back toward the house.

"He died because his hour had come."

And had the spell been broken? I asked him. Could the child walk afterward? But he had never heard, for Meriam had gone to Kenitra not much later to live with her sister.

When we were in the car, driving back down to the city, I
320  handed him the money. He stared at it for several seconds before slipping it into his pocket.

I let him off in town with a vague sense of disappointment, and I saw that I had not only expected, but actually hoped, to find someone on whom the guilt might be fixed. What constitutes a crime? There was no criminal intent—only a mother moving in the darkness of ancient ignorance. I thought about it on my way home in the taxi.

*Tim McCarthy*

⊶⊷⊶⊷⊶

# The Windmill Man

1    What was the premonition? It had been with him at least since the day old Clayton Hobbs fell off the mill and killed himself. Nearly a month ago now. Clayton had been astride the tail pouring fresh oil into that gear case. The simplest of jobs. But Clayton was over seventy years old and had vowed never to climb another windmill tower. "Hang it all. I ain't going to drag Justus across forty miles of desert just to pour a few quarts of oil into a gear case." Those might have been his words, talking to himself in the way of the lonely, tobacco

10  juice bubbling at his lip, bursting, staining his mustache. The simplest of jobs, yet something went wrong. The old man lost his balance, or his heart kicked up on him—something! He fell sixty feet to the ground. No one found him for three days, after the ravens and the coyotes had got to him, an oil can crushed in his fist. Justus sent flowers: "Condolences. Justus Knight." And that night he crept out of bed while his wife slept, went out and leaned against the windmill down by the corral, and cried.

        For fifty years Clayton had been a windmill man in that
20  part of the state and clear over into Arizona. He had been one of many to begin with. But gradually the others had died off or been killed or crippled, and no one had showed up to fill their shoes. Clayton was alone. In those last years he taught Justus everything he knew about windmills—including how to fear and love them, if such things can indeed be taught. Justus had the ten sections his father left him, but they were mostly sand and creosote bush and they wouldn't carry fifty head without feeding extra. He also had two daughters and a wife who wanted her slice of the American pie, so he had to find some
30  other way to earn money. The neighbors laughed at him when he finally went into the windmill business on his own. Windmills were on the way out; he would never make a living. That was six years ago. Clayton had referred his dwindling trade to

Justus and now the younger man had more work than he could handle. Six years had brought changes that were astonishing to most people. Gas was short, electricity threatened or curtailed. You couldn't buy anything when you wanted it, and what you did get hold of cost twice what it was worth. The country was going to pot, and some of its people were turning
40 back to the things they could more or less rely upon. Things like the windmill, a machine as simple as it was old upon the earth. And the wind to drive it, which for all its capriciousness was free and full of power. Now Clayton was dead, and Justus was the only good windmill man for a long way around.

He should have been content, and he supposed that for the most part he was. Until a month ago at least. He was keeping his wife happy. She had a new pickup, and they had recently moved from the adobe ranch house his father had built into a shiny, air-conditioned mobile home that had
50 arrived in two sections and was designed to look like a house. It almost succeeded, too, when it was set on a concrete foundation and surrounded by a trim lawn. A year of work and watering had turned the place into a regular oasis, with the towering antenna for the colored television filling in for a palm tree. Justus was glad that his wife liked the place, and he always felt cool and clean there himself. But there were days when he still preferred the corral and pens and old adobes down across the arroyo to the rear. Usually such things didn't trouble him one way or the other. He was on the road most of
60 the time. He had his work and he liked it. There was a solid, straightforward satisfaction in building a windmill from the ground up—lowering the drop pipe, cylinder, and sucker rod two, three, or even four hundred feet toward the bowels of the earth, cementing the anchor posts, and coaxing the tower up stage by stage until the stub tower clamped into its peak and you could set the gin pole to haul the mill up. Then before long he could throw the furl lever and watch that towering creation groan to life. Those first strokes never failed to pump up an edge of tension, of anticipation, that drew his belly a little
70 tight. For after all those years, all those windmills, he had not overcome the wonder, the sudden thrill he felt every time that first jet of water spurted from the lead pipe. That was the kind of satisfaction a man could stand upon, could build his life upon from the ground up.

If anyone had ever succeeded in getting Justus to talk seriously about his work, he probably would have told him something of the sort. Yet even that much was unlikely. Justus was a reserved man, a little shy in his ways. He thought he

knew himself pretty well. He was small and trim, with light
80   brown eyes and a straight look. His round chin bulged from a
squarish face and he kept his sandy hair cropped so close that
from a distance he appeared bald. On the ground his manner
was tight, even stiff at times. He didn't smoke, swear, or drink.
His voice was an even drawl, subdued, almost a hush, as if
there were something deep within himself that he feared to
awaken. But once up on a windmill tower his whole body and
bearing seemed to relax, to run with life. He swung out free as
a wild thing, silent and sure, and often those who watched
from below clamped their awe-hung jaws for fear of giving
90   themselves away. What most men found dangerous Justus
experienced as a kind of liberation.

That was his secret. He was hardly conscious of it himself, but even if he had been able to articulate it down to its last
wind-torn detail, he never would have done so. Justus was not
the kind of man to give so precious a thing away. He kept what
was his to himself and let others think what they would. There
was a kind of sideways satisfaction even in that. Anyway it all
held for him until the day Clayton Hobbs fell off the mill.
What was the premonition? At first it was only a shadow, a
100  certain darkness that he could all but feel in his chest, as if a
cloud had come between him and his heart. Then he got the
job of erecting what he had come to call the Royal Don windmill, and the shadow began to take shape. It was as if that
windmill were the voice of his premonition, an articulation of
it shaping itself girt by girt, angle brace by angle brace into the
sky.

The Royal Don windmill fought him from the start.
Clayton had warned him that might happen. "Cussed things
can get so ornery they might as well as be human," he said.
110  The mill was to pump a domestic well on a newly purchased
piece of land up off the old Royal Don Mine road. Once you
left the shade of the giant cottonwoods along the Mimbres
there was nothing up there but rocks and hills, rugged
arroyo-slashed rangeland, flood-heaved, wind-dried, and sun-
cracked. Oak, juniper, mesquite. No one had ever lived on it
before—no white man at any rate—then along came Jesse
Pruit and drilled a well on an impossible hill. Why in God's
name would anyone ever want to live out here? That was
Justus's first reaction as he turned off the mine road onto
120  Pruitt's track. But the place had its pull. Even Justus felt it, and
he was a man who usually saw land only in terms of wind,
water, and grazing potential. There was a subdued, even subtle

grandeur to it, if you can imagine such a thing. It stretched
north to the brooding Black Range, west and south along the
coppery Santa Rita hills, then past the granite jut of Cooke's
Peak and clear into Mexico. A long, lonely landscape that
could tumble your heart and in the next breath ache low in
your belly with the spirit of a half-forgotten place, an old
memory you could not quite catch and conquer. Justus hopped
130  out of his pickup, turned a quick circle, then let his gaze come
to rest on the rough, raw pyramid called Cooke's Peak, monu-
mental, anchoring the Mimbres Range to the plain. "Nice
place you got here," he said. Jesse Pruit seemed to ponder this.
He looked sideways at the ground, shoved his hands in his
jeans with his thumbs thrusting free, hunched his hulking
shoulders, spit, shifted his plug, lurched Justus a straight look,
and said, "Yup." Jesse had come over from Texas, but Justus
didn't hold that against him. He liked the man from the start.
Though Jesse was over fifty, you could tell at a glance that he
140  was still a working fool. He looked to have been carved from
oak, the whole of him, from his salted sideburns to his down-
at-the-heel boots. Solid. You would have had to roast him an
hour to get an ounce of fat off of him. His cap was the only
whimsical touch. He favored the same floppy, polka-dotted
affair that Justus liked to wear on the job. Justus had a sign
reading "I work alone" taped to the toolbox in the back of his
truck. But when Jesse offered to give him a hand, he did not
hesitate to accept. Good thing he did, too! He needed all the
help he could get with the Royal Don windmill.
150      It wasn't just the windmill, either. The land itself seemed
to resent the intrusion. It offered them about a foot of stony
topsoil, then crumbled to a rock-ribbed grainy substance that
looked more like ashes than dirt. It was like digging into the
record of some primordial conflagration deep as the earth. The
more you dug, the more there was to dig; the hole never got
any deeper. They finally had to drench it with river water so
they could take the anchor holes down to four feet. From there
the first two sections of the tower went up easily. Justus began
to feel better. But the ground around the well sloped two ways,
160  and they had a devil of a time squaring and leveling those
sections so they could cement them down. They'd get one leg
right only to throw another one off. Round and round they
wrestled it through an afternoon of ninety-degree heat, a
vicious circle that brought them both to the edge of cursing.
They kept looking to the west for wind but none came, and
they counted themselves lucky on that score. At five they got it

leveled and went down to Jesse's trailer for a drink of cold
water. Suddenly—out of a sky so calm that even the ravens
had forsaken it—a fierce wind gusted up, rocked into the hill,
170  snapped sotol stalks, swooshed like sixty through the juniper,
and died. In the silence that whirled like a second, soundless
wind into its wake both men turned to face the hill, knowing
full well what they would see. For a moment, neither could
draw a breath. There was no air! Up there on the hill the tower
lay on its side like the skeleton of some prehistoric beast. Jesse
spit and looked sideways at the ground. Justus yanked off his
polka-dotted cap and swabbed his glistening pate.

And that's the way it went with the Royal Don windmill.
Two anchor posts were bent beyond use. Parts were hard to
180  find. There was a delay of three days before they could heave
the tower back into place. Then they took it up, section by
section, girt by girt, fighting, it seemed, for every bolt and nut
they could punch or hammer home. After what seemed a
month of Sundays, Justus pried the ill-fitted stub tower close
enough to clamp, then worked the wooden platform down
over it. The tower was up! Justus looked down at the other
man and almost smiled. Jesse had been watching every move,
shading his eyes with a big brown hand, one cheek bulging
with tobacco. Now he looked aslant and rotated his shoulders,
190  the way a boxer does sometimes to loosen up, spat, then knelt
by one corner post to chain a block into place. With luck they
would haul the mill up before quitting time. But the first time
Justus swung up onto the platform he knocked a wrench off.
"Watch it!" The shout was too late. Jesse's forearm was
gashed to the bone, the wrench bloody by his knee. Justus had
to drive him into Silver for stitches. Another day shot. He
began to hate that windmill the way he would never had
allowed himself to hate another man. He'd already lost money
on it. Now it had cost him his helper. Next thing he knew he
200  would be losing his temper—something no windmill man
could safely allow himself to do.

The next day they got the tailbone, vane, and motor
assembled and the whole works onto the tower—Justus handling the tackle and a somewhat wan Jesse backing the pickup
with one hand. But of course the wind had gusted up at the
very moment Justus was anchoring the block on top of the gin
pole. He rocked there forty feet in the air, fighting for balance,
clinging like a lover to that wavering plastic pole, his heart
punching into his throat. And then the motor wouldn't slip
210  plump onto the mill pipe. Justus wrestled it every which way

until his belly burned with anger and the blood surged hot into his head. He could barely see for the sweat smarting his eyes. Finally he gripped the rim of the gear case, braced both feet against the motor and wrenched his whole weight into it, time after time, hunched parallel to the ground like some lesser primate raging at the mesh of his cage, heaving, twisting, until Jesse heard him screech something that sounded like shhee-at! and the motor clunked home. Jesse smiled, looked sideways at the ground, and spat.

220     The wheel went on without undue trouble, arm after arm, tediously but true, which for this windmill was something of a small miracle. By sunset the sucker rod was bolted to the pump pole, the connection made between the towering mill and the short brass cylinder three hundred feet into the earth. The wind was still up. Justus threw the furl lever, but for the first time that he could remember he did not keep watch for that first jet of water. He put his ear to the drop pipe, and as soon as he heard that both check valves were working properly, he turned his back on the clicking, clanking mill, hopped

230 into his pickup and began to make out Jesse's bill. For all he cared that windmill could spin itself off the face of the earth— even if he would have to replace it under his usual guarantee.

What was the premonition? It weighed heavy in him again as he crossed the divide into Silver City that afternoon. Jesse had caught up with him by phone at the Carlton ranch outside of Lordsburg: "That windmill of yours has gone crazy. Furl wire's broken, storm's coming, tank's full, and the water's wasting all over the ground."

*My* windmill. The protest rose in Justus's throat but he

240 forced it down. His heart fell, quaked. In a small, quiet voice he said, "I'm real busy right now. Can't you climb up there and brake it?"

There was a long silence. For a moment he thought Jesse had hung up. Then he pictured him looking slantwise at the floor, one hand holding the phone, the other stuffed in his pocket, thumb thrusting free. He waited, fought to gird his heart for what he knew he was about to hear. Finally Jesse spoke: "I could... but I'm not about to. Not the way that thing's turning... You *do* guarantee your work, don't you?"

250     "I'll be there directly."

Now he had crossed the Santa Ritas and was heading down the valley. He drove mechanically, watching the road but not really seeing it. He tried not to think, to imagine. The few thoughts that forced themselves upon him seemed to come from somewhere outside his head. Echoes. But always it was there. The premonition. Towering into a roiling sky. A runaway windmill. He hadn't realized until that afternoon how hard he had been fighting to put the Royal Don windmill behind him. Now it was there. A runaway. A premonition.

260　　　It hadn't rained for nearly a year. The grass was burned beyond feeding, the ground cracked like a dead skin. Today the first rain of the season was brewing over the Black Range. A runaway windmill was bad enough. But a runaway with lightning, a shifting wind ... Justus shrugged and felt a little better. It would be, *had* to be that way with the Royal Don windmill.

He was almost through the village before he realized where he was. Haphazard adobes, most of them unplastered, rusted tin roofs, mud walls bellying above crumbling stone

270　foundations, a rickety store with a single gas pump in front, a squat bar, its one small window bright with a neon beer sign. Only two miles to the turn. Not a soul in sight. Newspapers blowing down a dirt street. An election poster on a fence post, half the candidate's head flapping in the wind. A dying place. Yet up there in the hills a few miles above the valley Jesse Pruit was staking a claim on life. With a pick and shovel, some rocks and mud, he was starting the whole circle all over again. A man ought to take hope from that. Justus could not. His belly turned with dread.

280　　　Water was running in the Mimbres. First time in months. Justus took note as he crossed the bridge. Must have been raining in the mountains for hours. As he crossed the first cattle guard up from the valley the wind nearly tore the steering wheel from this hand, jolting him from his daze. He had to pull himself together. Get this job done. Go home and watch TV from a big chair, with the first rain clicking on the trailer roof. The image settled him somewhat. And then he caught sight of it. The Royal Don windmill. About a mile to the west across that humping time-slashed land. Barely visible against

290　the lowering day, the roiling blackness of the sky. He looked away, his stomach tightening again, as he turned onto Jesse's track.

Jesse was waiting at the foot of the tower, beneath the whir of the great wheel, in the swift fourbeat click-click-clank-click of the mill, the wind beating his yellow slicker about his legs. The moment Justus hopped from the pickup it began to rain. Cooke's Peak had vanished in the storm. Lightning jagged in a sudden simultaneous row of four across the Black

Range. All the land—the hills, the canyons, the arroyos, and
300 the valley—between the Emory Pass and Caballo Blanco in the
Santa Rita range was wind-rocked and thundered, heaving
with sound. The wind tore at Jesse's hill, wrenched the juni-
pers nearly flat to the rocks. Justus was soaked in the ten steps
it took him to reach the tower. "Where's it broke at?" he
shouted in response to Jesse's nod.

Jesse spat, the wind smearing his tobacco spit against the
storage tank behind. He seemed to consider the question for a
moment then shouted his response. "Right at the furl lever.
Only way you can hitch it is from the platform."
310 "We'll see," said Justus setting his jaw. But as he spoke
the wind shifted, gusted south, violently. The great wheel
heaved round, its tail thrashing, wind-whipped, as if the mill
were some monstrous sea creature beached in the storm. Justus
stared at it, rain drilling his face, and he realized that what he
felt swelling into his heart from the very pit of him was fear.

With a quick, slashing motion he turned and stepped to
the pickup, dug a short iron bar from the jumble in back.
Maybe he could pry the furl lever home from below the platform, brake the wheel. Supporting the bar like a stubby lance
320 against his hip, he advanced on the tower. "We'll get her," he
said with a glance toward Jesse. But the wind snatched his
words, smashed them back past his own ear, and Jesse, un-
hearing, spat and looked aslant. Justus's polka-dotted cap was
smeared to his head and pulled so far down over his ears that
nothing could blow it off. He tugged at it one last time, then
shoved the heavy bar into his belt and scampered up the corner
post ladder.

The wind seemed to redound, redouble as he climbed the
shuddering tower. The upper cross braces hummed and rat-
330 tled. The four-beat rhythm of the mill, louder, more immediate, click-click-clank-click. And the wheel, always the wheel,
whirring louder, fiercer, until those whirling arms cleaved just
above his head. He wrapped his legs around the stub tower
and hitched himself around beneath the platform until he
could arch the bar up over and probe for a hold on the furl
lever. The bar, the tower, everything was slick and slippery in
his hands. There! He'd almost had it. Again. Again. But no. It
was no good. The wheel was going too fast. He'd never be able
to brake it with the bar. Damn this windmill anyway. Damn it
340 all to hell. He would have to attach the furl wire then have
Jesse brake the mill from below. Lightning thundered onto the
valley, blazing, blinding deep behind his eyes—a cold, white

heat. *Rising.* Damn you! Damn you! He heaved himself up and beat at the furl lever with the bar. Beat at it. Beat at it. Damn you! Damn you! But nothing. He could barely hear the iron strike home. He was breathless, exhausted, trembling. He hurled the useless bar out into the blackness of the storm and inched back to the ladder. For a few moments he clung there, motionless, feeling foolish and afraid, despising himself to the
350 edge of tears, breathless, gathering strength. He would have to go up.

His breath was returning. He raised his head above the platform, so close to the raging wheel that its breath felt more powerful than the wind itself. He gauged his move, concentrating so hard that for a moment both the windmill and the storm faded to the recesses of his hearing. If the wind didn't decide to shift he would be all right. He turned his attention to the wind, gauging it, feeling it out. But that voice howling out of the black was dumb, deep as madness, and he could not
360 hear its intent. Now, Justus! He heaved himself onto the platform and in almost the same motion caught the furl lever with one boot and from that foothold swung up onto the tail. At first he merely held on for dear life, straddling that cold, ribbed giant as if it were some towering, insensible mutation of the horse. Then he gradually got his bearings. The wind clubbed and ripped at him, rain stung his face, but he felt he had firm hold. The wheel couldn't touch him here. He was on top! He had been there before, a thousand times, wind or no wind. Here the wheel's whir was a fiercesome roar. Its twelve-foot
370 span whirled so fast that the curving, cleaving blades were one. No. Faster yet! There was a tail of speed, of motion, an aureole of velocity ringing the wheel, making it appear larger than life. But suddenly he was not afraid. His cap was planted firmly, safely upon his ears. He felt light, almost happy—the way he used to feel in the old days, when Clayton was alive. He glanced confidently down at Jesse. The other man's face was in shadow, his slicker a yellow blur. Only his hands stood forth. They looked huge and very white on the corner post. Even from that height Justus could see that their grip was hard,
380 immovable, as if Jesse alone were holding up the tower. Justus clucked his tongue and twisted his upper body down toward the furl lever, the toe of one boot snagged in the ribbing for support. His heart thrilled to the whir and race of the wind. He had been here before! He had the wire hitched in a jiffy. "Brake the wheel!" he shouted as he arched himself back onto the tail. Then a blast of lightning, thunderous blaze. For a

blink of time Justus felt himself burned black against the jag-
ging light. His arms were already flailing, as if he sensed the
shift before it came. It came. A clubbing crosswind out of the
390 black. Whipping the tail round, flipping the man off like so
much jetsam. He turned once in the air, his body loosely awry,
as if it were already limp and lifeless. Yet he landed on his
hands and knees—at the last trying to rise even as he fell. The
shock was tremendous. His insides seemed to explode against
his spine, then collapse into his belly in a mush. Only the
polka-dotted cap held true.

What was the premonition? He felt it looming there in
the descending black, heard it above the storm in the four-beat
rhythm of the mill, in the great wheel whirring as if it would
400 turn forever. He had been there before. He puked a blackish
gob, smearing his mouth, the darkening earth, dying, dying
out, the windmill man.

*Joyce Carol Oates*

—·«·»— ·—·—· —·«·»—·

# *Under/Ground*

1 ## *CHARACTERS*

**NOLA HARVEY:**  *twenty-eight years old*
**MILES HARVEY:**  *forty to fifty years old*
**KEITH:**  *thirty to thirty-five years old*

*Lights up. Extreme stage right, KEITH, NOLA, and MILES are standing preparatory to entering the underground bomb shelter. Most of the stage is dark. KEITH, NOLA, and MILES may be standing on a raised platform to indicate "ground level"—a sidewalk—outside the shelter. There are double doors leading into the shelter; stairs, a landing, more*
10 *stairs, corridors, doors to rooms, etc. The shelter need not be represented realistically but should be suggestive in its labyrinthine, gloomy, sinister, surreal complexity. The play itself begins in apparent realism and moves gradually toward surrealism.*

*KEITH is a foreign-service officer of modest rank at the American embassy of this capital city of an unnamed European country: seemingly upbeat, optimistic, ebullient, "patriotic" in the professional manner of foreign-service employees abroad. NOLA HARVEY is the young wife of DR. MILES HARVEY, an American historian of some reputation. The HARVEYS are attractively dressed: NOLA in a tasteful,*
20 *"feminine" dress or suit; MILES more conservatively. KEITH wears regulation diplomatic attire—a dark blue suit, conservatively cut, a plain necktie. As these three descend into the bomb shelter, their personalities gradually shift—from their "daylight" or "social" personae to deeper, more primitive personalities.*

*As the lights come up, KEITH, NOLA, and MILES are laughing companionably. KEITH fumbles for his wallet and extracts two small plastic card-keys to unlock the shelter doors. The locks on the doors are prominent.*

NOLA:  Oh, I've had too much to drink—that luncheon
30  went on and *on*. Is it always like that at the
  embassy?

KEITH:  (*suavely, boyishly*) Only when our visitors are VIPs.

MILES:       We weren't treated half so well in Frankfurt after
             my lecture.

KEITH:       That's because it was Frankfurt—a major post.
             Here—(*lowering his voice, smiling*)—well, things
             are sort of *minor,* as maybe you've noticed.

NOLA:        This is a lovely country. The people are so—
             warm, and curious, and *interested* in us.

40 KEITH:    Yes, they adore Americans—at least our faces. (*As
             he peers at the card-keys and fits one into the lock
             of the outer door, without success*) They're eager
             for visas to "study"—to get scholarships to pay
             their way to the States. (*Smiling*) Wait'll you see
             this place—as the ambassador was saying, they
             lost most of the capital city's historic architecture
             in the war, so they've poured money into
             government buildings. (*Fussing with key-cards,
             still pleasant, but getting impatient*) This bomb
50           shelter is quite something, y'know, for a country
             so—limited in resources as this.

NOLA:        (*a bit apprehensive*) This—bomb shelter—is it big?

KEITH:       Mammoth!

NOLA:        I've never been in a bomb shelter before.

MILES:       Nor have I, come to think of it. They've lost
             popularity, back home.

KEITH:       (*sly smile*) They still exist, back home—but they're
             reserved for VIPs, you bet!

NOLA:        (*uneasily*) Well. I guess we don't like to think
60           about that.

KEITH:       That's the idea.

NOLA:        (*to MILES*) I—I'm wondering whether I really
             want to go in here. It's such a lovely, sunny day.

MILES:       Certainly you're coming along. We want to "share
             everything," don't we? (*Gives her a significant
             look, squeezes her hand*)

KEITH:       (*as a guide; "booster" voice*) When it was built in
             1964, this was as modern as any shelter in the
             world, even the Kremlin's—even our own
70           leaders'. Now, I guess it's outmoded in certain
             respects, like for instance a chemical attack—toxic
             chemicals *sink,* y'know—but in case of a
             conventional nuclear war, it should be adequate.
             Ah! (*Succeeds in unlocking the door; turns the
             knob and pushes the door in, producing a sharp,
             creaking, jarring noise*)

NOLA:      (*startled by the noise, laughs nervously*) I—
           I think I—

MILES      (*displeased*) Nola, dear, don't be silly.

80  NOLA:      —I'd rather wait in the car.

KEITH:     (*like a salesman*) Oh, the shelter is perfectly safe,
           Mrs. Harvey. (*Joking, with a gesture toward the
           sky*) Much safer than "reality."

NOLA:      (*apologetic, but willful*) My head aches, I must
           have drunk too much champagne.

MILES:     (*pulling gently but firmly at her arm*) We are not
           going to leave you in the car, and *I* want to see the
           shelter. If Ken says it's safe—

KEITH:     Keith.

90  MILES:    —if he's taken visitors through before—

KEITH:     Dozens of American VIPs! The most
           distinguished, last year, was Vice-President
           Quayle! And he loved it.

NOLA:      Loved it?

KEITH:     Mr. Quayle is *appreciative.*

(*NOLA acquiesces. The three step through the first doorway into a
small vestibule. KEITH is enjoying his role as guide.*)

KEITH:     (*playful finger to lips*) The existence of this shelter
           is a state secret, so we'll close the door—quickly.

100              (*Shuts outer door; NOLA makes an involuntary
           gesture, as of distress at being locked in.*)

MILES:     (*bemused*) A state secret? This gigantic door, in a
           wall fronting a street? Behind Parliament?

KEITH:     An open secret, for sure. But—it isn't spoken of.
           (*To NOLA*) Are you all right, Mrs. Harvey?

NOLA:      Oh—yes.

MILES:     (*overlapping with NOLA*) My wife is *fine.*

KEITH:     (*familiar, solicitous*) Gee, I used to be
           claustrophobic too, as a kid. Even through

110            college. Had dreams about being buried alive,
           choking for air, trapped—burr! (*Shudders, but
           reverts easily to cheerful tone as he inserts the
           second card in the inner door*) They say it's a basic
           human phobia—fear of being buried alive.

(*NOLA hugs herself, shudders; sniffs as if smelling something
unpleasant.*)

MILES:     (*professorial, pedantic*) No doubt because in the
           past, people often *were* buried alive—poor souls

who were believed to be dead but weren't. Before
120             modern medical technology. Before embalming.

NOLA:   (*nervous laugh*) That's what it smells like!

MILES:   What smells like—?

NOLA:   The air in here smells like formaldehyde.

MILES:   (*disapproving*) *I* don't smell anything.

KEITH:   (*cheerfully*) Oh, this is nothing, yet.

NOLA:   (*accommodating*) Of course, it could be
          my—imagination.

(*KEITH continues to try to fit the card into the lock, turning it upside-down, jamming it in harder or more gently, etc., but without success.*
130 *To cover his annoyance, he begins to whistle.*

MILES:   (*to KEITH*) Do many people have access to this
          shelter?

KEITH:   Naturally not. This is *the* bomb shelter in the
          country. The prime minister—high-ranking
          government officials and members of Parliament
          —a select number of diplomats and visitors.
          (*Smiles*) Everyone at the U.S. Embassy, for sure.
          They wouldn't keep *us* out. (*Muttering*) Damn
          this lock, I *know* it works.

140 NOLA:   (*an edge to her voice; schoolgirl sort of manner*)
          And what about the others?

KEITH:   What others?

NOLA:   The seventy million others in this country.

KEITH:   (*vaguely, blandly*) Oh, I'm sure they'd be taken
          care of. There are lots of bomb shelters, more
          conventional ones, built during the war. (*Pause*)
          Anyway, ordinary folks wouldn't expect to be
          included in *this* shelter.

MILES:   I should think not.

150 NOLA:   (*stubbornly*) I thought this was a "parliamentary
          democracy"—an "egalitarian" society.

KEITH:   So? That doesn't affect their tradition.

MILES:   (*to KEITH*) Keith—it *is* Keith, isn't it?—how long
          have you been posted here?

KEITH:   (*shrugging, pleasant*) Oh forever! . . . Naw, only a
          few years. They rotate us around. Prevent us from
          getting "attached." Before this I was stationed in
          Norway. Before that, Canada. (*Yawns*) Places
          where nothing much happens. Or if it does, you
160           don't notice. (*An old joke*) Like—tree rings

growing. (*Pause, more seriously*) Almost, y'know,
you wish for some kind of action—"history"—in
backwaters like this. Gee, I envy my colleagues in
the Mideast—I *do.*

NOLA: (*incensed*) You wouldn't want bombings, would
you? Missiles? *War?*

KEITH: (*quickly*) Oh, no, of course not. (*Reverts to an
earnest, official voice*) The goal of all U.S.
diplomacy is global peace.

170 (*KEITH has managed to unlock the door, with a cracking, creaking
sound, as before. As the three step through the inner door, MILES takes
a small camera out of his pocket.*)

KEITH: (*with sudden authority*) Uh, Dr. Harvey—better
not.

MILES: Not even for private use?

KEITH: This *is* an official classified zone.

MILES: But who would know?

KEITH: It's just forbidden.

MILES: (*smiling*) Yes, but who would know?

180 NOLA: (*embarrassed*) Oh, Miles, put it away. Please.

MILES: (*reluctantly*) Well. All right. But I don't see—

KEITH: It's all right that we're here so long as it isn't *known*
we're here. Y'know—diplomacy.

MILES: I understand. Sorry. (*Slips camera back into
pocket*)

KEITH: Thanks! (*Switches on fluorescent lights, shuts
second door, with a little difficulty.*)

NOLA: What if we're locked in here?

KEITH: Impossible, Mrs. Harvey. (*Waving cards*) What
190 got us in will get us out. Also—there are plenty of
telephones.

(*NOLA nudges herself against MILES, who slips an arm around her.
KEITH begins to lead them down the stairs, which are steep.*)

KEITH: (*ebulliently*) Hmmmm! It *does* smell a bit, doesn't
it? But you get used to it quickly. Nothing to be
worried about—it's perfectly empty, and it's
perfectly safe. In fact, I find it comforting. I feel so
*privileged.*

(*Lights out.*)
200 (*Lights up.*)
(*KEITH, NOLA, MILES are standing on a landing, illuminated
brightly while the rest of the stage remains darkened. NOLA and MILES*)

*glance up behind them a bit edgily, as if to indicate that they've*
*descended a considerable distance.)*
    *(Here, we see a large, glossy—though faded—poster giving*
*numbered instructions in a foreign language, an invented language*
*suggestive of Finnish and Russian: "Kyväuoppyio"—*
*"Hyvmespheere"—"Janisijäaratiaj"—"Vjtirkborg"—"Svenszeri"—*
*"Väajivilya"—"Reostrov"—"Ostrykyr"—etc. There is a life-sized*
210 *mannequin in full nuclear defense gear: khaki jacket and trousers, gas*
*mask, boots, gloves.)*

NOLA:      (*girlish reaction, seeing mannequin*) Oh! It's
             so—lifelike.

KEITH:    (*tapping mannequin on head*) Yeah, he's my
             buddy, Hiya, pal! (*To the HARVEYS*) He's wearing
             your basic issue, for when the bomb falls. I mean
             —uh, if—*if* the bomb falls. (*Chuckles*) I've had the
             gear on—actually, it's a lot more comfortable than
             it looks.

220 NOLA:      A gas mask can suffocate you, if it's defective.

KEITH:    Nah, more likely people put them on wrong. The
             human factor—no matter how they're educated,
             some people for sure are going to goof up in times
             of emergency.


    *(A deep, subterranean, near-inaudible throbbing and vibrating has*
*begun.)*

MILES:    (*cupping hand to ear*) What's that?

KEITH:    Generator, ventilation system, hydraulic pumps—
             everything running constantly, of course.
230              Twenty-four hours a day.

NOLA:      So—everything is ready. (*Shivers*)

KEITH:    Absolutely! There's a maintenance crew, for sure.
             And the whole thing is in the process of being
             computerized.

NOLA:      (*glancing back up behind her, uneasy*) How deep
             *is* this place?

KEITH:    Oh, we've hardly begun. We're down about
             twenty-five feet is all. The lowermost level is one
             hundred seventy-five feet. (*Gesturing expansively*)
240              A regular metropolis!

MILES:    (*has been examining poster*) What a language! I
             know German, and Russian, and some Swedish,
             but this hardly seems Indo-European.

KEITH:    Yeah, it's like Hungarian—a real linguistic
             challenge.

(MILES *stumbles through some of the words on the poster,*
*mispronouncing them:* KEITH *rattles them off with surprising fluency.*)

KEITH:  It's just directions in time of emergency. Routine
stuff—schoolchildren are drilled in it.

250  (*Fluorescent lights flicker subtly.* NOLA, KEITH, MILES *notice but say
nothing. Lights then stabilize.*)

MILES:  (*an air of profundity*) How—strange! After
millions of years of evolution, and the progress of
civilization, a man doesn't know—*really* know—
what he's made of. Until he's put to the test.

NOLA:  (*lightly ironic*) And a woman?

MILES:  By "man" I include woman. As in "mankind."

KEITH:  It's true, Dr. Harvey! And for entire nations, too.
Entire nations can be courageous, or cowardly.

260  MILES:  It's a process of evolution, I suppose.

KEITH:  Survival of the fittest!

MILES:  I'm a historian, not a scientist, but I've always seen
the basic pattern—adaptation or death.

NOLA:  (*shivering*) It *is* cold.

MILES:  Would you like my coat, dear? To drape over your
shoulders?

NOLA:  No, I'll be all right.

(KEITH *leads* NOLA *and* MILES *down another flight of stairs; or the
action is simulated. Lights behind them go out; others come on. The*
270  *throbbing and vibrating sound is more pronounced. We come to an
area of several shut doors; a television monitor; an old-fashioned wall
telephone, its receiver dangling loose. Signs on the wall "Út
Ysskräjivak-Ylla"—"Czijillo Bvtthlíomez."*)

KEITH:  (*chattering*) Above us—four-ton steel reinforced
shields. On all sides—steel and concrete. Tons of
dirt. (*Pointing*) Down that corridor, the
communications center; down here, the infirmary;
and this corridor (*pointing*) is a secret passageway
connecting the shelter with the prime minister's
280                residence. (*Turns on light switch, but corridor
remains dark*)

MILES:  Say, can we see that?

KEITH:  Well, Doctor, it's uh, *dark.*

MILES:  (*peering into corridor*) I believe I hear—dripping?

KEITH:  *I* don't hear anything.

NOLA:  (*wrinkling her nose*) That smell ...

MILES:  How far down are we now?

| | |
|---|---|
| KEITH: | Approximately one hundred feet. (*Cheerfully, glancing up*) You can feel it, sort of, can't you— |
| 290 | eardrums, eyeballs—a sort of—*force?* |
| NOLA: | ... like stagnant water. |
| MILES: | (*primly*) Leakage in here could be dangerous. |
| KEITH: | (*stiffly*) The shelter has *never* leaked, Dr. Harvey, in its entire history. |

*(NOLA has wandered to the telephone, lifts the receiver to her ear, out of curiosity. She catches MILES' eye, mouths the words "It's dead," shakes her head, and returns the receiver to its cradle.)*
    *(KEITH, oblivious of NOLA, has gone to a door to open it, switch on lights. The room is cell-like, very small. A single cot.)*

| | |
|---|---|
| 300 KEITH: | Here we have a typical room: a bit compact, but not bad, eh? And a single, if you like privacy. |
| NOLA: | (*holding her nose*) Oh, dear! The smell! |

*(MILES too reacts, but enters the room; bends to peer under the cot: recoils in disgust.)*

| | |
|---|---|
| MILES: | Ugh! |
| NOLA: | (*frightened*) What is it? |
| MILES: | Uh—nothing. |
| NOLA: | (*dreading*) Something—dead? |
| KEITH: | (*quickly*) Oh, I'm sure it's—nothing. |
| 310 NOLA: | (*voice rising*) Something dead? |
| MILES: | (*professorial irony, dry wit*) Darling, it isn't any danger to us in the condition it's in—let's put it that way. |
| KEITH: | (*peering under the cot too, similarly revolted; turns off lights, firmly shuts the door; apologetic, chagrined*) Whew! That's most unusual, I swear. |
| MILES: | (*pedantic*) Decomposition would be very slow in here, of course—no flies, very little bacteria. More likely, since the air is so dry, the process would be |
| 320 | like—mummification. |
| | (*A pause.*) |
| NOLA: | (*frightened*) A rat? |
| KEITH: | (*whistling*) *Most* unusual. |

*(NOLA looks around, alarmed, listening to the throbbing, vibrating sound.)*

| | |
|---|---|
| NOLA: | My God, isn't this—madness! This! Down here! How long could human beings survive down here, if there *was* a war? |

|        |        |                                                                                  |
|--------|--------|----------------------------------------------------------------------------------|
|        | MILES: | Now, Nola.                                                                        |
| 330    | KEITH: | Now, Mrs. Harvey.                                                                 |
|        | NOLA:  | (*pulling away from* MILES's *touch*) Think of the terror, the disorientation, the hopelessness— |
|        | KEITH: | (*ticking off on his fingers, matter-of-fact*) The alert sounds—you report to your station—the shelter is sealed—you wait out the results of the attack: what's so hopeless about that? Anyway, what's the alternative? |
|        | NOLA:  | (*angry*) You don't seem to realize, either of you, that we are surrounded by *earth*. This is a tomb, it's |
| 340    |        | for burial—burial alive.                                                         |
|        | KEITH: | (*smiling*) Why, no. It's for surviving. Surviving alive. |
|        | NOLA:  | I can feel the earth—the weight of it. The pressure. (*Swaying, hands to eyes*) It's horrible. |
|        | MILES: | (*embracing* NOLA, *addressing* KEITH *over her shoulder*) My poor darling interprets everything so *personally*. |
|        | KEITH: | My wife was the exact same way, Dr. Harvey! I guess that's how women are. |
| 350    | MILES: | They lack the gift of abstraction. Of detaching yourself from experience. |
|        | KEITH: | Exactly!                                                                          |
|        | MILES: | Nola, dear, it's just your imagination, whatever you're thinking of. Mmm? (*Whispers in her ear*) |
|        | KEITH: | Shall we continue?                                                               |
|        | NOLA:  | (*easing away from* MILES, *with an expression of dread yet resignation*) There's more? |
|        | KEITH: | The best is yet to come.                                                          |

(NOLA *stares at him, laughs incredulously.*)

|        |        |                                                                                  |
|--------|--------|----------------------------------------------------------------------------------|
| 360    | KEITH: | (*politely*) I gather you are a disarmament person, Mrs. Harvey? An "ecology" person? |
|        | NOLA:  | (*pertly*) And you are a war person?                                              |
|        | KEITH: | (*laughing pleasantly*) I don't care to be reduced to a political stance, Mrs. Harvey, any more than you do. I'm a realist. Americans are realists. Of course, the shelter isn't a luxury hotel, but the fact is, it *exits*. And if there's a nuclear war, you're either *in* or you're *out*. |

(*A pause.* MILES *nods professionally.* NOLA *glares at* KEITH, *then turns*
370 *away, to continue down the stairs.*)

|        |        |                                      |
|--------|--------|--------------------------------------|
|        | NOLA:  | (*grimly*) Let's get this over with. |

(KEITH *hurries to accompany* NOLA; *takes her arm on the steep stairs,* MILES *holds back, surreptitiously removes his camera from his pocket, takes two quick photographs of the secret passageway and the room. Neither* KEITH *nor* NOLA *notices.*

*Lights out.*

*Several beats. "Shelter" sounds—rustlings, scuttlings, echoes of footsteps, distorted voices, distant laughter or cries. An eerie sort of music, underlaid by the throbbing, vibrating pulse.*

380 *Lights up.*

KEITH *and* NOLA *are on the next level. There is a new rapport between them, as if their outburst has linked them emotionally.* MILES *in background.*)

| | |
|---|---|
| KEITH: | All sorts of Americans come through here, and the cultural attaché foists them off on— I mean, entrusts them to—me. But it's a lonely post. |
| NOLA: | Is it? You seem so sociable. |
| KEITH: | You and the professor are leaving tomorrow? |
| 390 NOLA: | Yes. For Stockholm. |
| KEITH: | Were you—a student of his? |
| NOLA: | Does it show? |
| KEITH: | It's the best kind of marriage, I'm sure. Marriage between equals never works. (*As* NOLA *looks at him, startled*) I mean—somebody always wants to be more equal than the other. |
| NOLA: | (*stiffly*) I have an advanced degree too—I'm just not using it right now. I'm (*pause*) ... just not using it right now. |
| 400 KEITH: | No kids, eh? |
| NOLA: | Miles has two sons, already grown. (*Pause*) He doesn't want more. |
| KEITH: | He dumped his old wife for you, eh? I don't blame him. |
| NOLA: | (*offended*) What did you say? |
| KEITH: | *I* was married, but it didn't last. Marriages sort of fall apart in the foreign service. |
| NOLA: | That's—too bad. |
| KEITH: | My wife hung on through Ottawa pretty well, just |
| 410 | about made it through Oslo: but here (*laughs*) she started speaking their language, suddenly!—like, y'know, the words would—*erupt*—in the midst of other things, in her sleep, or in—uh—intimate moments with me. (KEITH *emits harsh, crowing sounds, his eyes shut.*) |

"Kuhvavalaji!"—"Pyajuddik-ut!"—
"Uzkavajjikyyo!"

NOLA: (*staring at him*) How—

KEITH: (*when we think he has finished*)

420 "Hyvskyygizkyi!"

NOLA: —awful.

KEITH: (*wiping forehead*) It *was* awful. I'd hafta pacify her, like—(*a gesture as of pressing the flat of his hand over someone's mouth; then pause*) Poor li'l Bobbie went back to Tulsa, where she's from, with the kids. Got remarried to some ol' high-school sweetheart. (*Yawns*) That's how it is.

NOLA: You must miss your children.

KEITH: (*leaning closer to her*) I get lonely, but not for my

430 children.

NOLA: (*uneasy*) You—uh—must go back home occasionally, to the States?

KEITH: (*shrugs*) Once you leave, and live in other countries, you sort of forget about home. (*Slight sneer*) That's another secret everybody knows.

NOLA: (*stiffly*) I wouldn't forget my home. My birthplace. (*Pause, as if a bit vague*) My family ...

KEITH: (*with a sudden, curious ardor, seizing NOLA's hand*) In a place like this, (*drawing out word*)

440 *underground,* you forget your own name. It's easier that way.

(*Pause. NOLA and KEITH stare at each other. NOLA slowly withdraws her hand.*

*MILES, out of breath, joins them.*)

MILES: Wait for me! (*Pulling at necktie*) It's a little—close in here, isn't it?

(*KEITH, NOLA, and MILES descend stairs to another, lower level. The sounds of the shelter are more evident here, especially to MILES, who glances about with increasing unease. KEITH whistles cheerfully,*

450 *intermittently, in short outbursts.*

*NOLA loses her footing momentarily, grips KEITH's arm; he steadies her. MILES, grown querulous, seems not to notice.*)

MILES: Is the air fresh, coming in these vents? It smells like mold.

KEITH: (*as if a direct, ingenuous reply*) Mold manufactures oxygen, doesn't it, doctor? "The action of friendly bacteria in fungus." (*Chuckles*)

(MILES *stares at him.*)

MILES:       (*tugging at tie*) I—I'm thirsty.

(*During the following dialogue, while* KEITH *continues his tour,* MILES
460  *wanders off, toward stage right, to get water from a water cooler. He
has some difficulty getting the water to come out of the spout. His
hands tremble as he lifts the paper cup to his mouth. Then, when he
drinks, he reacts immediately to the water—spitting it out, gagging,
crying, "Ugh!—ugh!" He has spilled water on himself and dabs at it
with a handkerchief, muttering.* KEITH *and* NOLA *do not notice.*)

KEITH:      (*expansive, ebullient*) Yessir! This is one of many
                nations with a "tragic history." Hitler punished
                them for their neutrality—Stalin killed hundreds
                of thousands in slave labor camps—and the Allies,
470                  I'm afraid, bombed the hell out of them—couldn't
                be helped. That's how history is—cruel to losers.
                (*Chuckles*)

NOLA:      (*sympathetic*) The soil of Europe is drenched in
                blood ... World War II seems so *recent*.

KEITH:      Yeah. People hang on to their history, even when
                it's fucked them up. (*Shakes head, bemused*) It's
                an old-fashioned concept, like that's how they
                know who they *are*.

NOLA:      (*looking around, indicating door*) What's in here?

480  KEITH:      Medical supplies. But the door's locked.

(NOLA *nonetheless tries the door, which opens, startling them.*)

KEITH:      Oops! Guess I'm wrong.

(*It is a closet, with shelves of bottles, vials, first-aid equipment,
bedpans, enemas, rolls of gauze, etc. There is a sudden scuttling noise
as of rodents fleeing, and one of the enema bags is knocked to the
floor.*)

NOLA:      Oh!

KEITH:      Go*damn*. (*Kicks enema bag*)

NOLA:      What was that?

490  KEITH:      What was what?

NOLA:      Some—things—creatures—were in there. I could
                see them running.

KEITH:      A roach, maybe. A mouse.

NOLA:      (*weakly*) There were more than one. They were
     bigger than mice.

KEITH:      Nah, this shelter is vermin-proof.

MILES:      (*clutching at KEITH's arm*) Excuse me, is there
     maybe—distilled water in there?

KEITH:      (*shutting door firmly; officiously*) We can't be
500      breaking into the supplies, doctor. We aren't even
     citizens of this country.

NOLA:      (*dismayed, to MILES*) Miles, you look so—

MILES:      (*querulous, self-pitying*) I don't feel well. It's this
     impure air. (*To KEITH*) What about oxygen—is
     there, maybe, oxygen in there?

KEITH:      Pure oxygen is a depressant—you don't want that,
     doctor.

MILES:      I'm having difficulty—breathing.

KEITH:      Nah, you'll get used to it.

510 NOLA:      If you didn't—talk—so much, Miles dear. I mean—
     (*as if genuinely solicitous of him, like a concerned
     wife, even as he stares at her in disbelief*)—if you
     didn't take up so much *space.*

MILES:      So much space? (*Looking down at himself*) This is
     all I have.

NOLA:      (*poking fingers in ears, experimentally*) Oh—
     something feels so strange! Like—champagne
     bubbles!

KEITH:      It's the pressure—on the brain. Makes the brain
520      cells sort of fizzle and pop—feel it? (*Giddy, he too
     pokes fingers in his ears and wriggles them
     playfully.*)

NOLA:      (*giggling*) So straaange—!

MILES:      Nola, Ken—I—I—don't feel well. I—

NOLA:      (*to KEITH*) Where are we now? How far
     underground?

KEITH:      What's it matter? We're here.

MILES:      (*as they ignore him, as if he were invisible*) I—I'd
     like to go back to the hotel. I don't feel well.
530      (*Reeling backward, to stare up at the stairs they've
     descended*) But, my God, how can I ever
     climb . . . ?

NOLA:      I've never felt like this before. (*Sniffing*) I think
     there's something in the air. (*Sly smile*)

KEITH:      The best is yet to come.

NOLA:      (*pointing at door, childlike, mischievous*) Uh-oh,
     *that* door—what's behind it?

KEITH:      Better not open it!
NOLA:       Why not?
540 KEITH:   Mmmm—it's forbidden, that's why.
NOLA:       Yes, but why?
KEITH:      Maybe it's locked. Maybe there's nothing behind
            it.


*(NOLA tiptoes to the door, daringly.)*
MILES:      *(pleading)* Nola, Ken—*please*—I need oxygen—


*(NOLA opens the door, and a figure tumbles out. It is dressed in a gas
mask, khakis, etc.: but is it a dummy, or a corpse? NOLA shrieks and
leaps back into KEITH's arms; MILES nearly faints.)*
KEITH:      *(seems seriously alarmed, disapproving, crouches
550         over the figure)* It's a—dummy. Like the other.
NOLA:       *(frightened)* Oh, *who* is—?
KEITH:      *(insistent)* A dummy. Like the other. *(KEITH tries
            to lift the figure to push it back through the
            doorway; though lifeless, it seems to be resistant.)*
NOLA:       I'm so sorry! Let me help you.
MILES:      *(backing off, swaying, weakly)* Don't touch it,
            Nola. It's contaminated.


*(KEITH and NOLA struggle to lift the bulky figure. With some effort,
they push it back through the doorway, and KEITH quickly shuts the
560 door.)*
KEITH:      *(panting, wiping at forehead with handkerchief )*
            Only a dummy. We all saw.
MILES:      *(a bit wildly)* I saw! I saw what that was!
KEITH:      *(incensed)* The prime minister will hear about this.
            Things are getting shamefully lax. *(To NOLA)* Are
            you all right, Nola? Mrs. Harvey?
NOLA:       A little—out of breath.
KEITH:      *(staring at her)* Your eyes! Dilated like a cat's.
NOLA:       I'm so sorry I—interfered.
570 KEITH:   *I'm* sorry. Perhaps we should wash up.
MILES:      *(accusing, cowering at stage right)* Nola, how
            could you? You touched it. That thing. I saw.
NOLA:       Wash up? Is the guided tour over?
KEITH:      Almost.
NOLA:       I want to see everything.
MILES:      *(faintly)* I want to go back to the hotel.

KEITH:   Well! Let's see! (*Opens another door, resuming his
         official manner; switches on lights, which flicker*)
         Here is one of the jewels of the shelter—the
580      parliamentary assembly room, with a seating
         capacity of three hundred.
NOLA:    (*looking in*) Goodness, it's vast. I can't see the
         walls.
KEITH:   (*cups hands to mouth, makes a yodellike sound*)
         Halloo! Halloo in there! Syvkrikkoya omphysikr!
         (*Low, rippling, booming echo of* KEITH's *words*)
KEITH:   (*whistles, yodels*) Pskyooyiala-ptimi! (*To* NOLA)
         Hear 'em? The P.M. and the M.P. debating what
         to do, now the Big One got dropped, that
590      everybody said never would, and Northern
         Europe is zapped. (*As if listening*) Nothing left
         above ground, but down here,
         chatterchatterchatter, gobblygook talk—Jeezuz.
         (*We seem to hear low, murmurous, contentious
         voices.*)
NOLA:    Oh, dear. Is it—?
KEITH:   Yeah, it's sad. But, y'know—history. (*Shuts door,
         and the sounds vanish.*)
MILES:   (*cowering at stage right, almost inaudible*) Help—
600      can't breathe—

(KEITH *kisses* NOLA, *somewhat grossly, on the mouth.* NOLA *stiffens
in resistance but does not shove him away.*)
NOLA:    (*as if incensed*) You're—crude, that's what you
         are.
KEITH:   *You're* nice.
NOLA:    Oh!
KEITH:   Some meat on your bones, the way I like 'em.
         (*Pinches her buttocks*)

(NOLA *slaps at him, shocked.*)
610  NOLA:    How dare you! You know I'm married.
     KEITH:   (*gripping her wrist*) Every American cunt who
              comes through here is married, for sure.
     NOLA:    I'll report you to the ambassador!

*(KEITH advances upon NOLA, who retreats toward stage left. It is as if she were mesmerized by him, backing away, arms extended gropingly behind her. MILES watches helplessly, in anguish.)*

MILES:      Nola—Nola! Help me! Can't breathe! (*Opens shirt, sinks to knees*)

KEITH:      (*in his earlier, ebullient tone*) The luxury rooms
620               come equipped with *saunas*. But it's a state secret.

*(Lights out.*
*In the darkness, sinister sounds: vibrating, throbbing, echoes as of voices, laughter, erotic/anguished murmurs, cries.*
*Lights up. MILES alone, stage right, sitting dazed on the floor. He has taken his camera out of his pocket, raises it with shaking fingers, to take a flash shot of the audience.)*

MILES:      The only evidence. All the dead. No one will
believe, otherwise. (*He is breathing hoarsely; perspiration gleams on his face.*)

630 *(Lights out on MILES; Lights up on KEITH and NOLA, entering from stage left. They are wearing dazzling white terrycloth robes and are barefoot; seemingly naked beneath the robes. Their hair is damp: KEITH's is slicked back, and NOLA is combing hers. They are amorous, playful; oblivious of MILES, who, under cover of darkness, crawls to exit stage right.)*

KEITH:      (*as they enter, arms around each other's waist, nuzzling NOLA's neck*) Toldja, eh! What'd I tellya?

NOLA:      That hurts!

640 KEITH:      Eh, sweetheart! What'd I tellya?

NOLA:      (*glancing around nervously*) Not *here*. Goodness, is this a public place!

KEITH:      So? Everybody's *fried*, nobody's *left*.

NOLA:      You shouldn't have sealed that door. I can't believe you so selfishly *sealed that door*.

KEITH:      We can repopulate, you and me. (*Whistles cheerfully*)

NOLA:      (*pouting*) I don't know if I—if I love you that much. In that way.

650 KEITH:      (*grabbing NOLA's hips playfully, roughly*) That's what all the cunts say.

NOLA:     (*trying to slap him, but he restrains her*) I hate that
          kind of talk, I really do. I *do*.
KEITH:    (*discovering camera on floor, whistling sharply*)
          What's this? (*He snatches it up, opens it, takes out
          the roll of film and pitches it into the darkness*)
NOLA:     (*closing robe at throat, as if her modesty were
          being threatened*) Oh, is that a *camera*?


(KEITH *stuffs the camera into his pocket. Offstage, in the darkness*
660  *stage right, an ominous chewing and crunching sound has begun,
nearly inaudible at first, then building.*)
NOLA:     What's that?
KEITH:    What's what?

(KEITH *goes to fetch a bottle of wine and two glasses.* NOLA
*approaches the darkness at stage right but holds back, fearfully.*)
NOLA:     I hear something—strange.
KEITH:    (*pouring wine into glasses*) I don't hear anything.
          Just the generator. (*Pause*) When that goes out, *we*
          go out. (*Amorous, cheerful, handing* NOLA *her*
670       *glass*) But not for billions of years!
NOLA:     (*distracted by sounds offstage*) Oh, dear, it sounds
          like—something eating? chewing? (*Listens*) Or
          being chewed. (*Squints into darkness*)
KEITH:    Aw, it's all dark there. It's oblivion. "The darkness
          upon the face of the deep." (*Smirks*) But the Spirit
          of God isn't coming this time. *Zap.*
NOLA:     (*listening, blinking*) Hear it? Little jaws, teeth—so
          many—grinding. Brrr! (*Turning to* KEITH) Oh,
          protect me!

680  (KEITH *slides an arm around* NOLA; *she rests her head against his
shoulder; after a moment, they raise their glasses, clink them together,
drink.*)
KEITH:    It's great, eh? From the P.M.'s private cellar.
          (*Chuckles*) We're *in* the cellar.
NOLA:     I'm so ashamed, I seem to have forgotten your
          name.
KEITH:    Nah, it's all right.
NOLA:     But it isn't like me at all.
KEITH:    Down here, honey, we don't have names.
690  NOLA:  Don't?
KEITH:    It's easier that way.

*(Lights flicker and dim, but remain steady.)*

NOLA:     And if the generator goes out?

KEITH:    It never has, yet.

NOLA:     *(gazing up at him, urgently)* But—if it does?

KEITH:    *(firmly, ebulliently)* We still have each other.
          There's always—love. And—I have this. *(Takes
          from his pocket a candle, which he lights)*

*Lights slowly out. Noises of chewing, etc., in background. Finally only*
700 *the candle flame remains, illuminating the lovers' radiant faces.*

*(THE END)*

*Philip Appleman*

# Gathering at the River

1  Is it
crossing over Jordan
to a city of light, archangels
ceaselessly trumpeting over
the heavenly choirs: perpetual Vivaldi,
jasper and endless topaz and amethyst,
the Sistine ceiling seven days a week,
the everlasting smirk
of perfection?

10  Is it
the river Styx,
darkness made visible, fire
that never stops: endless murder
too merciless to kill,
massacres on an endless loop,
the same old victims always
coming back for more?

Or is it the silky muck
of Wabash and Maumee, the skirr
20  and skim of blackbirds,
fields of Queen Anne's lace
and bumblebees? Well,
go out once more, and feel
the crumble of dry loam,

fingers and soil slowly becoming
the same truth: there in the hand
is our kinship with oak, our bloodline
to cattle. Imagine,
not eons of boredom or pain,
30  but honest earth-to-earth;
and when our bodies rise again,
they will be wildflowers, then rabbits,
then wolves, singing a perfect love
to the beautiful, meaningless moon.

# Mark Doty

# *Noir*

1 It's the hotel balcony, after midnight
    and though the station below's deserted
      there's an engine idling black

as the current under the bridge,
    and chimes echo from the warehouses,
      the moon and the clock flashing back

from factory windows. That's how much
    is leaning toward your eyes,
      and I'm leaning too, dangerously.

10 This town's in tatters, dead
    since the trains stopped mattering,
      and though I've stopped for the night it's no place

I expect to encounter my life. *Come out
to the balcony,* you said, and then
      it's one of those forties' movies,

the city grid awry and black and white,
    the late marquees benevolent
      but ambiguous. In the film I'm imagining

a woman on some minor mission, a journey
20 she'd rather not take, lands in a strange town
      and somewhere between the crazy streets

by the depot and the lobby's cool welcome
    she feels what she couldn't have known yet
      open around her. This unfamiliar burg's

more catacombed with possibility
   than she knew; you can see it in the drape
      of her coat, the way she's trying to protect

herself with her collar. There's a reason
   for going behind the scenes, into the depths
30      of roominghouses, alleys where the streetlamps

stripe the pavement like venetian blinds.
   Something's been hidden all along, though
      she must have felt it, the narrative

insistent as the forward pull of a novel.
   The river signs a dozen false names
      in neon. The hands of the clock stop,

signalling the moment we didn't know
   we were waiting for, or else
      they rush forward: the calendar's amphetamined,

40  shedding pages like there's no tomorrow.
   Sooner or later everything must rush
      at the character in this story,

the smoking engine, the clockface and the hour,
   every whole or broken moon flashing
      hypnotically above a life strangely up

for grabs. And in the last moments
   the truth that appears is something
      we could have known all along,

if only we'd been able to piece the clues,
50     or even recognize them. Anything
      can matter: a cigarette

lit to kill time, the decision
   to sit in the hotel bar just a little
      longer, ice in the scotch,

all the instants before the instant
   we met, before we walked onto the balcony.

## Bruce Bond

# Gallery of Rivers

1　In your watercolors of Texas, a mosquito floats
in a glass of milk. Hot light pours
through the memoirs of trees,
imagining how the street-tar softens
or the vaguely bruised shade of brick.

The scene lays down its magnificent burden
of affection, having come so far,
and appeals to us, the way lovers
appeal to each other's silence.
10　Morning sun hurls across the widest day of the year.

When I look in your breezeways,
their sparse stories, the abundance
of white, it's Sunday.
No one dies or gets married:
I cannot know your stories, where to begin,

how they lead like one story
through the walls of a summer
boathouse, its warm lock. This morning
you call me back to bed, stretch your legs.
20　We are slipping words inside each other's words,

turning against the solace of rivers,
the belief that we never step in the same
word twice, the same story, the same
hot Texas street. Your story's horizon
wavers in the heat as though the very air

resists us: where the river thickens
and bends, a girl sketches in the mud
with a stick. Above her the August afternoon
nearly pauses in its canvas, then draws
30 away, broad, white, refusing to be filled.

## Jay Parini

# *Working the Face*

  1  On his belly with a coal pick
mining underground:
the pay was better for one man
working the face.
Only one at a time could get
so close, his nose
to the anthracite, funneling
light from a helmet, chipping,
with his eyes like points of fire.
10  He worked, a taproot
tunneling inward, layer
by layer, digging
in a world of shadows,
thick as a slug against the floor,
dark all day long.
Wherever he turned, the facets
showered a million stars.
He was prince of darkness,
stalking the village at 6 P.M.,
20  having been to the end of it,
core and pith
of the world's rock belly.

# Al Young

# *New Autumn, New York*

1 Late in the day when light is sandwiched
softly between slices of daytime and night,
I stroll around Gramercy Park, locked as usual
and all keyed up again for the real autumn.

To the falling of leaves in time-lapse slow
motion, I follow my feet, each crackling step
nudging me into a vaster present than this
friendly seasonal chill can circumscribe.

There is no end to the inward adventure of
10 journeying October to the edge of November.

# WRITING ASSIGNMENTS

1. Write a story in which an American tourist becomes involved in a strange occurrence in an exotic foreign setting, such as Tangier (used by Paul Bowles), Hong Kong, Singapore, Casablanca, Cairo, or Johannesburg. Do the necessary research if you do not have the direct experience. Use your imagination.

2. Write a play or story that uses a symbolic setting, such as those used in "The Windmill Man" by Tim McCarthy or *Under/Ground* by Joyce Carol Oates. For instance: the ruins of a lost city in a remote jungle, a bleak landscape, a smoldering volcano, a huge unexplored cave, an oasis, an industrial wasteland of smokestacks and toxic fumes, an unspoiled paradise.

3. Write a play or story that takes place in a generic setting, such as a living room, a barn, a bar, a boat. Make everything happen in a limited period of time without a change of scene. Analyze television situation comedies to see how much can happen on a single set.

4. Write a poem about a big city that captures the essential qualities of the place.

5. Write a poem about a special place that has some significance and evokes strong feelings. For instance, a rocky shore, a river bank, a meadow, a misty lake, an old house, a summer place, a lover's leap, the hanging tree, an old cemetery, an old boatyard, a lighthouse.

# *Character*

## *Introduction*

## *Fiction*

Joyce Carol Oates      *Nairobi*
Jennifer Egan      *Sacred Heart*

## *Drama*

A.R. Gurney, Jr.      *The Problem*

## *Poetry*

Ai      *The Mortician's Twelve-Year-Old Son*
Susan Astor      *Dame*
Mary B. Campbell      *Sexual Terrorist*
James Tate      *I Am a Finn*
            *I Am Still a Finn*

## *Writing Assignments*

A character in literature is not a real person, any more than a portrait hanging on the wall is a real person. Like the subject of the portrait, the character is a part of a work of art and is limited by other factors which go to make up the whole.

A character is an imagined being with the appearance of reality, drawn from the writer's observation of actuality, and given life by the writer's own feeling of empathy with his or her creation. Let us say the character is a murderer; writers can relate to that. We have all *had* the impulse to kill, and if we have been close observers, we have all *seen* the impulse to kill. Observation and empathy are the tools of imaginative creation.

There are many devices for breathing humanity into an imagined character. A description of the individual's appearance may be the beginning. The Aryan exterminator in "Killing the Bees" (Chapter 1), for instance, is introduced as "tall, narrow-hipped and rangy," with "wonderful golden-haired wrists and big hands" as well as "noteworthy muscles." He is a minor character; nevertheless we have a vivid sense of him. The French writer Honoré de Balzac frequently uses one startling physical characteristic to bring his characters to life—a glaring eye, a nose, a bulging vein—and to underline their obsessions. And in "The Windmill Man" (Chapter 2), the windmill is so passionately described as to become a second character, the enemy perhaps.

Dialogue is another means of breathing life into a character. In plays, of course, characters are created by the way they speak, by the attitudes and desires they express, by the way other characters react to them, and by the actions they take. In Max Apple's play in Chapter 1, Grandpa reveals himself as a curmudgeon when he refuses to go to Larry's Bar Mitzvah; an idealist when he says, "And I want you to care about the whole world, at least about all the workers"; and a loving man when he says, "Larry, my *boychik*, you know I love you." In A.R. Gurney's *The Problem,* both husband and wife reveal themselves, in a comic mode, as deliciously salacious and inveterate gameplayers.

In "Sacred Heart," Jennifer Egan's story about a turning point in a young girl's life, Sarah's character is explored through her own thoughts and observations. She is restless, excited. She longs to visit "a world of ecstasy and violence."

> During Mass I would sit and imagine the infant
> Christ on his bale of straw, the barn animals with
> burrs and bits of hay caught in their soft fur. I
> would gaze at our thin Jesus perched above the
> altar and think of what violence he had suffered
> since his day of birth, what pity he deserved. And
> I found to my confusion that I was jealous of him.

Later her mood has changed, and she sees the crossed
ankles of Jesus as a pair of "neatly folded drumsticks on a
roasting chicken," an image that may indicate to the reader that
her religious feelings have undergone a change. Sarah's own
finely detailed perceptions make her "come alive" as a character, and give her depth.

Action, too, defines a character. Sarah, for instance—
wanting to be more like a girl with whom she is momentarily in
love—cuts the inside of her arm with a razor. It is entirely
plausible. She doesn't want to die; she wants to do something
perverse. The act frightens her. It is the climax of the story, and
it causes her to resolve her life in a more mature way.

Ginny, in Joyce Carol Oates' "Nairobi," is described by
her actions. She allows Oliver to dress her as someone else, in
beautiful clothes and shoes that she admires and wants. She
plays her part in his little drama, and afterwards is sent packing.
At the end, however, it is her thoughts that help the reader to
grasp something of the essential Ginny. She suffers from a sense
of loss: " … of loss tinged with a queer cold sickish knowledge."
The reader must wonder, knowledge of what? of Oliver? of
reality? of herself? of a sort of prostitution? If the latter, then the
last sentence of the story is surely ironic: "All she had lost, in a
sense, was her own pair of shoes."

Thoughts, dialogue, images, all equip the author to give
the character more depth. In "Sacred Heart," the character's
thoughts are easy for the author to express, since the story is
written in the first person. In "Nairobi," however (written in
the third person), we see that Ginny's thoughts may also be
expressed.

A writer will generally not wish to give all his characters
depth. There are major and minor characters, and there are

"flat" and "round" characters. The flat characters do not have to be stereotypes (like the incorruptible sheriff or the cruel landlord) but may be sufficiently endowed with life in a sentence or two. The "wonderful golden-haired wrists" of the exterminator in "Killing the Bees" (Chapter 1) is one example. Another is Julius, in "Sacred Heart": "He was the sort of man who stayed warm when it was cold out, who kept important tickets and slips inside his wallet when you needed them."

Round or flat, a character must be plausible. Let's say that you are writing that story about a murderer, a woman. The reader must believe that she has the capacity to kill. She will probably not be a passive personality, for instance. Or if she is, then her passivity will mask a repressed violence. She must have sufficient motivation to do the deed. Sarah, as we have noted, is *motivated* to cut her arm. It is a plausible act, and one that we can all understand. It has universality: It expresses in some way the experience of adolescence.

Poetry, of course, may also deal with character, although it is not as important an element there as it is in fiction. In "Dame," Susan Astor laughingly, affectionately, describes the character of her dog. In "The Mortician's Twelve-Year-Old Son," the appearance of inaccessibility in a woman is undermined in death. In "Sexual Terrorist," Mary B. Campbell projects a character or persona—the "I" of the poem—who is both violent and comical. Or, possibly, the persona is violent and the tone is comical. There is a world of possibility in the speech and thoughts of characters: How much are they speaking for themselves, how much for the author?

Joyce Carol Oates

# *Nairobi*

1    Early Saturday afternoon the man who had introduced himself
as Oliver took Ginny to several shops on Madison Avenue
above 70th Street to buy her what he called an appropriate
outfit. For an hour and forty-five minutes she modeled clothes,
watching with critical interest her image in the three-way
mirrors, unable to decide if this was one of her really good
days or only a mediocre day. Judging by Oliver's expression
she looked all right, but it was difficult to tell. The salesclerks
saw too many beautiful young women to be impressed, though
10   one told Ginny she envied her her hair—not just that shade of
chestnut red but the thickness too. In the changing room she
told Ginny that her own hair was "coming out in handfuls"
but Ginny told her it didn't show. It will begin to show one of
these days, the salesgirl said.

     Ginny modeled a green velvet jumpsuit with a brass
zipper and oversized buckles, and an Italian knit dress with
bunchy sleeves in a zigzag pattern of beige, brown, and cream,
and a ruffled organdy "tea dress" in pale orange, and a navy-
blue blazer made of Irish linen, with a pleated white linen skirt
20   and a pale blue silk blouse. Assuming she could only have one
costume, which seemed to be the case, she would have preferred the jumpsuit, not just because it was the most expensive
outfit (the price tag read $475) but because the green velvet
reflected in her eyes. Oliver decided on the Irish linen blazer
and the skirt and blouse, however, and told the salesclerk to
remove the tags and to pack up Ginny's own clothes, since she
intended to wear the new outfit.

     Strolling uptown, he told her that with her hair down
like that, and her bangs combed low on her forehead, she
30   looked like a "convent schoolgirl." In theory, that was.
Tangentially.

     It was a balmy, windy day in early April. Everyone was
out. Ginny kept seeing people she almost knew. Oliver waved
hello to several acquaintances. There were baby buggies, dogs
being walked, sports cars with their tops down. In shop

windows—particularly in the broad windows of galleries—
Ginny's reflection in the navy-blue blazer struck her as unfamiliar and quirky but not bad: the blazer with its built-up
shoulders and wide lapels was more stylish than she'd thought
40　at first. Oliver too was pleased. He had slipped on steel-frame
tinted glasses. He said they had plenty of time. A pair of good
shoes—really good shoes—might be an idea.

But first they went into a jewelry boutique at 76th Street,
where Oliver bought her four narrow silver bracelets, engraved in bird and animal heads, and a pair of conch-shaped
silver earrings from Mexico. Ginny slipped her gold studs out
and put on the new earrings as Oliver watched. Doesn't it hurt
to force those wires through your flesh? He was standing
rather close.

50　No, Ginny said. My earlobes are numb, I don't feel a
thing. It's easy.

When did you get your ears pierced? Oliver asked.

Ginny felt her cheeks color slightly—as if he were asking
a favor of her and her instinct wasn't clear enough, whether to
acquiesce or draw away just perceptibly. She drew away, still
adjusting the earrings, but said: "I don't have any idea, maybe
I was thirteen, maybe twelve, it was a long time ago. We all
went out and had our ears pierced.

In a salon called Michel's she exchanged her chunky-
60　heeled red shoes for a pair of kidskin sandals that might have
been the most beautiful shoes she'd ever seen. Oliver laughed
quizzically over them: they were hardly anything but a few
straps and a price tag, he told the salesman, but they looked
like the real thing, they were what he wanted. The salesman
told Oliver that his taste was "unerring."

Do you want to keep your old shoes? Oliver asked
Ginny.

Of course, Ginny said, slightly hurt, but as the salesman
was packing them she changed her mind. No, the hell with
70　them, she said. They're too much trouble to take along.—
Which she might regret afterward: but it was the right thing to
say at that particular moment.

In the cab headed west and then north along the park,
Oliver gave her instructions in a low, casual voice. The main
thing was that she should say very little. She shouldn't smile
unless it was absolutely necessary. While he and his friends
spoke—if they spoke at any length, he couldn't predict Marguerite's attitude—Ginny might even drift away, pick up a

magazine and leaf through it if something appropriate was
80  available, not nervously, just idly, for something to do, as if
she were bored; better yet, she might look out the window or
even step out on the terrace, since the afternoon was so warm.
Don't even look at me, Oliver said. Don't give the impression
that anything I say—anything the three of us say—matters
very much to you.

Yes, said Ginny.

The important thing, Oliver said, squeezing her hand
and releasing it, is that you're basically not concerned. I mean
with the three of us. With Marguerite. With anyone. Do you
90  understand?

Yes, said Ginny. She was studying her new shoes. Kidskin in a shade called "vanilla," eight straps on each shoe,
certainly the most beautiful shoes she'd ever owned. The price
had taken her breath away too. She hadn't any questions to
ask Oliver.

When Ginny had been much younger—which is to say, a
few years ago, when she was new to the city—she might have
had some questions to ask. In fact she had had a number of
questions to ask, then. But the answers had invariably disap-
100  pointed. The answers had contained so much less substance
than her own questions, she had learned, by degrees, not to
ask.

So she told Oliver a second time, to assure *him:* Of
course I understand.

The apartment building they entered at Fifth and 88th
was older than Ginny might have guessed from the outside—
the mosaic murals in the lobby were in a quaint ethereal style
unknown to her. Perhaps they were meant to be amusing, but
she didn't think so. It was impressive that the uniformed door-
110  man knew Oliver, whom he called "Mr. Leahy," and that he
was so gracious about keeping their package for them while
they visited upstairs: it was impressive that the black elevator
operator nodded and murmured hello in a certain tone. Smiles
were measured and respectful all around, but Ginny didn't
trouble to smile; she knew it wasn't expected of her.

In the elevator—which was almost uncomfortably
small—Oliver looked at Ginny critically, standing back to examine her from her toes upward and finding nothing wrong except
a strand of hair or two out of place. The Irish linen blazer was an
120  excellent choice, he said. The earrings too. The bracelets. The
shoes. He spoke with assurance though Ginny had the idea he
was nervous, or excited. He turned to study his own reflection

in the bronze-frosted mirror on the elevator wall, facing it with
a queer childlike squint. This was his "mirror face," Ginny
supposed, the way he had of confronting himself in the mirror
so that it wasn't *really* himself but a certain habitual expression that protected him. Ginny hadn't any mirror face herself.
She had gone beyond that, she knew better, those childish
frowns and half-smiles and narrowed eyes and heads turned
130 coyly or hopefully to one side—ways of protecting her from
seeing "Ginny" when the truth of "Ginny" was that she required being seen head-on. But it would have been difficult to
explain to another person.

Oliver adjusted his handsome blue-striped cotton tie and
ran his fingers deftly through his hair. It was pale, fine, airily
colorless hair, blond perhaps, shading into premature silver,
rather thin, Ginny thought, for a man his age. (She estimated
his age at thirty-four, which seemed "old" to her in certain
respects, but she knew it was reasonably "young" in others.)
140 Oliver's skin was slightly coarse; his nose wide at the bridge,
and the nostrils disfigured by a few dark hairs that should have
been snipped off; his lower jaw was somewhat heavy. But he
was a handsome man. In his steel-rimmed blue-tinted glasses
he was a handsome man, and Ginny saw for the first time that
they made an attractive couple.

Don't trouble to answer any questions they might ask,
Oliver said. In any case the questions won't be serious—just
conversation.

I understand, Ginny said.
150     A Hispanic maid answered the door. The elevator and
the corridor had been so dimly lit, Ginny wasn't prepared for
the flood of sunlight in the apartment. They were on the eigh-
teenth floor overlooking the park and the day was still
cloudless.

Oliver introduced Ginny to his friends Marguerite and
Herbert—the last name sounded like Crews—and Ginny
shook hands with them unhesitatingly, as if it were a customary gesture with her. The first exchanges were about the
weather. Marguerite was vehement in her gratitude since the
160 past winter, January in particular, had been uncommonly long
and dark and depressing. Ginny assented without actually
agreeing. For the first minute or two she felt thrown off balance, she couldn't have said why, by the fact that Marguerite
Crews was so tall a woman—taller even than Ginny. And she
was, or had been, a very beautiful woman as well, with a pale
olive-dark complexion and severely black hair parted in the

center of her head and fixed in a careless knot at the nape of her neck.

170    Oliver was explaining apologetically that they couldn't stay. Not even for a drink, really: they were in fact already late for another engagement in the Village. Both the Crewses expressed disappointment. And Oliver's plans for the weekend had been altered as well, unavoidably. At this announcement the disappointment was keener, and Ginny looked away before Marguerite's eyes could lock with hers.

But Oliver was working too hard, Marguerite protested.

But he *must* come out to the Point as they'd planned, Herbert said, and bring his friend along.

180    Ginny eased discreetly away. She was aloof, indifferent, just slightly bored, but unfailingly courteous: a mark of good breeding. And the Irish linen blazer and skirt were just right.

After a brief while Herbert Crews came over to comment on the view and Ginny thought it wouldn't be an error to agree: the view of Central Park was, after all, something quite real. He told her they'd lived here for eleven years "off and on." They traveled a good deal, he was required to travel almost more than he liked, being associated with an organization Ginny might have heard of—the Zieboldt Foundation. He had just returned from Nairobi, he said. Two days ago. And
190    still feeling the strain—the fatigue. Ginny thought that his affable talkative "social" manner showed not the least hint of fatigue but did not make this observation to Herbert Crews.

She felt a small pinprick of pity for the way Marguerite Crews's collarbones showed through her filmy muslin Indian blouse, and for the extreme thinness of her waist (cinched tight with a belt of silver coins or medallions), and for the faint scolding voice—so conspicuously a "voice"—with which she was speaking to Oliver. She saw that Oliver, though smiling nervously, and standing in a self-conscious pose with the
200    thumb of his right hand hooked in his sports coat pocket, was enjoying the episode very much—she noted for the first time something vehement and cruel though at the same time unmistakably boyish in his face. Herbert Crews was telling her about Nairobi but she couldn't concentrate on his words. She was wondering if it might be proper to ask where Nairobi was—she assumed it was a country somewhere in Africa—but Herbert Crews continued, speaking now with zest of the wild animals, including great herds of "the most exquisitely beautiful gazelles," in the Kenya preserves. Had she ever been there,
210    he asked. No, Ginny said. Well, said Herbert, nodding

vigorously, it really *is* worth it. Next time Marguerite promised to come along.

Ginny heard Oliver explain again that they were already late for an appointment in the Village, unfortunately they couldn't stay for a drink, yes it was a pity but he hoped they might do it another time: with which Marguerite warmly agreed. Though it was clearly all right for Oliver and Ginny to leave now, Herbert Crews was telling her about the various animals he'd seen—elands, giraffes, gnus, hippopotami, croc-
220 odiles, zebras, "feathered monkeys," impalas—he had actually eaten impala and found it fairly good. But the trip was fatiguing and his business in Nairobi disagreeable. He'd discovered—as in fact the Foundation had known from certain clumsily fudged reports—that the microbiological research being subsidized there had not only come to virtually nothing, but that vast sums of money had "disappeared" into nowhere. Ginny professed to feel some sympathy though at the same time, as she said, she wasn't surprised. Well, she said, easing away from Herbert Crews's side, that seems to be human
230 nature, doesn't it. All around the world.

Americans and Swedes this time, Herbert Crews said—equally taken in.

It couldn't be avoided that Herbert tell Oliver what he'd been saying—Oliver in fact seemed to be interested, he might have had some indirect connection with the Foundation himself—but unfortunately they were late for their engagement downtown, and within five minutes they were out of the apartment and back in the elevator going down.

Oliver withdrew a handkerchief from his breast pocket,
240 unfolded it, and carefully wiped his forehead. Ginny was studying her reflection in the mirror and felt a pinprick of disappointment—her eyes looked shadowed and tired, and her hair wasn't really all that wonderful, falling straight to her shoulders. Though she'd shampooed it only that morning, it was already getting dirty—the wind had been so strong on their walk up Madison.

On Fifth Avenue, in the gusty sunlight, they walked together for several blocks. Ginny slid her arm through Oliver's as if they were being watched, but at an intersection
250 they were forced to walk at different paces and her arm slipped free. It was time in any case to say good-bye: she sensed that he wasn't going to ask her, even out of courtesy, to have a drink with him: and she had made up her mind not to feel even tangentially insulted. After all, she hadn't been insulted.

He signaled a cab for her. He handed over the pink cardboard box with her denim jumper and sweater in it and shook her hand vigorously. You were lovely up there, Oliver said—just perfect. Look, I'll call you, all right?

260 She felt the weight, the subtle dizzying blow, of the "were." But she thanked him just the same. And got into the cab. And wasn't so stricken by a sudden fleeting sense of loss—of loss tinged with a queer cold sickish knowledge— that, as the cab pulled away into the traffic stream, she couldn't give him a final languid wave of her hand, and even shape her mouth into a puckish kiss. All she had really lost, in a sense, was her own pair of shoes.

Jennifer Egan

# Sacred Heart

1   In ninth grade I was a great admirer of Jesus Christ. He was everywhere at Sacred Heart: perched over doorways and in corners, peering from calendars and felt wall hangings. I liked his woeful eyebrows and the way his thin, delicate legs crossed at the ankles. The stained-glass windows in our chapel looked like piles of wet candy to me, and from the organ came sounds which seemed to rise from another world, a world of ecstasy and violence. I longed to visit that place, wherever it was, and when they told us to pray for our families I secretly prayed for
10 the chance.

  We had a new girl in class that year whose name was Amanda. She had short red hair and wore thin synthetic knee-socks tinted different colors from the wash. She wore silver bracelets embedded with chunks of turquoise, and would cross her legs and stare into space in a way that gave the impression she lived a dark and troubled life. We had this in common, I thought, though no one else knew it.

  During mass I once saw her scrape something onto the pew with the sharp end of a pin she was wearing. Later I
20 sneaked back when the chapel was empty to see what it was, and found her single first initial, "A." To leave one's mark on a church pew seemed a wondrous and terrible thing, and I found myself watching Amanda more often after that. I tried talking to her once, but she twirled her pen against her cheek and fixed her gaze somewhere to my left. Close up her eyes looked cracked and oddly lifeless, like mosaics I'd seen pictures of in our religion class.

  Though we were only girls at Sacred Heart, there were boys to contend with. They came from St. Pete's, our compan-
30 ion school three blocks away, and skulked relentlessly at the entrances and exits of our building. Unlike Christ, who was gentle and sad, these boys were prone to fits of hysterical laughter without cause. I was disturbed by stories I had heard of them tampering with the holy wafers and taking swigs of

the sacred wines Father Damian kept in his cabinet. They reminded me of those big dogs that leap from nowhere and bark convulsively, stranding young children near fences. I kept my distance from these boys, and when the girls began to vie for their attention, I avoided them too.

40     Late in the fall of that ninth grade year I saw Amanda cutting her arm in the girls room. I pretended not to notice, but when I left the stall and began washing my hands she was still there with her wrist laid out on the wood box which covered the radiator. She was jamming a bobby pin into the skin of her forearm, bunching it up.

"What are you doing?" I said.

Amanda glanced at me without expression, and I moved a step closer. She was working her arm in the fierce, quiet way she might work a splinter from her foot.

50     "It's not sharp enough," she said, raising the bobby pin. It was straightened, and the plastic nubs at its ends had been removed. Amanda seemed unembarrassed by my presence, as though trying to cut her arm were no different from braiding her hair with ribbons. This amazed me, and her urgency drew me in.

I was wearing a pin, a white goat my mother's husband Julius had bought me on a trip to Switzerland. I wore it to please my mother, for although it was hard to imagine a nicer man than Julius, I just couldn't like him. It was as if my not 60 liking him had been decided beforehand by someone else, and I were following orders. Now as I touched this present from him I wanted Amanda to use it—I craved it like you crave a certain taste. It was wrong and bad and yet perfect, somehow. I felt a pleasant twisting in my stomach, and my hands shook as I unhooked the pin from my dress.

"Here," I said, holding it up, "this might work."

Amanda's face looked softer than normal and puffy; as if she had been sleeping. She held me with her eyes while I looked for a match to sterilize the pin. A lot of furtive smoking went 70 on in that bathroom, and I found a book wedged behind the mirror. I clasped my goat's head and held the pin in the flame until it turned black. Then I held it out to Amanda, but she shook her head.

"You," she said.

I stood there a moment, the goat between my fingers. Although I was frightened, there was something raw and splendid in the sight of Amanda's arm against the chipped paint of the radiator cover. Her skin was white and smooth.

Gently I held her wrist and touched the pin to the scratch she
80  had already made. Then I pulled it away. "I can't," I said.
    Her face went slack. When I tried to give her the pin she
turned away from me, embarrassed. I felt like a coward, and I
knew that unless I helped Amanda now, she would never be
my friend.
    "Wait," I said.
    I took her wrist and held it. I scraped the pin hard this
time and made a thin, bleeding scratch along her skin. I kept
going, no longer afraid, and was surprised to find that the
point made a sound against her as though I were scraping a
90  piece of thick fabric. It was hard work, and soon my arms were
shaking. Sweat gathered on my forehead. I did not look once
at Amanda until I had finished an "A" like the one she carved
on the pew. When I did look I found her eyes squeezed shut,
her lips drawn back as if she were smiling.
    "It's finished," I told her, and let go.
    When Amanda opened her eyes, tears ran from them,
and she rubbed them away with her other hand. I found that I
was crying too, partly with relief at having finished, partly
from some other sadness I didn't understand. In silence we
100  watched her arm, which looked small and feverish under its
bright tattoo. I was aware of the hot light overhead, a smell of
chalk in the air and my own pounding heart. Finally Amanda
smoothed her hair and pulled her sweater-sleeve down. She
smiled at me—a thin smile, and kissed me on the check. For an
instant I felt her weight against me, the solidness of her, then
she was gone.
    Alone in the bathroom I noticed her blood on my
fingers. It was reddish-orange, sticky and thin like the residue
of some sweet. A wave of sadness made me shut my eyes and
110  lean against the sink. Slowly I washed my hands and my goat
pin, which I stuck in my pocket. Then I stood for a while and
looked at the radiator, trying to remember each thing, the
order of it all. But already it had faded.
    From that day on when I looked at Amanda a warm
feeling rose from my stomach to my throat. When I walked
into class the first place I looked was her desk, and if she were
talking to somebody else I felt almost sick. I knew each detail
of Amanda: her soiled-looking hands with their bitten nails,
the deep and fragile cleft at the base of her neck. Her skin was
120  dry and white around the kneecaps, and this got worse as fall
wore on. I adored these imperfections—each weakness made
Amanda seem more tender, more desperate for my help. I was

haunted by the thought that I had seen her blood, and would search her distracted eyes for some sign of that event, some hint of our closeness. But her look was always vague, as if I were someone she had met once, a long time ago, and couldn't quite place.

At that time I lived in a tall apartment building with my mother and Julius, her husband of several months. Julius was a
130   furrier, and the Christmas before he had given me a short fox coat which still draped a padded hanger in my closet. I hadn't worn it. Now that it was fall I worried my mother would make me put it on, saying Julius' feelings would be hurt. His lips seemed unnaturally wet, as though he'd forgotten to swallow for too long. He urged me to call him Dad, which I avoided by referring to him always as "you" and looking directly at him when I spoke. I would search the apartment until I found him, rather than have to call out. Once, when I was telephoning from school, Julius answered the phone. I said, "Hello ..." and
140   then panicked over what to call him. I hung up and prayed he hadn't recognized my voice. He never mentioned it.

It was getting near Christmas. Along the wind-beaten streets of downtown the windows were filled with cotton-bearded Santas and sleighs piled high with gifts. It was darker inside our chapel, and candles on thin gold saucers covered the stone walls with halos of light. During Mass I would sit and imagine the infant Christ on his bale of straw, the barn animals with burrs and bits of hay caught in their soft fur. I would gaze at our thin Jesus perched above the altar and think of what
150   violence he had suffered since his day of birth, what pity he deserved. And I found to my confusion that I was jealous of him.

Amanda grew thinner as winter wore on. Her long knee-socks slipped and pooled in folds around her ankles. Her face was drawn to a point and often feverish, so her eyes seemed glossy as white marbles against its flush. Sister Wolf let her wear a turquoise sweater studded with yellow spots after Amanda explained that neither one of her parents was home and she had shrunk her uniform. That same day her nose
160   began to bleed in science class, and I watched Sister Donovan stand for thirty minutes behind her desk, cupping Amanda's small head in her palm while another girl caught the dark flow of her blood in a towel. Amanda's eyes were closed, the lids faintly moist. As I stared at her frail hands, the blue chill which marbled the skin of her calves, I felt that nothing mattered more to me than she did. My mouth filled with a salty taste I

couldn't swallow and my head began to ache. I knew that I would do anything for her. And sitting there, in the familiar dull surroundings of my classroom, I was suddenly afraid.

170      Later that day I found her resting outside on a bench, and forced myself to sit beside her.

"Are your parents on vacation?" I asked. It made me nervous, approaching her like this. I glanced at her arm, but her sweater-sleeves reached the tops of her wrists.

"They're getting a divorce," she said.

Uttered by Amanda the word sounded splendid to me, like a chain of bright railway cars sliding over well-oiled tracks. Divorce.

"My parents are divorced," I told her, but it hissed when
180 I said it, like something being stepped on.

Amanda looked at me directly for the first time since that day in the girl's room, weeks before. Her irises were piles of broken glass in clean, still water. "They are?" she asked.

"My father lives in California."

I felt an urge to describe my entire life to Amanda, beginning with the "Devil's Paint Pots" I had seen with my father at Disneyland when I was six. These were craters filled with thick, bubbling liquid, each a different color. They gave off steam. My father and I had ridden past them on the backs of
190 donkeys. I hadn't seen him since.

"I have a brother," Amanda said.

In my mind the Devil's Paint Pots bubbled lavishly, but I said nothing about them. Amanda crossed her legs and rapidly moved the foot which hung suspended. She fiddled with her bracelets.

"Why do you watch me all the time?" she asked.

A hot blush flooded my face and neck. "I don't know," I told her.

Our silence filled with the shouts of younger children
200 swinging on the rings and bars. I thought of the days when I, too, used to hang upside down from those bars, their cold metal stinging the backs of my knees. I hadn't cared if my dress flopped past my head and flaunted my underwear. But it was ninth grade now, and nothing was the same.

"If you could have one wish," said Amanda, looking at me sideways with her broken eyes, "what would it be?"

I considered this. I wanted plenty of things: to poke freely through the cupboards of our altar, to eat communion wafers by the fistful and take a swig of the sacred wine. But I
210 told Amanda, "I'd wish I were you."

I had never seen her really smile before. Her teeth were slightly discolored, and her gums seemed redder than most people's. "You're crazy," she said, shaking her head. "You're really nuts."

She hunched over and made a high, thin sound like a damp cloth wiping a mirror. I thought at first that her nose was bleeding again, but when I leaned over, I saw she was only laughing.

220 Each morning, as the arc of frost on my windowpane grew wider, I worried about the coat. It hung in my closet, like an eager pet I knew I would have to feed eventually. When I touched the soft fur it swung a little. I had an urge sometimes to stroke it.

While I was dressing for school my mother came into my room. Her face was puffed with sleep, her lips very pale. It still amazed me to think that she and Julius shared the big bed where she had slept alone for so many years, where I had slept too when I had nightmares. I imagined an extra room back there where Julius slept, an inner door where he and my mother 230 kissed goodnight and did not meet again until morning.

"It's cold outside," my mother said.

I nodded, scanning my closet for a sweater. I could feel her watching the coat. She was quiet while I unrolled my kneesocks over my legs.

"You know," she said, "Julius really likes you. He thinks you're terrific." Her voice was filled with irrepressible pleasure, as if just saying his name felt good.

"I know it," I said, and I did—he fixed me pancakes in the morning and had offered many times to take me to his 240 warehouse, where I pictured row after row of soft, beckoning furs. So far I'd refused.

"Sarah," my mother said, waiting for me to look at her. "Please won't you wear it?"

She had flat hair and an open, pleading face. When she was dressed up and wearing her makeup my mother could look beautiful to me, but now, in the early white light of a winter day as she balanced her cup on her kneecap, she looked as if she had been badly damaged once, a long time ago, and never fully recovered.

250 "I will," I said, meaning it now. "I'll wear the coat when it's freezing."

Two weeks before the start of Christmas vacation, Amanda wasn't in school. When I saw her empty chair I felt a flicker of dread. I came inside the classroom and sat at my desk, but without Amanda to hook my attention to, the room felt baggy. I worried, before the teacher had even called her absent, that she would not be back.

A special assembly was called. Our headmistress, Sister Brennan, announced to the school that Amanda had run away
260 from home with her brother, a high school dropout who worked at Marshall Fields. As she spoke there, a vast stirring around me, the same I remembered from the day when we learned that Melissa Shay, two years below me with long gold braids, had died of leukemia during summer vacation. That stirring was laced with collective delight, a jittery pleasure at news so shocking that it briefly banished all traces of normal life. I twisted around with the other girls, exchanging pantomimed amazement. It comforted me to feel like one of them, to pretend that the news of Amanda meant no more than a
270 shorter math class. By the time Sister Brennan was finished an invisible mist of awe had risen among us, frail and delicate as steam, at the terrible thing Amanda had dared to do.

After that I found it hard to concentrate. I was obsessed with the thought that she had left me behind with the rest: Father Damian in his robes, the old chalkboards and desks, the solemn chapel. I felt physical pain in my stomach and arms as I walked through the doors to Sacred Heart, this place Amanda had discarded. The chapel stank of old lint and damp stone, the same words endlessly repeated. As Father Damian lectured
280 to us on Amanda's sin, I noticed how the clerical collar squashed and wrinkled his neck to look like a turkey's, how his eyes were thick and clouded as fingernails. I looked at Jesus and saw, where his crossed ankles should have been, the neatly folded drumsticks on a roasting chicken. After that I kept my eyes averted.

What compelled me instead was her desk. For weeks and weeks—who knew how long?—Amanda had sat before it, twirling her pen against her cheek and planning her escape. After school sometimes when the shadowy halls had emptied, I
290 would sit in her chair and feel the ring of her absence around me. I opened the desk and fingered her chewed pencils, the grimy stub of her eraser, a few haphazard notes she had taken in class. One by one I took these items home with me, lined them carefully along my windowsill and watched them as I went to sleep. I imagined Amanda and her brother walking through thick dunes of sand or climbing the turrets of castles. In my thoughts this brother bore a striking resemblance to

Jesus. As for Amanda, she grew more unearthly with every day, until what amazed me was not that she had vanished, but
300 that she had ever really been here.

One night when my mother had gone to a meeting and Julius was reading, I took a razor blade from the pack he kept in his cabinet. I held it between my fingers and brought it to my room, where I sat on the edge of my bed and took off my sweater. I was still in my school jumper with the short-sleeved blouse underneath, and I lay a pillow across my lap and placed my bare arm on top of it. My forearm was white as milk, smooth, full of pale, snaking veins. I touched it with the blade and found that I was terrified. Around me were my childhood
310 bears, my bubbling aquarium and ballerina posters. They were someone else's—a girl whose idea of mischief had been chasing those fish through their tank with her wet arm, touching their slippery tails. For a moment I felt her horror at what I was about to do, and it made me pause. But I had to do something, and this was all I could think of.

Gently but steadily, I sank one corner of the blade into the skin halfway between my elbow and wrist. The pain made tears rush to my eyes, and my nose began to run. I heard an odd humming noise but I continued cutting, determined not to
320 be a baby, determined to be as fierce with myself as I had seen Amanda be. The razor went deeper than the pin had. For a moment the thin cut sat bloodless on my arm—for an instant, and then, like held breath, blood rose from it suddenly and soaked the pillowcase. The white fabric bloomed with red. This happened so fast that at first I was merely astonished, as though I were watching a dazzling science film. Then I grew dizzy and frightened by the mess, this abundance of sticky warmth I could not contain.

I'd done something wrong, that was obvious. In the next
330 room I heard the kettle boil and the crack of Julius' chair as he rose to take it off the stove. I wished my mother were home. I stood up to go to him and ask for help, but my arm seemed huge and heavy to me now, an elephant's arm, and I couldn't carry it.

"Julius," I called. The name sounded unfamiliar, and it struck me that I hadn't said it aloud in nearly a year. The kettle was still whistling, and Julius didn't hear me.

"Dad," I hollered, which sounded even stranger than "Julius" had.
340 From the next room I heard the stillness of a pause. "Dad," I called again. The wet warmth was soaking through

to my legs, and I'd grown lightheaded. As I leaned back I remembered the Devil's Paint Pots with their wisps of steam, the man beside me on a donkey. Then the door to my room burst open, and Julius ran in.

I was shivering now. My teeth knocked together so hard that I bit my tongue. Julius wrapped me in the fox-fur coat and carried me to the car. I fell asleep before we reached it.

At the hospital they stitched my arm and wrapped it in
350 white gauze. They hung it in a sling of heavy fabric, and despite my shock over what I'd done to myself, I couldn't help predicting the stir my sling would cause in homeroom. Julius spoke to my mother on the phone. From what he said I could tell she was frantic, but Julius stayed calm throughout.

When we were ready to go, he held up the coat. It was squashed and matted, covered with blood. I thought with satisfaction that I had ruined it for good.

"I think we can clean it," said Julius, glancing at me.

He was a big man, with olive skin and hair that shone like
360 plastic. Each mark of the comb was visible on his head. I knew why my mother loved him then—he was the sort of man who stayed warm when it was cold out, who kept important tickets and slips inside his wallet until you needed them. The coat looked small in his hands, like a tiny animal he had shot by mistake. Julius held it a moment, looking at the matted fur. He glanced at me again, and without even meaning to I shook my head. I hated that coat, and it wasn't going to change in a minute.

To my amazement, Julius began to laugh. His wide, wet lips parted in a grin, and a loud chuckle shook him. I smiled
370 back, although I was uneasy.

In a single movement, Julius stuffed the coat into the white cylinder of the hospital garbage can. "What the hell," he said, still laughing, as the silver flap moved back into place. "What the hell." Then he took my hand and walked me back to the parking lot.

Months later, in early summer, Sacred Heart and St. Peter's joined to give a formal dance. I was invited by a boy named Stuart, who had the habit of flicking the hair from his eyes more often than necessary. Stuart's cheeks were smooth
380 and freckled and lifeless, but he seemed as frightened as I was, so I accepted.

I needed white shoes. After school one day in our last week of classes I went to a large store downtown which sold shoes at a discount. Just inside the door I shut my eyes.

Amanda was seated on a small stool, guiding a woman's foot into a green high-heel. There were crumpled tissue papers beside her. I noticed that her hair was longer now, and she was not so thin as before.

390 I had an urge to duck back out the door before she saw me. Although I hardly thought of Amanda anymore, I still held the vague belief that she had risen from the earth and floated off somewhere. What I felt, seeing her now, was a jolt of disappointment.

"Amanda," I said.

She twisted to face me and squinted a moment. Her confusion amazed me: for all the time I'd devoted to thinking of her, she had barely known who I was.

"Oh, yeah," she said, smiling now. "Sacred Heart."

She told me to wait while she finished with her client,
400 and I went to look for my shoes. I picked white satin, with tiny designs of pearl embroidered on top. I brought them to the register, where Amanda was waiting, and she rang them up.

"Where do you go to school?" I asked her.

She named a large public school and said she liked it better there. Her fingers moved rapidly over the keys.

Lowering my voice I said, "Where did you go?"

Amanda flipped the cash drawer open and counted out my change, mouthing the numbers. "Hawaii," she said, handing me the bills.

410 My mind filled with a vision of grass skirts, flower necklaces and tropical drinks crowded with umbrellas and canned cherries. Julius had been there, and this was how he described it.

"Hawaii?" I said. It was not what I'd imagined.

"We were there two weeks," Amanda said. "Then my dad came and got us."

She did not sound ashamed of this. As she handed me my box in its plastic bag she said, "He came all the way over, he had to. We would've stayed otherwise."

420 Amanda closed the register and walked me to the street, where we stood for a moment in silence. The day was warm, and both of us wore short sleeves. Her arms were smooth and lightly tanned. On my own arm, the thin pink scar was nearly invisible now.

Amanda leaned over and kissed me on the cheek. I caught her smell—the warm, bready smell that comes from inside people's clothes. Then she was gone, back at the door to the shoe store, waving. I thought her face looked pink.

430 I felt a sudden longing not to move from that spot. I could feel where her arms had pressed, where her hands had touched my neck. The smell was still there, warm and rich like the odor a lawn gives off after hours of sunlight. I turned to look back at her, but light hit the window so I couldn't see inside.

Finally, I began to walk, swinging my bag of shoes. I breathed deeply, catching the last of her smell, and it was only after several more blocks that I knew what I smelled was not Amanda. It was this day of early summer—the fresh, snarled leaves and piles of sunlit dirt. I was almost fifteen years old.

## A. R. Gurney, Jr.

# *The Problem*

1 CHARACTERS

THE HUSBAND   *In his thirties.*
THE WIFE   *Also in her thirties.*

SETTING

*As simple a set as possible: the suggestion of a study. A leather chair with a matching footstool, a reading light behind it. A bookcase.*

*At curtain the* HUSBAND *is sitting in the chair, feet up on the footstool, reading a book, smoking a pipe, taking notes into a notebook comfortably propped on his knee. After a moment, the* WIFE *comes in*
10 *from the left, hugely pregnant. She stands looking at him. He continues to read.*

| | |
|---|---|
| WIFE | Hey. |
| HUSBAND | *(Not looking at her.)* I'm reading, dear. |
| WIFE | *(Sticking out her stomach.)* I know. |
| | But look at me. |
| HUSBAND | *(Still reading.)* I'm preparing for a class, dear. |
| WIFE | I know, but just look. *(She crosses to him, stands by his chair, and sticks out her stomach.)* Just take a gander. |
| 20  HUSBAND | *(Turns his head and looks right into her stomach. He starts, takes off his glasses, looks again, and then looks up into her face.)* Well, well. |

|  |  |
|---|---|
| WIFE | Yes. |
| HUSBAND | Surprise, surprise. |
| WIFE | Yes. |
| HUSBAND | Merry Christmas. |
| WIFE | Exactly. *(Pause.)* |
| HUSBAND | Why have I never noticed before? |
| WIFE | Because I wear loose-fitting clothes. |
| 30 HUSBAND | That's true. |
| WIFE | Clothes without waists. Merri-mekkos. Sack dresses. Granny gowns. |
| HUSBAND | That's true. |
| WIFE | Large, shapeless flannel nightgowns. |
| HUSBAND | True enough. |
| WIFE | So only now, tonight, does it seem to show. |
| HUSBAND | I see. *(Pause. They smile at each other. Then he looks at his watch.)* I've got to teach a class in an hour. |
| 40 WIFE | Oh, I know. And I've got to go out to a meeting on Open Housing. |
| HUSBAND | So ... |
| WIFE | I just wanted you to know. *(Pause.)* So you could plan. |
| HUSBAND | Yes. I will. I'll plan accordingly. *(Smiles at her again, puts on his glasses, and returns to his book. She starts off left, and then stops.)* |
| WIFE | Oh, there's one thing, though. |
| HUSBAND | *(Reading.)* Mmmmmm? |
| 50 WIFE | One small problem. |
| HUSBAND | *(Reading.)* Mmmmmm. And what's that, dear? |
| WIFE | I don't know whether you've thought about this, or not. |
| HUSBAND | *(Looking up.)* State the problem. And I'll tell you whether I've thought about it. |
| WIFE | It's a little tricky. |
| HUSBAND | Well. We're married, after all. |
| WIFE | Yes. That's why it's a little tricky. |
| HUSBAND | Perhaps. But that's also why you should feel free to speak out. |
| 60 |  |
| WIFE | All right. *(Pause.)* You see, I'm not absolutely sure that this ... *(She looks down at her stomach.)* is yours. *(Pause. He marks his place in his book, puts it down carefully, takes off his glasses, and then looks up.)* |

| | |
|---|---|
| HUSBAND | Ah. So that's the problem |
| WIFE | Yes. That's the problem. |
| HUSBAND | I think I'll trust you on this one, dear. |
| WIFE | That's sweet of you, darling. *(Pause.)* But do I |
| 70 | trust myself? |
| HUSBAND | I think you should. So there we are. |
| WIFE | But ... |
| HUSBAND | But what? |
| WIFE | The thing is ... Now how do I put this? |
| HUSBAND | Speak frankly now. |
| WIFE | I'll try. The thing is ... that you and I ... haven't made love very much. Recently. |
| HUSBAND | Is that true? |
| WIFE | I think it is. Not very much. Not recently. |
| 80 HUSBAND | Hmmm. Define "recently." |
| WIFE | Well, I mean ... five years, more or less ... give or take a month or two. |
| HUSBAND | Is that true? |
| WIFE | I think it is. *(Pause.)* |
| HUSBAND | *(Lighting his pipe.)* My gosh, has it been that long? |
| WIFE | Oh, yes. |
| HUSBAND | Well, well. And so ... |
| WIFE | And so ... |
| HUSBAND | And so you mind, obviously. |
| 90 WIFE | Mind? |
| HUSBAND | Mind that we haven't. Much. Recently. |
| WIFE | Oh, no. Oh, no, no. I don't *mind*. Why should I *mind*? |
| HUSBAND | Well, then ... |
| WIFE | *(Pointing to her stomach.)* I'm just thinking of *this*, that's all. |
| HUSBAND | Oh, I *see!* |
| WIFE | *(Smiling.)* You see? |
| HUSBAND | Of *course*. I see the connection! *(He slaps his* |
| 100 | *head.)* For*give* me. I was thinking about my class. |
| WIFE | Oh, heavens. I forgive you. You love your work. |
| HUSBAND | Yes, but I'm with you now. I'm on your wavelength now. |
| WIFE | Oh, good. |
| HUSBAND | Yes, yes. I understand now. What you're really saying is ... now stop me if I'm wrong ... but what you're really saying is that you think someone else might have impregnated you. |

|  |  |  |
|---|---|---|
|  | WIFE | More or less. Yes. |
| 110 | HUSBAND | I see, I see, I see. |
|  | WIFE | It's possible, after all. |
|  | HUSBAND | Yes. It's possible. |
|  | WIFE | On these evenings that you have to go teach. |
|  | HUSBAND | Yes. When you go out to your meetings. |
|  | WIFE | Yes. Exactly. |
|  | HUSBAND | So we do have a problem there, don't we? |
|  | WIFE | Yes. We really do. |

*(Pause; he looks at her, looks at her stomach, scratches his head, taps his teeth with a pencil, lights his pipe, twirls his glasses.)*

|  |  |  |
|---|---|---|
| 120 | HUSBAND | You know, darling ... it occurs to me ... that I should have made love to you more. |
|  | WIFE | Oh, no, no ... |
|  | HUSBAND | I'm kicking myself now. |
|  | WIFE | Oh, don't, don't ... |
|  | HUSBAND | I am. Things would have been much simpler. |
|  | WIFE | Oh, sweetheart, stop punishing yourself. |
|  | HUSBAND | But why didn't I? Darn it! Darn it all! |
|  | WIFE | Darling, you have your work. |
|  | HUSBAND | Oh, sure, but ... |
| 130 | WIFE | You have your intellectual life ... |
|  | HUSBAND | That's all very well, but ... |
|  | WIFE | You had your book to get out ... |
|  | HUSBAND | Yes, yes, but, darling, that doesn't really answer the question. The question is, why haven't I made love to you in the past five years? That's the question. *(Pause.)* |
|  | WIFE | Well. You used to laugh too much, maybe. |
|  | HUSBAND | Laugh? |
|  | WIFE | Yes. In the old days. Whenever we started to make |
| 140 |  | love, you'd start to chuckle. |
|  | HUSBAND | I did, didn't I? I remember now. *(He chuckles.)* |
|  | WIFE | Yes. You'd chuckle. |
|  | HUSBAND | *(Chuckling.)* Because the whole thing struck me as being slightly absurd. *(Chuckling.)* When you think about it. *(Chuckling.)* I should learn to control myself. *(He chuckles louder; controls himself stoically; then bursts into loud laughter; then forces himself to subside; looks at her.)* I'm sorry. |

| | | |
|---|---|---|
| 150 | WIFE | Oh, don't be sorry. I was just as bad. |
| | HUSBAND | Did you chuckle? |
| | WIFE | No. Actually I'd cry. |
| | HUSBAND | I don't remember your crying. |
| | WIFE | Well, I'd whimper. |
| | HUSBAND | Yes, yes! You would. You'd whimper. *(Chuckles.)* |
| | WIFE | Well, I felt so sad! Making love. While all these horrible things are going on in the world. |
| | HUSBAND | Yes. So you'd whimper. I remember now. |
| | WIFE | Vietnam ... Urban blight ... all that ... I felt |
| 160 | | so guilty! |
| | HUSBAND | And I felt so absurd. |
| | WIFE | Yes. You chuckling, me whimpering ... |
| | HUSBAND | Yes. Oh, yes. |
| | WIFE | And so it wasn't very conducive. |
| | HUSBAND | Right. So we gave it up. That answers that. *(Pause; picks up his book and starts to read.)* |
| | WIFE | But now there's this. *(Indicates her stomach.)* |
| | HUSBAND | *(Reading; taking notes.)* Keep it. |
| | WIFE | What? |
| 170 | HUSBAND | Keep it. Bear it. Bring it home. |
| | WIFE | Oh, darling ... |
| | HUSBAND | Give it my name. Consider me its father. |
| | WIFE | Oh, sweetheart. |
| | HUSBAND | I've let you down. Now I'll make it up. Keep it. |
| | WIFE | But I'm partly to blame. |
| | HUSBAND | But I'm the man. |
| | WIFE | You certainly are! You certainly are the man! |
| | HUSBAND | And now I'm afraid that I must prepare for my class. |
| | WIFE | Yes. And I've got to go to my meeting. |

180 *(They smile at each other; then she starts out left; then she stops, and stands reflectively. After a moment, he looks at her.)*

| | | |
|---|---|---|
| | HUSBAND | But you're not satisfied. |
| | WIFE | Oh, I am, I am. |
| | HUSBAND | Darling, we've been married ten years. You are not satisfied. |
| | WIFE | You've got a class. |
| | HUSBAND | My wife comes first. Come on. What's the problem now? |
| | WIFE | I'm embarrassed even to bring it up. |
| 190 | HUSBAND | *(Tenderly.)* Come on. Out with it. Tell Daddy. |
| | WIFE | All right. *(Pause.)* What if this ... *(She looks at her stomach)* turns out to be black? *(Pause.)* |

| | |
|---|---|
| HUSBAND | Black? |
| WIFE | Black. Or at least mulatto. Depending on how the chromosomes line up. |
| HUSBAND | *(Pause. Lights his pipe again.)* Mmmmm. |
| WIFE | You see? You see the problem? |
| HUSBAND | *(Nodding.)* Mmmmm. |
| WIFE | I mean, can you still act as its father if it's black? |
| 200 HUSBAND | *(Puffing away.)* Mmmmmm. *(Looks at her wryly.)* Yes, well, that puts a different complexion on things. |
| WIFE | *(Giggling.)* Funny. |
| HUSBAND | *(Chuckling.)* That's a horse of a different color. |
| WIFE | *(Laughing.)* Now cut it out. You're awful. *(Stops laughing.)* Try to be serious. |
| HUSBAND | *(Pause. Settles down.)* Black, eh? |
| WIFE | I should have told you before. |
| HUSBAND | No, no. I should have assumed it. |
| 210 WIFE | It just slipped my mind, I guess. |
| HUSBAND | I'm glad it did. That says something for America these days. |
| WIFE | Yes. But it's still a problem. |
| HUSBAND | In this case, yes. I'd say so. *(Pause.)* So you must let me think it out. |
| WIFE | But your class . . . |
| HUSBAND | I'll just be less prepared than I like to be. Which may be good. Which may be very good. Which may make things more lively and spontaneous. So let |
| 220 | me think about this other problem. *(Puffs on his pipe; she stands watching him.)* I could still adopt it. |
| WIFE | How? |
| HUSBAND | We could tell the world that you had a blue baby. Which died. And then we could bring home the black one. Which we say we adopted. |
| WIFE | That sounds awfully complicated. |
| HUSBAND | I know it. |
| WIFE | Awfully baroque. |
| HUSBAND | I know it. |
| 230 WIFE | Besides, the real father might object. He might take pride in it himself. |
| HUSBAND | Need he know? |
| WIFE | Oh, yes. Because he'll see it, after all. |
| HUSBAND | You mean, he'll continue to come around. |
| WIFE | Oh, yes. After I'm home from the hospital. And capable of sexual intercourse again. |

|  | HUSBAND | I see. |
|---|---|---|
|  | WIFE | So that pretty well puts a damper on the adopting idea. |
| 240 | HUSBAND | Yes, it does. *(He thinks.)* |
|  | WIFE | But you have your class ... |
|  | HUSBAND | No, no. Now wait a minute ... *(He thinks carefully, then suddenly pounds his fist on the arm of his chair.)* Sweetheart, I'm going to be honest with you. *(Points to the footstool.)* Sit down. |
|  | WIFE | *(Looking at the footstool.)* I can't sit down. Your feet are there. |
|  | HUSBAND | I'll remove my feet. *(He does.)* Now sit down. |
| 250 | WIFE | All right. I'll sit down. *(Sits on the footstool in front of him.)* |
|  | HUSBAND | Now don't look at me. Face forward. Because this is going to be hard for me to tell, and hard for you to hear. |
|  | WIFE | All right. I won't look at you. |
|  | HUSBAND | And if I'm inarticulate about his, you must try to understand that this is a difficult thing for a man to tell his wife. I'm only doing it—I'm only telling you—because it seems to be the only way to solve this problem. |
| 260 | WIFE | *(Smoothing her skirt over her stomach.)* Yes. This problem. |
|  | HUSBAND | Now try not to interrupt, darling, unless you have to. Unless you're unclear about anything. Save your remarks and comments for the end. All right? |
|  | WIFE | I'll try. |
|  | HUSBAND | All right. *(He takes a deep breath.)* Now. To begin with, I've been lying to you this evening. |
|  | WIFE | Lying? |
| 270 | HUSBAND | Ssshhh. Lying. I don't have a class tonight. I've never had a class at night. I don't believe in evening classes. All these years I've been lying. The class that I've told you meets at night actually meets on Mondays, Wednesdays, and Fridays at ten A.M. |
|  | WIFE | I see. |
| 280 | HUSBAND | You may well ask, therefore, where I go on these nights when I say I have classes. *(Pause.)* And that is what is so difficult to tell you. *(Pause.)* The fact is, I don't leave this house. Not really. Oh, I leave by the front door, all right. But I immediately |

circle around in back and go down into the cellar
by means of the bulkhead.

WIFE  I see.

HUSBAND  Now. What do I do in the cellar? You are probably
asking yourself that. What do I do in the cellar? ...
Don't look at me, darling! *(Pause; then grimly:)*
Here's what I do in the cellar. I make my way to a
small space behind the furnace. And in that small
space, I have hidden ... certain things. *(Pause.)* What
290  have I hidden? I'll tell you. *(He counts them off on
his fingers.)* Some black theatrical makeup. A woolly
wig. A complete change of clothes. And a small
mirror. That's what I have hidden in the cellar.

WIFE  I see ...

HUSBAND  Yes. You see, my darling, or you're beginning to.
When I go into the cellar, I set the mirror up on
an adjacent water pipe. I strip myself to the buff. I
daub myself from head to toe with that dusky
makeup. I glue on that curly wig. I don those
300  makeshift clothes. I leave the cellar. Go to the
front door. Ring the bell. And reappear to you. So
you see, my poor darling, I am your Negro visitor,
and have been all along.

WIFE  You.

HUSBAND  Me.

WIFE  But—

HUSBAND  Oh, I know it sounds implausible. But remember
how you always lower the lights. Remember, too,
that I played Othello in high school. Somehow I
310  was able to pass. I have deceived you for these past
years. Deceived my own wife! Disguising myself
as a Negro and capitalizing on the sympathies you
naturally feel for that unhappy race!

WIFE  But ... why?

HUSBAND  Because I wanted to make love to you. And
somehow this seemed to be the only way I could
do it. You'll have to admit it worked.

WIFE  *(Looking at her stomach.)* Oh, yes. It worked.

HUSBAND  So out of all this depravity, at least a child will be
320  born. And I was its father, after all.

WIFE  I'm somewhat ... stunned ... by all this.

HUSBAND  I know you are, darling. *(Gets up.)* Try to
assimilate it while I'm gone.

|  | | |
|---|---|---|
| WIFE | Gone? |
| HUSBAND | I'm going down to the cellar now. |
| WIFE | To put on your costume? |
| HUSBAND | No. To burn it. |
| WIFE | Burn it? |
| HUSBAND | Yes. It's all over now. Because you know. The |

330     mask is off. Any attempt to wear it again would be foolish. I'd be nothing but a self-conscious amateur. Our love life would be as absurd as it was before I found this way around it. So I'm going to destroy my role. *(Pause; he looks at her.)* And when I come back, I want you gone.

WIFE     Gone?

HUSBAND     You must leave me now.

WIFE     No.

HUSBAND     You must. Oh, my darling, this urge to love you is
340     still in me. I don't know what ... oblique form ... it will take next. Take the child and go.

WIFE     Never.

HUSBAND     Please. Listen: I don't know what I'll think of next, in the cellar. I've got Genet down there. And a complete de Sade. I'll reread them both, looking for increasingly complicated arabesques of sexual perversion. I may reappear with a whip. Wearing riding boots. Or dressed as a woman. Get out, darling. Run to the suburbs. Give my child a
350     normal home. Go!

WIFE     Normal? Normal? *(She laughs uneasily.)* What is normal?

HUSBAND     You're normal, my love.

WIFE     Me? Oh, my God, how little do you know! *(Grimly.)* Sit down, I have a tale to tell-o.

HUSBAND     Nothing you could say ...

WIFE     Sit down.

HUSBAND     Nothing ...

WIFE     I've known all along you were my dark lover!
360     HUSBAND     *(Sits down.)* You've known?

WIFE     From the beginning.

HUSBAND     But ... how?

WIFE     Five years ago, when you announced to me that you had scheduled some evening classes, I became suspicious. And so when you left for the first class, I ... followed you.

| | | |
|---|---|---|
| HUSBAND | | Followed me? |
| WIFE | | Yes. I followed my own husband. Followed you to that tacky little theater-supply shop downtown |
| 370 | | where you bought your disguise. Followed you back here. Followed you into the cellar, hid behind the hot-water heater, watched you change into your poor, pathetic imitation of a Negro. |
| HUSBAND | | You spied on me ... |
| WIFE | | Yes, I spied on you, my darling. Furtively, suspiciously, like some aging matron. But when I saw what you were doing, when I understood that you were doing it for me, my heart went out to you. With a great rush of longing, I dashed back |
| 380 | | upstairs, eager to receive you, but at the same time terrified that you would see that I recognized you. Frantically, I dimmed the lights, to make things easier for both of us. |
| HUSBAND | | I thought it was because you were romantic. |
| WIFE | | I know you did, darling. And I let you think that. But no: it was simply so I wouldn't give myself away. |
| HUSBAND | | You were acting? The whole time? |
| WIFE | | Yes. Wasn't I good? Pretending that you were |
| 390 | | someone new and strange? I, I, who am no actress, improvising like a professional during that whole scene! |
| HUSBAND | | *(Shaking his head.)* It's hard to believe ... You seemed so ... excited! |
| WIFE | | I was! I was terribly excited. I'll admit it. That strange, sly courtship, the banter, the give-and-take, with all those peculiar racial overtones. I threw myself into it with a vengeance. But then ... when you carried me into the bedroom ... |
| 400 | | everything changed. |
| HUSBAND | | What do you mean? I was a tiger! |
| WIFE | | You were, darling. You were a tiger. But I wasn't. |
| HUSBAND | | You said you loved me. |
| WIFE | | I was only pretending. I really hated you. |
| HUSBAND | | Hated me? |
| WIFE | | Hated myself. It was awful. I felt so guilty. All my old sexual agonies were magnified, as it were, by a gallery of mirrors. I wanted at least to whimper, as I did normally, with you, when you were white, |
| 410 | | but now you were black, I had to stifle my own |

|         |                                                                                 |
|---------|---------------------------------------------------------------------------------|
|         | sighs. Worse: I had to pretend, to play, to *fake* the most authentic experience a woman can have! And all the time, I felt like a thing, an object, a creature without a soul, a poor, pathetic concubine in the arms of an Ethiopian potentate. And when you left—finally left—I just lay on the bed, arms folded across my breast, like a stone carving on my own tomb. It took every ounce of energy I could muster to rise and greet you at the door when you returned from your supposed class. *(Pause.)* |

420

HUSBAND  So. For the past five years you have been through hell.

WIFE  No. After that first ghastly evening, I suffered nothing.

HUSBAND  You mean, you grew accustomed ...

WIFE  I mean, I wasn't there.

HUSBAND  You weren't there?

WIFE  No. I left the house right after you went into the cellar.

430

HUSBAND  But then who ... was here ... with me?

WIFE  I got a substitute.

HUSBAND  I see.

WIFE  Oh, darling, try to understand. I simply could not endure another evening like that. The sham, the pretense—it revolted me. And yet I knew how much it meant to you! All the next day, I racked my brain, trying to figure out something which would satisfy us both. I took a long walk. I wandered all over town. Finally, about an hour before I was due home, I saw a woman. Who looked a little like me. Same hair, same height ... roughly the same age. It was a least a chance. Before I really knew what I was doing, I approached her and asked her whether she'd like to sleep with a Negro. Naturally she said she would. And so now, for the past five years, this good woman has come here while you were in the cellar changing your clothes, and in the dim light, she has pretended to be me.

440

450

HUSBAND  I see.

WIFE  Do you hate me very much?

HUSBAND  No. I don't hate you. But I must say I'm somewhat ... surprised.

| | |
|---|---|
| WIFE | I suspected you would be. |
| HUSBAND | But what about that? *(Points to her stomach.)* |
| WIFE | *(Clutching her stomach.)* Ah, this ... |
| HUSBAND | Yes. That. Whose is that? |
| WIFE | Now bear with me, darling. On these nights while |

460 you're in the cellar, and while this good woman
is preparing herself for your return, I go off with a
real Negro. There it is. In a nutshell. His Cadillac
pulls up quietly in front. He flashes his lights. And
I sneak out and drive off with him into the black
ghetto. There, on an old mattress infested with
lice, nibbled at by rats, we make love. Love which
for the first time in my life I can give myself up to,
since I feel that with him I am expiating not only
my own guilt but the guilt of all America.

| | |
|---|---|
| 470 HUSBAND | I see. And so he is the father of that. |
| WIFE | No. |
| HUSBAND | No? |
| WIFE | Somehow, even that relationship wasn't enough. |

Somehow, in the ghetto, with all that soul music
pulsing around me, all that frustration, all that
anger, I still felt as if I were not playing my part.
So I betrayed my lover for his friend. And his
friend for another. And so on and so forth, with
Puerto Ricans, Mexican-Americans, and Indians
480 on relief. Oh, darling, for the past five years, I've
been offering myself as an ecstatic white sacrifice
to anyone with an income of less than five
thousand.

| | |
|---|---|
| HUSBAND | And so the father is ... |
| WIFE | Social Injustice, on a large and general scale. |
| HUSBAND | I see. |
| WIFE | And now you'll leave me, won't you? |
| HUSBAND | Me? Leave you now? *(Laughs peculiarly.)* I want |

to stay more than ever. *(Cleans his pipe carefully.)*
490 What would you say ... if I said ... that everything
you've told me ... excites me?

| | |
|---|---|
| WIFE | Excites you? |
| HUSBAND | Sets my blood boiling. Gives me strange, wild |

frissons of desire.... What would you say if I said
that your ghetto experiences have lit a lurid light
in my own loins?

| | |
|---|---|
| WIFE | Really? |
| HUSBAND | *(Still cleaning his pipe; not looking at her.)* What |

would you say ... if I said ... that I suddenly want

500                  to exercise—how shall I put it?—a *droit de seigneur* on you? That I want to steal you from the peasants and carry you into my bedroom and ravage you with the reading lights going full blaze? *(Looks at her carefully.)* What would you say if I said that? *(Pause; she looks at him coyly.)*

WIFE     I'd say ... do it.

HUSBAND     Mmmm.

WIFE     *(Hastily.)* And let me add this: Let me add that a woman, too, is capable of weird desires. This is

510                hard to say, but looking at you now, slouched in that chair, surrounded by your books and papers, I suddenly have the strange urge to experience the stale comforts of bourgeois married love. They say that Americans in Paris, surfeited by the rich food, yearn for the simple hamburger. So it is with me. For you. Tonight.

HUSBAND     *(Getting up slowly.)* Then ...

WIFE     *(Backing away from him.)* But there's still this! *(Indicating her stomach.)* This problem!

520 HUSBAND     *(Moving toward her.)* That's no problem.

WIFE     No problem?

HUSBAND     That's just the premise to the problem. Now we've solved the problem, we no longer need the premise.

WIFE     I fail to follow.

HUSBAND     That's just the starting mechanism. Now the motor's going, we no longer need the starter.

WIFE     *(Looking down at her stomach.)* Oh.

HUSBAND     *(Stalking her.)* That's not really a baby you have in

530                there.

WIFE     *(Backing away.)* Not really a baby?

HUSBAND     No. That's a balloon you have in there.

WIFE     A balloon?

HUSBAND     A balloon. Or a bladder. Or an old beach ball.

WIFE     It's a baby. I'm practically positive.

HUSBAND     No, no. Look. I'll show you. *(Takes the pointed metal prong of his pipe cleaner and gives her a quick, neat jab in the stomach.)* Touché! *(There is a pop, and then a hissing sound. She slowly*

540                *deflates. They both watch.)* You see? The problem was simply academic. *(Pause.)*

WIFE     *(Looking at him sheepishly.)* Aren't we awful?

HUSBAND     *(Going to his chair, closing his book, carefully marking the place.)* You started it.

|  |  |
|---|---|
| WIFE | I know. It was my turn. You started the last one. |
| HUSBAND | *(Neatening his books and papers.)* Well, it's fun. |
| WIFE | Shouldn't we see a psychiatrist? |
| HUSBAND | *(Tapping out his pipe; putting his glasses in his glasses case.)* Why? We're happy. *(Turns off his light. The stage is now lit only from a light off left.)* |
| WIFE | But we're de*praved!* *(He looks at her, then throws back his head and gives a long Tarzan-like whoop; then he pounds his chest like a gorilla; she giggles.)* Quiet! You'll wake the children! *(He picks her up in his arms; she pummels him melodramatically; speaks in an English accent.)* No, Tarzan! White men do not take women by force! No, Tarzan! White men *court* their women! They are civilized, Tarzan. It's very complicated. Do you understand what I am saying? Com-pli-ca-ted.... Com-pli- ... *(She giggles and kicks as he carries her off left.)* |

550

560

*Curtain.*

*Ai*

# The Mortician's Twelve-Year-Old Son

1   Lady, when you were alive
I'd see you on the streets,
the long green dress with the velvet flower
sewn dead center between your breasts
so tightly I could never get a look inside.

Now the gas lamps half-light the table,
washing the sheet that covers you with shadows.
A few strands of your dyed red hair
hang nearly to the floor,
10   as if all your blood had run there to hide.

I lift the sheet, rub the mole on your cheek
and it comes off black and oily on my hand.
I bend over your breasts and sing,
*love, sister, is just a kiss away.*
I cover each nipple with my mouth.
Tonight, just a kiss away.

*Susan Astor*

# Dame

1  That dog was always a dizzy blonde:
Nearsighted
Anxious to please
Confused.
Every night she slept under the bed
Dreaming of open fields;
Every morning banged awake against a wooden sky.
Males found her irresistible:
They sniffed and paced for hours in the yard
10  Until she broke away and ran to them
Windblown, breathless as a star,
Posing for the mounts as for so many quick pictures.
She would return parched and exhausted,
Tail in a half smile.

She made odd mistakes for an animal:
Growled at her own reflection;
Fell unexpectedly into holes of her own digging.
Once she spent all afternoon confined by an imaginary leash.
Even when she died she was mixed up;
20  Nested in the kitchen, pacing herself for the pain,
Thinking she was in another labor.
She panted to a stop, still scatterbrained,
Misinterpreting the last rough spasm,
Waiting for pups.

*Mary B. Campbell*

# *Sexual Terrorist*

1   I want to be in a rock and roll band so bad.
    I want to make my sins public
    In a special little dress made of gold or fur
    With one of those nuclear violins
    Strapped on around my neck
    And a couple thousand watts for a halo.
    I want to make so much noise
    That even God can't interrupt
    And the 24-hour business of heaven
10  Just grinds to a halt, and the angels
    Dangle in the sky like secretaries
    In an air raid.
    I want to make those tight wires
    Scream under my hands like bombs
    Dropping for miles over miles
    Of empty Arizona sand, and whimper
    Like animals when the sky goes black
    And the scales stampede
    And there's no cover to run for
20  Cause the cover's on fire and the earth is so hot
    The lizards have to dance to stay alive.
    And when I stop I'm gonna go backstage
    Where it's real, real dark and take prisoners
    All night. It could be you
    Or anyone. Get ready.
    If the ransom's rich enough I'll sing
    That long, low note that makes the sun come up.

*James Tate*

# I Am a Finn

1   I am standing in the post office, about
    to mail a package back to Minnesota, to my family.
    I am a Finn. My name is Kasteheimi (Dewdrop).

    Mikael Agricola (1510–1557) created the Finnish language.
    He knew Luther and translated the New Testament.
    When I stop by the Classé Café for a cheeseburger

    no one suspects that I am a Finn.
    I gaze at the dimestore reproductions of Lautrec
    on the greasy walls, at the punk lovers afraid

10  to show their quivery emotions, secure
    in the knowledge that my grandparents really did
    emigrate from Finland in 1910—why

    is everybody leaving Finland, hundreds of
    thousands to Michigan and Minnesota, and now Australia?
    Eighty-six percent of Finnish men have blue

    or gray eyes. Today is Charlie Chaplin's
    one hundredth birthday, though he is not
    Finnish or alive: "Thy blossom, in the bud

laid low." The commonest fur-bearing animals
20   are the red squirrel, musk-rat, pine-marten
and fox. There are about 35,000 elk.

But I should be studying for my exam.
I wonder if Dean will celebrate with me tonight,
assuming I pass. Finnish literature

really came alive in the 1860s.
Here, in Cambridge, Massachusetts,
no one cares that I am a Finn.

They've never even heard of Frans Eemil Sillanpää,
winner of the 1939 Nobel Prize in Literature.
30   As a Finn, this infuriates me.

# *I Am Still a Finn*

1  I failed my exam, which is difficult
for me to understand because I am a Finn.
We are a bright, if slightly depressed, people.

Pertti Palmroth is the strongest name
in Finnish footwear design; his shoes and boots
are exported to seventeen countries.

Dean bought champagne to celebrate
my failure. He says I was just nervous.
Between 1908 and 1950, 33 volumes

10  of *The Ancient Poetry of the Finnish People*
were issued, the largest work of its kind
ever published in any language.

So why should I be nervous? Aren't I
a Finn, descendant of John Ludvig Runeberg
(1804–1877), Finnish national poet?

I know he wrote in Swedish, and this
depresses me still. Harvard Square
is never "empty." There is no chance

that I will ever be able to state honestly
20  that "Harvard Square is empty tonight."
A man from Nigeria will be opening

his umbrella, and a girl from Wyoming
will be closing hers. A Zulu warrior
is running to catch a bus and an over-

painted harlot from Buenos Aires will
be fainting on schedule. And I, a Finn,
will long for the dwarf birches of the north

I have never seen. For 73 days the sun
never sinks below the horizon. O
30    darkness, mine! I shall always be a Finn.

# WRITING ASSIGNMENTS

1. Write a story about a brief encounter with a character whom the narrator will remember for the rest of his or her life.

2. Write a play or story about two people who have a serious disagreement on the eve of their wedding. What new things do they find out about each other and themselves?

3. Write a story in the first-person from the point of view of someone who is planning a murder. Reveal the character's motivation and psychological peculiarities. Does the plot succeed or fail? It might be helpful to use the framework of a confession or a diary with dated entries.

4. Write a poem about one of the following characters:
   a) a rock star who died young.
   b) a bag lady who lives in the bus terminal.
   c) an old fisherman or mariner.
   d) an athlete at the peak of his or her powers.
   e) an old Indian on a modern reservation.
   f) a child playing in the rubble of a ghetto.

# Chapter 4

# Plot

## Introduction

## Fiction

Margaret Atwood     *Happy Endings*
Kit Reed     *Winter*
Nadine Gordimer     *A Find*

## Drama

Horton Foote     *The One-Armed Man*

## Poetry

Kate Barnes     *The Old Lady's Story*
Robert Cooperman     *Isabella Bird Rides in a Round-Up,*
                *Colorado Territory, 1873*
Brigit Pegeen Kelly     *Young Wife's Lament*
Ursula K. LeGuin     *The Maenads*
Robert J. Levy     *Paradise Fish*

## Writing Assignments

In literature plot is not merely action; it is *significant* action *arranged* in an artistically meaningful way. An account of your trip to India or your holiday in Africa might be full of action, but unless you convert experience into art it will not be *A Passage to India* or *The Heart of Darkness.*

Many poems have a narrative element, but few have a fully formed plot. Drama and fiction, on the other hand, depend heavily on a sequence of events and the characters who are involved in these events. A poem might be simply an observation, a meditation, or reverie, an expression of emotion presented through certain images and patterns of sound. There are often poetic elements in drama and fiction, of course, but without a plot, however minimal, you cannot have a play or a story.

The essential ingredient in the plot is what we usually call the *conflict,* which means not only the clashing of forces, as in the classical struggle between good and evil, but any problem, external or internal, that troubles the characters and needs a resolution. It is this need for a resolution that motivates the characters and drives the whole play or story. It is also the ingredient that arouses the interest of the audience or reader.

Conflict gives rise to *suspense,* which is a state of curiosity, uncertainty, or anxiety about how the problem will be resolved. Since we are, by nature, problem-solving creatures with a capacity for empathy, we become involved in the affairs of others, even fictional characters. We want to know who will win or lose, who will live or die, how it will all end, and what it all means.

The usual pattern for a plot is to (1) introduce the problem, (2) develop it, and then (3) resolve it.

The problem should be clear from the beginning or the work will lack dramatic tension. Development is necessary because you can't go directly from a problem to a resolution without destroying the suspense. A problem usually gives rise to a series of complications, a sequence of events, which moves with a certain inevitability towards a logical resolution. The resolution has to be logical because it must grow out of what has gone before. It should not be purely gratuitous or implausible.

Among the selections in this chapter you will find an unusual "story" by Margaret Atwood called "Happy Endings."

It is a story designed to make a point about plot (one might argue that it is really an essay). In any case, it explores, in terms of *problem–development–resolution,* some amusing variations on a simple plot. There is a somewhat satirical treatment here of the John-loves-Mary happy ending, but there is also a lesson in writing.

Kit Reed's "Winter" is a very good example of the well-made story with a logical sequence of events and a bizarre ending. Two old maid sisters live alone on the family farm. A young vagrant arrives and they agree to let him stay a while, because it's useful and exciting to have a man around the house. The young man turns out to be a thief, and what the elderly sisters do about it is an ending too good to reveal.

In "A Find," Nadine Gordimer plunges into the plot with the refreshing clarity usually found in folk tales: "A man who had bad luck with women decided to live alone for a while." One day he finds a beautiful ring on the beach. His quest for the owner develops considerable suspense and leads to a significant conclusion.

A traditional device for creating suspense is simply to withhold information from the reader. In "Nairobi" (Chapter 3) a man has apparently hired a young woman to go with him to have a drink with some friends. He instructs her how to act out a certain role he has in mind. What is it all about? The reader wonders, and keeps on reading. As it happens, we never do find out, but it's hard to put the story down.

Perhaps the best example here of raw suspense can be found in Horton Foote's one-act play called *The One-Armed Man.* The year is 1928. The place is a cotton gin in Texas. A grief-crazed worker who has lost his arm in an accident comes to the manager's office with a gun and says, "Give me back my arm." There is social commentary in the conflict, but it is the threat of violence that grips the audience.

A good example of the narrative poem is "The Old Lady's Story," by Kate Barnes. It is a tale that could have been told in prose. It is about a peasant woman who nearly dies. Her soul leaves her body temporarily and she has a vision. In the end she survives and lives for a long time. Her story is told and retold by the local people.

Robert Cooperman's poem is a narrative account of an English woman's exciting adventure riding in a round-up in

Colorado in 1873 beside "the finest horseman in North America." It's told in the first person by the "British lady." It is not a fully plotted story, but a vivid experience described poetically and somewhat erotically.

Brigit Pegeen Kelly's "Young Wife's Lament" has most of the characteristics of a story, except that it is "a lament" and, therefore, rather static. A wife looks back in sorrow at her dreary life on the farm. She recalls her loneliness and regrets that she was not able to run away from it all.

"The Maenads" by Ursula K. LeGuin is not really a story, but it has a narrative element. It is a contemplative reference to the female attendants of Dionysus in Greek mythology. When the frenzied, drunken, exhausted maenads are "sprawled helpless" on the ground after their revels, "the middle-aged women, respectable housewives," watch over them all night to keep away the men.

"Paradise Fish" by Robert J. Levy could have been a short story, but it works well as a poem, with all the advantages of distillation and imagery. The narrator buys an exotic "girlish" tropical fish and falls in love with her. The other fish in the tank are hostile to her, and she seems too fragile to survive. Her master feeds her in the palm of his hand and strokes her affectionately, but "the affair" is destined to end tragically.

*Margaret Atwood*

# *Happy Endings*

1    *John and Mary meet. What happens next?*
     *If you want a happy ending, try* **A.**

**A**

John and Mary fall in love and get married. They both have
worthwhile and remunerative jobs which they find stimulating
and challenging. They buy a charming house. Real estate
values go up. Eventually, when they can afford live-in help,
they have two children, to whom they are devoted. The children turn out well. John and Mary have a stimulating and
10   challenging sex life and worthwhile friends. They go on fun
vacations together. They retire. They both have hobbies which
they find stimulating and challenging. Eventually they die.
This is the end of the story.

**B**

Mary falls in love with John but John doesn't fall in love with
Mary. He merely uses her body for selfish pleasure and ego
gratification of a tepid kind. He comes to her apartment twice
a week and she cooks him dinner, you'll notice that he doesn't
even consider her worth the price of a dinner out, and after
20   he's eaten the dinner he fucks her and after that he falls asleep,
while she does the dishes so he won't think she's untidy, having all those dirty dishes lying around, and puts on fresh
lipstick so she'll look good when he wakes up, but when he
wakes up he doesn't even notice, he puts on his socks and his
shorts and his pants and his shirt and his tie and his shoes, the
reverse order from the one in which he took them off. He
doesn't take off Mary's clothes, she takes them off herself, she
acts as if she's dying for it every time, not because she likes sex
exactly, she doesn't, but she wants John to think she does
30   because if they do it often enough surely he'll get used to her,
he'll come to depend on her and they will get married, but
John goes out the door with hardly so much as a goodnight

and three days later he turns up at six o'clock and they do the whole thing over again.

Mary gets run down. Crying is bad for your face, everyone knows that and so does Mary but she can't stop. People at work notice. Her friends tell her John is a rat, a pig, a dog, he isn't good enough for her, but she can't believe it. Inside John, she thinks, is another John, who is much nicer. This other John
40　will emerge like a butterfly from a cocoon, a Jack from a box, a pit from a prune, if the first John is only squeezed enough.

One evening John complains about the food. He has never complained about the food before. Mary is hurt.

Her friends tell her they've seen him in a restaurant with another woman, whose name is Madge. It's not even Madge that finally gets to Mary: it's the restaurant. John has never taken Mary to a restaurant. Mary collects all the sleeping pills and aspirins she can find, and takes them and half a bottle of sherry. You can see what kind of a woman she is by the fact
50　that it's not even whiskey. She leaves a note for John. She hopes he'll discover her and get her to the hospital in time and repent and then they can get married, but this fails to happen and she dies.

John marries Madge and everything continues as in **A**.

**C**
John, who is an older man, falls in love with Mary, and Mary, who is only twenty-two, feels sorry for him because he's worried about his hair falling out. She sleeps with him even though she's not in love with him. She met him at work. She's
60　in love with someone called James, who is twenty-two also and not yet ready to settle down.

John on the contrary settled down long ago: this is what is bothering him. John has a steady respectable job and is getting ahead in his field, but Mary isn't impressed by him, she's impressed by James, who has a motorcycle and a fabulous record collection. But James is often away on his motorcycle, being free. Freedom isn't the same for girls, so in the meantime Mary spends Thursday evenings with John. Thursdays are the only days John can get away.
70　John is married to a woman called Madge and they have two children, a charming house which they bought just before the real estate values went up, and hobbies which they find stimulating and challenging, when they have the time. John tells Mary how important she is to him, but of course he can't leave his wife because a commitment is a commitment. He goes

on about this more than is necessary and Mary finds it boring,
but older men can keep it up longer so on the whole she has a
fairly good time.

80 One day James breezes in on his motorcycle with some
top grade California hybrid and James and Mary get higher
than you'd believe possible and they climb into bed. Everything becomes very underwater, but along comes John, who
has a key to Mary's apartment. He finds them stoned and
entwined. He's hardly in any position to be jealous, considering Madge, but nevertheless he's overcome with despair. Finally he's middle-aged, in two years he'll be bald as an egg and
he can't stand it. He purchases a handgun, saying he needs it
for target practice—this is the thin part of the plot, but it can
be dealt with later—and shoots the two of them and himself.

90 Madge, after a suitable period of mourning, marries an
understanding man called Fred and everything continues as in
**A,** but under different names.

**D**

Fred and Madge have no problems. They get along exception-
ally well and are good at working out any little difficulties that
may arise. But their charming house is by the seashore and one
day a giant tidal wave approaches. Real estate values go down.
The rest of the story is about what caused the tidal wave and
how they escape from it. They do, though thousands drown.
100 Some of the story is about how the thousands drown, but Fred
and Madge are virtuous and lucky. Finally on high ground
they clasp each other, wet and dripping and grateful, and
continue as in **A.**

**E**

Yes, but Fred has a bad heart. The rest of the story is about
how kind and understanding they both are until Fred dies.
Then Madge devotes herself to charity work until the end of **A.**
If you like, it can be 'Madge,' 'cancer,' 'guilty and confused'
and 'bird watching.'

110 **F**

If you think this is all too bourgeois, make John a revolutionary and Mary a counterespionage agent and see how far that
gets you. Remember, this is Canada. You'll still end up with **A,**
though in between you may get a lustful brawling saga of
passionate involvement, a chronicle of our times, sort of.

\*

You'll have to face it, the endings are the same however you slice it. Don't be deluded by any other endings, they're all fake, either deliberately fake, with malicious intent to deceive, or just motivated by excessive optimism if not by downright
120 sentimentality.

The only authentic ending is the one provided here:
*John and Mary die. John and Mary die. John and Mary die.*

\*

So much for endings. Beginnings are always more fun. True connoisseurs, however, are known to favour the stretch in between, since it's the hardest to do anything with.

That's about all that can be said for plots, which anyway are just one thing after another, a what and a what and a what.

Now try How and Why.

*Kit Reed*

# *Winter*

1 It was late fall when he come to us, there was a scum of ice on all the puddles and I could feel the winter cold and fearsome in my bones, the hunger inside me was already uncurling, it would pace through the first of the year but by spring it would be raging like a tiger, consuming me until the thaw when Maude could hunt again and we would get the truck down the road to town. I was done canning but I got the tomatoes we had hanging in the cellar and I canned some more; Maude went out and brought back every piece of meat she could shoot
10 and all the grain and flour and powdered milk she could bring in one truckload, we had to lay in everything we could before the snow could come and seal us in. The week he come Maude found a jack-rabbit stone dead in the road, it was frozen with its feet sticking straight up, and all the meat hanging in the cold room had froze. Friday there was rime on the grass and when I looked out I seen footprints in the rime, I said Maude, someone is in the playhouse and we went out and there he was. He was asleep in the mess of clothes we always dressed up in, he had his head on the velvet gown my mother wore to the
20 Exposition and his feet on the satin gown she married Father in, he had pulled her feather boa around his neck and her fox fur was wrapped around his loins.

Before he come, Maude and me would pass the winter talking about how it used to be, we would call up the past between us and look at it and Maude would end by blaming me. I could of married either Lister Hoffman or Harry Mead and left this place for good if it hadn't been for you, Lizzie. I'd tell her, Hell, I never needed you. You didn't marry them because you didn't marry them, you was scared of it and you
30 would use me for an excuse. She would get mad then. It's a lie. Have it your way, I would tell her, just to keep the peace.

We both knew I would of married the first man that asked me, but nobody would, not even with all my money, nobody would ask me because of the taint. If nobody had of known then some man might of married me, but I went down

to the field with Miles Harrison once while Father was still alive, and Miles and me, we almost, except that the blackness took me, right there in front of him, and so I never did. Nobody needed to know, but then Miles saw me fall down in the
40 field. I guess it was him that put something between my teeth, but when I come to myself he was gone. Next time I went to town they all looked at me funny, some of them would try and face up to me and be polite but they was all jumpy, thinking would I do it right there in front of them, would I froth much, would they be hurt, as soon as was decent they would say Excuse me, I got to, anything to get out of there fast. When I run into Miles that day he wouldn't look at me and there hasn't been a man near me since then, not in more than fifty years, but Miles and me, we almost, and I have never stopped
50 thinking about that.

Now Father is gone and my mother is gone and even Lister Hoffman and Miles Harrison and half the town kids that used to laugh at me, they are all gone, but Maude still reproaches me, we sit after supper and she says If it hadn't been for you I would have grandchildren now and I tell her I would have had them before she ever did because she never liked men, she would only suffer them to get children and that would be too much trouble, it would hurt. That's a lie, Lizzie, she would say. Harry and me used to ... and I would tell her
60 You never, but Miles and me ... Then we would both think about being young and having people's hands on us but mem-
ory turns Maude bitter and she can never leave it at that, she says, It's all your fault, but I know in my heart that people make their lives what they want them, and all she ever wanted was to be locked in here with nobody to make demands on her, she wanted to stay in this house with me, her dried-up sister, cold and safe, and if the hunger is on her, it has come on her late.

After a while we would start to make up stuff: Once I
70 went with a boy all the way to Portland ... Once I danced all night and half the morning, he wanted to kiss me on the place where my elbow bends ... We would try to spin out the winter but even that was not enough and so we would always be left with the hunger; no matter how much we laid in, the meat was always gone before the thaw and I suppose it was really our lives we was judging but we would decide nothing in the cans looked good to us and so we would sit and dream and hunger and wonder if we would die of it, but finally the thaw would come and Maude would look at me and sigh: If only we had
80 another chance.

Well now perhaps we will.

We found him in the playhouse, maybe it was seeing him being in the playhouse, where we pretended so many times, asleep in the middle of my mother's clothes or maybe it was but there was this boy, or man, and something about him called up our best memories, there was promise wrote all over him. I am too old, I am all dried out, but I have never stopped thinking about that one time and seeing that boy there, I could pretend he was Miles and I was still young. I guess he sensed
90 us, he woke up fast and went into a crouch, maybe he had a knife, and then I guess he saw it was just two big old ladies in Army boots, he said, I run away from the Marines, I needed a place to sleep.

Maude said, I don't care what you need, you got to get out of here, but when he stood up he wobbled. His hair fell across his head like the hair on a boy I used to know and I said, Maude, why don't you say yes to something just this once.

He had on this denim shirt and pants like no uniform I ever seen and he was saying, Two things happened, I found
100 out I might have to shoot somebody in the war and then I made a mistake and they beat me so I cut out of there. He smiled and he looked open. I stared hard at Maude and Maude finally looked at me and said, All right, come up to the house and get something to eat.

He said his name was Arnold but when we asked him Arnold what, he said Never mind. He was in the kitchen by then, he had his head bent over a bowl of oatmeal and some biscuits I had made, and when I looked at Maude she was watching the way the light slid across his hair. When we told
110 him our names he said, You are both beautiful ladies. I could see Maude's hands go up to her face and she went into her room and when she come back I saw she had put colour on her cheeks. While we was alone he said how good the biscuits was and wasn't that beautiful silver, did I keep it polished all myself and I said well yes, Maude brings in supplies but I am in charge of the house and making all the food. She come back then and saw us with our heads together and said to Arnold, I guess you'll be leaving soon.

I don't know, he said, they'll be out looking for me with
120 guns and dogs.

That's no never mind of ours.

I never done nothing bad in the Marines, we just had different ideas. We both figured it was something worse but he looked so sad and tired and besides, it was nice to have him to talk to, he said, I just need a place to hole up for a while.

Maude said, You could always go back to your family.

He said, They never wanted me. They was always mean-hearted, not like you.

I took his side and said, It wouldn't kill you to let him
130 stay on, Maude, it's time we had a little life around here.

There won't be enough food for three.

He won't stay long. Besides, he can help you with the chores.

She was looking at his bright hair again, she said, like it was all my doing, If you want to let him stay I guess we can let him stay.

He was saying, I could work for my keep.

All right, I said, you can stay on until you get your strength.

140 My heart jumped. A man, I thought. A man. How can I explain it? It was like being young, having him around. I looked at Maude and saw some of the same things in her eyes, hunger and hope, and I thought, You are ours now, Arnold, you are all ours. We will feed you and take care of you and when you want to wander we will let you wander, but we will never let you go.

Just until things die down a little, he was saying.

Maude had a funny grin. Just until things die down.

Well it must of started snowing right after dark that
150 afternoon, because when we all waked up the house was surrounded. I said, Good thing you got the meat in, Maude, and she looked out, it was still blowing snow and it showed no signs of stopping, she looked out and said, I guess it is.

He was still asleep, he slept the day through except he stumbled down at dusk and dreamed over a bowl of my rabbit stew, I turned to the sink and when I looked back the stew was gone and the biscuits was gone and all the extra in the pot was gone, I had a little flash of fright, it was all disappearing too fast. Then Maude come over to me and hissed, The food, he's
160 eating all the food and I looked at his brown hands and his tender neck and I said, It don't matter, Maude, he's young and strong and if we run short he can go out into the snow and hunt. When we looked around next time he was gone, he had dreamed his way through half a pie and gone right back to bed.

Next morning he was up before the light, we sat together around the kitchen table and I thought how nice it was to have a man in the house, I could look at him and imagine anything I wanted. Then he got up and said, Look, I want to thank you

170  for everything, I got to get along now and I said, You can't, and he said, I got things to do, I been here long enough, but I told him You can't, and took him over to the window. The sun was up by then and there it was, snow almost to the window ledges, like we have every winter, and all the trees was shrouded, we could watch the sun take the snow and make it sparkle and I said, Beautiful snow, beautiful, and he only shrugged and said, I guess I'll have to wait till it clears off some. I touched his shoulder. I guess it will. I knew not to tell him it would never clear off, not until late spring; maybe he

180  guessed, anyway he looked so sad I gave him Father's silver snuffbox to cheer him up.

    He would divide his time between Maude and me, he played Rook with her and made her laugh so hard she gave him her pearl earrings and the brooch Father brought her back from Quebec. I gave him Grandfather's diamond stickpin because he admired it, and for Christmas we gave him the cameos and Father's gold-headed cane. Maude got the flu over New Year and Arnold and me spent New Year's Eve together, I mulled some wine and he hung up some of Mama's jewelry

190  from the center light, and touched it and made it twirl. We lit candles and played the radio, New Year's Eve in Times Square and somebody's Make-believe Ballroom, I went to pour another cup of wine and his hand was on mine on the bottle, I knew my lips was red for once and next day I gave him Papa's fur-lined coat.

    I guess Maude suspected there was something between us, she looked pinched and mean when I went in with her broth at lunch, she said, Where were you at breakfast and I said, Maude, it's New Year's Day, I thought I would like to

200  sleep in for once. She was quick and spiteful. You were with him. I thought, If she wants to think that about me, let her, and I let my eyes go sleepy and I said, We had to see the New Year in, didn't we? She was out of bed in two days, I have never seen anybody get up so fast after the flu. I think she couldn't stand us being where she couldn't see what we was up to every living minute. Then I got sick and I knew what torture it must have been for her, just laying there, I would call Maude and I would call her, and sometimes she would come and sometimes she wouldn't come and when she finally did look in on me I would

210  say, Maude, where have you been and she would only giggle and not answer. There was meat cooking all the time, roasts and chops and chicken fricassee, when I said Maude, you're going to use it up, she would only smile and say, I just had to

show him who's who in the kitchen, he tells me I'm a better cook than you ever was. After a while I got up, I had to even if I was dizzy and like to throw up, I had to get downstairs where I could keep an eye on them. As soon as I was up to it I made a roast of venison that would put hair on an egg and after that we would vie with each other in the kitchen, Maude and me.

220  Once I had my hand on the skillet handle and she come over and tried to take it away, she was saying, Let me serve it up for him. I said, you're a fool, Maude, I cooked this and she hissed at me, through the steam, it won't do you no good, Lizzie, it's me he loves, and I just pushed her away and said, you goddam fool, he loves me, and I give him my amethysts just to prove it. A couple of days later I couldn't find neither of them nowhere. I thought I heard noises up in the back room and I went up there and if they was in there they wouldn't answer, the door was locked and they wouldn't say nothing, not even when I

230  knocked and knocked and knocked. So the next day I took him up in my room and we locked the door and I told him a story about every piece in my jewel box, even the cheap ones, when Maude tapped and whined outside the door we would just shush, and when we did come out and she said, All right, Lizzie, what was you doing in there, I only giggled and wouldn't tell.

She shouldn't of done it, we was all sitting around the table after dinner and she looked at me hard and said, You know something, Arnold, I wouldn't get too close to Lizzie,

240  she has fits. Arnold only tried to look like it didn't matter, but after Maude went to bed I went down to make sure it was all right. He was still in the kitchen, whittling, and when I tried to touch his hand he pulled away.

I said, Don't be scared, I only throw one in a blue moon.

He said, That don't matter.

Then what's the matter?

I don't know, Miss Lizzie, I just don't think you trust me.

Course I trust you, Arnold, don't I give you everything?

250  He just looked sad. Everything but trust.

I owe you so much, Arnold, you make me feel so young.

He just smiled for me then. You look younger, Miss Lizzie, you been getting younger every day I been here.

You did it.

If you let me, I could make you really young.

Yes, Arnold, yes.

But I have to know you trust me.

Yes, Arnold.

So I showed him where the money was. By then it was
past midnight and we was both tired, he said, Tomorrow, and
I let him go off to get his rest.

I don't know what roused us both and brought us out
into the hall but I bumped into Maude at dawn, we was both
standing in our nightgowns like two ghosts. We crept downstairs together and there was light in the kitchen, the place
where we kept the money was open, empty, and there was a
crack of light in the door to the coldroom. I remember looking
through and thinking, The meat is almost gone. Then we
opened the door a crack wider and there he was, he had made
a sledge, he must of sneaked down there and worked on it
every night. It was piled with stuff, our stuff, and now he had
the door to the outside open, he had dug himself a ramp out of
the snow and he was lashing some home-made snowshoes on
his feet, in another minute he would cut out of there.

When he heard us he turned.

I had the shotgun and Maude had the axe.

He said, You can have all your stuff.

We said, We don't care about the stuff, Arnold, How
could we tell him it was our youth he was taking away?

He looked at us, wall-eyed. You can have it all, just let
me out.

You said you loved us, Arnold.

He was scrabbling up the snow ramp. Never mind what
I told you, let me out of here.

He was going to get away in another minute, so Maude
let him have it with the axe.

Afterward we closed the way to the outside and stood
there and looked at each other, I couldn't say what was in my
heart so I only looked at Maude, we was both sad, sad, I said.
The food is almost gone.

Maude said, Everything is gone. We'll never make it to
spring.

Maude looked at him laying there. You know what he
told me? He said, I can make you young.

Me too, I said. There was something in his eyes that
made me believe it.

Maude's eyes was aglitter, she said, The food is almost
gone.

I knew what she meant, he was going to make us young.

260

270

280

290

300 I don't know how it will work in us, but he is going to make us young, it will be as if the fits had never took me, never in all them years. Maude was looking at me, waiting, and after a minute I looked square at her and I said, I know.

So we et him.

*Nadine Gordimer*

# A Find

1   To hell with them.

A man who had bad luck with women decided to live alone for a while. He was twice married for love. He cleared his house of whatever his devoted second wife had somehow missed out when she left with the favorite possessions they had collected together—paintings, rare glass, even the best wines lifted from the cellar. He threw away books on whose fly-leaf the first wife had lovingly written her new name as a bride. Then he went on holiday without taking some woman along.

10   For the first time he could remember; but those tarts and tramps with whom he had believed himself to be in love had turned out unfaithful as the honest wives who had vowed to cherish him forever.

He went alone to a resort where the rocks flung up the sea in ragged fans, the tide sizzled and sucked in the pools. There was no sand. On stones like boiled sweets, striped and flecked and veined, people—women—lay on salt-faded mattresses and caressed themselves with scented oils. Their hair was piled up and caught in elastic garlands of artificial flow-

20   ers, that year, or dripped—as they came out of the water with crystal beads studding glossy limbs—from gilt clasps that flashed back and forth to the hoops looped in their ears. Their breasts were bared, that year. They wore inverted triangles of luminescent cloth over the pubis, secured by a string that went up through the divide of the buttocks to meet two strings coming round from over the belly and hip-bones. In his line of vision, as they walked away down to the sea they appeared totally naked; when they came up out of the sea, gasping with pleasure, coming towards his line of vision, their breasts

30   danced, drooped as the women bent, laughing, for towels and combs and the anointing oil. The bodies of some were patterned like tie-dye fabric: strips and patches white or red where garments had covered bits of them from the fiery immersion of sun. The nipples of others were raw as strawberries, it could be observed that they could scarcely bear to touch them with

balm. There were men, but he didn't see men. When he closed his eyes and listened to the sea he could smell the women—the oil.

40　　He swam a great deal. Far out in the calm bay between windsurfers crucified against their gaudy sails, closer in shore where the surf trampled his head under hordes of white water. A shoal of young mothers carried their infants about in the shallows. Denting its softness, naked against their mothers' flesh the children clung, so lately separated from it that they still seemed part of those female bodies in which they had been planted by males like himself. He lay on the stones to dry. He liked the hard nudging of the stones, fidgeting till he adjusted his bones to them, wriggling them into depressions until his contours were contained rather than resisted. He slept. He
50　　woke to see their shaven legs passing his head—women. Drops shaken from their wet hair fell on his warm shoulders. Sometimes he found himself swimming underwater beneath them, his tough-skinned body grazing past like a shark.

As men do at the shore when they are alone, he flung stones at the sea, remembering—regaining—the art of making them skip and skip across the water. Lying face-down out of reach of the last rills, he sifted handsful of sea-polished stones and, close up, began to see them as adults cease to see: the way a child will look and look at a flower, a leaf—a stone, follow-
60　　ing its alluvial stripes, its fragments of mysterious color, its buried sprinklings of mica, feeling (he did) its egg- or lozenge-shape smoothed by the sea's oiled caressing hand.

Not all the stones were really stones. There were flattish amber ovals the gem-cutter ocean had buffed out of broken beer bottles. There were cabochons of blue and green glass (some other drowned bottle) that could have passed for aquamarines and emeralds. Children collected them in hats or buckets. And one afternoon among these treasures mixed with bits of styrofoam discarded from cargo ships and other plastic
70　　jetsam that is cast, refloated and cast again, on shores all round the world, he found in the stones with which he was occupying his hand like a monk telling his beads, a real treasure. Among the pebbles of colored glass was a diamond and sapphire ring. It was not on the surface of the stony beach, so evidently had not been dropped there that day by one of the women. Some darling, some rich man's treasure (or ensconced wife), diving off a yacht, out there, wearing her jewels while she fashionably jettisoned other coverings, must have felt one of the rings slipped from her finger by the water. Or didn't feel

80 it, noticed the loss only when back on deck, rushed to find the insurance policy, while the sea drew the ring deeper and deeper down; and then, tiring of it over days, years, slowly pushed and washed it up to dump on land. It was a beautiful ring. The sapphire a large oblong surrounded by round diamonds with a baguette-cut diamond set horizontally on either side of this brilliant mound, bridging it to an engraved circle.

Although it had been dug up from a good six inches down by his random fingering, he looked around as if the owner were sure to be standing over him.

90 But they were oiling themselves, they were towelling their infants, they were plucking their eyebrows in the reflection of tiny mirrors, they were sitting cross-legged with their breasts lolling above the squat tables where the waiter from the restaurant had placed their salads and bottles of white wine. He took the ring up to the restaurant; perhaps someone had reported a loss. The patronne drew back. She might have been being offered stolen goods by a fence. It's valuable. Take it to the police.

Suspicion arouses alertness; perhaps, in this foreign 100 place, there was some cause to be suspicious. Even of the police. If no-one claimed the ring, some local would pocket it. So what was the difference—he put it into his own pocket, or rather into the shoulder-bag that held his money, his credit cards, his car keys and sunglasses. And he went back to the beach and lay down again, on the stones, among the women. To think.

He put an advertisement in the local paper. Ring found on Blue Horizon Beach, Tuesday 1st, and the telephone and room number at his hotel. The patronne was right; there were 110 many calls. A few from men, claiming their wives, mothers, girl-friends had, indeed, lost a ring on that beach. When he asked them to describe the ring, they took a chance: a diamond ring. But they could only prevaricate when pressed for more details. If a woman's voice was the wheedling, ingratiating one (even weepy, some of them) recognizable as that of some middleaged con-woman, he cut off the call the moment she tried to describe her lost ring. But if the voice was attractive and sometimes clearly young, soft, even hesitant in its lying boldness, he asked the owner to come to his hotel to identify the ring.

120 Describe it.

He seated them comfortably before his open balcony, with the light from the sea interrogating their fears. Only one convinced him that she really had a lost a ring; she described it

in detail and went away, sorry to have troubled him. Others—some quite charming and extremely pretty, dressed to seduce—would have settled for something else come of the visit, if they could not get away with their invented descriptions of a ring. They seemed to calculate that a ring is a ring; if it's valuable, it must have diamonds, and one or two were
130 ingenious to say, yes, there were other precious stones with it, but it was an heirloom (grandmother, aunt) and they didn't really know the names of the stones.

But the color? The shape?

They left as if affronted; or they giggled guiltily, they'd come just for a dare, a bit of fun. And they were quite difficult to get rid of politely.

Then there was one with a voice unlike that of any of the other callers, the controlled voice of a singer or actress, maybe, expressing diffidence. I have given up hope. Of finding it ...
140 my ring. She had seen the advertisement and thought no, no, it's no use. But if there were a million to one chance ... He asked her to come to the hotel.

She was certainly forty, a born beauty with great, still, grey-green eyes and no help needed except to keep her hair peacock-black. It grew from a peak like a beak high on her round forehead and fell shinily to her shoulders. There was no sign of a fold where her breasts met, firmly spaced in the neck of a dress black as her hair. Her hands were made for rings; she spread long thumbs and fingers, turned palms up: And then it
150 was gone, I saw a gleam a moment in the water—

Describe it.

She gazed straight at him, turned her head to direct those eyes away and began to speak. Very elaborate, she said, platinum and gold ... you know, it's difficult to be precise about an object you've worn so long you don't notice it any more. A large diamond ... several. And emeralds, and red stones ... rubies, but I think they had fallen out before ...

He went to the drawer in the hotel desk-cum-dressing-table and from under folders describing restaurants, cable TV
160 programs and room service available, he took an envelope. Here's your ring, he said.

Her eyes did not change. He held it out to her.

Her hand wafted slowly towards him as if under water. She took the ring from him and began to put it on the second finger of her left hand. It would not fit but she corrected the movement with a swift conjuring and it slid home over the third finger.

He took her out to dinner and the subject was not referred to. Ever again. She became his third wife. They live together with no more unsaid, between them, than any other couple.

## Horton Foote

··-··■■·■■··-··-··■■·■■··-··

# *The One-Armed Man*

1 *CAST*

**C. W. Rowe    Pinkey Anderson    Ned McHenry**
*Place:* Harrison, Texas
*Time:* Summer, 1928

*An office in a cotton gin. The manager of the cotton gin, C. W. Rowe, in his early fifties, is behind the desk. There are various photographs around the room of C. W. with staff heads and dignitaries, and a stalk of cotton is tacked on the wall. He is working at his desk and is surrounded by letters and papers. There is a knock on the door. C. W.*
10 *(calling): "Come in." Pinkey Anderson enters. C. W. continues with his work. Pinkey stands by the door.*

| | |
|---|---|
| C. W. | Pinkey, look out the window and see how many cotton wagons are in the gin yard. |

*(Pinkey looks out the window.)*

| | |
|---|---|
| Pinkey | Seven. |
| C. W. | How many bales have they ginned so far today? |
| Pinkey | Fifteen. |
| C. W. | They might as well leave it to rot in the field the prices they're paying. If it were my cotton I would |
20 | | store it until the price goes up again. Tell anyone that asks you that my advice is to store the cotton for a year if necessary. |
| Pinkey | What if they don't have a place to store it? |
| C. W. | Tell them to rent space. |
| Pinkey | Do you think cotton will ever hit forty cents a pound again like it did in 1912? |
| C. W. | Might. This country is on a curve of prosperity. Anything might happen. The way they are discovering oil in this country, someday you might |
30 | | look out in the gin yard and see oil wells. I had a |

dream the other night ... *(A noise is heard in the outer office.)* Is that somebody out there?

PINKEY  Yes. That's what I came in to tell you.

C. W.  Who is it? *(PINKEY pantomimes a man with one arm.)* Oh, my God. Get rid of him.

PINKEY  I can't get rid of him.

C. W.  Yes, you can. Use your wits. Tell him I'm very busy.

PINKEY  I told him that.

40 C. W.  Then distract him some way. This is the height of the cotton season.

PINKEY  I can't fool him anymore. Oh, see him and get it over with. He's harmless.

C. W.  He may be harmless, but how would you like it if a man came in here every other week asking you to give him his arm back?

PINKEY  He soon leaves after that. All you have to do is to say you haven't got it, and he leaves.

C. W.  Well, I don't want to do that anymore. Tell him I
50  said to go away.

*(PINKEY leaves. C. W. goes back to his work. PINKEY comes back in.)*

PINKEY  He insists on seeing you. He says he won't leave until he does.

C. W.  Oh, my God, I swear I think he's crazy. *(A pause.)* Tell him I know what he wants. Tell him I haven't got his damn arm and tell him if he doesn't stop worrying and driving me crazy I am going to call the sheriff and have him arrested.

PINKEY  Yes sir. *(He starts away.)*

60 C. W.  Wait a minute. Forget about saying that. He always leaves after I offer him five dollars. *(He takes a bill out of his pocket.)* Here, give this to him, but tell him if I hear of his getting drunk like he did on the last five dollars I gave him, it will be the last he ever gets from me. *(PINKEY starts out.)* And Pinkey ... *(PINKEY pauses.)* Tell him he doesn't have to come back here anymore asking about his arm. Tell him I'll send five dollars every week up to Christmas as long as I hear he stays
70  sober. *(He starts away.)* Oh, by the way. Jeff Lyons was here this morning when you were uptown for coffee—and incidentally, you were

|   |   |
|---|---|
|  | gone over an hour. I know because Jeffrey waited at least an hour here for you, and an hour is too long to be away. |
| PINKEY | Yes sir. *(He starts away.)* |
| C. W. | Hold your horses, Pinkey. He left you a bill. *(He gets the bill and hands it to PINKEY. PINKEY puts it in his pocket.)* He calls you "dearie." Why does he call you that? |
| PINKEY | That's what my wife calls me. Jeffrey Lyons is a member of my Boy Scout troop, and when they heard my wife calling me that, they started calling me that too. |
| C. W. | Well, I think that's a lot of foolishness. Ask him not to call you that anymore when he comes around here. It doesn't sound dignified. *(He starts out.)* Pinkey. |
| PINKEY | Yes sir. |
| C. W. | He told me the bill was three months old. |
| PINKEY | Yes sir. |
| C. W. | How much is it for? |
| PINKEY | Eight dollars. |
| C. W. | Eight dollars? |
| PINKEY | Yes sir. |
| C. W. | My God, you haven't been able to pay back eight dollars in three months? *(A pause.)* How many bills do you have? |
| PINKEY | Quite a bit. |
| C. W. | What do you mean quite a bit? |
| PINKEY | Three hundred dollars. |
| C. W. | Three hundred dollars. That's a fortune now for someone in your position. How in the name of God did you ever get that much in debt? I pay you a decent salary here, I think. I mean, I know you can't get rich on it, but you should be able certainly to live comfortably with a wife and only one child on forty dollars a week. At Christmastime you get a turkey and a fifteen-dollar bonus. How much is your house rent? |
| PINKEY | Twenty-five dollars a month. |
| C. W. | Cut out the cigarettes. That would save you quite a bit. How many packages a day do you smoke? |
| PINKEY | Two. |
| C. W. | Two too many. All right, two packages of cigarettes a day, twenty-five dollars a month for rent. Where does the rest go? |

80

90

100

110

| | | |
|---|---|---|
| | Pinkey | There's food and clothes. A man has to eat, you know. |
| | C. W. | Do you have your own garden? |
| 120 | Pinkey | No sir. |
| | C. W. | That's another extravagance. Grocery stores rob you blind. I grow my own food, at least I hire a nigra to do it. I pay him two dollars a week and he can take home any of the vegetables we can't use. Do you belong to any fraternal organizations? |
| | Pinkey | No sir. |
| | C. W. | I know you're not a member of the Lions Club. |
| | Pinkey | No sir. |
| 130 | C. W. | Or the Chamber of Commerce. |
| | Pinkey | No sir. |
| | C. W. | I belong to them all, and I contribute personally to my church. I drive a car, and my wife drives a car, and I still save money every month. |
| | Pinkey | Yes sir. |
| | C. W. | I am only able to take five hundred dollars a month out of the business, you know. Of course you know that. You keep the books. |
| | Pinkey | That's three hundred more than I do. |
| 140 | C. W. | Yes, but I'm an executive. I run the oil mill and the cotton gin. You're only a bookkeeper. I have to be a leader in this town. I pay dues every month to the Lions, the Chamber of Commerce, I'm the third most generous giver to the Baptist church. I own my own home which I paid three thousand dollars for in cash. I go day and night. I am past president of the Chamber of Commerce, past president of the Lions Club, and its present tail twister. I teach the men's Bible class at the Baptist church, I am deacon |
| 150 | | of the church, a member of the choir, helped to start a building and loan association and am an officer in the White Man's Union. |
| | Pinkey | Yes sir, I know, sir. |
| | C. W. | And you are three hundred dollars in debt. Not me. |
| | Pinkey | Yes sir. |
| | C. W. | I owe not a penny in this world. |
| | Pinkey | Yes sir. |

*(There is another noise outside.)*

| | | |
|---|---|---|
| 160 | Pinkey | I better get out to him. *(PINKEY goes. C.W. goes back to work at his desk. PINKEY comes back in.)* |

C. W.    And I'd like to say further, there is no excuse for a man to be in debt in this great little town of ours. Nature endowed us with abundance. We have cotton land that is as fertile as anything in the Valley of the Nile. We have rice fields, oil, sulphur. I have a vision for this beloved town and county of ours, and you need a vision in life, Pinkey.

PINKEY    Yes sir. I'm sure, but the McHenry boy ...

170  C. W.    What about him?

PINKEY    He said he won't leave until he sees you.

C. W.    Did you give him the five dollars?

PINKEY    Yes sir. He said he didn't want it. He wants to see you.

C. W.    My God. I guess I'll have to see him to get rid of him. Well, I might as well get it over with. Send him in here.

PINKEY    Yes sir. *(He starts out.)*

C. W.    First give me back the five dollars.

180  PINKEY    Yes sir.

*(He gives him the money, then goes.* MCHENRY, *21, comes in. His left arm has been severed at the elbow, and only a stump is left.)*

C. W.    Hello, son. *(No answer.)* How are you today? *(Still no answer.)* Well, you certainly seem to have recovered nicely from your accident. Home again? *(Still no response.)* I don't smoke cigarettes. You can get one though from Pinkey if you'd like a cigarette. He smokes two packs a day. I've been lecturing him about it. He can't afford two packs

190    a day. He owes everybody in town. Of course, he has an extravagant wife, and he's spineless, no backbone. He just lets her spend like she was the wife of a millionaire, which she certainly ain't. *(A pause.)* Well now, I was telling my wife Billie Joe the other night, I said the thing I hated most of all about ... what is your first name again, son? I always get you McHenry boys mixed up. *(A pause.)* Now let's see. Don't tell me. I believe you're Ned. Isn't that right? Ned? I said, "Billie

200    Joe, what I hate the most about Ned's accident is that I had to let him go from his job at the cotton gin." I don't sleep nights worrying about letting you go, son. But like I said to Billie Joe, there is

just no way in the world we can use a one-arm
man on a cotton gin. All that machinery is
dangerous enough for a man with two arms. Why,
shoot, you ought to certainly know about that.
*(A pause.)* Well, I guess Pinkey told you this is a
busy time of the year for me; it will get busier and
210 busier all through September, as we have a
bumper cotton crop, so I would appreciate it so
much if you would take this five dollars now and
excuse me, and I asked Pinkey to tell you that you
needn't come back here anymore as every week I
am going to ... *(McHenry takes out a gun. C. W.
sees it, but tries to ignore it.)* I'll send five dollars
over to your house every week from now to
Christmas, but I do hope you will not use it for
whiskey, but for nourishing food. *(McHenry lifts
220 up the gun.)* Of course, if you want to use it for
whiskey it would sadden me, but that is your
entire business. *(He gets up. He's even more
cheerful now.)* So, now, son, if you'll excuse me
and let me get on to my work, I will give you the
five dollars for this week in advance.

| | |
|---|---|
| McHenry | I don't want your damn five dollars. |
| C. W. | You don't? |
| McHenry | No, keep your goddamned five dollars. Give me my arm back. |
| 230 C. W. | Now, son. Talk like a sane man. Take the two five-dollar bills. |
| McHenry | I said keep your goddamned bills. Give me back my arm. |
| C. W. | How in the world am I going to do that? |
| McHenry | You figure that out. |
| C. W. | How can I figure that out? |
| McHenry | That's your problem. Tell your damn machinery to figure it out. It took it. Chewed it up. |
| C. W. | Was that my fault? I have had nigras working here |
| 240 | for years that can't even read or write and none of them ever lost so much as a hair of their heads. When I was in Russia showing the Bolsheviks how to run a cotton gin ... Did I ever tell you about the time I went to Russia, son? I spent a year there. *(He goes to the wall and takes down a picture.)* Here I am with the Bolsheviks teaching them about cotton gins. *(McHenry doesn't even glance* |

|        |          |                                                                                                                          |
|--------|----------|--------------------------------------------------------------------------------------------------------------------------|
| 250    |          | *at the picture. C. W. is becoming extremely nervous. He puts the picture on the desk.)* I got a Russian hat still someplace around here. *(He opens desk drawer looking for it.)* If I can find it, I'll make a present of it to you. |
|        | MᴄHᴇɴʀʏ  | I don't want no damn Russian hat.                                                                                         |
|        | C. W.    | Give you a Russian hat and ten dollars and five dollars every week until Christmas.                                      |

*(MᴄHᴇɴʀʏ moves down with the gun.)*

|        |          |                                                                                                                          |
|--------|----------|--------------------------------------------------------------------------------------------------------------------------|
|        | MᴄHᴇɴʀʏ  | Give me back my arm.                                                                                                      |
|        | C. W.    | Son, be reasonable. I can't do that. You know I can't do that, son.                                                      |
| 260    | MᴄHᴇɴʀʏ  | Don't call me son.                                                                                                        |
|        | C. W.    | Say, I meant no offense, Ned.                                                                                             |
|        | MᴄHᴇɴʀʏ  | Don't call me Ned.                                                                                                        |
|        | C. W.    | What can I call you then?                                                                                                 |
|        | MᴄHᴇɴʀʏ  | Knub.                                                                                                                     |
|        | C. W.    | Why in the world would I want to call you that?                                                                          |
|        | MᴄHᴇɴʀʏ  | Call me Knub.                                                                                                             |
|        | C. W.    | Why in the name of God?                                                                                                  |
|        | MᴄHᴇɴʀʏ  | Because that's what they call me now in the pool hall.                                                                   |
| 270    | C. W.    | Well, then stay out of the pool hall.                                                                                    |
|        | MᴄHᴇɴʀʏ  | I work in the pool hall. That's the only work I can get as a one-armed man.                                              |
|        | C. W.    | Well, that surely upsets me. I hate to hear of you going into a pool hall, much less working there. Now sit down and let's talk this over like reasonable men. Let me call Pinkey and have him go to the corner for Coca-Colas. *(He starts for the door. MᴄHᴇɴʀʏ stops him with the gun.)* |
| 280    | MᴄHᴇɴʀʏ  | I don't want any goddamned Coca-Colas. I want my arm back.                                                               |
|        | C. W.    | My God, son. Talk sense. I'd sure give you back your arm if I could. How in this world can I do that? Use that head. Use your . . . |

*(MᴄHᴇɴʀʏ raises the gun and C. W. backs into the room.)*

|        |          |                                                                                                                          |
|--------|----------|--------------------------------------------------------------------------------------------------------------------------|
|        | MᴄHᴇɴʀʏ  | The day I lost my arm I begged them not to cut it off. I said, "For God sakes don't cut off my arm. Kill me first." "It's already gone," they said. "We have to cut off what's left." "Where's my arm?" |

| | | |
|---|---|---|
| 290 | | I said. "Mixed up in somebody's bale of cotton," they said. |
| | C. W. | Well, that's how it goes, son. My oldest boy had his toe froze off while he was over in France fighting the Germans, but he don't let it get him down, not Delbert. He's a fine boy. He's an example to us all. Why, Whitney Taylor lost a leg in a hunting accident, but that doesn't keep him from getting around. He rides horseback every day just like other men. Thomas Edison is deaf as |
| 300 | | a post and look at all he's done in spite of his handicap. |
| | McHenry | I heard yesterday at the pool hall you said whoever got the bale of cotton with my arm chopped up didn't get much. |
| | C. W. | I didn't say that. Who said I said that? |
| | McHenry | That I probably ruined the cotton and that whoever it was you will give them their next bale free. |
| | C. W. | I didn't say that. Whoever said I said that is a liar. |

310    *(McHenry moves closer with the pistol.)*

| | | |
|---|---|---|
| | C. W. | *(In terror now.)* Knub. |
| | McHenry | Mr. Knub. |
| | C. W. | Mr. Knub. |
| | McHenry | Mr. Knub please. |
| | C. W. | Mr. Knub please. |
| | McHenry | Mr. Knub please sir. |
| | C. W. | Mr. Knub please sir. |
| | McHenry | Mr. Knub in the name of God, please. |
| | C. W. | Mr. Knub in the name of God, please. |
| 320 | McHenry | Mr. Knub in the name of God, please sir. |
| | C. W. | Mr. Knub in the name of God, please sir. |
| | McHenry | Please what? |
| | C. W. | Please don't kill me. |
| | McHenry | Mr. Knub sir. |
| | C. W. | Mr. Knub sir. |
| | McHenry | Mr. Knub sir, please don't kill me. |
| | C. W. | Mr. Knub sir, please don't kill me. |
| | McHenry | Get on your knees. *(C. W. gets on his knees.)* Pray. |
| | C. W. | Our Father . . . |
| 330 | McHenry | Louder. |
| | C. W. | *(Loud.)* Now I lay me down to sleep. I pray the Lord my soul to keep. |

| | | |
|---|---|---|
| McHenry | Not that one. The other one. | |
| C. W. | Our Father ... | |
| McHenry | Louder ... | |
| C. W. | Pinkey ... | |
| McHenry | Why do you want Pinkey? | |
| C. W. | To go for the Coca-Colas. I am very thirsty ... | |
| McHenry | You don't need any Coca-Colas. Pray ... | |

340    C. W.    Our Father ...

McHenry    You said that.

C. W.    Now I lay me down to sleep ...

McHenry    I told you I didn't want to hear that one.

C. W.    Our Father ...

McHenry    You said that.

C. W.    I can't remember the rest of it. Our Father ... Our Father ... *(He screams.)* Pinkey ... *(He runs towards the door. Again McHenry stops him with the gun.)* I tell you what, I think all this has

350    affected your mind. You are not yourself. I think we'd better get you to a doctor, and I'll pay for it. And I tell you what else—I bet I can find you some kind of a job again around here at the gin. What do they pay you at the pool hall? *(No answer.)* Whatever it is I certainly bet I can do better. If they pay you twelve a week I'll make it fifteen. I could make you night watchman. I always figured we needed two of them anyway. *(A pause.)* I remember it now. I remember the Lord's Prayer.

360    Now I lay me down to sleep. I pray the ... I'm sorry. I got that wrong. I got mixed up again. Our Father which art in Heaven. Hallowed be thy name ...

McHenry    Give me back my arm.

C. W.    Our Father which art in heaven, hallowed be thy name, thy kingdom come, thy will be done on earth as it is in heaven ...

*(McHenry shoots him. He slumps over. He is killed. Pinkey comes in. He looks in horror at what has happened.)*

370    McHenry    He wouldn't give me back ... *(He sees Pinkey. He raises the gun.)* Pray ...

Pinkey    Yes sir. *(A pause.)* How in the hell does it go? My God, how does it go? You killed him. Why did you kill him? *(McHenry moves toward him.)* I'm

gonna pray. I'll think of something. Our Father
... which art in heaven. Our Father. Hallowed be
thy name. Our Father. Hallowed be thy name.
Our Father ... Our Father ...

*(He is crying. MCHENRY is pointing the gun at him as the lights fade.)*

## Kate Barnes

# The Old Lady's Story

1   When my friend Clementina
Was growing up in Honduras
There was an old lady in the village
Who had died and come back to life.

As her body lay on the cot
Her soul got up and left it;
She walked out into the village street
Which was somewhat different from usual

Because instead of ending
10   In a muddy track into the hills,
It now ended at the edge
Of a wide, swift-flowing river.

And what was that green land
On the opposite shore
With such inviting shady trees?
Perhaps it was an island—

She couldn't quite tell—
But one thing was certain:
Happiness blew toward her from that place
20   With a scent like vanilla flowers.

Looking anxiously around,
The old lady saw that she was not alone:
Other people just like her
Were walking down to the bank

And as soon as each little soul
Strolled uncertainly to the water's edge,
A dog would swim up
To carry it over on its back.

The dogs were as busy as sidewheelers
30  Ferrying souls across the river.
The old lady stood watching a long while
But no canine psychopomp

Hurried up to *her*,
And then—she remembered!
The kicks as she cooked the beans:
Get away, you curs, there's none for you!

So she sadly turned around,
Sadly walked up the street again.
It was hard to climb back into that body
40  So old and fever-wasted

But she managed to blink her eyes,
And then she drank a little cold tea,
And after a while
She got quite well again

So that she lived on for years
Telling her story over and over,
A source of deep interest to the whole village—
And a notable friend to its dogs.

*Robert Cooperman*

# Isabella Bird Rides in a Round-up, Colorado Territory, 1873

1   What exhilaration to thunder along
the mountain grass of Estes Park beside a man
proclaimed the finest horseman in North America,
and give him stride for stride of the wildest
race he admitted ever having, what joy
in turning the frenzied cattle, some wild
as bisons, one having to be shot by Mr. Evans,
for attacking any drover who made the mistake
of riding between her and the stupid calf
10  she was always losing in a maternal funk.
In the end the calf lowed so piteously
obstinate over her corpse, Mr. Evans
had to shoot it as well. We feasted
like Queen Elizabeth and her court
that night, off an open mountain fire,
the aroma of burning pine logs driving me
quite unladylike in anticipation, luring
wolves down from the snowy peaks,
their craven howling making the meal
20  that much more thrillingly succulent.

In England, I'd have to ride side-saddle,
as if a British lady were too fragile to sit
her horse astraddle, as sign of low breeding.
No one in these mountains has ever mistaken me
for anyone less than a lady, the equal of the Queen

of England, as one man put it, saluting me
with as graceful a bow as I've seen,
and with far more real gallantry than any
delivered by a lord or officer handing down
30  a lady from a carriage, as he reckons
her fortune to the shilling.

I slept like exhausted innocence that night,
in the unchinked cabin Mr. Evans lets me
keep for free, my base while I explore these peaks
and canyons, ride the finest horse I've ever
sat, her gait melting the miles, her hooves
nimble as the mountain sheep that bound
from rock to rock and make me hold
my breath for fear they will slip
40  and shatter on the boulders below,
or be trampled by the hooves of cattle
wild as elk, emaciated creatures used
to the dizzying shimmer of dawn and dusk.

My legs want to straddle the very highest
peaks, ride them like a goddess horsewoman,
not a hero in the world able to catch me
on the fire-darting mare responding to the least
touch of my naked knees, my hair flying behind me,
a comet too hot for any man but one to touch.

## Brigit Pegeen Kelly

# Young Wife's Lament

1　The mule that lived on the road
　　where I was married
　　would bray to wake the morning,
　　but could not wake me.
　　How many summers I slept
　　lost in my hair. How many
　　mules on how many hills singing.
　　Back of a deep ravine
　　he lived, above a small river
10　on a beaten patch of land.
　　I walked up in the day and walked down,
　　having been given nothing
　　else to do. The road grew no longer,
　　I grew no wiser, my husband
　　was away selling things to people who buy.
　　He went up the road, too, but
　　the road was full of doors for him,
　　the road was his belt and,
　　one notch at a time, he loosened it
20　on his way. I would sit
　　on the hill of stones and look down
　　on the trees, on the lake
　　far away with its boats and those
　　who ride in boats
　　and I could not pray. Some of us
　　have mule minds,

are foolish as sails whipping
in the wind, senseless
as sheets rolling through the fields,
30　some of us are not given
even a wheel of the tinker's cart
upon which to pray.
When I came back I pumped water
in the yard under the trees
by the fence where the cows came up,
but water is not wisdom
and change is not made by wishes.
Else I would have ridden something,
even a mule, over
40　those hills and away.

*Ursula K. LeGuin*

·+·=+=·+· ·+·+· =+=· ·+·

# *The Maenads*

1    Somewhere I read
    that when they finally staggered off the mountain
    into some strange town, past drunk,
    hoarse, half-naked, blear-eyed,
    blood dried under broken nails
    and across young thighs,
    but still jeering and joking, still trying
    to dance, lurching and yelling, but falling
    dead asleep by the market stalls,
10  sprawled helpless, flat out, then
    middle-aged women,
    respectable housewives,
    would come and stand nightlong in the agora
    silent
    together
    as ewes and cows in the night fields,
    guarding, watching them
    as their mothers
    watched over them.
20  And no man
    dared
    that fierce decorum.

*Robert J. Levy*

# *Paradise Fish*

1    Purchased on a whim, plunged recklessly
into my cramped aquarium,
      she was the perfect girlfish, a pink chiffon
of fins adrift in artificial light.
  Black mollies blanched and neon tetras
      dimmed perceptibly as she trailed
her silent taffeta past rigid swordtails,
      pudgy cichlids, lowly snails. Endless nights
watching her hover midway between

10   gravel and glass sky—a living jewel
nestled in black velvet—I would marvel
      at loveliness so unearthly, and think:
How amazing she was *all mine*. Restive,
  listless and plagued by less effulgent fish,
      she spent her days avoiding tankmates
who found her plumage something good to eat.
      Unable to seize the tubifex worms
and daphnia I offered her for fear

    of being ripped to shreds, she languished
20  among leaves—hollow-bellied, starved.
      One time I pinched some dried food between
my fingertips and held it out to her.
  With soft fins, she brushed my hand—a briny
      butterfly kiss—then nibbled daintily,

and soon, accustomed to this finger-food,
    she pressed against my wrist. Cupping her
in my hand, I raised her from the tank:

  In the safe haven of my palm-sized pool,
I stroked the length of her body
30    with one finger. She lay completely still.
When I released her, she swam off
  without the slightest urgency,
    done with her flirtation in parched heaven.
  Once returned, her torments only worsened:
  Guppies slashed her fins to tattered flags
of finery while stray catfish

  hounded her in corners. And then,
one day at feeding time, I found her
    beached on the floor in front of the fishtank,
40 gone mad from too much personhood too soon.
  The thin, pink crepe of her body crackled
    like a dried leaf when I lifted her.
    *All mine*, I thought, as I sent her off,
    far from any human aquarium,
back to the ocean of her origin.

# WRITING ASSIGNMENTS

1.  Write a story that starts out with a serious problem but winds up with a happy ending. For instance, John and Mary are in love, but their families hate each other. Somehow the problem is resolved.

2.  Write a story or play about a young husband who persuades his wife that they must drop out of the urban rat-race for a while and spend a year in the wilderness. Write about one of the experiences they have in the depths of winter. This situation lends itself to a one-set one-act play.

3.  Write a story about an elderly, well-educated gentleman who takes advantage of lonely women with money. Perhaps he is even a "Bluebeard"-type killer. He finally meets his match. Make your plot intricate and try for an ironic or surprise ending.

4.  Write a tale about a fisherman who finds a magnificent ring inside a fish. Perhaps the ring has a name on it or says, "I will grant your wish."

5.  Write a narrative poem with a folk-story quality (see the poem by Kate Barnes).

6.  Write a poem about one of the following:
    a) the sinking of the *Titanic*.
    b) Amelia Earhart.
    c) someone who makes friends with a wild animal.
    d) being lost in the wilderness.
    e) an encounter with a ghost.

# _Chapter 5_

# _Point of View_

## Introduction

## Fiction

Alberto Alvaro Ríos    _Waltz of the Fat Man_
Leo Litwak    _Mouth to Mouth_

## Poetry

Margaret Atwood    _Variations on the_ Word Sleep
Lisel Mueller    _Statues_
Ishmael Reed    _Grizzly_
William Stafford    _A Proposition_
Jean Nordhaus    _My Life in Hiding_

## Writing Assignments

A narrative implies a narrator. Somebody has to tell the story, whether it is someone who participates in the action or someone who heard about it or someone so anonymous as to become merely the voice that speaks the tale. At times that anonymous speaker is God-like and omniscient, as James Joyce pointed out. The reader is asked to see things through the eyes of the teller of the story. That is what we mean by *point of view.*

In drama, of course, the situation is different, since the work is performed. The story is acted out on a stage and we see it all from the point of view of the audience.

In fiction and poetry we often refer to the teller of the story as the *persona*. We cannot assume that the person speaking to us is the author, although sometimes that seems to be the case. Often an author will create a voice that is not his or her own, a voice better suited for the purpose. The created voice is part of the fiction and should be referred to as the *persona*. Even in very personal or *confessional* poetry the voice the author uses in his work is part of the artifact and not necessarily the voice he might use in a private conversation over a cup of coffee.

In "What She's Saying Now," for instance (Chapter 10), the voice that is telling the story has a peculiar and personal style. It appears to belong to one of Trudy's friends or relations. This person is relating Trudy's story to us partly as Trudy herself has told it and partly as the storyteller. The author has invented a speaker who uses vigorous figures of speech such as " ... hers was a story with the smell and shape of rotting fruit," or "As seems now inevitable ... they became a pair, inseparable as bird and song." The author may have chosen to tell the story from this point of view because it enabled him to editorialize in this manner, creating a story-telling atmosphere.

The usual points of view can be classified as: *first person, second person, third person limited,* and *third person omniscient.* The second person is rarely used. One is most likely to find it in old private eye stories that begin something like this: "You are sitting in your office when the telephone rings. You pick it up and listen to the sultry voice of a woman...."

What we are mainly left with are the first person and the third person. There are several varieties of each of these points of view.

The first person narrator can seem to be the author or one of the characters, or someone not involved who heard the story from someone else. Sometimes even several voices are used in the first person to put together the story.

The third person narrator can seem to be totally objective, telling the reader only what was said or happened, as if it were all seen on a stage or screen. More often the narrator will see events through the eyes of one of the characters. This is called *limited objectivity*. "Nairobi" (Chapter 3) serves as a good example of this. The action is written in the third person ("he" or "she," not "I"), but it is limited to what Ginny perceives. The reader does not know how Oliver sees things, except through his dialogue.

If the narrator seems to know more than can be seen through the eyes of one central character—perhaps the reactions of some of the other characters and some events that take place "offstage"—then the point of view is called *limited omniscient*. Finally, that God-like narrator who knows it all can reveal facts and make comments without any restrictions. This is the *omniscient* point of view.

An example of omniscience is "Takes" (Chapter 9) by Stephen Dixon. Here the author is able to reveal what *everybody* is thinking: the girl, her mother, her sister, her roommate, her date, the rapist, and another tenant. Often the author cannot afford the omniscient point of view because the plot depends on *not* revealing what each character is thinking. In this case, however, the point of view heightens the suspense and intensifies the reader's concern. Such a totally omniscient point of view is seldom used because it is difficult to handle the thoughts of so many characters; those of two or three are usually enough.

There are two stories in this chapter that illustrate point of view, one written in the third person and the other in the first person. Keep in mind, however, that the point of view of every poem and story in this book is worth analyzing. A brief survey would reveal certain patterns and variations.

In "Waltz of the Fat Man" by Alberto Alvaro Ríos we have a good example of a story that is told in the third person, but through the eyes of the main character, Noé. What the reader is told is always something that Noé knows or feels or thinks. For instance: "He did not think himself fat, but he felt himself heavy, in a manner he could not explain to anyone." We never enter the minds of the other characters, the townspeople, or the soldiers. All we get occasionally is a description of them through Noé's eyes: "In whatever part of the town he walked, people spoke behind their hands, and pointed when they didn't think Noé could see them. But his eyes were fat as well, and because of that he could see more."

Stories that deal with memories of childhood seem to favor the first person point of view. The approach is understandable. The memories often deal with personal matters, early joys and sorrows. To hear such things described in the voice of the person who experienced them can be very effective. The reader has to keep in mind, however, that this is the voice of a fictional character and not the author, even if much of the material is autobiographical. Leo Litwak's "Mouth to Mouth" is a perfect example of the first person point of view used in a story that recalls childhood experiences. The narrator remembers his days at the Mary Tessler Orphanage and his strong attachment to Miss Wyman. "There were more than a hundred of us. She knew all our griefs and enthusiasms and bent ways." The story touches on a few significant early incidents and then leaps forward to the release of Eugene (the narrator) and his difficult adjustment to the outside world. A story such as this might also have been written in the third person, but the point of view used here was a good choice.

Since poetry also often deals with personal matters, the first person point of view is used with great frequency. Of our selections, the poems by Atwood, Nordhaus, and Stafford are all in the first person. The very openings of these poems reveal the point of view and the personal nature of the material. In "Variations on the Word *Sleep*" by Margaret Atwood the opening line is: "I would like to watch you sleeping." In "My Life in Hiding" Jean Nordhaus says "My life in hiding /is not unlike your own." In William Stafford's "A Proposition" we find the first person used mainly in the plural (the singular, of course, is implied in this): "Pretend our house is on an ordinary street—/locust trees, and firs, cars in each drive." The effect of this use of the plural is to suggest that the poem is addressed to one specific other person (wife or husband in this case.)

There are times in poetry when the third person is clearly preferable. In "Statues" by Lisel Mueller, for instance, we have a commentary on the liberation of Eastern Europe from Communism. "In Prague, or perhaps Budapest, /the heroes have fallen off their horses." The point of the fantasy is fairly obvious. The oppressors fall off their horses, and the liberated animals step down from their pedestals, get used to free movement, and eventually gallop joyfully away.

Ishmael Reed's "Grizzly" is also told in the third person. The central image is a grizzly bear with a rather lecherous appetite for honey. Eventually Mrs. Grizzly catches him and he winds up down and out as a dancing bear being led by a rope. The human parallels are obvious but amusing.

Choosing the most effective point of view is important. The choice clearly depends to some extent on the nature of the material and the degree of objectivity or subjectivity that the author wants to achieve.

*Alberto Alvaro Ríos*

···+··· ···+···

# *Waltz of the Fat Man*

1 Noé's house trim was painted blue, good blue, deep and neat, with particular attention to the front door, that it should stand against spirits. He kept the house in repair, and hired a gardener in the three seasons, spring and summer, a little in autumn. In this place it was a gray wind after that, a time for planting things in the ground to save them, or to hide them.

His personal appearance suffered nothing from the attentions to his house, as Noé kept on himself a trim mustache and a clean face, neat clothes for which he thanked Mrs.
10 Martínez, patronizing her for a quarter of a century. From ironing his clothing, she knew the shape of his body more than he did, and for her consequent attention to detail in that regard he was appreciative—just the right fold in the collars, a crease moving a little to the left along his right leg, the minor irregularities and embarrassments. And he was doubly thankful as she never said a word to him about it.

His body was full of slow bones, after all, and Noé moved as if long fish swam in a small place.

He did not think himself fat, but he felt himself heavy, in
20 a manner he could not explain to anyone. His body to be sure was overweight, but he did not feel it to be something of the stomach or thighs; rather, it was heaviness that came from the inside out, manifesting itself to the world as the body of a fat man.

On his best days, Noé could make that weight look like muscles. On his best days he could make his stomach go into his chest and his shoulders, and people would believe anything he had to say.

Noé had a business as a butcher, but it was too much for
30 him, a sadness cutting the meats. He had become a butcher, after all, purely for social reasons. It was a civic service, and he

wanted to do good things. But it was not a good choice, given what he desired, which was simply to be part of the town.

To be sure, people patronized his shop, and took him up on his offer of extra services and niceties, but they did not finally stay very long to talk, not in the way they stayed for coffee and to warm themselves at the baker's. He could see them in there, with their mouths open and their eyes rolling along a line of laughter.

40    He could not say why the townspeople were like this, exactly. Perhaps it was his full size, or something about his looks, or about being the butcher in a town and being too good at his trade. But, the whole of his life was that no one cared much for him, or even spoke to him very much, and when he attended wakes, which he did because he was a courteous man, he left indentations in the kitchen linoleum, which would not go away.

Noé knew that, though he tried not to be, in the people's minds he was simply an irritation.

50    In whatever part of the town he walked, people spoke behind their hands, and pointed when they didn't think Noé could see them. But his eyes were fat as well, and because of that he could see more.

When Noé danced, he wore a blue suit, and was always alone, always at the same place outside of town, by the river reeds.

He danced with the wind, which was also cruel like the women of the town, but the wind at least did not have a face. He locked the trunks of his arms with the branch arms of the
60  black walnut trees, which also like the women of the town did not bend around to hold him, did not invite him to another, softer room.

But neither could these arms of a tree leave Noé so easily. They could not so quickly give him over cruelly to the half-hot tongues of the weeds so that they might talk about him, and make their disapproving sounds.

When he danced this dance he let out with a small noise his thin girl, which he kept inside himself. This is what had made him look fat, the holding in, the keeping in of the noise
70  inside himself, his desire to freely speak his needs as a human

being in the company of other human beings. This was his thin girl.

And Noé would let her out and they would dance the dance of weddings into the night.

··-··-·-··-··-··

Noé took to wearing his blue suit to the shop, because he thought he looked better. He did this in case someone would look at him, and think the better of him, think him something of a fine man after all.

Then his plan of the blue suit grew into a great deal
80   more, taking as he did the wearing of his suit as some small license. It was the license, he thought, of a regular man. And he tried what he imagined to be the secret work of a regular man in the company of a regular woman.

When he shook the hands of women, he did so vigor-ously, hoping to see movement on their bodies, some small adventure to take his breath, some nodding yes, some quiet dance of the upper body. This first adventure of a man.

His was a modest plan, and worked a little. The shaking of the hands was, however, the most Noé did. It gave to him so
90   much, and he thought the intimate movements of a woman to be so loud, there in front of everybody, that he could go no further.

But it is why Noé attended wakes so faithfully as well, sometimes as if they were the whole of his social life: how in comforting a bereaved wife he could—properly and in front of everyone so that there was no question of propriety—kiss her on the cheek.

Even then, after the hour of praying for the deceased and thinking about what he would do, by the time his moment was
100   at hand, his attempt at kissing was a dizzied missing of the mark. His lips to the cheek were so clumsy and so fast that the kiss was more of something else, something not quite any-thing, something in keeping with his life after all.

··-··-·-··-··-··

The butcher shop through the slow years began to change, as did Noé himself. He had taken up in his house the collection and caring of clocks, because, he said to himself, they had hands, and in so many clocks was a kind of heaven, a dream of sounds to make the hours pass in a manner that would allow him to open up shop again the next day.

110    His nighttime dream became a daytime dream as well. He did not keep them, could not keep the clocks, finally, only at home. Along with Noé in his blue suit, the shop also began to find itself dressed differently, hung with clocks, first one, a plain dark wood, and then two, and then a hundred. Each of them with two hands for him.

There was a blue clock. Cuckoos and 28-day, anniversary clocks to the side of the scale, large-faced numbers where once there had been letters in the sections of an illustrated cow.

What Noé knew and did not say was that here was the
120 anniversary Mariquita, the schoolhouse Mariette, Marina the singular blue, Caras with her bird tongue. Armida had hands that sometimes rose outstretched to the two and ten like the blessing arms of Christ, and sometimes lowered to the five and seven of desire, one hand shorter, in the act of beckoning him, a come here, Noé. A come here, I've got something to tell you, Noé, come on, don't be afraid.

This was no butcher shop, the townspeople would say to themselves, not with clocks. One or two clocks maybe, but not so many as this. It would not have been so bad, except that he
130 was the only butcher in town, and people had to make use of his services. An unofficial inquiry was opened as to whether or not there was perhaps a law, some ordinance, prohibiting such abuses of the known world, but no one could find any reference that applied to the walls of a butcher shop, other than cleanliness. And of that, there could be no discussion. Noé did not neglect the clocks, and therefore did not neglect the white-sheeted bed of his walls.

One evening in winter as Noé was closing up his shop, having wound the clocks for the night and having left just
140 enough heat in the stove that they would not suffer, he heard the blue clock falter. So much like a heartbeat had the sounds of the clocks come to be for him, that he was alarmed and stumbled in his quickness to reach the clock, though it could not move and was not falling. It called to him nonetheless as a wife in pain might call to her husband: honey, it said, please.

He reached it too late, he thought, though it was simply a clock, and he laughed at himself.

He tried winding the clock again, thinking the unthinkable, that perhaps he had missed its turn in his haste to leave.
150 But that was not it: the spring was taut, and there was no play.

He took it down from its nail, and looked at it from different angles in his hands, but he could see nothing extraordinary. There was no obvious damage, no one had dropped it without telling him and rehung it, no insect had been boring into its side. Its blue was still blue, without blemish.

He took it to the counter and measured out some butcher's paper in which to wrap it, deciding that he would take it home to see to its difficulty. He put string around it and made a good blanket of the paper, which should comfort, he always said, what was inside. As he picked it up he could hear the workings move, and he resolved to be wary of its delicacy.

He need not have done it, but he warned himself, as if he were his own mother. He put the clock in the crook of his arm, closed and locked his door, took a deep breath in the cold air, hunched his shoulders and began his walk toward home.

He had errands, but they could wait. And he was, in any event, the last of the merchants to close for the evening, so he would have been out of luck anyway. Save for the clock, this was how his evenings most often came to an end, the closing of the door and the walk toward home.

An occasional voice greeted him, and he returned the hello, but it was the conversation of single words, friendly enough, and that was all.

·—·⊨⊹⊨·—·—··—·⊨⊹⊨·—·

Some theorized later it was the soldiers who were common in those days and who hung around with nothing better to do, that it was they who had been paid, because they never did anything for nothing, but would do anything for something, those soldiers from that kind of army.

There was nothing tragic, of course, nothing for which any charges could be drawn, in much the same manner that nothing could be legally said about what Noé had done to his butcher's shop. You get back what you give, someone was later reported as having said, someone but not anyone in particular. That's how it was told to the captain of the police.

Noé was walking home with his package, which no one could have known was the blue clock. No one but perhaps the soldiers, and only then if they had been nosy enough to have been watching through his window, which had been recently broken and was full of cardboard patches, easy enough to hide behind.

The package's aspect was of a ham or a roast of some sort, a good rabbit, something simple and natural in the arm of a big man walking home to dinner.

Darkness had set and the moon was new. He cast no shadow and made his way quickly as he left the last of the downtown buildings. The ground was neither muddy nor dry, resembling something closer to a woody mulch, and through him passed a moment of gardens from sometime in his life, gardens he had passed through, or that his mother had kept. It was a simple feeling, and brought a prickling to his skin.

He next passed by the stand of walnut trees and wild oleander which was white-flowered in the summer.

The oleander called to him, *Noé.*

At first it was so quiet he said to himself he did not hear it, *Noé.*

*Noé,* the oleanders said, louder this time, and he stopped to look. Though it was dark and the moon was hidden, he was not afraid.

His size was such that he had never been made to be afraid, not at a moment like this. It was, if one could read his face, a curiosity, this sound which was reminiscent of his name. It was like the mulch and his mother's garden, and it gave him a prickling of the skin once more.

*Noé.* He heard it again, and stopped, and turned to it, saying who was there, what did they want, that perhaps he could be of some service.

No one answered, so he reached his free hand into the leaves and moved them around. He heard the sound and then saw what seemed like, in the dimness, a rabbit, running into the underbrush.

Ha, he said, and let it go. He turned again to walk, pulling his coat back up onto his neck.

*Noé.* It was a whisper, this time he was sure. Not a voice, but more of a breath. A half-breath, but unmistakable in its enunciation.

As a child, Noé might have crossed himself, and as he was sometimes his own mother, he had the impulse, but he just stood there, once more.

He put down the clock in order to enter the oleander more fully, and see what was what, but he found nothing, only branches and the small noises of startled birds and lizards.

When he came out he could not find his package, though he concentrated with his eyes and with his hands. It was not there.

A voice whispered once more, *Noé. You know me,* it said, *you know who I am.*

Noé no longer moved around. He listened, and he waited.

*Noé.* He did know the whisper. He had in fact heard it
240 many times. He knew the whisper more than the voice of his neighbor, whom he had seen a thousand times.

He would not have believed any of it had this not been the blue clock. Marina his blue, who had made so many places for herself in his life. Not big places, but so many, her hair color on the trim of his house, the color of her eyes in his suit, and so on. She was the blueness inside him, the color of his appetite, the color both of what filled him and what he needed more of.

*Marina,* he said.
250 *Noé.*

He stood there and waited.

*Do you love me?*

Noé did not answer.

*You can love me if you love me like a horse,* said the whisper. *Can you be a horse, Noé? Can you show me how you are a horse?*

Noé stood there, quietly.

He stamped his foot, gingerly at first, unsure and sure at the same time.
260 *Is that it, Noé, is that all the horse you are?*

Noé stamped his foot harder, and made a noise with his nose, and partway through his mouth.

*Yes, Noé. And are you more of a horse still?*

If this were anything but his blue clock, Marina, he would have gone, and given the moment up as the ghosts of this place. Or children, or who knew what. But he could not.

And then he heard the laughter of the soldiers as they could no longer contain themselves camouflaged so well otherwise in the oleanders. He heard the laughter, but did not
270 bother with it. He turned and went home, without the clock.

⸻

He had gone away from home once before, from his family. He had to. One thing and another, right or wrong, these things didn't matter. It was simply too much to stay.

He had in some manner become an exponent to a regular number. He was ordinary times ten or times twenty, always

too much. And his desire carried an exponent as well. He wanted everything to be nice, to be only the Golden Rule, but times ten, and that is too much. He had no sense of himself, and yet he was everything. In that sea of mathematics he had
280 drowned a sailor's death.

And now he had to go away again. The tide had come up, and caught him once more. He sold what was left of his business at a loss finally to Mr. Molina, who had a scarred face and who wanted to do the work. There was an art in the cutting, and it took Noé, because he was a courteous man, the afternoon to teach the profession's immediate intricacies to Mr. Molina, who had had no idea there was so much.

And that same night Noé bought a brown horse and rode it as far into the following days and weeks, as far into the
290 future as he could because he could not wait to see what was there. He arrived at the circus, and in it he made his life again.

But he almost did not make it. A man and a sparrow— each puts a shoulder to the wind, each to his own intention: a sparrow to fly, a man to run. Noé on this night was in be- tween, and even with his weight he felt himself lifted, as if he were in league with angels at the edge of heaven, not quite deserving, but sneaking in with some help through a back door, hoping to go unnoticed again, as he had felt when he had come to this town. But it was not heaven, these places.

300 He stopped because the circus people were the first to wave him down, all of them standing near the road, as if this were the place, and they knew him, and they had been waiting, and what took him so long, had he not heard them calling into the night for him.

But they had called him without telegraph or telephone. Something stronger.

His mustache curled up from the wind and his body, which had sometimes seemed fat, was hardened, tense in that moment from the cold which had made him hold his breath
310 and flex his muscles for the whole distance of the ride.

He arrived as a beast, almost, something crazed and unshaven, out of breath.

Or as a beast on top of a man, as if the horse itself was more human, and asking for help.

His was a body full of slow bones still, but if it had taken his lifetime up to now to be slow, now the other foot was coming down, and it was fast.

It was the other half of himself now, for the rest of his years.

320　　　This was, after all, the place. And in that moment of dust kicked up and of noise, he began his real career, this life with a whole company of half-size men, two-bodied women, and all the rest of the animals who danced.

*Leo Litwak*

# Mouth to Mouth

1 Miss Wyman instructed us in first aid. When she demonstrated the new method of resuscitation, mouth to mouth, breath to breath, heart joined to heart, she knelt beside a recumbent Lenny Lucca. Her skirt rode up her thighs and we saw the tabs of her garters. She lowered herself on Lenny and didn't touch his mouth, but came close. She explained that somehow the breathless body would learn its own living rhythm through this act of sympathy.

She was in charge and no one dared snicker. Afterwards
10 in the dorm Lenny said, "If I died and Miss Wyman stuck her tongue in me, boy! I'd come alive! You bet your ass! I'd puke her right out!"

I hated that image of himself and Miss Wyman. Her mouth on his? The everted lips with a wisp of mustache, clumps of hair on his chin, acne pustules at the bursting point, touching her mouth? I despised him for having the notion.

We weren't eager to do such service to the dying. To link our own breath with someone corrupted—by god knows what disease, what foulness—would poison our souls. We specu-
20 lated about other possibilities. If it were a breathless Hedy Lamarr or Lana Turner with whom we joined mouths we might take from their honeyed vitality the power to transform ourselves from toads to something princely.

The demonstration ended in these jokey speculations. Then, a few weeks later, as if a model had been provided for the fates, our janitor, Mr. Harkness, collapsed while hauling in the flag. He staggered under billowing stars and stripes. We watched his comic dance as he batted at the flag and then sank beneath it. We tentatively giggled. But he was no clown. He
30 was a dour, simple man who insisted on respect for the flag. He would fold the flag in precise triangles, concluding in a tight package he devoutly carried to its place in the office. He was a churlish man, easy to provoke. The boys were annoyed by his way with the flag. We knew almost nothing about Mr. Harkness except that he'd been a doughboy and had served in

France and remained a patriot. The shabby old man in dirty overalls assumed a proud ceremonial attitude as he lowered the flag. He pressed one of the younger boys into service while he folded. It was someone like Mr. Harkness whom we imag-
40 ined when we thought of the horrors of mouth to mouth.

Miss Wyman rushed to him when he collapsed. She knelt among the billows, spread aside the flag, pried into his mouth with a handkerchief. She waved us off. "Give him air!" Then she lowered her mouth and blew into him and drew him into her and listened while her breath rattled somewhere inside him and was lost. She blew and blew and only gave up when the firemen arrived. They attached oxygen; his chest was convulsed by forced air. He was covered with a Mary Tessler blanket. His feet protruded. Miss Wyman hustled us
50 back on schedule. It was time to clean up and it was a subdued dinner. When we were done Miss Wyman clinked her glass and announced that our janitor had died of a heart attack. She asked us to lower our heads. He'd had no family of his own. We were his family. He considered us to be his children. She wanted us to think of all the orphaned people of the world who didn't have anyone with whom to share their lives. She asked us to thank god that we at Mary Tessler's had each other.

I thanked God, but not that we had each other. Only
60 through her did we have each other. She was what we had in common. She was with us every day of the week. She was only gone from Mary Tessler's on an occasional weekend night. The night she would go out she showed up on her rounds wearing a tweed suit rather than her customary skirt and smock. Her dense reddish hair was down to her shoulders instead of in a bun. She'd stand at the threshold of the dorm room checking us out and we'd be comforted by that sturdy military posture she encouraged us to assume. She seemed to me so firmly grounded nothing could unbalance her, not even
70 Mr. Harkness dying in her mouth. When she arose from his dying she was as clear and unaffected as if she'd blown away death and remained pure and uncorrupted.

There were more than a hundred of us. She knew all our griefs and enthusiasms and bent ways. She meant to straighten us while we were in her hands. On those nights when she was gone, Mary Tessler's didn't feel secure. It didn't matter who else was in charge—Mr. Atkins or Mrs. Hempleman or Miss Sample—it was only a holding action until the commander returned. Miss Wyman did the planning. We lived by her

80   schedule. She introduced what novelty there was—the Christmas visits to the Ford Rotunda, the showing of *Fantasia* in the refectory, the free trips to Brigg's stadium and the Barnum and Bailey circus, the performance of *Alice in Wonderland* by a troupe from Wayne University.

When I left the orphanage she had been there for twenty years, director for fifteen. In that time, she must have released more than five hundred of us to Detroit. She made sure we were settled before she let go the tether. Interviews began during our last year, which was for some as early as age 90  sixteen, and for a few, like myself, as late as eighteen.

I didn't want to give her trouble, but it wasn't easy releasing me. She couldn't get me pegged. I could type. I was good at math. I knew how to keep books. I had no mechanical skills. I was too young for the kind of jobs that might have used my talents. I refused to work at the fountain of George V's pharmacy. I turned down a job as stock boy at A&P. I wouldn't accept a scholarship to the Ford vocational trade school. I told her I was too old and would never learn.

"If you don't try, Eugene, how do you know what you 100  can do?"

She was increasingly annoyed. I caused her as much trouble as any boy she could remember.

"You're not going to be president at the start. You have to begin somewhere."

I wanted to go to Wayne University. I'd read the bulletin and it promised me Troy and Athens and Rome and Renaissance Florence.

"That's fine," she said. "But what are you going to do about a place to live? How are you going to eat?" She found 110  me an opening in the shoe department of Sam's Cut Rate.

I refused to work in a store. My father and mother were grocers in Syracuse.

It was my heart's desire to please Miss Wyman, but I couldn't accept her notion of a safe place. She found a position she thought perfect, a bookkeeper at Clamage's Radio Emporium on Livernois Avenue. Clamage, himself a Mary Tessler graduate, was a chunky crew-cut man. He wore spectacles secured by a thong. He wore white overalls. His name was in red yarn over his pocket. He had been in Miss Wyman's first 120  classes. She began as the gym teacher and history instructor twenty years before. He told me he considered Mary Tessler's to be his first home. He wanted to return a little of what had been given to him so he hired orphans. He showed me the cubicle where I would work. It contained a battered steel desk and an ancient adding machine set among what seemed to be a ruin of radio parts—speakers, coils, tubes, cabinets. There were piles of withered manuals and circuit diagrams.

He offered me the job. "Kate says you can do it and her word's good enough for me."

130    I told him I'd call and let him know.

"What do you mean you'll call? Don't you want the job?"

I went back to Mary Tessler's and told her I couldn't work at Clamage's.

"You can do it. You will do it. There's nothing else." She said I was a snob. What right did I have to look down on people like Al Clamage? He was a wonderful man, loyal to the Home. There were three Mary Tessler graduates now in his employ. "You don't have to stay forever. Start there and when

140    you get a better offer move on."

I told her I couldn't do it.

I feared such a start would be my finish. I'd never get out of that cubicle. I'd be buried in a smell of grease, the absence of daylight, the sputtering fluorescence. The other workers were more kin to pliers and screwdrivers than to orphans.

She said, "All right, Eugene. You're on your own. I've got nothing else for you."

On the last day she told me that the offer was still open and I again refused. I had twenty-five dollars. Everything I

150    owned was in a cardboard suitcase. I wore a suit that, though new to me, was someone's cast-off, and too heavy for the summer weather. She accompanied me to the outer gate, took my hand, and squeezed.

"Don't be your own worst enemy, Eugene. You're very talented. You're very bright. You have it in your power to make something of yourself. I expect great things from you. Don't disappoint me."

And then she let me go. Once beyond the threshold of Mary Tessler's I was on my own. It was sink or swim and if I

160    went down she wouldn't be around to give me mouth to mouth.

I stayed briefly with Mr. and Mrs. Sutton. He had been a foreman at the Briggs Bodyworks until felled by arthritis. In the week I knew him I never saw him without a newspaper. Even when he got up to greet me he carried it in his left hand. They had taken other orphans. None could have been less forthcoming than I was. "Well," he said, after we came to an abrupt halt, "it's going to be a long summer for the Tigers. I'm afraid this isn't their year."

170     I was so stunned by the world outside Mary Tessler's I couldn't speak.

She led me to an attic room. One of the windows was closed off by an exhaust fan. She didn't have a key for me. She said they'd have one made. Meanwhile, I'd have to be in by their eleven o'clock bedtime. It turned out that I had arrived in the midst of a quarrel that in the next few days reached its crisis. Her ferocious monotone penetrated ceilings and walls and I stayed away as much as I could, looking for work.

I found nothing as good as Clamage's offer.

180     I saw a range of positions on a sidewalk blackboard outside an employment office—short order cook, handyman, welder, mechanic, Fuller Brush salesman—I didn't bother going in.

I wasted time riding buses, waiting for appointments in personnel offices. I barely managed three or four applications a day. Of the positions that seemed interesting, most were taken before I arrived. The two leads I found—busboy at Greenfield's Cafeteria and helper on a laundry truck—I didn't follow up.

190     Each afternoon about five I sat at the counter of Blakeney's Chili Parlor across from the Mary Tessler grounds and watched the day end. I heard her distant whistle, summoning them to dinner. The playground emptied. The janitor lowered the flag, then shut the great carved double doors after them. Shadows spread over the ironwork fence and the elaborate gate with the letters MT scripted in brass, then the hedges of forsythia and the great elms and the blood red brick with the sandstone coping, the towers, the gables. At dusk lights appeared, first in the refectory then spreading above and below

200 until all Mary Tessler was ignited. At nine-thirty she began her rounds. In her wake light vanished, first on the top floor where the youngest slept, then on the third floor. By ten everything was blanked out except the red exit lights on each floor and her rooms on the ground floor and the threshold lanterns and the street lights on Six Mile Road and the reversed Blakeney Chili Parlor sign.

One night the counterman at Blakeney's leaned over and in a low pleasant voice so as not to offend the other customers, said to me, "You've been using up that chair for three days

210 now. I've got customers waiting." He nodded toward the bowling crowd that had arrived. "You come in every night,

spend fifty cents for a bowl of soup, load up on oyster crackers, leave a nickel tip. Listen, Big Spender, why don't you take your business someplace else? I can afford the loss."

I was an orphan in the world. I had no place to light. I had to keep moving. I was breathless as if I'd been running. Dreams devoured my sleep. I awoke in panic and started moving again. I looked for work in the neighborhood of Wayne University. The summer session had just finished. The campus was empty.
220 Clerks manned the admissions office. I didn't have the appropriate credits for admission. I barely missed a job at a bookstore.

A week after leaving the orphanage I was down to twelve dollars.

Out of necessity—I was exhausted, it was a boiling day, my shirt was soaked, I limped from tight shoes—I found a room near Wayne. There was a For Rent sign in the window of a three-story Victorian. The door was open. I looked into a dark cool vestibule and a carpeted stairway. The landlady was out front watering the lawn. Something Prussian in her man-
230 ner was confirmed by the German accent. She softened "t's" and hardened "th's" and put dents in "w's".

There was a room available for a clean, reliable tenant. She didn't want drinkers or noise makers. She guessed I was a Wayne student. She had other students as tenants. It was a good place to study, quiet, cool, clean. The rooms were furnished. Each had kitchen facilities. Rent was eight dollars a week. There was a shared bath in the corridor.

I followed her to the second floor where there were three rooms and a bath. My room was at a corner adjoining the
240 bath. There was a cot by the wall with a crocheted spread. There was a round oak table in the center of the room. There were two straight chairs and a rattan arm chair. The kitchen alcove was the size of a large closet. It contained a counter and sink with cabinets above. There was a countertop refrigerator and a two-jet gas burner. The braided rug on the floor was unfurled. The rattan was broken on the arm chair. The table was unsteady.

I paid on the spot.

"In this room," she said, "you will write books and
250 become famous. Take my word for it, Professor. This is a house of good luck."

I left the Suttons that afternoon. He was locked into silence behind the spread sheets of the Free Press. She ran the vacuum around his feet. They were barely interested in my going.

"Leave an address," she said, "if someone wants to get in touch."

I left Tuchler's name and address and spent the night in my own place.

260 I dreamed of my father. I entered my room and he was sitting at the round table, dressed in a robe, his face in his hands. I said, "Dad, you're alive." He turned to me and burst into tears. "Oh, my boy," he said. "I've missed you so." I picked him up and sat with him on my lap and I hugged him and said, "I miss you too, Daddy." I woke up. The old man next door was coughing. It was still night. I felt dreadfully orphaned. I yearned for the sounds of Mary Tessler's—the morning prayers and exercise, footsteps on waxed linoleum tiles, the echo of Mr. Atkins' tenor in the small amphitheater 270 adjoining the shop. Our breath at night. I dwelt inside the noise and smell of the Home as if they were my skin. The sound of buckets in the corridor signalled the rituals of Sunday morning inspection, then chapel, and afterward the best meal of the week. The stillness of Harold Mitchell in the cot beside me was promise of trouble ahead. There were uncalculated inferences to be made about my future state from slight changes in the skin of noise that located me.

At Tuchler's every creak, every rattle, every clank needed attention because I wasn't at home.

280 The next day I didn't go out. I had four dollars left after paying the rent. I drifted into fantasy. I imagined a heart-shaped island. I stood on a quivering pier. I saw a line of cottages above the beach. There was dense forest. I began to create my dream of Arcadia. Benign days, a lovely breeze, lemon-scented air, fish-dappled water, blackberry bushes, wild strawberries, gull cries, my island.

I don't know how far into my dreams I would have declined if I hadn't been summoned by Mrs. Tuchler in her German English. "Mr. Smith! The telephone! Downstairs. It's 290 for you." When I came down she said, "Next time give them the number of the upstairs phone. My phone is not for the use of the tenants." I walked through her lacy pillowed bedroom to the phone. Miss Wyman was at the other end.

Had I found work yet?

I gloried in her voice. I would have done anything to have ready access to it. Did she want me for Clamage? I was willing to serve.

"Eugene, I think I've found something tailor-made for you. It's perfect."

300     And the next day I entered those gates again. I was back
in her office which I knew better than most, always from the
perspective of a straight chair, looking through the innards of
an ancient Smith Corona across a huge walnut desk at an
erect, matronly woman in a squealing swivel chair, the fish
tank perking, a fluorescent light illuminating a miniature sea-
scape with caves and swaying plants and snails glued to the
glass. Eisenhower had replaced Truman on the wall near the
window. Above the desk, Mary Tessler was ornately framed, a
prettified young lady with protuberant eyes and a creamy
310 bosom and full lips and chestnut hair. Taken in the flower of
her youth, the Home endowed in her memory. Every other
object in that room subdued.

     "Well, Eugene. How do you like being a free man?" A
large innocent smile as though she hadn't choreographed my
destiny and brought me to this moment in precisely the attitude she wanted.

     I was available for anything she had for me.

     A job with Elton Kramer, proprietor of ELKRAM REAL
ESTATE.

320     She told me about Elton Kramer before he arrived. He
was a real hustler from the day he had come to the Home, eight
years old, undersized, underweight, eyes so huge they seemed
to be devouring the rest of him. He was called Knobby by the
other kids. He had knobs on his cheeks, a knob on his chin,
knobs on collar bones and shoulders. She used to be relieved to
see him eat. He hustled to be first in line. He was first for
seconds. He ate and ate but his bones never vanished from
sight. She considered his survival her triumph. As she described it, he insinuated himself into a crowd, wiggling and
330 elbowing, and arrived up front, his tray at the ready.

     His success was a tribute to the Home. After serving as
an agent for a large developer, he had started his own real
estate business and at twenty-four he was on the verge of a
great success. "Believe me, Eugene. The world will hear of
Elton."

     He was her boy. He returned to see her two or three
times a year. I saw her pleasure when he entered, lighting up
that worn room. He wore a checked suit, a hankie in his lapel
pocket. He brought a bouquet of roses for Miss Wyman. He
340 kissed her on the cheek.

     "Business? Terrific!" As much as he could handle. Right
here in the Mary Tessler neighborhood. A hot area, in transition from Catholic to Jew. The Catholics were heading for

Royal Oak and Birmingham, while the Jews moved to Six and Seven Mile Roads.

"Miss Wyman tells me you're smart, one of the brightest. Terrific. But can you sell? Without hustle you could be Albert Einstein and you'd go down like a lead balloon." I was pretty young to be selling. Maybe I could grow a mustache. A

350  blazer and grey flannels would help. He liked the college look. We could have terrific fun, two Mary Tessler boys taking on the city of Detroit. But he gave me warning. He wasn't going to carry me. It was a tough world. I would sink or swim on my own. I wouldn't get a free ride just because of the Mary Tessler connection.

"Well, kid. Are you interested?"

Miss Wyman stared at me and I said, "Terrific. Yes. I will," despite the protest of my heart which longed to be free of her breath in the land of my dreams.

# Margaret Atwood

# *Variations on the* Word Sleep

1  I would like to watch you sleeping,
which may not happen.
I would like to watch you,
sleeping. I would like to sleep
with you, to enter
your sleep as its smooth dark wave
slides over my head

and walk with you through that lucent
wavering forest of bluegreen leaves
10  with its watery sun & three moons
towards the cave where you must descend,
towards your worst fear

I would like to give you the silver
branch, the small white flower, the one
word that will protect you
from the grief at the center
of your dream, from the grief
at the center. I would like to follow
you up the long stairway
20  again & become
the boat that would row you back

carefully, a flame
in two cupped hands
to where your body lies
beside me, and you enter
it as easily as breathing in

I would like to be the air
that inhabits you for a moment
only. I would like to be that unnoticed
30  & that necessary.

*Lisel Mueller*

# *Statues*

1    In Prague, or perhaps Budapest,
the heroes have fallen off their horses.
Here lies a general's profile
and here a helmet, there
a ferrous glove still holding the reins.
The horses, so long inert
under the heavy bodies,
are not used to wind and sun,
nor to the tenderness of their flanks
10   now that the boots are gone,
and their eyes, so long overcast
by bronze or stone, are slow
to take in the gray city,
the heavyset houses. Gradually
they start to move, surprised
by their new lightness. There's a scent
of rain in the air, and something clicks
inside their heads; it has to do
with green, with pasture. They step down
20   from their pedestals, unsteady as foals
beginning to walk. No one pays attention
to riderless horses walking
through city streets; these are
supernatural times. Near the edge of town,

where the sky expands, they trust themselves
to break into a run
and then drop out of sight
behind a bank of willows
whose streamers promise water.

*Ishmael Reed*

# *Grizzly*

1  He always prided himself on
never being caught with his paws down
The flying grizzly left his bear
tracks at fifty thousand feet
his life, a daily peach blossom
He always managed to find some
hot honey to dip into
He was smiling all the time
Licking his lips, till Mrs.
10  Grizzly discovered him in the
bush with some outside trim of
a wonderful red cabbage and Mrs.
Grizzly grounded her
Teddy Bear
the rough rider under her fur coat
she was not taken in by his sweet
word-bees
Last trip back to the cave
he felt like he'd entered customs
20  after a return from an enemy city
What are these claw marks doing on your back?
Are those huckleberry stains on the front
of your pants?
Why do you have that fishy smell?
The divorce left him belly-up
He's somewhere right now

dressed in white and black
checkered pants
being led at the neck by a rope
30  While he bangs on a dirty
bass drum
a little monkey toots a whistle
and little dogs taunt him
and little children tug at
his ears

# William Stafford

# *A Proposition*

1   Pretend our house is on an ordinary street—
locust trees, and firs, cars in each drive.
Pretend you like me. Pretend the neighbors
accept us and we go on living here.
A long summer has surrounded the town.

Pretend we have become old. Every day
batters against houses, pavement, and even the sky.
Every part of life has worked out—we have
children, even grandchildren. Our parents—
10   after full lives—have died. We have mourned.

Our regular jobs have ended; retirement pay
takes care of all reasonable needs, and our health
is ok. Pretend a stranger stops by while we
are working in the yard and asks us how things
are going, whether we have any questions or complaints.

What could we answer? Have we forgotten to turn on, or off,
any important part of our house? Is there
more we should have done about our yard or parents
or children? What can this stranger mean? Why
20   does anyone raise questions like that? What shall we say?

## Jean Nordhaus

# *My Life in Hiding*

1  My life in hiding
is not unlike your own.
Each morning, I clap a tame face
over my wild one, dress as you dress,
train my gestures to resemble yours.

Time touches me,
brushing my skin. Money
slides through my hands.
Eggs siphon through my body,
10  sand through glass.

There are days when nothing happens,
evenings when the winter sun
turns the sky to a city in flames.
Sometimes I speak to myself
and a stranger answers.

When the child began to grow inside me,
clambering from deeper into lighter shade,
to crown from hiding

into hiding, I saw how camouflage
20  contains disclosure, how each unveiling
draws us

into deeper disguise. And so I rise
from caves of wrath to live
as one of you, a woman wrapped
in silence, bearing alive
my buried name.

# WRITING ASSIGNMENTS

1.   Write a story, using the third person point of view, about someone who is miserable but does not know why until some event results in a revelation that completely changes his or her life.

2.   Using the first person point of view, write a story about an orphan, perhaps focusing on an emotional attachment to someone at the orphanage or the trauma of leaving the place to face the world.

3.   Write a courtroom play in which two or more witnesses see the same event from different points of view. What is the verdict?

4.   Write a poem on one of the following:
     a) A mother seen differently through the eyes of her daughter and her son; told, perhaps, by the mother in the first person or directly by the children.
     b) A visit to an old battlefield or some other historical place that recalls the past.
     c) "My Life in Hiding" (see the poem by Jean Nordhaus). Write about your own secret life.
     d) A letter to a dead lover (use your imagination).

# Chapter 6

# Tone and Style

## Introduction

## Fiction

Stuart Dybek     *Pet Milk*
Tim O'Brien     *The Things They Carried*

## Poetry

Mary B. Campbell     *Money*
Maxine Chernoff     *The New Money*
Robert Kelly     *Farewell Letter*
W.S. Merwin     *At Home*
Charles Wright     *Dog Yoga*

## Writing Assignments

When we talk about tone, we approach one of the great intangibles of literature. Just as individual as a person's signature, the *tone* of any literary work reflects the feelings and attitudes of the author. That stance is revealed in many ways, both obvious and subtle.

It may take days or even weeks before a writer finds that first sentence or chapter that will establish exactly the right tone. Many writers cannot proceed until that has happened, until a clear approach to the material has been established. It might be farcical, say, or mysterious, gloomy, charming, witty, ironic, realistic, whatever. As many descriptive words might apply as there are words to describe someone's temperament.

Writers achieve such a tone by the manner in which they express themselves. A writer makes use of several of myriad stylistic techniques, some of them so basic that we barely notice them. The way a writer puts words together, or constructs sentences, are matters of personal style. Ernest Hemingway, for example, often uses a very basic vocabulary and short sentences which generate a recognizable rhythm. Such simplicity of style lends a poetic tone to his work. William Faulkner, on the other hand, depends on a rich vocabulary and complicated, not to say labyrinthine, sentences which generate a passionate tone and flowing cadence. Hemingway and Faulkner are extremes; all good writers, nevertheless, develop a style that is idiosyncratic while remaining adaptable to different subjects. Style, in a literary sense, refers not only to word choice or syntax, but to imagery, figurative language, the handling of dialogue, and point of view and further techniques such as repetition and alliteration, rhyme, meter, and other formal matters.

The kind of imagery employed by the author may lend a certain tone to the work. In Stuart Dybek's "Pet Milk" an old love affair is described—almost by thought association—in conjunction with a series of images that "swirl" and "cloud" and "steam" and "stream," that "hover ghostlike" and bloom in "kaleidoscopic clouds." Here the imagery induces a tone and even a worldview, of suggestive richness. It is reinforced by a careful choice of both words and details: the words are evocative, the details nostalgic. In the end the lovers are seen "streaming by" on a train, as though the affair were as tantalizing and as full of potential as the images themselves.

The content, one might say, is the love story. The style depends on imagery (among other things). The tone is laconic, controlled, and suggestive.

The tone of Charles Wright's "Dog Yoga," both mournful and musical, arises, not only from the imagery, but from devices that are largely (but by no means exclusively) the tools of the poet: alliteration, repetition, internal rhyme, and sporadic use of strict meter. W.S. Merwin's poem, on the other hand, demonstrates stern simplicity of language and form. The tone, measured, ordinary, and compelling, arises from a listing of domestic images and the suppression of "loaded" words, those which might suggest emotion. Nevertheless, the poem packs a punch as basic as its title, "At Home." Is there a human being who does not respond in some way to these words?

Lists figure as well in Tim O'Brien's "The Things They Carried." The story is propelled by a series of lists of military equipment carried by "grunts" in the Vietnam war—equipment that becomes heavier with each repetition—and lists that widen to include the human burdens of each soldier. Each additional list provides the impetus for a deepening exploration of the central incident.

The entire story is infused with an ironic tone arising from a discrepancy between the flat, businesslike tone of the lists and the actuality of human suffering and desire. Another notable stylistic technique here is repetition itself. Circling ever closer to the heart of his story, O'Brien introduces the fact of Ted Lavender's death early on—in connection with the lists—repeats it, always with more detail, and develops it until it is central both thematically and in terms of plot. In the end "grief, terror, love and longing" have flooded out the dry voice of the military invoice, and the central image of military baggage has come to represent what the author calls "the emotional baggage of men who might die."

As O'Brien develops his lists, the reader begins to understand them as a commentary on war rather than a realistic description. The ironic point of view expressed by the story depends on this gradual enlightenment on the part of the reader. A similar irony may be perceived in the poems of Maxine Chernoff and Mary Campbell (do they *really* love money?) and even in the incongruity of the images in Robert Kelly's "Farewell Letter."

A different form of irony—the irony of fate—is not exemplified here, but we might call to mind Somerset Maugham's famous story "The Appointment in Samarra." In this miniscule fable, a merchant's servant, having seen the figure of Death reach out to him at the marketplace, leaves Baghdad and flees to Samarra to avoid him. The merchant asks Death why he frightened the servant. Death replies that he did not mean to frighten him, he was only surprised: "I was astonished to see him in Baghdad, for I have an appointment with him tonight in Samarra."

Irony, beyond a doubt, is one of the truly powerful tools for creating tone.

*Stuart Dybek*

# *Pet Milk*

1 Today I've been drinking instant coffee and Pet milk, and watching it snow. It's not that I enjoy the taste especially, but I like the way Pet milk swirls in the coffee. Actually, my favorite thing about Pet milk is what the can opener does to the top of the can. The can is unmistakable—compact, seamless looking, its very shape suggesting that it could condense milk without any trouble. The can opener bites in neatly, and the thick liquid spills from the triangular gouge with a different look and viscosity than milk. Pet milk isn't *real* milk. The color's
10 off, to start with. There's almost something of the past about it, like old ivory. My grandmother always drank it in her coffee. When friends dropped over and sat around the kitchen table, my grandma would ask, "Do you take cream and sugar?" Pet milk was the cream.

There was a yellow plastic radio on her kitchen table, usually tuned to the polka station, though sometimes she'd miss it by half a notch and get the Greek station instead, or the Spanish, or the Ukrainian. In Chicago, where we lived, all the incompatible states of Europe were pressed together down at
20 the staticky right end of the dial. She didn't seem to notice, as long as she wasn't hearing English. The radio, turned low, played constantly. Its top was warped and turning amber on the side where the tubes were. I remember the sound of it on winter afternoons after school, as I sat by her table watching the Pet milk swirl and cloud in the steaming coffee, and noticing, outside her window, the sky doing the same thing above the railroad yard across the street.

And I remember, much later, seeing the same swirling sky in tiny liqueur glasses containing a drink called a King
30 Alphonse: the crème de cacao rising like smoke in repeated explosions, blooming in kaleidoscopic clouds through the layer of heavy cream. This was in the Pilsen, a little Czech restaurant where my girlfriend, Kate, and I would go sometimes in the evening. It was the first year out of college for both

of us, and we had astonished ourselves by finding real jobs—
no more waitressing or pumping gas, the way we'd done in
school. I was investigating credit references at a bank, and she
was doing something slightly above the rank of typist for
Hornblower & Weeks, the investment firm. My bank showed
40  training films that emphasized the importance of suitable
dress, good grooming, and personal neatness, even for employees like me, who worked at the switchboard in the basement. Her firm issued directives on appropriate attire—skirts,
for instance, should cover the knees. She had lovely knees.

Kate and I would sometimes meet after work at the
Pilsen, dressed in our proper business clothes and still feeling
both a little self-conscious and glamorous, as if we were im-
postors wearing disguises. The place had small, round oak
tables, and we'd sit in a corner under a painting called "The
50  Street Musicians of Prague" and trade future plans as if they
were escape routes. She talked of going to grad school in
Europe; I wanted to apply to the Peace Corps. Our plans for
the future made us laugh and feel close, but those same plans
somehow made anything more than temporary between us
seem impossible. It was the first time I'd ever had the feeling of
missing someone I was still with.

The waiters in the Pilsen wore short black jackets over
long white aprons. They were old men from the old country.
We went there often enough to have our own special waiter,
60  Rudi, a name he pronounced with a rolled *R*. Rudi boned our
trout and seasoned our salads, and at the end of the meal he'd
bring the bottle of crème de cacao from the bar, along with
two little glasses and a small pitcher of heavy cream, and make
us each a King Alphonse right at our table. We'd watch as he'd
fill the glasses halfway up with the syrupy brown liqueur, then
carefully attempt to float a layer of cream on top. If he failed to
float the cream, we'd get that one free.

"Who was King Alphonse anyway, Rudi?" I sometimes
asked, trying to break his concentration, and if that didn't
70  work I nudged the table with my foot so the glass would jiggle
imperceptibly just as he was floating the cream. We'd usually
get one on the house. Rudi knew what I was doing. In fact,
serving the King Alphonses had been his idea, and he had also
suggested the trick of jarring the table. I think it pleased him,
though he seemed concerned about the way I'd stare into the
liqueur glass, watching the patterns.

"It's not a microscope," he'd say. "Drink."

He liked us, and we tipped extra. It felt good to be there
and to be able to pay for a meal.

80      Kate and I met at the Pilsen for supper on my twenty-second birthday. It was May, and unseasonably hot. I'd opened my tie. Even before looking at the dinner menu, we ordered a bottle of Mumm's and a dozen oysters apiece. Rudi made a sly remark when he brought the oysters on platters of ice. They were freshly opened and smelled of the sea. I'd heard people joke about oysters being aphrodisiac but never considered it anything but a myth—the kind of idea they still had in the old country.

90      We squeezed on lemon, added dabs of horseradish, slid the oysters into our mouths, and then rinsed the shells with champagne and drank the salty, cold juice. There was a beefy-looking couple eating schnitzel at the next table, and they stared at us with the repugnance that public oyster-eaters in the Midwest often encounter. We laughed and grandly sipped it all down. I was already half tipsy from drinking too fast, and starting to feel filled with a euphoric, aching energy. Kate raised a brimming oyster shell to me in a toast: "To the Peace Corps!"

        "To Europe!" I replied, and we clunked shells.

100     She touched her wineglass to mine and whispered, "Happy birthday," and then suddenly leaned across the table and kissed me.

        When she sat down again, she was flushed. I caught the reflection of her face in the glass-covered "The Street Musicians of Prague" above our table. I always loved seeing her in mirrors and windows. The reflections of her beauty startled me. I had told her that once, and she seemed to fend off the compliment, saying, "That's because you've learned what to look for," as if it were a secret I'd stumbled upon. But, this time, seeing her reflection hovering ghostlike upon an imaginary Prague was like seeing a future from which she had vanished. I knew I'd never meet anyone more beautiful to me.

        We killed the champagne and sat twining fingers across the table. I was sweating. I could feel the warmth of her through her skirt under the table and I touched her leg. We still hadn't ordered dinner. I left money on the table and we steered each other out a little unsteadily.

        "Rudi will understand," I said.

120     The street was blindingly bright. A reddish sun angled just above the rims of the tallest buildings. I took my suit coat off and flipped it over my shoulder. We stopped in the doorway of a shoe store to kiss.

        "Let's go somewhere," she said.

My roommate would already be home at my place, which was closer. Kate lived up north, in Evanston. It seemed a long way away.

We cut down a side street, past a fire station, to a small park, but its gate was locked. I pressed close to her against the
130 tall iron fence. We could smell the lilacs from a bush just inside the fence, and when I jumped for an overhanging branch my shirt sleeve hooked on a fence spike and tore, and petals rained down on us as the sprig sprang from my hand.

We walked to the subway. The evening rush was winding down; we must have caught the last express heading toward Evanston. Once the train climbed from the tunnel to the elevated tracks, it wouldn't stop until the end of the line, on Howard. There weren't any seats together, so we stood swaying at the front of the car, beside the empty conductor's
140 compartment. We wedged inside, and I clicked the door shut.

The train rocked and jounced, clattering north. We were kissing, trying to catch the rhythm of the ride with our bodies. The sun bronzed the windows on our side of the train. I lifted her skirt over her knees, hiked it higher so the sun shone off her thighs, and bunched it around her waist. She wouldn't stop kissing. She was moving her hips to pin us to each jolt of the train.

We were speeding past scorched brick walls, gray windows, back porches outlined in sun, roofs, and treetops—the
150 landscape of the El I'd memorized from subway windows over a lifetime of rides: the podiatrist's foot sign past Fullerton; the bright pennants of Wrigley Field, at Addison; ancient hotels with TRANSIENTS WELCOME signs on their flaking back walls; peeling and graffiti-smudged billboards; the old cemetery just before Wilson Avenue. Even without looking, I knew almost exactly where we were. Within the compartment, the sound of our quick breathing was louder than the clatter of tracks. I was trying to slow down, to make it all last, and when she covered my mouth with her hand I turned my face to the window and
160 looked out.

The train was braking a little from express speed, as it did each time it passed a local station. I could see blurred faces on the long wooden platform watching us pass—businessmen glancing up from folded newspapers, women clutching purses and shopping bags. I could see the expression on each face, momentarily arrested, as we flashed by. A high school kid in shirt sleeves, maybe sixteen, with books tucked under one arm and a cigarette in his mouth, caught sight of us, and in the

instant before he disappeared he grinned and started to wave.
170 Then he was gone, and I turned from the window, back to
Kate, forgetting everything—the passing stations, the glowing
late sky, even the sense of missing her—but that arrested wave
stayed with me. It was as if I were standing on that platform,
with my schoolbooks and a smoke, on one of those endlessly
accumulated afternoons after school when I stood almost outside of time simply waiting for a train, and I thought how
much I'd have loved seeing someone like us streaming by.

*Tim O'Brien*

# *The Things They Carried*

1 First Lieutenant Jimmy Cross carried letters from a girl named Martha, a junior at Mount Sebastian College in New Jersey. They were not love letters, but Lieutenant Cross was hoping, so he kept them folded in plastic at the bottom of his rucksack. In the late afternoon, after a day's march, he would dig his foxhole, wash his hands under a canteen, unwrap the letters, hold them with the tips of his fingers, and spend the last hour of light pretending. He would imagine romantic camping trips into the White Mountains in New Hampshire. He would
10 sometimes taste the envelope flaps, knowing her tongue had been there. More than anything, he wanted Martha to love him as he loved her, but the letters were mostly chatty, elusive on the matter of love. She was a virgin, he was almost sure. She was an English major at Mount Sebastian, and she wrote beautifully about her professors and roommates and midterm exams, about her respect for Chaucer and her great affection for Virginia Woolf. She often quoted lines of poetry; she never mentioned the war, except to say, Jimmy, take care of yourself. The letters weighed ten ounces. They were signed "Love,
20 Martha," but Lieutenant Cross understood that "Love" was only a way of signing and did not mean what he sometimes pretended it meant. At dusk, he would carefully return the letters to his rucksack. Slowly, a bit distracted, he would get up and move among his men, checking the perimeter, then at full dark he would return to his hole and watch the night and wonder if Martha was a virgin.

The things they carried were largely determined by necessity. Among the necessities or near necessities were P-38 can openers, pocket knives, heat tabs, wrist watches, dog tags,
30 mosquito repellent, chewing gum, candy, cigarettes, salt tablets, packets of Kool-Aid, lighters, matches, sewing kits, Military Payment Certificates, C rations, and two or three canteens of water. Together, these items weighed between fifteen and twenty pounds, depending upon a man's habits or rate of

metabolism. Henry Dobbins, who was a big man, carried extra rations; he was especially fond of canned peaches in heavy syrup over pound cake. Dave Jensen, who practiced field hygiene, carried a toothbrush, dental floss, and several hotel-size bars of soap he'd stolen on R&R in Sydney, Aus-
40   tralia. Ted Lavender, who was scared, carried tranquilizers until he was shot in the head outside the village of Than Khe in mid-April. By necessity, and because it was SOP, they all carried steel helmets that weighed five pounds including the liner and camouflage cover. They carried the standard fatigue jackets and trousers. Very few carried underwear. On their feet they carried jungle boots—2.1 pounds—and Dave Jensen carried three pairs of socks and a can of Dr. Scholl's foot powder as a precaution against trench foot. Until he was shot, Ted Lavender carried six or seven ounces of premium dope,
50   which for him was a necessity. Mitchell Sanders, the RTO, carried condoms. Norman Bowker carried a diary. Rat Kiley carried comic books. Kiowa, a devout Baptist, carried an illustrated New Testament that had been presented to him by his father, who taught Sunday school in Oklahoma City, Oklahoma. As a hedge against bad times, however, Kiowa also carried his grandmother's distrust of the white man, his grandfather's old hunting hatchet. Necessity dictated. Because the land was mined and booby-trapped, it was SOP for each man to carry a steel-centered, nylon-covered flak jacket, which
60   weighed 6.7 pounds, but which on hot days seemed much heavier. Because you could die so quickly, each man carried at least one large compress bandage, usually in the helmet band for easy access. Because the nights were cold, and because the monsoons were wet, each carried a green plastic poncho that could be used as a raincoat or ground sheet or makeshift tent. With its quilted liner, the poncho weighed almost two pounds, but it was worth every ounce. In April, for instance, when Ted Lavender was shot, they used his poncho to wrap him up, then to carry him across the paddy, then to lift him into the chopper
70   that took him way.

They were called legs or grunts.

To carry something was to "hump" it, as when Lieutenant Jimmy Cross humped his love for Martha up the hills and through the swamps. In its intransitive form, "to hump" meant "to walk," or "to march," but it implied burdens far beyond the intransitive.

Almost everyone humped photographs. In his wallet, Lieutenant Cross carried two photographs of Martha. The first was a Kodachrome snapshot signed "Love," though he

80 knew better. She stood against a brick wall. Her eyes were gray and neutral, her lips slightly open as she stared straight-on at the camera. At night, sometimes, Lieutenant Cross wondered who had taken the picture, because he knew she had boyfriends, because he loved her so much, and because he could see the shadow of the picture taker spreading out against the brick wall. The second photograph had been clipped from the 1968 Mount Sebastian yearbook. It was an action shot— women's volleyball—and Martha was bent horizontal to the floor, reaching, the palms of her hands in sharp focus, the
90 tongue taut, the expression frank and competitive. There was no visible sweat. She wore white gym shorts. Her legs, he thought, were almost certainly the legs of a virgin, dry and without hair, the left knee cocked and carrying her entire weight, which was just over one hundred pounds. Lieutenant Cross remembered touching that left knee. A dark theater, he remembered, and the movie was *Bonnie and Clyde,* and Martha wore a tweed skirt, and during the final scene, when he touched her knee, she turned and looked at him in a sad, sober way that made him pull his hand back, but he would
100 always remember the feel of the tweed skirt and the knee beneath it and the sound of the gunfire that killed Bonnie and Clyde, how embarrassing it was, how slow and oppressive. He remembered kissing her good night at the dorm door. Right then, he thought, he should've done something brave. He should've carried her up the stairs to her room and tied her to the bed and touched that left knee all night long. He should've risked it. Whenever he looked at the photographs, he thought of new things he should've done.

What they carried was partly a function of rank, partly of field
110 specialty.
    As a first lieutenant and platoon leader, Jimmy Cross carried a compass, maps, code books, binoculars, and a .45-caliber pistol that weighed 2.9 pounds fully loaded. He carried a strobe light and the responsibility for the lives of his men.
    As an RTO, Mitchell Sanders carried the PRC-25 radio, a killer, twenty-six pounds with its battery.
    As a medic, Rat Kiley carried a canvas satchel filled with morphine and plasma and malaria tablets and surgical tape
120 and comic books and all the things a medic must carry, including M&M's for especially bad wounds, for a total weight of nearly twenty pounds.

As a big man, therefore a machine gunner, Henry Dobbins carried the M-60, which weighed twenty-three pounds unloaded, but which was almost always loaded. In addition, Dobbins carried between ten and fifteen pounds of ammunition draped in belts across his chest and shoulders.

As PFCs or Spec 4s, most of them were common grunts and carried the standard M-16 gas-operated assault rifle. The
130 weapon weighed 7.5 pounds unloaded, 8.2 pounds with its full twenty-round magazine. Depending on numerous factors, such as topography and psychology, the riflemen carried anywhere from twelve to twenty magazines, usually in cloth bandoliers, adding on another 8.4 pounds at minimum, fourteen pounds at maximum. When it was available, they also carried M-16 maintenance gear—rods and steel brushes and swabs and tubes of LSA oil—all of which weighed about a pound. Among the grunts, some carried the M-79 grenade launcher, 5.9 pounds unloaded, a reasonably light weapon except for
140 the ammunition, which was heavy. A single round weighed ten ounces. The typical load was twenty-five rounds. But Ted Lavender, who was scared, carried thirty-four rounds when he was shot and killed outside Than Khe, and he went down under an exceptional burden, more than twenty pounds of ammunition, plus the flak jacket and helmet and rations and water and toilet paper and tranquilizers and all the rest, plus the unweighed fear. He was dead weight. There was no twitching or flopping. Kiowa, who saw it happen, said it was like watching a rock fall, or a big sandbag or something—just
150 boom, then down—not like the movies where the dead guy rolls around and does fancy spins and goes ass over teakettle—not like that. Kiowa said, the poor bastard just flat-fuck fell. Boom. Down. Nothing else. It was a bright morning in mid-April. Lieutenant Cross felt the pain. He blamed himself. They stripped off Lavender's canteens and ammo, all the heavy things, and Rat Kiley said the obvious, the guy's dead, and Mitchell Sanders used his radio to report one U.S. KIA and to request a chopper. Then they wrapped Lavender in his poncho. They carried him out to a dry paddy, established
160 security, and sat smoking the dead man's dope until the chopper came. Lieutenant Cross kept to himself. He pictured Martha's smooth young face, thinking he loved her more than anything, more than his men, and now Ted Lavender was dead because he loved her so much and could not stop thinking about her. When the dust-off arrived, they carried Lavender aboard. Afterward they burned Than Khe. They marched until

dusk, then dug their holes, and that night Kiowa kept explaining how you had to be there, how fast it was, how the poor guy just dropped like so much concrete. Boom-down, he said. Like
170  cement.

In addition to the three standard weapons—the M-60, M-16, and M-79—they carried whatever presented itself, or whatever seemed appropriate as a means of killing or staying alive. They carried catch-as-catch-can. At various times, in various situations, they carried M-14s and CAR-15s and Swedish Ks and grease guns and captured AK-47s and Chi-Coms and RPGs and Simonov carbines and black-market Uzis and .38-caliber Smith & Wesson handguns and 66 mm LAWs and shotguns and silencers and blackjacks and bayonets and C-4
180  plastic explosives. Lee Strunk carried a slingshot; a weapon of last resort, he called it. Mitchell Sanders carried brass knuckles. Kiowa carried his grandfather's feathered hatchet. Every third or fourth man carried a Claymore antipersonnel mine—3.5 pounds with its firing device. They all carried fragmentation grenades—fourteen ounces each. They all carried at least one M-18 colored smoke grenade—twenty-four ounces. Some carried CS or tear-gas grenades. Some carried white-phosphorus grenades. They carried all they could bear, and then some, including a silent awe for the terrible power of the
190  things they carried.
     In the first week of April, before Lavender died, Lieutenant Jimmy Cross received a good-luck charm from Martha. It was a simple pebble, an ounce at most. Smooth to the touch, it was a milky-white color with flecks of orange and violet, oval-shaped, like a miniature egg. In the accompanying letter, Martha wrote that she had found the pebble on the Jersey shoreline, precisely where the land touched water at high tide, where things came together but also separated. It was this separate-but-together quality, she wrote, that had inspired her
200  to pick up the pebble and to carry it in her breast pocket for several days, where it seemed weightless, and then to send it through the mail, by air, as a token of her truest feelings for him. Lieutenant Cross found this romantic. But he wondered what her truest feelings were, exactly, and what she meant by separate-but-together. He wondered how the tides and waves had come into play on that afternoon along the Jersey shoreline when Martha saw the pebble and bent down to rescue it from geology. He imagined bare feet. Martha was a poet, with the poet's sensibilities, and her feet would be brown and bare,

210 the toenails unpainted, the eyes chilly and somber like the ocean in March, and though it was painful, he wondered who had been with her that afternoon. He imagined a pair of shadows moving along the strip of sand where things came together but also separated. It was phantom jealousy, he knew, but he couldn't help himself. He loved her so much. On the march, through the hot days of early April, he carried the pebble in his mouth, turning it with his tongue, tasting sea salts and moisture. His mind wandered. He had difficulty keeping his attention on the war. On occasion he would yell at his men to
220 spread out the column, to keep their eyes open, but then he would slip away into daydreams, just pretending, walking barefoot along the Jersey shore, with Martha, carrying nothing. He would feel himself rising. Sun and waves and gentle winds, all love and lightness.

What they carried varied by mission.

When a mission took them to the mountains, they carried mosquito netting, machetes, canvas tarps, and extra bug juice.

If a mission seemed especially hazardous, or if it in-
230 volved a place they knew to be bad, they carried everything they could. In certain heavily mined AOs, where the land was dense with Toe Poppers and Bouncing Betties, they took turns humping a twenty-eight-pound mine detector. With its headphones and big sensing plate, the equipment was a stress on the lower back and shoulders, awkward to handle, often useless because of the shrapnel in the earth, but they carried it anyway, partly for safety, partly for the illusion of safety.

On ambush, or other night missions, they carried peculiar little odds and ends. Kiowa always took along his New
240 Testament and a pair of moccasins for silence. Dave Jensen carried night-sight vitamins high in carotin. Lee Strunk carried his slingshot; ammo, he claimed, would never be a problem. Rat Kiley carried brandy and M&M's. Until he was shot, Ted Lavender carried the starlight scope, which weighed 6.3 pounds with its aluminum carrying case. Henry Dobbins carried his girlfriend's pantyhose wrapped around his neck as a comforter. They all carried ghosts. When dark came, they would move out single file across the meadows and paddies to their ambush coordinates, where they would quietly set up the
250 Claymores and lie down and spend the night waiting.

Other missions were more complicated and required special equipment. In mid-April, it was their mission to search

out and destroy the elaborate tunnel complexes in the Than Khe area south of Chu Lai. To blow the tunnels, they carried one-pound blocks of pentrite high explosives, four blocks to a man, sixty-eight pounds in all. They carried wiring, detonators, and battery-powered clackers. Dave Jensen carried earplugs. Most often, before blowing the tunnels, they were ordered by higher command to search them, which was
260 considered bad news, but by and large they just shrugged and carried out orders. Because he was a big man, Henry Dobbins was excused from tunnel duty. The others would draw numbers. Before Lavender died there were seventeen men in the platoon, and whoever drew the number seventeen would strip off his gear and crawl in head first with a flashlight and Lieutenant Cross's .45-caliber pistol. The rest of them would fan out as security. They would sit down or kneel, not facing the hole, listening to the ground beneath them, imagining cobwebs and ghosts, whatever was down there—the tunnel walls
270 squeezing in—how the flashlight seemed impossibly heavy in the hand and how it was tunnel vision in the very strictest sense, compression in all ways, even time, and how you had to wiggle in—ass and elbows—a swallowed-up feeling—and how you found yourself worrying about odd things—will your flashlight go dead? Do rats carry rabies? If you screamed, how far would the sound carry? Would your buddies hear it? Would they have the courage to drag you out? In some respects, though not many, the waiting was worse than the tunnel itself. Imagination was a killer.
280     On April 16, when Lee Strunk drew the number seventeen, he laughed and muttered something and went down quickly. The morning was hot and very still. Not good, Kiowa said. He looked at the tunnel opening, then out across a dry paddy toward the village of Than Khe. Nothing moved. No clouds or birds or people. As they waited, the men smoked and drank Kool-Aid, not talking much, feeling sympathy for Lee Strunk but also feeling the luck of the draw. You win some, you lose some, said Mitchell Sanders, and sometimes you settle for a rain check. It was a tired line and no one laughed.
290     Henry Dobbins ate a tropical chocolate bar. Ted Lavender popped a tranquilizer and went off to pee.
    After five minutes, Lieutenant Jimmy Cross moved to the tunnel, leaned down, and examined the darkness. Trouble, he thought—a cave-in maybe. And then suddenly, without willing it, he was thinking about Martha. The stresses and fractures, the quick collapse, the two of them buried alive

under all that weight. Dense, crushing love. Kneeling, watching the hole, he tried to concentrate on Lee Strunk and the war, all the dangers, but his love was too much for him, he felt
300  paralyzed, he wanted to sleep inside her lungs and breathe her blood and be smothered. He wanted her to be a virgin and not a virgin, all at once. He wanted to know her. Intimate secrets —why poetry? Why so sad? Why that grayness in her eyes? Why so alone? Not lonely, just alone—riding her bike across campus or sitting off by herself in the cafeteria. Even dancing, she danced alone—and it was the aloneness that filled him with love. He remembered telling her that one evening. How she nodded and looked away. And how, later, when he kissed her, she received the kiss without returning it, her eyes wide
310  open, not afraid, not a virgin's eyes, just flat and uninvolved.

    Lieutenant Cross gazed at the tunnel. But he was not there. He was buried with Martha under the white sand at the Jersey shore. They were pressed together, and the pebble in his mouth was her tongue. He was smiling. Vaguely, he was aware of how quiet the day was, the sullen paddies, yet he could not bring himself to worry about matters of security. He was beyond that. He was just a kid at war, in love. He was twenty-two years old. He couldn't help it.

    A few moments later Lee Strunk crawled out of the
320  tunnel. He came up grinning, filthy but alive. Lieutenant Cross nodded and closed his eyes while the others clapped Strunk on the back and made jokes about rising from the dead.

    Worms, Rat Kiley said. Right out of the grave. Fuckin' zombie.

    The men laughed. They all felt great relief.

    Spook City, said Mitchell Sanders.

    Lee Strunk made a funny ghost sound, a kind of moaning, yet very happy, and right then, when Strunk made that high happy moaning sound, when he went *Ahhooooo,* right
330  then Ted Lavender was shot in the head on his way back from peeing. He lay with his mouth open. The teeth were broken. There was a swollen black bruise under his left eye. The cheekbone was gone. Oh shit, Rat Kiley said, the guy's dead. The guy's dead, he kept saying, which seemed profound—the guy's dead. I mean really.

---

The things they carried were determined to some extent by superstition. Lieutenant Cross carried his good-luck pebble.

Dave Jensen carried a rabbit's foot. Norman Bowker, otherwise a very gentle person, carried a thumb that had been
340 presented to him as a gift by Mitchell Sanders. The thumb was
dark brown, rubbery to the touch, and weighed four ounces at
most. It had been cut from a VC corpse, a boy of fifteen or
sixteen. They'd found him at the bottom of an irrigation ditch,
badly burned, flies in his mouth and eyes. The boy wore black
shorts and sandals. At the time of his death he had been
carrying a pouch of rice, a rifle, and three magazines of
ammunition.

You want my opinion, Mitchell Sanders said, there's a
definite moral here.
350 He put his hand on the dead boy's wrist. He was quiet
for a time, as if counting a pulse, then he patted the stomach,
almost affectionately, and used Kiowa's hunting hatchet to
remove the thumb.

Henry Dobbins asked what the moral was.

Moral?

You know. *Moral.*

Sanders wrapped the thumb in toilet paper and handed
it across to Norman Bowker. There was no blood. Smiling, he
kicked the boy's head, watched the flies scatter, and said, It's
360 like with that old TV show—Paladin. Have gun, will travel.

Henry Dobbins thought about it.

Yeah, well, he finally said. I don't see no moral.

There it *is,* man.

Fuck off.

They carried USO stationery and pencils and pens. They carried
Sterno, safety pins, trip flares, signal flares, spools of wire, razor
blades, chewing tobacco, liberated joss sticks and statuettes of
the smiling Buddha, candles, grease pencils, *The Stars and
Stripes,* fingernail clippers, Psy Ops leaflets, bush hats, bolos,
370 and much more. Twice a week, when the resupply choppers
came in, they carried hot chow in green Mermite cans and large
canvas bags filled with iced beer and soda pop. They carried
plastic water containers, each with a two-gallon capacity.
Mitchell Sanders carried a set of starched tiger fatigues for
special occasions. Henry Dobbins carried Black Flag insecticide.
Dave Jensen carried empty sandbags that could be filled at night
for added protection. Lee Strunk carried tanning lotion. Some
things they carried in common. Taking turns, they carried the
big PRC-77 scrambler radio, which weighed thirty pounds with
380 its battery. They shared the weight of memory.

They took up what others could no longer bear. Often, they carried each other, the wounded or weak. They carried infections. They carried chess sets, basketballs, Vietnamese-English dictionaries, insignia of rank, Bronze Stars and Purple Hearts, plastic cards imprinted with the Code of Conduct. They carried diseases, among them malaria and dysentery. They carried lice and ringworm and leeches and paddy algae and various rots and molds. They carried the land itself—Vietnam, the place, the soil—a powdery orange-red dust that covered

390  their boots and fatigues and faces. They carried the sky. The whole atmosphere, they carried it, the humidity, the monsoons, the stink of fungus and decay, all of it, they carried gravity. They moved like mules. By daylight they took sniper fire, at night they were mortared, but it was not battle, it was just the endless march, village to village, without purpose, nothing won or lost. They marched for the sake of the march. They plodded along slowly, dumbly, leaning forward against the heat, unthinking, all blood and bone, simple grunts, soldiering with their legs, toiling up the hills and down into the

400  paddies and across the rivers and up again and down, just humping, one step and then the next and then another, but no volition, no will, because it was automatic, it was anatomy, and the war was entirely a matter of posture and carriage, the hump was everything, a kind of inertia, a kind of emptiness, a dullness of desire and intellect and conscience and hope and human sensibility. Their principles were in their feet. Their calculations were biological. They had no sense of strategy or mission. They searched the villages without knowing what to look for, not caring, kicking over jars of rice, frisking children

410  and old men, blowing tunnels, sometimes setting fires and sometimes not, then forming up and moving on to the next village, then other villages, where it would always be the same. They carried their own lives. The pressures were enormous. In the heat of early afternoon, they would remove their helmets and flak jackets, walking bare, which was dangerous but which helped ease the strain. They would often discard things along the route of march. Purely for comfort, they would throw away rations, blow their Claymores and grenades, no matter, because by nightfall the resupply choppers would

420  arrive with more of the same, then a day or two later still more, fresh watermelons and crates of ammunition and sunglasses and woolen sweaters—the resources were stunning—sparklers for the Fourth of July, colored eggs for Easter. It was the great American war chest—the fruits of science, the smokestacks,

the canneries, the arsenals at Hartford, the Minnesota forests, the machine shops, the vast fields of corn and wheat—they carried like freight trains; they carried it on their backs and shoulders—and for all the ambiguities of Vietnam, all the mysteries and unknowns, there was at least the single abiding
430    certainty that they would never be at a loss for things to carry.

After the chopper took Lavender away, Lieutenant Jimmy Cross led his men into the village of Than Khe. They burned everything. They shot chickens and dogs, they trashed the village well, they called in artillery and watched the wreckage, then they marched for several hours through the hot afternoon, and then at dusk, while Kiowa explained how Lavender died, Lieutenant Cross found himself trembling.

He tried not to cry. With his entrenching tool, which weighed five pounds, he began digging a hole in the earth.
440    He felt shame. He hated himself. He had loved Martha more than his men, and as a consequence Lavender was now dead, and this was something he would have to carry like a stone in his stomach for the rest of the war.

All he could do was dig. He used his entrenching tool like an ax, slashing, feeling both love and hate, and then later, when it was full dark, he sat at the bottom of his foxhole and wept. It went on for a long while. In part, he was grieving for Ted Lavender, but mostly it was for Martha, and for himself, because she belonged to another world, which was not quite
450    real, and because she was a junior at Mount Sebastian College in New Jersey, a poet and a virgin and uninvolved, and because he realized she did not love him and never would.

······ ··· ·····

Like cement. Kiowa whispered in the dark. I swear to God— boom-down. Not a word.

I've heard this, said Norman Bowker.

A pisser, you know? Still zipping himself up. Zapped while zipping.

All right, fine. That's enough.

Yeah, but you had to see it, the guy just—
460    I *heard*, man. Cement. So why not shut the fuck *up?*

Kiowa shook his head sadly and glanced over at the hole where Lieutenant Jimmy Cross sat watching the night. The air was thick and wet. A warm, dense fog had settled over the paddies and there was the stillness that precedes rain.

After a time Kiowa sighed.

One thing for sure, he said. The Lieutenant's in some deep hurt. I mean that crying jag—the way he was carrying on—it wasn't fake or anything, it was real heavy-duty hurt. The man cares.

470 Sure, Norman Bowker said.

Say what you want, the man does care.

We all got problems.

Not Lavender.

No, I guess not, Bowker said. Do me a favor, though.

Shut up?

That's a smart Indian. Shut up.

Shrugging, Kiowa pulled off his boots. He wanted to say more, just to lighten up his sleep, but instead he opened his New Testament and arranged it beneath his head as a pillow.

480 The fog made things seem hollow and unattached. He tried not to think about Ted Lavender, but then he was thinking how fast it was, no drama, down and dead, and how it was hard to feel anything except surprise. It seemed un-Christian. He wished he could find some great sadness, or even anger, but the emotion wasn't there and he couldn't make it happen. Mostly he felt pleased to be alive. He liked the smell of the New Testament under his cheek, the leather and ink and paper and glue, whatever the chemicals were. He liked hearing the sounds of night. Even his fatigue, it felt fine, the stiff muscles

490 and the prickly awareness of his own body, a floating feeling. He enjoyed not being dead. Lying there, Kiowa admired Lieutenant Jimmy Cross's capacity for grief. He wanted to share the man's pain, he wanted to care as Jimmy Cross cared. And yet when he closed his eyes, all he could think was Boom-down, and all he could feel was the pleasure of having his boots off and the fog curling in around him and the damp soil and the Bible smells and the plush comfort of night.

After a moment Norman Bowker sat up in the dark.

What the hell, he said. You want to talk, *talk*. Tell

500 it to me.

Forget it.

No, man, go on. One thing I hate, it's a silent Indian.

For the most part they carried themselves with poise, a kind of dignity. Now and then, however, there were times of panic, when they squealed or wanted to squeal but couldn't, when they twitched and made moaning sounds and covered their heads and said Dear-Jesus and flopped around on the

earth and fired their weapons blindly and cringed and sobbed and begged for the noise to stop and went wild and made
510 stupid promises to themselves and to God and to their mothers and fathers, hoping not to die. In different ways, it happened to all of them. Afterward, when the firing ended, they would blink and peek up. They would touch their bodies, feeling shame, then quickly hiding it. They would force themselves to stand. As if in slow motion, frame by frame, the world would take on the old logic—absolute silence, then the wind, then sunlight, then voices. It was the burden of being alive. Awkwardly, the men would reassemble themselves, first in private, then in groups, becoming soldiers again. They would repair
520 the leaks in their eyes. They would check for casualties, call in dust-offs, light cigarettes, try to smile, clear their throats and spit and begin cleaning their weapons. After a time someone would shake his head and say, No lie, I almost shit my pants, and someone else would laugh, which meant it was bad, yes, but the guy had obviously not shit his pants, it wasn't that bad, and in any case nobody would ever do such a thing and then go ahead and talk about it. They would squint into the dense, oppressive sunlight. For a few moments, perhaps, they would fall silent, lighting a joint and tracking its passage from man to
530 man, inhaling, holding in the humiliation. Scary stuff, one of them might say. But then someone else would grin or flick his eyebrows and say, Roger-dodger, almost cut me a new asshole, *almost.*

There were numerous such poses. Some carried themselves with a sort of wistful resignation, others with pride or stiff soldierly discipline or good humor or macho zeal. They were afraid of dying but they were even more afraid to show it.

They found jokes to tell.

They used a hard vocabulary to contain the terrible soft-
540 ness. *Greased,* they'd say. *Offed, lit up, zapped while zipping.* It wasn't cruelty, just stage presence. They were actors and the war came at them in 3-D. When someone died, it wasn't quite dying, because in a curious way it seemed scripted, and because they had their lines mostly memorized, irony mixed with tragedy, and because they called it by other names, as if to encyst and destroy the reality of death itself. They kicked corpses. They cut off thumbs. They talked grunt lingo. They told stories about Ted Lavender's supply of tranquilizers, how the poor guy didn't feel a thing, how incredibly tranquil he
550 was.

There's a moral here, said Mitchell Sanders.

They were waiting for Lavender's chopper, smoking the dead man's dope.

The moral's pretty obvious, Sanders said, and winked. Stay away from drugs. No joke, they'll ruin your day every time.

Cute, said Henry Dobbins.

Mind-blower, get it? Talk about wiggy—nothing left, just blood and brains.

560    They made themselves laugh.

There it is, they'd say, over and over, as if the repetition itself were an act of poise, a balance between crazy and almost crazy, knowing without going. There it is, which meant be cool, let it ride, because oh yeah, man, you can't change what can't be changed, there it is, there it absolutely and positively and fucking well *is*.

They were tough.

They carried all the emotional baggage of men who might die. Grief, terror, love, longing—these were intangibles, 570    but the intangibles had their own mass and specific gravity, they had tangible weight. They carried shameful memories. They carried the common secret of cowardice barely restrained, the instinct to run or freeze or hide, and in many respects this was the heaviest burden of all, for it could never be put down, it required perfect balance and perfect posture. They carried their reputations. They carried the soldier's greatest fear, which was the fear of blushing. Men killed, and died, because they were embarrassed not to. It was what had brought them to the war in the first place, nothing positive, no 580    dreams of glory or honor, just to avoid the blush of dishonor. They died so as not to die of embarrassment. They crawled into tunnels and walked point and advanced under fire. Each morning, despite the unknowns, they made their legs move. They endured. They kept humping. They did not submit to the obvious alternative, which was simply to close the eyes and fall. So easy, really. Go limp and tumble to the ground and let the muscles unwind and not speak and not budge until your buddies picked you up and lifted you into the chopper that would roar and dip its nose and carry you off to the world. A 590    mere matter of falling, yet no one ever fell. It was not courage, exactly; the object was not valor. Rather, they were too frightened to be cowards.

By and large they carried these things inside, maintaining the masks of composure. They sneered at sick call. They spoke bitterly about guys who had found release by shooting off their own toes or fingers. Pussies, they'd say. Candyasses. It was fierce, mocking talk, with only a trace of envy or awe, but even so, the image played itself out behind their eyes.

 They imagined the muzzle against flesh. They imagined
600 the quick, sweet pain, then the evacuation to Japan, then a hospital with warm beds and cute geisha nurses.

 They dreamed of freedom birds.

 At night, on guard, staring into the dark, they were carried away by jumbo jets. They felt the rush of takeoff. *Gone!* they yelled. And then velocity, wings and engines, a smiling stewardess—but it was more than a plane, it was a real bird, a big sleek silver bird with feathers and talons and high screeching. They were flying. The weights fell off, there was nothing to bear. They laughed and held on tight, feeling the
610 cold slap of wind and altitude, soaring, thinking *It's over, I'm gone!*—they were naked, they were light and free—it was all lightness, bright and fast and buoyant, light as light, a helium buzz in the brain, a giddy bubbling in the lungs as they were taken up over the clouds and the war, beyond duty, beyond gravity and mortification and global entanglements—*Sin loi!* they yelled, *I'm sorry, motherfuckers, but I'm out of it, I'm goofed, I'm on a space cruise, I'm gone!*—and it was a restful, disencumbered sensation, just riding the light waves, sailing that big silver freedom bird over the mountains and oceans,
620 over America, over the farms and great sleeping cities and cemeteries and highways and the golden arches of McDonald's. It was flight, a kind of fleeing, a kind of falling, falling higher and higher, spinning off the edge of the earth and beyond the sun and through the vast, silent vacuum where there were no burdens and where everything weighed exactly nothing. *Gone!* they screamed, *I'm sorry but I'm gone!* And so at night, not quite dreaming, they gave themselves over to lightness, they were carried, they were purely borne.

 On the morning after Ted Lavender died, First Lieutenant
630 Jimmy Cross crouched at the bottom of his foxhole and burned Martha's letters. Then he burned the two photographs. There was a steady rain falling, which made it difficult, but he used heat tabs and Sterno to build a small fire, screening it with his body, holding the photographs over the tight blue flame with the tips of his fingers.

 He realized it was only a gesture. Stupid, he thought. Sentimental, too, but mostly just stupid.

 Lavender was dead. You couldn't burn the blame.

640 Besides, the letters were in his head. And even now, without photographs, Lieutenant Cross could see Martha playing volleyball in her white gym shorts and yellow T-shirt. He could see her moving in the rain.

When the fire died out, Lieutenant Cross pulled his poncho over his shoulders and ate breakfast from a can.

There was no great mystery, he decided.

In those burned letters Martha had never mentioned the war, except to say, Jimmy, take care of yourself. She wasn't involved. She signed the letters "Love," but it wasn't love, and all the fine lines and technicalities did not matter.

650 The morning came up wet and blurry. Everything seemed part of everything else, the fog and Martha and the deepening rain.

It was a war, after all.

Half smiling, Lieutenant Jimmy Cross took out his maps. He shook his head hard, as if to clear it, then bent forward and began planning the day's march. In ten minutes, or maybe twenty, he would rouse the men and they would pack up and head west, where the maps showed the country to be green and inviting. They would do what they had always 660 done. The rain might add some weight, but otherwise it would be one more day layered upon all the other days.

He was realistic about it. There was that new hardness in his stomach.

No more fantasies, he told himself.

Henceforth, when he thought about Martha, it would be only to think that she belonged elsewhere. He would shut down the daydreams. This was not Mount Sebastian, it was another world, where there were no pretty poems or midterm exams, a place where men died because of carelessness and 670 gross stupidity. Kiowa was right. Boom-down, and you were dead, never partly dead.

Briefly, in the rain, Lieutenant Cross saw Martha's gray eyes gazing back at him.

He understood.

It was very sad, he thought. The things men carried inside. The things men did or felt they had to do.

He almost nodded at her, but didn't.

Instead he went back to his maps. He was now determined to perform his duties firmly and without negligence. It 680 wouldn't help Lavender, he knew that, but from this point on he would comport himself as a soldier. He would dispose of his good-luck pebble. Swallow it, maybe, or use Lee Strunk's

slingshot, or just drop it along the trail. On the march he would impose strict field discipline. He would be careful to send out flank security, to prevent straggling or bunching up, to keep his troops moving at the proper pace and at the proper interval. He would insist on clean weapons. He would confiscate the remainder of Lavender's dope. Later in the day, perhaps, he would call the men together and speak to them
690 plainly. He would accept the blame for what had happened to Ted Lavender. He would be a man about it. He would look them in the eyes, keeping his chin level, and he would issue the new SOPs in a calm, impersonal tone of voice, an officer's voice, leaving no room for argument or discussion. Commencing immediately, he'd tell them, they would no longer abandon equipment along the route of march. They would police up their acts. They would get their shit together, and keep it together, and maintain it neatly and in good working order.

He would not tolerate laxity. He would show strength,
700 distancing himself.

Among the men there would be grumbling, of course, and maybe worse, because their days would seem longer and their loads heavier, but Lieutenant Cross reminded himself that his obligation was not to be loved but to lead. He would dispense with love; it was not now a factor. And if anyone quarreled or complained, he would simply tighten his lips and arrange his shoulders in the correct command posture. He might give a curt little nod. Or he might not. He might just shrug and say Carry on, then they would saddle up and form
710 into a column and move out toward the villages west of Than Khe.

*Mary B. Campbell*

# *Money*

1  We need more money.
There isn't enough, and life
Is too short to waste
On being poor.

Money in all its beautiful forms:
The pale wampum, the bright doubloon
Cowries blinking on the dawn shore
The tawny oxen, the rupee
With its ten colors.

10  We need to give each other money
Till we are rich beyond our wildest dreams
Until the banks of the world can't hold it
Until we have to melt it down into spoons.

There should be money on every tree
Nestled in the buds for safe keeping
Or in summer hanging heavy from the branches.
The leaves should clink as they fall
And the squirrels hoard nuggets of gold.

We could buy everything
20  If we had the money:
We could buy each other's freedom.
It would mean the end of rock and roll.

It would give us time to walk hand in hand
Through the forest with our lovers,
Like rich people do in a time of peace,
Naming the animals.

## Maxine Chernoff

# *The New Money*

1 *Ones:* white for purity. A white man says his prayers in a white room. White nightshirt. White hair. In the background (raised velveteen relief) is an altar. Impaled on a stalagmite: the old money. "Self-reference is our motto" is reflected in a real mirror shaped like the continental forty-eight. Squint and you can see the Rockies. Cost: $49.98, discounted for summer white sale.

*Fives:* Colossal black olives rest in a bed of generals and wanted men who appear agitated, anonymous as canned
10 goods. They are the first designer bills with Salvador Dali's signature in gold leaf. There's a run on the Chase Manhattan as they are bought up by counter-agents trying to strengthen the zloty. They are duplicated by forgers in developing nations where unemployed Ph.D.'s are used as cheap labor. Finally replaced by Norman Rockwell money, familiar and comfortable. Nobody wants to steal it.

*Tens:* out of circulation. Fear of decimals in high places. The president sleeps with mittens and wingtips. What
20 more can be said of the intimate nature of currency?

*Thirteens:* largest of bills. Featuring football fields, battleships named after women in the thirties, hair fetishes, arenas where flamenco dancers practice voluntary metabolism. Reverse side: an appeal to sentiment. Paw raised in a friendly salute, everyone's favorite pet is quoted (in Latin) as saying, "I am snowing on your capital, a lost Caravaggio, a taxidermist's dream of islands in relief."

*Robert Kelly*

# *Farewell Letter*

1 There are not many ways
to tell you this. The cat
jumped over the moon,
I married the spoon.

The machine of difference
has ground us apart. You
are blue and I am west.
Only the brass & silver bell

in the middle of the sky
10 keeps us together
by hearing it. Already
I can't tell it from the rain.

## W.S. Merwin

# *At Home*

1 As the ants know
where the honey is
I know the way to you

—

where we live
we look far out to sea
and our clothes are behind us in the bedroom

—

here on a shirt is a scar
of your round stitches
pulling apart again

—

10 we saved some of the old calendars
for their beauty
I look at the numbers

—

one year on your birthday
after years together
we planted that big tree

—

we remember each other
as we will never
be again

—

I think of you with nothing on
20 leaning across the sink
looking into the mirror

—

I find you cooking
in your torn
underpants worn low
—

each time you
set the table
it is a world never repeated
—

you read lying on the mattress
wearing nothing
30 but your glasses
—

sometimes it is true
we do not go out enough
we stay home

## Charles Wright

# Dog Yoga

1   A spring day in the weeds.
A thread of spittle across the sky, and a thread of ash.
Mournful cadences from the clouds.

Through the drives and the cypress beds,
                                                                25 years of sad news.

Mother of Thrushes, Our Lady of Crows,
Brief as a handkerchief,
                                                25 years of sad news.

Later, stars and sea winds in and out of the open window.
Later, and lonesome among the sleepers,
                                                the day's thunder in hidden places,
One lissome cheek a notch in the noontide's leash,

10  A ghostly rain of sunlight among the ferns.

Year in, year out, the same loom from the dark.
Year in, year out, the same sound in the wind.

Near dawn, the void in the heart,
The last coat of lacquer along the leaves,
                                                the quench in the west.

# WRITING ASSIGNMENTS

1.  Write a short story in which a farmer, in despair, holds his family hostage to prevent a foreclosure on his farm. Use a tone and style that are appropriate to this situation.

2.  Write a story or one-act play that is *light and witty*. The following are some possible situations:
    a)  An attractive former college roommate comes to visit a married woman and flirts outrageously with her husband.
    b)  A young graduate student in sociology plans to spend a few weeks living with homeless people as a way to research a thesis.
    c)  A mother-in-law comes to visit and tries to re-decorate the young couple's house.
    d)  An urban couple go hiking in the mountains and find themselves lost in a remote place where there are rumored to be dangerous people.
    e)  A woman gets fed up with her eccentric husband, who is an unemployed inventor of fantastic gadgets.

3.  Write a war story in which three men, cut off from the rest of their company, have captured an enemy soldier and can not agree what to do with him—let him go, take him along, or kill him. Make sure your tone reflects their desperate circumstances.

4.  Write a satirical poem about one of the following:
    a)  money
    b)  health foods
    c)  violence on television
    d)  recreational shopping
    e)  educational fads
    f)  the behavior of adolescents
    g)  our romance with the automobile

_____*Chapter 7*

# Description

## Introduction

## Fiction

James McKinley     *Ozark Episode*
Amy Bloom     *Love Is Not a Pie*

## Poetry

Margaret Atwood     *Last Day*
Alice Jones     *Anorexia*
Richard Kenney     *Aubade*
Philip Levine     *Keats in California*
Jay Parini     *Coal Train*

## Writing Assignments

We live in a show-and-tell age, when everything is supposed to take place in a flash. We crave action, results. We tend towards the moment rather than exhumations of the past, or exhaustive descriptions of a character or setting. We want a slice of living flesh, but not the whole cow. We distrust a proliferation of words. It may be that television has influenced us in this way.

The Victorians and earlier twentieth-century writers lavished a lot of prose on descriptive elements. Now, in general, more economy prevails, but the basic principle underlying the use of description is and always has been the same. It's not a *mass* of detail that makes a good description, but carefully *selected* details.

It is the well-chosen detail that makes a character leap into life, a thought crystallize; that gives a sense of place or period; that creates a swift image which may stay with the reader long after the scene has faded from his mind. A yellow towel draped over a chair, for instance, the feel of bricks in the rain: Such things help the writer to establish the reality of a scene.

Writers are observers. They notice things, often jot them down. They use the five senses (smell, touch, taste, sight, and hearing) in a daily and often unconscious way to record their impressions of real life, and later they use this information in their writing.

Description is the language that is used to convey such perceptions to the reader. It may be realistic, presenting what is generally called "concrete detail." It may be abstract, as in "there was a hint of cruelty in his face." It may be figurative (making use of metaphors, similes, allusions, and symbols). It may also be direct ("He had a cruel mouth") or indirect ("She thought he had a cruel mouth").

Notice the careful selection of details—of the concrete variety—in "Nairobi," by Joyce Carol Oates, in Chapter 3. Oliver is described (indirectly, through Ginny's thoughts) as a handsome man, although his "skin was slightly coarse; his nose [was] wide at the bridge, and the nostrils disfigured by a few dark hairs that should have been snipped off; his lower jaw was somewhat heavy." Such accurate observation goes far in giving the reader a sense of the physical presence of the character.

Sensuous detail in Margaret Atwood's "Last Day" suggests beauty, fertility and evanescence, while the hens making "egg after egg, warty-shelled and perfect" underline the ongoing vitality of the natural cycle. In the first stanza there is a careful selection of descriptive elements—the feel of air on our skins, sweetness of the air, moths with "powdery wings," "fluting voices" from the pond, its web of spawn, the moon. Touch, smell, sight, and hearing are called on to suggest an erotic mood. Most of these details are somewhat figurative, involving the use of simile and metaphor—the evenings, for instance, that touch our skins "like plush," or things that "lean toward" the pulpy moon. "Pulpy" suggests a piece of overripe fruit. Nevertheless, we recognize the real and familiar details of an early summer night. Further on the imagery becomes more symbolic (the oval, the egg, the sun, the sky, the self-repeating day) and will serve as an example of highly charged description that carries the meaning of the poem.

In "Keats in California," the contrast between Levine's descriptions of Detroit ("under a soiled sky") and California ("blazing in the foolish winds of April") forms the substance of the poem. And, of course, it's possible that those places themselves may be descriptive metaphors for states of mind.

Description is vital in "Ozark Episode," a story by James McKinley in which fear-arousing details create the suspense. The boy, Simon, is fishing. "Natural noises" of the countryside are obliterated by a "twig-crushing crash behind him." The strange dog has a "sharp, ugly muzzle" and "flaring amber eyes." The man speaks out of a "thin mouth and stubbled black-gray chin," emitting "an odor like a rotten apple." Simon shuffles his feet "in the chilly mud." Here instances of noise, sight, smell, and touch combine to produce dread.

In "Love Is Not a Pie," Amy Bloom creates a warm family atmosphere through her use of descriptive detail. She also evokes a sense of place, in this case, of a summer place by a lake. "The two small bedrooms had big beds with pastel chenille spreads; yellow with red roses in my parents' room, white with pansies in the other ... The pillows were always a little damp and smelled like salt and pine and mine smelled of Ma Griffe perfume as well, because I used to sleep with my mother's scarf tucked under my pillow. The shower was outside, with a thin green plastic curtain around it. . . ."

The homely details of the cottage give it reality; furthermore, its simplicity is important to the theme. This unconventional family, in which the parents form a clearly described triangle with Mr. DeCuervo, does not live in a sybaritic or disgusting way; all live simply. Mr. DeCuervo does not appear as the Other Man, the Latin Lover, or other clichés of adultery; he is described as a simple man, ". . . his curly brown hair making him look like a giant dandelion, with his yellow T-shirt and brown jeans." Ellen's father goes to meet him, "his freckled back pink and moist in the sun, as it was every summer. The sun caught the red hair on his head and shoulders and chest and he shone." The affection between the two men who share a woman is the more believable because they are described throughout as both sensuous and innocent.

The use of concrete detail in "Aubade," by Richard Kenney, sharpens an experience of wintry pre-dawn hours, carefully observed by the author ("vinyl seat cracks, cold and brittle") and then softens into metaphor as emotions are introduced. In "Coal Train," on the other hand, Jay Parini tends to use figurative language when he describes the trains that pass in terms of their effect on a person lying in bed at night. As he piles detail on detail, the passage of the train appears to be both real and "the thunder of wheel and bone," an imagined death.

"Anorexia," by Alice Jones, a psychiatrist, describes the mental and physical condition of an anorexic, "a cannibal of self." We may take that almost literally, although most of the detail is more figurative, implying a delicate balance between life and death.

## James McKinley

# *Ozark Episode*

1   The boy's line arced against the stream's pull, a tie between that swirling, fishy world and the brown clay-mud where he stood. The pull was steady, so he knew it was no fish, only the stream. The fish were there all right. Sometimes he could see them in the shallows, now brown, now silver, darting in the mosses and the shelter of stones. With patience he would catch one. His daddy had taught him that. Be steadfast, his father said. They will come to you. He hauled in the line to check the bit of cheese. Funny, how these trout like cheese, most of all
10   the Velveeta he bought in Thompson's store, the cellophane pack as shiny and slippery in his hand as the fish themselves. Ol' Thompson, he asked for part of the catch, always grinning, knowing that if there was one it went straight home. Without the stream and woods, the supper table would be mighty barren. His daddy didn't make much with his teaching and it seemed like there was always a hungry stranger or two. The boy dabbed a cheese ball on the number-four hook, then flipped the monofilament out with a swish of the cane pole. The slight plop came, blending with the bird noise and squirrel
20   squawk and leaf rustle. Then, like a snake going down a hole, the natural noises vanished in a twig-crushing crash behind him.

"Whoa, now! Whoa, Luke!" the man hollered as he broke the brush line at the streambank's upper edge. "Whoa!" sounded harsh and high, but the dog pelted past the boy, beneath his now slackened line, and splashed into the water. It thrust its sharp, ugly muzzle deep and drank. The boy'd never seen a badder dog. Black and low to the ground, with sharp ears and a wedge-head set with flaring amber eyes, a dog like
30   the one on the moviehouse poster in Springfield that time he'd gone with his daddy. "Picture about an evil dog," his daddy had told him. Now this dog lifted its dripping muzzle, and the boy felt cold. He lowered the pole to pull in, feeling the man's chill, too, moving close to him.

"You havin' luck, boy?" the man hissed. "Here! Luke! Here!" The dog trotted toward them. The man spoke out of a thin mouth and stubbled black-gray chin. His eyes were silt-colored, with fine red lines running out to brown wrinkled corners. "Hey, nigger boy, I said, you doin' any good?"

40    "Nosir." He was twisting the line around the pole. The cheese ball dropped to the speckled gravel at the water's edge, bobbed in an eddy, and started down the stream. The dog watched it.

"Mebbe you do better with this, huh? You think?" The man waved his gun at the boy. Shiny and black, a soldier's rifle gun. He'd seen them before, ones like this. He'd seen men like this before, too. At Thompson's, and the Dairy Drive-In, and the post office in town. Thin, hard white men with cold eyes, all dressed in the green army clothes, with the boots and the

50    big knife in its leather case on the belt. In town they left the shiny guns in their pickups. His daddy called them Zealots, but the boy didn't know why, only that they lived out on a farm, praying all the time and keeping everybody out.

"You think?" the man hollered again.

"Nosir. Pole's good enough."

The man cackled and kicked the gravel. It scattered into the stream, making pockmarks. The dog jumped and growled.

"Easy, Luke. What's you name, boy?"

"Simon, sir."

60    "You fish here much, Simon? You know this here is the Lord's water. Belongs to the Godly. Fish, too. They belong to the Godly. Are you Godly, boy?"

"Yessir, I think so. My daddy taught me."

The man scratched his belly.

"He did, did he? Thass good. You sure you ain't got any of the Godly's fish?"

Simon didn't know what to say. For sure not what his daddy said, that all things belonged to everybody.

"Nosir," he answered.

70    "Thass good," the man said.

Then the man's thin body bent quick as an eye blink. He picked up a stone and cast it twenty feet downstream. Fast as heat lightning, he threw the gun to his shoulder and fired—Crack! Crack!—at the ripples. Simon felt the blast roll out from the gun barrel. The shot echoed over the water, blotting out everything except the thump of his heart. The dog recoiled against Simon's legs, twisted, then howled and sidled stiff-legged toward the still-widening circles. The man slung the rifle on his shoulder.

80    "Godly, boy. You know us?" he said.

"Yessir. From the Farm." His daddy said they didn't grow anything much.

The man's mouth split to show stained teeth.

"No Farm. It's God's Country. We protect it. Keep it away from sinners. Put it away for the Rapture. You know Rapture, Simon? You heard of that? Luke! Hush! Come here now!"

Simon shuffled his feet on the chilly mud. His shoes were up the bank behind him. He had his pole ready. He ached with

90   wanting to leave. Simon took a small step backwards. The man pushed belly-close and grabbed his pole

"I asked you, nigger, if you know the Rapture? You answer now." An odor like a rotten apple came out of the man's mouth. Simon could see the dirt in the cracks of his face and hand, could smell the oil on the gun and knife case, the sweat from the stained green shirt. U.S. Army, it said in black over the left pocket.

"Nosir."

The man shook the pole.

100    "Rapture! You gotta know that, boy. Rapture's when us Godly go to heaven, whisked up like by a spaceship. Ain't you a Christian? Don't you believe? Are you a Sinner? I hope not, boy, 'cause Sinners gonna burn. Burn when the A-tom Apocalypse comes, burn more at Rapture time. But the Godly, we gonna live, we gonna eat the fishes and the squirrels and the deers, gonna hole up in God's Country until Rapture time. You hear, boy, you hear? You ain't no Sinner, are you?"

The man had hold of Simon now, shaking him by the shoulders. Simon felt his teeth rattling against each other. The

110   stream, sky, woods, the man's pink open mouth and brown, broken teeth moved around, up and down. His head felt like a fish flopping on the bank.

"Nosir. No Sinner. Not me. Mister, let go, please. Let go."

The man dropped his hands and folded them in front like he was praying.

"You sure? Praise God?"

"Yessir. I'm a Christian. No Sinner." Simon took another small step toward his shoes. His daddy'd skin him if he

120   lost them shoes.

"Praise God, then. Praise God. Boy?"

"Yessir. Praise God! Praise God!"

"You hate Sin, boy?"

Simon moved another foot backwards.

"Yessir. My daddy, he say hate the sin, love the sinner."

The man seemed not to hear. He was looking downstream, past where the dog was muzzling near where the bullets hit.

"Boy, I don't believe you're a saved Christian," he said,
130  still looking away. "Not saved. You're tribe of Ham, ain't you? Curse of Canaan and Cush. Slave folk. The Book says you ain't saved. Not black ones. Black is the Devil's color, you know that?" The man unslung his rifle. His eyes seemed nailed to a spot downstream. Simon felt his back go colder, the hairs on his arms raise. He wanted to run, that was sure. No shoes. Just run.

"Tribe of Ham," the man whispered, "for sure." Simon saw him move, step carefully into the stream, holding the rifle crossways against his chest like guards do. "We the Warriors,
140  you know that, boy? Compact of Christ and Sword of the Almighty is us. Crusaders of the Godly." Simon felt the rasp of saw grass and weed underfoot. He'd made the bank edge. The man stood in a foot of water now. Simon's hand cramped around his pole.

"Hallelujah!" the man shouted, and the gun flashed up. Simon felt his body stop, like someone had shot a ray and paralyzed him. Crack! the shiny gun spit. Crack! again. Simon's head swiveled to watch the squirrel leap from one tree trunk to another just beyond the dog. Bits of bark flew. The
150  dog howled, whirled, leaped. Crack! Crack! The dog howled and fell backwards, twisted as a fishhook, and started tearing at his bleeding side. Chunks of fur fell way, then flesh. The dog's scream ricocheted through the pin oaks and pines, piercing Simon like he'd not been pierced since his momma went to Heaven. The man gazed at the dog, his eyes wide and puzzled.

"Luke!" he called. "Come here, Luke!" The dog lay now in the water, amber eyes rolled up. Blood colored the stream. "Luke!" the man called, moving toward the dog. Simon slid a foot onto the forest floor, and turned halfway toward the
160  trees. The man's head flared to him. "This your work, boy. Devil's work. You possessed, boy. Possessed! Tribe of Slaves! You a Sinner, boy."

The shiny gun barrel came down. Simon saw the muzzle hole leading back to the man's hand, and he could not move. He felt his mouth work, lips forming words, but it seemed he could not hear them, they came from so far away.

"No, Mister. Not me. You got it wrong. You. You the one."

The gun stayed on him, waggling a little, then flew from
170 the man like it had been snatched away. "O, Lord, O, Lord,"
the man screamed. Simon watched him fall to his knees in the
shallow water, hands clasped over his stained dirty face, his
body shaking, his mouth working like a bellows, racked with
something like what the boy had seen when the women came
to grieve and the men to sing sad hymns. Simon saw the
soldier-gun cartwheel toward him slowly as a blown leaf, saw
it fall, and at the same time, almost, heard the sharp crack as
the gun hit the stony water edge. Then he felt the hot sting, the
slash at his side, the warm flow begin.
180        "O, Lord," the man cried.
Simon seemed to see the words ascend from the man
toward the cloud-flecked blue. They were round and orange.
He could see everything clearly, the insects settling on the
dog's eyes and mouth, the waterstain soaking black on the
man's pants. He saw the squirrel scolding them all. His hand
went to the warm, dark blood.
"O, Lord, forgive me, Lord," the man shouted, his face
now uncovered, thrust at the sky like a sword. "Forgive me,
Lord, forgive me."
190        "Mister," Simon called. "Help me, please, I'm hurt." He
took a step toward the man. He felt weak, like he had when
he'd fallen into the creek from his daddy's arms at his Baptism.
The man's face rolled down to look at him. Red surged
round the dark pupils of his cold eyes.
"Help me, Mister. Please. I got to get help."
The man cried out again, this time to Simon.
"Forgive me, please forgive me. In the Savior's name,
forgive me. I am Godly, truly."
Simon took another step. He pushed his shirt harder
200 against his side, but still he felt the flow.
"Mister," he hollered. "I forgive you, honest. I forgive
you. Please, help me."
A strange glow, maybe the sun through the flying water,
settled on the man's sweaty face. He threw his arms
heavenward.
"God, Almighty, I thank you," the man cried. "I'm
shrived and forgiven. Thank you, O, Lord." Then he was
bounding like a deer, splashing the stream, coming past Simon
now, his boots pounding imprints in the mud, up through the
210 bank edge brush and into the forest's shade, running, running
as if Satan himself were after him, singing suddenly in a harsh,
high voice, "Hallelujah! Hallelujah! I'm saved, O, Lord.

Hallelujah! Hallelujah!" until it trailed off into just noise, like moans or animal cries, and then he and the noise were gone. Simon looked again at the dog, almost peaceful in the stream. A fish nuzzled the carcass. Simon felt weak, lightheaded but good, like he had once after he'd run a long way from school and come into the kitchen and found his daddy there with fresh greens and spring water. Carefully, he turned his face
220 toward the forest. He'd have to leave his pole and his shoes, but he'd come back another day to the stream and the fish. Another day he'd retrieve his fisherman shoes. He moved up the bank, surprised at how steep it felt, and stepped into the quiet, cool woods.

## Amy Bloom

# *Love Is Not a Pie*

1   In the middle of the eulogy at my mother's boring and heart-breaking funeral, I started to think about calling off the wedding. August 21 did not seem like a good date, John Wescott did not seem like a good person to marry and I couldn't see myself in the long white silk gown Mrs. Wescott had offered me. We had gotten engaged at Christmas, while my mother was starting to die. She died in May, earlier than we had expected. When the minister said, "She was a rare spirit, full of the kind of bravery and joy that inspires others ... ," I stared at
10 the pale blue ceiling and thought, "My mother would not have wanted me to spend my life with this man." He had asked me if I wanted him to come from Boston to the funeral, and I said no. So he didn't, respecting my autonomy and so forth. I think he should have known that I was just being considerate.

    After the funeral, we took the little box of ashes back to the house and entertained everybody who came by to pay their respects. Lots of my father's colleagues, other law professors, a few of his former students, my Uncle Steve and his new wife, my cousins (whom my sister and I always referred to as Thing
20 One and Thing Two), friends from the old neighborhood, before my mother's sculpture started selling, my mother's art world friends, her sisters, some of my friends from high school, some people I used to baby-sit for, my best friend from college, some friends of my sister's, a lot of people I didn't recognize. I've been living away from home for a long time, first at college, now at law school.

    My sister, my father and I worked the room. And everyone that came in, my father embraced. It didn't matter whether they started to pat him on the back or shake his hand, he
30 pulled them to him and hugged them so hard, I saw some people's feet lift right off the floor. My sister and I took the more passive route, letting people do whatever they wanted to us—patting, stroking, embracing, cupping our faces in their hands.

My father was in the middle of squeezing Mrs. Ellis, our cleaning lady, when he saw Mr. DeCuervo come in, still carrying his suitcase. He about dropped Mrs. Ellis and went charging over to Mr. DeCuervo, wrapped his arms around him, and the two of them moaned and rocked together, in a passionate,
40  musicless waltz. My sister and I sat down on the couch, our arms pressed against each other, watching our father cry all over his friend, our mother's lover.

When I was eleven and my sister was eight, her last naked summer, Mr. DeCuervo and his daughter, Gisela, who was just about to turn eight, spent part of the summer with us at the cabin in Maine. The cabin was from the Spencer side, my father's side of the family, and he and my Uncle Steve were co-owners. We went there every July (colder water, better weather) and they came in August. My father felt about his
50  brother the way we felt about our cousins, so we would only overlap for lunch on the last day of our stay.
    That July, the DeCuervos came, but without Mrs. De-Cuervo, who had to go visit a sick someone in Argentina, where they were from. That was okay with us; Mrs. DeCuervo was a professional mother, a type that made my sister and me very uncomfortable. She told us to wash the berries before we ate them, to rest after lunch, to put on more suntan lotion, to make our beds. She was a nice lady; she was just always in our way. My mother had a few very basic summer rules: don't eat
60  food with mold or insects on it; don't swim alone; don't even think about waking your mother before 8 A.M., unless you are fatally injured or ill. That was about it and Mrs. DeCuervo was always amending and adding to the list, one apologetic eye on my mother. Our mother, as usual, was pleasant and friendly and did things the way she always did. She made it pretty clear that if we were cowed by the likes of Mrs. De-Cuervo, we were on our own. They got divorced when Gisela was a sophomore at Mount Holyoke.
    We liked pretty, docile Gisela, and bullied her a little bit,
70  and liked her even more because she didn't squeal on us, on me in particular. We liked her father, too. We saw the two of them, sometimes the three of them, at occasional picnics and lesser holidays. He always complimented us, never made stupid jokes at our expense and brought us unusual, perfect little presents. Silver barrettes for me, the summer I was letting my hair grow out from my pixie cut; a leather bookmark for Lizzie, who learned to read when she was three. My mother

would stand behind us as we unwrapped the gifts, smiling and shaking her head at his extravagance.

80    When they drove up, we were all sitting on the porch; Mr. DeCuervo got out first, his curly brown hair making him look like a giant dandelion, with his yellow T-shirt and brown jeans. Gisela looked just like him, her long, curly brown hair caught up in a bun, wisps flying around her tanned little face. As they walked toward us, she took his hand and I felt a rush of warmth toward her, for showing how much she loved her daddy, like I loved mine, and for showing that she was a little afraid of us, of me, probably. People weren't often frightened of Lizzie, she never left her books long enough to bother 90   anyone.

My parents got down from the porch, my big father in his faded blue trunks, drooping below his belly, his freckled back pink and moist in the sun, as it was every summer. The sun caught the red hair on his head and shoulders and chest and he shone. The Spencers were half Viking, he said. My mother was wearing her summer outfit, a black two-piece bathing suit. I don't remember her ever wearing a different suit. At night, she'd add one of my father's shirts and wrap it around her like a kimono. Some years, she looked great in her 100  suit, waist nipped in, skin smooth and tan; other years, her skin looked burnt and crumpled and the suit was too big in some places and too small in others. Those years she smoked too much and went out on the porch to cough. But that summer, the suit fit beautifully, and when she jumped off the porch into my father's arms, he whirled her around and let her black hair whip his face, while he smiled and smiled.

They both hugged Mr. DeCuervo and Gisela; my mother took her little flowered suitcase and my father took his duffel bag and they led them into the cabin.

110   The cabin was our palace; Lizzie and I would say, very grandly, "We're going to the cabin for the summer, come visit us there, if it's okay with your parents." And we loved it and loved to act as though it was nothing special, when we knew, really, that it was magnificent. The pines and birches came right down to the lake, with just a thin lacing of mossy rocks before you got to the smooth, cold water, and little gray fish swam around the splintery dock and through our legs, or out of reach of our oars when we took out the old blue rowboat.

The cabin itself was three bedrooms and a little kitchen 120  and a living room that took up half the house. The two small bedrooms had big beds with pastel chenille spreads; yellow

with red roses in my parents' room, white with blue pansies in the other. The kid's room was much bigger, like a dormitory, with three sets of bunk beds, each with its own mismatched sheets and pillowcases. The pillows were always a little damp and smelled like salt and pine and mine smelled of Ma Griffe perfume as well, because I used to sleep with my mother's scarf tucked under my pillow. The shower was outside, with a thin green plastic curtain around it, but there was a regular
130 bathroom inside, next to my parents' room.

Mr. DeCuervo and Gisela fit into our routine as though they'd been coming to the cabin for years, instead of just last summer. We had the kind of summer cabin routine that stays with you forever as a model of leisure, of life being enjoyed. We'd get up early, listening to the birds screaming and trilling, and make ourselves some breakfast: cold cereal or toast if the parents were up, cake or cold spaghetti or marshmallows, if they were still asleep. Then the parents would get up, my mother first, usually. She'd make a cup of coffee and brush and
140 braid our hair and set us loose. If we were going exploring, she'd put three sandwiches and three pieces of fruit in a bag, with an army blanket. Otherwise, she'd just wave to us as we headed down to the lake.

We'd come back at lunchtime and eat whatever was around and then go out to the lake, or the forest, or down the road to see if the townie kids were around and in a mood to play with us. I don't know what the grown-ups did all day; sometimes they'd come out to swim for a while, and sometimes we'd find my mother in the shed she used for a studio. But when we
150 came back at around five or six, they all seemed happy and relaxed, drinking gin-and-tonics on the porch, watching us run toward the house. It was the most beautiful time.

At night, after dinner, the fathers would wash up and my mother would sit on the porch, smoking a cigarette, listening to Aretha Franklin or Billie Holiday or Sam Cooke, and after a little while, she'd stub out her cigarette and the four of us would dance. We'd twist and lindy and jitterbug and stomp, all of us copying my mother. And pretty soon, the daddies would drift in, with their dishtowels and their beers, and
160 they'd lean in the doorway and watch. My mother would turn first to my father, always to him, first.

"What about it, Danny? Care to dance?" And she'd put her hand on his shoulder and he'd smile, tossing his dishtowel to Mr. DeCuervo, resting his beer on the floor. And my father

would lumber along, gamely, shuffling his feet and smiling. Sometimes, he'd wave his arms around and pretend to be a fish or a bear, while my mother swung her body, easily and dreamily, sliding through the music. They'd always lindy together, to Fats Domino. That was my father's favorite and then he'd sit
170 down, puffing a little.

My mother would stand there, snapping her fingers, shifting back and forth.

"Gaucho, you dance with her, before I have a coronary," said my father.

Mr. DeCuervo's real name was Bolivar, which I didn't know until Lizzie told me after the funeral. We always called him Mr. DeCuervo because we felt embarrassed to call him by a nickname.

So, Mr. DeCuervo would shrug gracefully, and toss the
180 two dishtowels back to my father. And then he'd bop toward my mother, his face still turned toward my father.

"We'll go running tomorrow, Dan, get you back into shape, so you can dance all night."

"What do you mean, 'back'? I've been exactly this same svelte shape for twenty years. Why fix it if it ain't broke?"

And they all laughed and Mr. DeCuervo and my mother rolled their eyes at each other and my mother walked over and kissed my father, where the sweat was beading up at his temples. Then she took Mr. DeCuervo's hand and they walked to
190 the center of the living room.

When she and my father danced, my sister and I giggled and interfered and treated it like a family badminton game in which they were the core players but we were welcome participants. When she danced with Mr. DeCuervo, we'd sit on the porch swing or lean on the windowsill and watch, not even looking at each other.

They only danced the fast dances, and they danced as though they'd been waiting all their lives for each song. My mother's movements got deeper and smoother and Mr. De-
200 Cuervo suddenly came alive, as though a spotlight had hit him. My father danced the way he was—warm, noisy, teasing, a little overpowering; but Mr. DeCuervo, who was usually quiet and thoughtful and serious, became a different man when he danced with my mother. His dancing was light and happy and soulful, edging up on my mother, turning her, matching her every step. They would smile at all of us, in turn, and then face each other, too transported to smile.

"Dance with Daddy some more," my sister said, speaking for all three of us. They had left us too far behind.

210        My mother blew Lizzie a kiss. "Okay, sweetheart."

She turned to both men, smiling, and said, "That message was certainly loud and clear. Let's take a little break, Gauch', and get these monkeys to bed. It's getting late, girls."

And the three of them shepherded the three of us through the bedtime rituals, moving us in and out of the kitchen for water, the bathroom for teeth, potty and calamine lotion, and finally to our big bedroom. We slept in our underwear and T-shirts, which impressed Gisela.

"No pajamas?" she had said, the first night.

220        "Not necessary," I said smugly.

We would lie there after they kissed us, listening to our parents talk and crack peanuts and snap cards; they played gin and poker while they listened to Dinah Washington and Odetta.

One night, I woke up at around midnight and crossed the living room to get some water in the kitchen and see if there was any strawberry shortcake left. I saw my mother and Mr. DeCuervo hugging, and I remember being surprised, and puzzled, too. I had seen movies; if you hugged someone like you'd

230    never let them go, surely you were supposed to be kissing, too. It wasn't a Mommy-Daddy hug, partly because their hugs were defined by the fact that my father was eight inches taller and a hundred pounds heavier than my mother. These two looked all wrong to me; embraces were a big pink-and-orange man enveloping a smaller, leaner black-and-white woman who looked up at him. My mother and Mr. DeCuervo looked like sister and brother, standing cheek-to-cheek, with their broad shoulders and long, tanned, bare legs. My mother's hands were under Mr. DeCuervo's white T-shirt. She must

240    have felt my eyes on her because she opened hers slowly.

"Oh, honey, you startled us. Mr. DeCuervo and I were just saying goodnight. Do you want me to tuck you in after you go potty?" Not quite a bribe, certainly a reminder that I was more important to her than he was. They had moved apart so quickly and smoothly I couldn't even remember how they had looked together. I nodded to my mother; what I had seen was already being transformed into a standard goodnight embrace, the kind my mother gave to all of her close friends.

When I came back from the bathroom, Mr. DeCuervo

250    had disappeared and my mother was waiting, looking out at the moon. She walked me to the bedroom and kissed me, first on my forehead, then on my lips.

"Sleep well, pumpkin pie. See you in the morning."

"Will you make blueberry pancakes tomorrow?" It seemed like a good time to ask.

"We'll see. Go to sleep."

"Please, Mommy."

"Okay, we'll have a blueberry morning. Go to sleep, now. Goodnight, nurse." And she watched me for a moment, 260 from the doorway, and then she was gone.

My father got up at five to go fishing with some men at the other side of the lake. Every Saturday in July, he'd go off, with a big red bandanna tied over his bald spot, his Mets T-shirt, and his tackle box, and he'd fish until around three. Mr. DeCuervo said that he'd clean them, cook them and eat them, but he wouldn't spend a day with a bunch of guys in baseball caps and white socks to catch them.

I woke up smelling coffee and butter. Gisela and Liz were already out of bed and I was aggrieved; I was the one who had 270 asked for the pancakes and they were probably all eaten by now.

Mr. DeCuervo and Liz were sitting at the table, finishing their pancakes. My mother and Gisela were sitting on the blue couch in the living room, while my mother brushed Gisela's hair. She was brushing it more gently than she brushed mine, not slapping her on the shoulder to make her sit still. Gisela didn't wiggle and she didn't scream when my mother hit a knot.

I was getting ready to be mad when my mother winked at me over Gisela's head and said, "There's a plate of pancakes for you on top of the stove, bunny. Gauch', would you please 280 lift them for Ellen? The plate's probably hot."

Mr. DeCuervo handed me my pancakes, which were huge brown wheels studded with smashed, purply berries; he put my fork and knife on top of a folded paper towel and patted my cheek. His hand smelled like coffee and cinnamon. He knew what I liked and pushed the butter and the honey and the syrup toward me.

"Juice?" he said.

I nodded, trying to watch him when he wasn't looking; he didn't look like the man I thought I saw in the moonlight, 290 giving my mother a funny hug.

"Great pancakes, Lila," he said.

"Great, Mom." I didn't want to be outclassed by the DeCuervos' habitual good manners. Even Gisela remembered her please and thank you for every little thing.

My mother smiled and put the barrettes in Gisela's hair. It was starting to get warm, so I swallowed my pancakes and kicked Liz to get her attention.

"Let's go," I said.

"Wash your face, then go," my mother said.

300    I stuck my face under the kitchen tap and my mother and Mr. DeCuervo laughed. Triumphantly, I led the two little girls out of the house, snatching our towels off the line as we ran down to the water, suddenly filled with longing for the lake.

"Last one in the water's a fart," I screamed, cannonballing off the end of the dock. I hit the cold blue water, shattering its surface. Liz and Gisela jumped in beside me and we played water games until my father drove up in the pickup with a bucket of fish. He waved to us and told us we'd be eating fish for the next two days, and we groaned and held our noses as

310    he went into the cabin, laughing.

There was a string of sunny days like that one: swimming, fishing with Daddy off the dock, eating peanut-butter-and-jelly sandwiches in the rowboat, drinking Orange Crush on the porch swing.

And then it rained for a week. We woke up the first rainy morning, listening to it tap and dance on the roof. My mother stuck her head into our bedroom.

"It's monsoon weather, honeys. How about cocoa and cinnamon toast?"

320    We pulled on our overalls and sweaters and went into the kitchen, where my mother had already laid out our mugs and plates. She was engaged in her rainy-day ritual: making sangria. First she poured the orange juice out of the big white plastic pitcher into three empty peanut-butter jars, then she started chopping up all the oranges, lemons and limes we had in the house. She let me pour the brandy over the fruit, Gisela threw in the sugar and Lizzie came up for air long enough to pour the big bottle of red wine over everything. I cannot imagine drinking anything else on rainy days.

330    That day, my mother went out onto the porch for her morning cigarette and when my father came down, he joined her on the porch, while we played Go Fish; I could see them snuggling on the wicker settee. After a while, Mr. DeCuervo came down, looked out on the porch and picked up an old magazine and started reading.

We decided to play Monopoly in our room, since the grown-ups didn't want to entertain us. After two hours, in which I rotted in jail and Lizzie forgot to charge rent, little Gisela beat us and the three of us went back to the kitchen for

340    snacks. Rainy days were basically a series of snacks, more and less elaborate, punctuated by board games, card games, and

whining. We drank soda and juice all day, ate cheese, bananas, cookies, bologna, graham crackers, Jiffy popcorn, hard-boiled eggs. The grown-ups ate cheese and crackers and drank sangria.

The daddies were reading in the two big armchairs; my mother had gone off to her room to sketch. We were getting bored, so I started writing my name in the honey that had spilled on the kitchen table, while Gisela and Liz pulled the
350 stuffing out of the hole in the bottom of the blue couch.

My mother came downstairs for a cigarette and started swearing. "Jesus Christ, Ellen, get your hands out of the goddamned honey. Liz, Gisela, that's absolutely unacceptable, you know that. Leave the poor couch alone. If you're so damned stir-crazy, go outside and dance in the rain."

The two men looked up, slowing focusing, from a great distance.

"Lila, really," said my father.
360 "Lila, it's pouring. We'll keep an eye on them, now," said Mr. DeCuervo.

"Right. Like you were." My mother was grinning.

"Can we, Mommy, can we go in the rain? Can we take off our clothes and go in the rain?"

"Sure, go naked, there's no point in getting your clothes wet and no point in suits. There's not likely to be a big crowd in the yard."

We ran to the porch and, before my mother could get rational, stripped and ran whooping into the rain, leaping off
370 the porch onto the muddy lawn, screaming and feeling superior to every child in Maine who had to stay indoors.

We played goddesses-in-the-rain, which consisted of caressing our bodies and screaming the names of everyone we knew, and we played ring-around-the-rosie and tag and red light, green light and catch, all of which were deliciously slippery and surreal in the sheets of gray rain. Our parents watched us from the porch.

When we finally came in, thrilled with ourselves and the extent to which we were completely, profoundly wet, in every
380 pore, they bundled us up and told us to dry our hair and get ready for dinner.

My mother brushed our hair and then she made sauce for spaghetti, while my father made a salad and Mr. DeCuervo made a strawberry tart, piling the berries into a huge, red, shiny pyramid in the center of the pastry. We were in heaven.

The grown-ups were laughing a lot, sipping their rosy drinks, tossing the vegetables back and forth.

After dinner, my mother took us into the living room to dance and then the power went off.

390    "Shit," said my father in the kitchen.

"Double shit," said Mr. DeCuervo, and we heard them stumbling around in the dark, laughing and cursing until they came in with two flashlights.

"The cavalry is here, ladies," said Daddy, bowing to us all and twirling his flashlight.

"American and Argentinian divisions, senora y senoritas." I had never heard Mr. DeCuervo speak Spanish before, not even that little bit.

"Well, then, I know I'm safe—from the bad guys, any-
400 way. On the other hand . . ." My mother laughed, and the daddies put their arms around each other, and they laughed, too.

"On the other hand, what? What, Mommy?" I tugged at her the way I did when I was afraid of losing her in a big department store.

"Nothing, honey. Mommy was just being silly. Let's get ready for bed, munchkins. Then you all can whisper in bed for a while. We're shut down for the night, I'm sure."

The daddies accompanied us to the bathroom and whis-
410 pered that we could skip everything except peeing, since there was no electricity. The two of them kissed us goodnight, my father's moustache tickling, Mr. DeCuervo's sliding over my cheek. My mother came into the room a moment later, and her face was as smooth and warm as a velvet cushion. We didn't whisper for long; the rain dance and the eating and the storm had worn us out.

It was still dark when I woke up, but the rain had stopped and the power had returned, so that there was a light burning in our hallway. It made me feel very grown-up and
420 responsible, getting out of bed and going around the house turning out the lights that no one else knew were on; I was conserving electricity.

I went into the bathroom and was squeezed by stomach cramps, probably from all the burnt popcorn kernels I had eaten. I sat on the toilet for a long time, watching a brown spider crawl along the wall; I'd knock him down and then watch him climb back up again toward the towels. My cramps were better, but not gone, so I decided to wake my mother. My father would have been more sympathetic, but he was the

430 heavier sleeper, and by the time he understood what I was telling him my mother would have her bathrobe on and be massaging my stomach, kindly, but without the excited concern that I felt was my due as a victim of illness.

I walked down to my parents' room, turning the hall light back on. I pushed open the creaky door and saw my mother spooned up against my father's back, as she always was, and Mr. DeCuervo spooned up against her, his arm over the covers, his other hand resting on the top of her head.

I stood up and looked and then backed out of the bed-
440 room. They hadn't moved, the three of them breathing deeply, in unison. What was that, I thought, what did I see? I wanted to go back and take another look, to see it again, to make it disappear, to watch them carefully, until I understood.

My cramps were gone. I went back to my own bed, staring at Liz and Gisela, who looked, in their sleep, like little girl versions of the two men I had just seen. Just sleeping, I thought, the grown-ups were just sleeping. Maybe Mr. De-Cuervo's bed collapsed, like ours did two summers ago, or maybe it got wet in the storm. I thought I would never be able
450 to fall asleep, but the next thing I remember is waking up to more rain and the sounds of Liz and Gisela begging my mother to take us to the movies in town. We went to see *The Sound of Music,* which had been playing at the Bijou for about ten years.

I don't remember much else about the summer; all of the images run together. We went on swimming and fishing and taking the rowboat out for little adventures, and when the DeCuervos left, I hugged Gisela, but wasn't going to hug him, until he whispered in my ear, "Next year, we'll bring up a
460 motorboat and I'll teach you to water-ski," and then I hugged him very hard and my mother put her hand on my head, lightly, giving benediction.

The next summer, I went off to camp in July and wasn't there when the DeCuervos came. Lizzie said they had a good time without me. Then they couldn't come for a couple of summers in a row, and by the time they came again, Gisela and Lizzie were at camp with me in New Hampshire; the four grown-ups spent about a week together, but then I heard my father say that another vacation with Elvira DeCuervo would kill him or
470 he'd kill her. My mother said she wasn't so bad.

We saw them a little less after that. They came, Gisela and Mr. DeCuervo, to my high school graduation, to my mother's opening in Boston, to my father's fiftieth birthday party and then to Lizzie's graduation. When my mother went down to New York, she'd have dinner with the three of them, she said, but sometimes her plans would change and they'd have to substitute lunch for dinner.

Gisela couldn't come to the funeral; she was in Argentina for the year, working with the architectural firm that Mr.
480  DeCuervo's father had started.

After all the mourners left, Mr. DeCuervo gave us a sympathy note from Gisela, with a beautiful pen-and-ink of our mother inside it. The two men went into the living room and took out a bottle of Scotch and two glasses. It was like we weren't there; they put on Billie Holiday singing "Embraceable You," and they got down to serious drinking and grieving. Lizzie and I went into the kitchen and decided to eat everything sweet that people had brought over: brownies, strudel, pfeffernuss, sweet potato pie, Mrs. Ellis' chocolate cake, with
490  chocolate mousse in the middle. We laid out two plates and two mugs of milk and got to it.

Lizzie said, "You know, when I was home in April, he called every day." She jerked her head toward the living room.

I couldn't tell if she approved or disapproved, and I didn't know what I thought about it either.

"She called him 'Bolivar.' "

"What? She always called him 'Gaucho' and so we didn't call him anything."

"I know, but she called him 'Bolivar.' I heard her talk to
500  him every fucking day, El; she called him 'Bolivar.'" Tears were running down Lizzie's face, and I wished my mother was there to pat her soft, fuzzy hair and keep her from choking on her tears. I held her hand across the table. I was still holding my fork in my other hand and I could feel my mother looking at me, smiling and narrowing her eyes a little, the way she did when I was balking. I dropped the fork onto my plate and went over and hugged Lizzie, who leaned into me as though her spine had collapsed.

"I asked her, after the third call, about his calling," she said, into my shoulder.
510  "What'd she say?" I straightened Lizzie up, so I could hear what she was saying.

"She said, 'Of course, he calls at noon, he knows that's when I'm feeling strongest.' And I told her that's not what I meant, that I hadn't known they were so close."

"You said that?"

"Yeah. And she said, 'Honey, nobody loves me more than Bolivar.' And I didn't know what to say, so I just sat there

feeling like 'Do I really want to hear this?' and then she fell
asleep."

520    "So what do you think?"

"I don't know. I was getting ready to ask her again . . ."

"You're amazing, Lizzie," I interrupted. She really is,
she's so quiet but she goes out and has conversations that I
can't even imagine having.

"But I didn't have to ask because she brought it up
herself, the next day after he called. She got off the phone,
looking just so exhausted, she was sweating, but she was smiling. She was looking out at the crabapple trees in the yard,
and she said, 'There were apples trees in bloom when I met

530    Bolivar, and the trees were right where the sculpture needed to
be in the courtyard, so he offered to get rid of the trees, and I
said that seemed arrogant, and he said that they'd replant
them. So I said okay and he said, 'What's so bad about arro-
gance?' And the first time he and Daddy met, the two of them
drank Scotch and watched soccer while I made dinner. And
then they washed up, just like at the cabin. And when the two
of them are in the room together and you two girls are with us,
I know that I am living in a state of grace.'"

"She said that? She said 'in a state of grace'? Mommy

540    said that?"

"Yes, Ellen. Christ, what do you think, I'm making up
interesting deathbed statements?" Liz hated to be interrupted,
especially by me.

"Sorry. Go on."

"Anyway, we were talking and I sort of asked what were
we actually talking about. I mean, close friends or very close
friends, and she just laughed. You know how she'd look at us
like she knew exactly where we were going when we said we
were going to a friend's house for the afternoon but we were

550    really going to drink Boone's Farm and skinny-dip at the
quarry? Well, she looked just like that and she took my hand.
Her hand was so light, El. And she said that the three of them
loved each other, each differently, and that they were both
amazing men, each special, each deserving love and apprecia-
tion. She said that she thought Daddy was the most wonderful
husband a woman could have and that she was very glad that
we had him as a father. And I asked her how she could do it,
love them both, and how they could stand it. And she said,
'Love is not a pie, honey. I love you and Ellen differently,

560    because you are different people, wonderful people, but not at
all the same. And so who I am with each of you is different,
unique to us. I don't choose between you. And it's the same

way with Daddy and Bolivar. People think that it can't be that way, but it can. You just have to find the right people.' And then she shut her eyes for the afternoon. Your eyes are bugging out, El."

"Well, Jesus, I guess so. I mean, I knew . . ."

"You knew and you didn't tell me?"

570 "You were eight or something, Lizzie, what was I supposed to say? I didn't even know what I knew then."

"So what did you know?" Lizzie was very serious. It was a real breach of our rules not to share inside dirt about our parents, especially our mother; we were always trying to figure her out.

I didn't know how to tell her about the three of them; that was even less normal than her having an affair with Mr. De-Cuervo with Daddy's permission. I couldn't even think of the words to describe what I had seen, so I just said, "I saw Mommy and Mr. DeCuervo kissing one night after we were in bed."

580 "Really? Where was Daddy?"

"I don't know. But wherever he was, obviously he knew what was going on. I mean, that's what Mommy was telling you, right? That Daddy knew and that it was okay with him."

"Yeah. Jesus."

I went back and sat down and we were halfway through the strudel when the two men came in. They were drunk, but not incoherent. They just weren't their normal selves, but I guess we weren't either, with our eyes puffy and red and all this destroyed food around us.

590 "Beautiful girls," Mr. DeCuervo said to my father. They were hanging in the doorway, one on each side.

"They are, they really are. And smart, couldn't find smarter girls." My father was going on and on about how smart we were. Lizzie and I just looked at each other, embarrassed but not displeased.

"Ellen has Lila's mouth," Mr. DeCuervo said. "You have your mother's mouth, with the right side going up a little more than the left. Exquisite."

My father's nodding his head, like this is the greatest truth ever told. And Daddy turns to Liz and says, "And you have your mother's eyes. Since the day you were born and I looked right into them, I thought, 'My God, she's got Lila's eyes, but blue, not green.'"

And Mr. DeCuervo is nodding away, of course. I wondered if they were going to do a complete autopsy, but they stopped.

My father came over to us at the table and put one hand on each of us. "You girls made your mother incredibly happy. There was nothing she ever created that gave her more pride
610  and joy than you two. And she thought that you were both so special..." He started crying and Mr. DeCuervo put an arm around his waist and picked up for him.

"She did, she had two pictures of you in her studio, nothing else. And you know, she expected us all to grieve, but you know how much she wanted you to enjoy, too. To enjoy everything, every meal, every drink, every sunrise, every kiss . . ." He started crying too.

"We're gonna lie down for a while, girls. Maybe later we'll have dinner or something." My father kissed us both,
620  wet and rough, and the two of them went down the hall.

Lizzie and I just looked at each other.

"Wanna get drunk?" I said.

"No, I don't think so. I guess I'll go lie down for a while unless you want my company." She looked like she was about to sleep standing up, so I shook my head. I was planning on calling John anyway.

Lizzie came over and hugged me, hard, and I hugged her back and brushed the chocolate crumbs out of her hair.

Sitting alone in the kitchen, I thought about John, about
630  telling him about my mother and her affair and how the two men were sacked out in my parents' bed, probably snoring. And I could hear John's silence and I knew that he would think my father must not have really loved my mother, if he'd let her go with another man; or that my mother must have been a real bitch, forcing my father to tolerate an affair "right in his own home," John would think, maybe even say. I thought I ought to call him, before I got myself completely enraged over a phone call that hadn't taken place. Lizzie would say I was projecting anyway.

640  I called John and he was very sweet, asking how I was feeling, how the memorial service had gone, how my father was. And I told him all that and then I knew I couldn't tell him the rest and that I couldn't marry a man I couldn't tell this story to.

"I'm so sorry, Ellen," he said. "You must be very upset. What a difficult day for you."

I realize that that was a perfectly normal response; it just was all wrong for me. I didn't come from a normal family, I wasn't ready to get normal.

650  I felt terrible, hurting John, but I couldn't marry him just

because I didn't want to hurt him, so I said, "And that's not the worst of it, John. I can't marry you, I really can't. I know this is pretty hard to listen to, over the phone . . ." I couldn't think of what else to say.

"Ellen, let's talk about this when you get back to Boston. I know what kind of a strain you must be under. I had the feeling that you were unhappy about some of Mother's ideas. We can work something out when you get back."

660 "I know that you think this is because of my mother's death and it is, but not the way you think, John, I just can't marry you. I'm not going to wear your mother's dress and I'm not going to marry you and I'm very sorry." He was quiet for a long time and then he said, "I don't understand, Ellen. We've already ordered the invitations." And I knew that I was right. If he had said, "Fuck this, I'm coming to see you tonight," or even "I don't know what you're talking about, but I want to marry you anyway," I would have probably changed my mind before I got off the phone. But as it was I said goodbye sort of quietly and hung up.

670 It was like two funerals in one day. I sat at the table, poking the cake into little shapes and then knocking them over. My mother would have sent me out for a walk. I started to clear the stuff away when my father and Mr. DeCuervo appeared, looking more together.

"How about some gin, El?" my father said.

"If you're up for it," said Mr. DeCuervo.

"Okay," I said. "I just broke up with John Wescott."

"Oh?" I couldn't tell which one spoke.

"I told him that I didn't think we'd make each other 680 happy." Which was what I had meant to say.

My father hugged me and said, "I'm sorry if it's hard for you." Then he turned to Mr. DeCuervo and said, "Did she know how to call them or what? Your mother knew you weren't going to marry that guy."

"She was almost always right, Dan."

"Almost always, not quite," said my father, and the two of them laughed at some private joke and shook hands like a pair of old boxers.

"So it's your deal," my father said, leaning back in his 690 chair.

"Penny a point," said Mr. DeCuervo.

*Margaret Atwood*

# *Last Day*

1   This is the last day of the last week.
It's June, the evenings touching
our skins like plush, milkweed sweetening
the sticky air which pulses
with moths, their powdery wings and velvet
tongues. In the dusk, nighthawks and the fluting
voices from the pond, its edges
webbed with spawn. Everything
leans into the pulpy moon.

10  In the mornings the hens
make egg after egg, warty-shelled
and perfect; the henhouse floor
packed with old shit and winter straw
trembles with flies, green and silver.

Who wants to leave it, who wants it
to end, water moving
against water, skin
against skin? We wade
through moist sun-
20  light towards nothing, which is oval

and full. This egg
in my hand is our last meal,
you break it open and the sky
turns orange again and the sun rises
again and this is the last day again.

## *Alice Jones*

# *Anorexia*

1  Not everyone is so skilled
at the ancient art, not everyone
can exist on air, refusing
the burden of flesh. Hating

the yellow globs of fat in any
form—under the skin, padding
the heart, cushions for the eyes'
globes, but mostly those

that mark her as her mother's—
10  the encumbering curves of hip
or breast, she eats only
oranges and water, a cannibal

of self. Trying to undo all
the knots the female body has
tied, the cyclical obligations
to gush, to feed, she chooses

to hone her shape down,
her scapulae prepared like
thin birds, to fly away from
20  the spine. Barely held together

by silk and liquid and air,
she floats, flightless, the water's
iciness along her back;
she tries not to be sucked

down by the black cold,
its deadliness pulling
at the nape of her long neck,
biting at her unfeathered heels.

## *Richard Kenney*

# *Aubade*

1 Cold snap. Five o'clock.
Outside, a heavy frost—dark
footprints in the brittle
grass; a cat's. Quick coffee,
jacket, watch-cap, keys.
Stars blaze across the black
gap between horizons;
pickup somehow strikes
its own dim spark—an arc—
10 starts. Inside, familiar
metal cab, an icebox
full of lightless air,
limns green with dash-light. Vinyl
seat cracks, cold and brittle;
horn ring gleams, and chrome
cuts hard across the wrist
where the sleeve falls off the glove,
as moon-track curves its cool tiara
somewhere underneath your sleep
20 this very moment, love—

*Philip Levine*

# Keats in California

1  The wisteria has come and gone, the plum trees
have burned like candles in the cup of earth,
the almond has shed its pure blossoms
in a soft ring around the trunk. Iris,
rose, tulip, hillsides of poppy and lupin,
gorse, wild mustard, California is blazing
in the foolish winds of April. I have been
reading Keats—the poems, the letters, the life—
for the first time in my 59th year, and I
10  have been watching television after dinner
as though it could bring me some obscure,
distant sign of hope. This morning I rose
late to the soft light off the eucalyptus
and the overbearing odor of orange blossoms.
The trees will give another year. They are giving.
The few, petty clouds will blow away
before noon, and we will have sunshine
without fault, china blue skies, and the bees
gathering to splatter their little honey dots
20  on my windshield. If I drive to the foothills
I can see fields of wildflowers on fire until
I have to look away from so much life.
I could ask myself, Have I made a Soul
today, have I sucked at the teat of the Heart
flooded with the experience of a world like ours?
Have I become a man one more time? At twenty

it made sense. I put down *The Collected Poems,*
left the reserve room of the Wayne library
to wander the streets of Detroit under a gray
30　soiled sky. It was spring there too, and the bells
rang at noon. The out-patients from Harper
waited timidly under the great stone cross
of the Presbyterian church for the trolly
on Woodward Avenue, their pinched faces flushed
with terror. The black tower tilted in the wind
as though it too were coming down. It made sense.
Before dark I'll feel the lassitude enter
first my arms and legs and spread like water
toward the deep organs. I'll lie on my bed
40　hearing the quail bark as they scurry from
cover to cover in their restless searching
after sustenance. This place can break your heart.

*Jay Parini*

# Coal Train

1   Three times a night it woke you
in middle summer, the Erie Lackawanna,
running to the north on thin, loud rails.
You could feel it coming a long way off:
at first, a tremble in your belly,
a wire trilling in your veins, then diesel
rising to a froth beneath your skin.
You could see the cowcatcher,
wide as a mouth and eating ties,
10   the headlight blowing a dust of flies.
There was no way to stop it.
You lay there, fastened to the tracks
and waiting, breathing like a bull,
your fingers lit at the tips like matches.
You waited for the thunder of wheel and bone,
the axles sparking, fire in your spine.
Each passing was a kind of death,
the whistle dwindling to a ghost in air,
the engine losing itself in trees.
20   In a while, your heart was the loudest thing,
your bed was a pool of night.

# WRITING ASSIGNMENTS

1.  Write a story about a terrifying experience that charges the
    atmosphere with danger and suspense. Use details in your
    description that reflect the fear and danger, the heightened
    awareness of reality.

2.  Write a story that takes place at a house in the country
    where a family has spent its summers for many years. In
    your description give us a clear sense of the place. Make
    something happen one summer that leaves a deep
    impression on one of the characters—a love affair, a death,
    a loss of innocence, terror in the night.

3.  Write a descriptive poem about one or more of the seasons
    of the year. Make sure there is some significance in your
    poem. Use some metaphors and similes and appeals to the
    five senses.

4.  Write a descriptive poem about an unusual place, perhaps a
    place that evokes memories or fantasies. One of the
    following might prove interesting:
    a)  an old mill
    b)  a waterfall
    c)  a Pacific island
    d)  a murky swamp
    e)  the scene of a murder
    f)  a hilltop with an ancient tree blasted by lightning
    g)  an abandoned railroad station

5.  Write a descriptive poem about an unusual character,
    someone exotic or beautiful or old and wise; someone
    doomed to die young or destined to achieve a great deal;
    someone with mystical powers, perhaps saintlike or God-
    like or satanic.

# _Chapter 8_

# _Dialogue_

## Introduction

## Fiction

## Drama

## Poetry

## Writing Assignments

It is essential for a writer to know how to deal with the way that people talk, whether it's in a monologue or in a dialogue.

A *monologue* is something spoken by one person, usually to an audience rather than to another person. It is an age-old stage convention that has been used to let the audience know what is on the character's mind or what is going on offstage or what has happened in the past. In fiction the "internal monologue" serves the same purpose, except that it is not spoken aloud (see Chapter 9, "Thoughts").

A *dialogue* is a conversation between two or more people. Dialogue is important in all three genres. In drama it is essential. A play without dialogue becomes something else—pageantry or mime. In fiction it is at least as useful as description in fleshing out a skeleton of events. It makes the bare recital of events come to life. Dialogue is used in poetry, but less frequently than in drama or fiction, since poetry is usually briefer and contains less narrative.

Dialogue is useful in drama and fiction because it can supply the audience or reader with a great deal of information. Characters can be defined not only by what they say, but *how* they say it. Their thoughts can be revealed, and they can also comment on the thoughts of others. We can learn what is happening in the present and what has happened in the past; even what might happen in the future. In Shakespeare's plays, whole battles are described in a few passages of dialogue. Since stage plays have their limitations, dialogue can fill in the gaps in material that might be shown visually in the movies or on television. In certain high-tech entertainments, in fact, special effects sometimes become more important than dialogue.

There are ways in all three genres to isolate the words that are spoken directly by the characters. For all the mechanical details of dialogue form see an appropriate handbook, such as *The College Handbook of Creative Writing* (Harcourt, 1991).

A major problem in writing dialogue is to capture the distinct way in which a character speaks. On the screen it is a lot easier to deal with characters who have accents or who speak in dialect. It is part of the actor's job to know how to speak appropriately. On paper it's another matter. Some writers try to capture an accent by making their spelling a bit more phonetic. A New York character might say: "So, ya wanna go or what?

C'mon, we're gonna be late." Other writers prefer to maintain the standard spelling but remind the reader periodically that the character has a New York or Southern or Western accent, or perhaps a foreign accent of some kind. With such a reminder, it is perfectly possible to avoid the often cumbersome phonetic approach. On the other hand, writers such as Mark Twain have shown us how colorful local accents and dialects can be. Student writers should be very careful about the phonetic approach. One has to be thoroughly familiar with an accent to write it well. It is safer to use a hint of an accent here and there, and perhaps an occasional reminder.

Remember that neither accent nor dialect depend entirely on phonetics. As often as not, the way a sentence is constructed will do the job, as in "I have my notebook forgotten," to imply a German accent. Sometimes the lilt or rhythm of a whole paragraph will suggest a dialect—Caribbean, for instance, or Irish. When it comes to dialogue, it is necessary to develop an ear—that is, to learn to hear in detail how different kinds of people speak.

When the narrator tells us what the characters said, instead of allowing the characters to speak for themselves, we have what is called *indirect dialogue,* or *indirect discourse.* Compare, for instance: *"I love you," said John* with *John said that he loved her.* Furthermore, it is even possible for the narrator merely to *summarize* a whole conversation: "They talked all night in romantic whispers about their love for one another and their plans for the future." There are times when *indirect dialogue* and *summaries* are useful, though *direct dialogue* is usually more immediate and dramatic.

The most important thing to keep in mind about dialogue is that it must be *selective* and *significant.* It is virtually impossible to include, in any genre, every word of a "real-life" conversation. People simply talk too much! And, as we all know, not everything they say is significant. The modern master of minimalist dialogue was Hemingway. Certain contemporary writers are also fond of this sort of suggestive conciseness. It is, however, not the only approach to dialogue, and it runs the risk, at times, of seeming self-conscious or affected.

In "Sawdust," by Chris Offutt, we can find illustrations of several points just made about dialogue. To begin with, the story is in the first person and is told by the main character. This means that we hear the voice of the character throughout, and that character speaks in the accent of Appalachia. His opening line is: "Not a one on this hillside finished high school." They call him Junior. He wants to take the G.E.D. test to get a high school diploma. His brother Delmer says to him: "Hear you're eat up with the smart bug." The language is regional and colorful. The dialogue is *selective* and *significant,* often very brief. Sometimes indirect dialogue is used: "He [Delmer] said the one thing I'm good for was taking care of Mom." The way people talk in this story is part of the theme. These are rural, poor, and uneducated people in one of the most depressed and neglected areas of America. The backwoods quality of the dialogue establishes the environment immediately and effectively. Junior's attempt to become educated and thus vindicate his father is, in a small way, heroic.

In "Should Wizard Hit Mommy?" John Updike handles a complicated problem in dialogue. The father, Jack, is in the habit of telling his young daughter Jo stories that are made up out of his head. She is about four years old, and the stories are usually about animals. One night he tells her about Roger Skunk, who is rejected by the other animals because of his smell. A wizard sets things right and makes him smell like roses. Roger is happy because the other animals like him now. However, his Mommy takes him back and hits the wizard, making him restore Roger's original smell. The question is, should a skunk smell like a skunk? Or should he please his playmates? Should he be himself, or should he change himself to be happy?

The theme of this story-within-a-story relates to the human characters in the larger story. The little girl wants Roger Skunk to smell like roses. Perhaps she too has playmates who don't like her. Perhaps her parents, too, would like to smell nice, but find themselves limited by their own distinctive characters and values.

There are many complexities of dialogue here. Jack talks with Jo as he puts her to bed. They talk about what story he should tell. Jack tells the story, which itself has dialogue in it. Jo keeps interrupting, so that we go back and forth from the skunk story to present action. To complicate things further, Jack has memories of certain past events as all this is happening. Updike keeps all three levels (his own life, his daughter's life, and that of young Roger Skunk) firmly in place, and the theme emerges largely through the dialogue, as in a play. One might speculate as to whether this story would be as effective if the direct dialogue were replaced with narrative or descriptive passages.

Wendy Wasserstein's *Tender Offer* is practically all dialogue, not unusual for a one-act play. The conversation is between Paul and his daughter Lisa, who is nine years old. He has come to pick her up at a dance studio. The dialogue is concise, selective, significant, and absolutely convincing. This play is a good example of how much can be revealed about the characters and the situation without leaving the stage. And it is the dialogue that provides the problem, the development, and the resolution.

Nikki Giovanni's "Poem for a Lady Whose Voice I Like" is entirely a he said–she said dialogue, with a skillful handling of black accents, occasionally a bit phonetic on paper, as in: "you pretty full of yourself ain't chu." There is a very good balance here between standard spelling and phonetic pronunciation.

More extreme is the Caribbean dialect in David Dabydeen's "Coolie Mother." The sound and peculiar vocabulary and grammar of this poem are all essential to the total effect—the cadence especially, but also the meaning.

The incidental use of dialogue in a poem that has a narrative element is nicely illustrated in "The Sweetness of Bobby Hefka," by Philip Levine. The narrator recalls a schoolroom exchange between a naive boy named Bobby, who is afraid of Negroes, and a liberal teacher named Jaslow, who is outraged at this confession of racism. Innocent Bobby explains that he comes from Finland, where the only black person they ever heard of was Joe Louis, the boxer.

In Leonard Nathan's "Ragged Sonnets" we find some incidental dialogue—actually a quote from an anonymous poet—and, in one of the sonnets, an amusing example of how a foreign accent might be captured. This sonnet is, supposedly, a letter from Arthur Schopenhauer to Nathan (the author). The blend of English and German results in genuine comedy: "I warned you beauty ist ein trick conjured/ by Natur up to fool you into love . . ."

"The Blues Don't Change" by Al Young is a poem addressed to the blues by someone who speaks that language. There is no phonetic adjustment in the spelling, and yet we imagine we can hear the rhythm and proper pronunciation. A whole way of speaking and maybe a whole way of life is suggested in passages such as, ". . . you mean old grudgeful-hearted, table-/turning demon, you, you sexy soul-sucking gem."

## *Chris Offutt*

# *Sawdust*

1   Not a one on this hillside finished high school. Around here, a man is judged by how he acts, not how smart he's supposed to be. I don't hunt, fish, or work. Neighbors say I think too much. They say I'm like my father, and Mom worries that maybe they're right.

When I was a kid we had a dog that got into a skunk, then had the gall to sneak under the porch. He whimpered in the dark and wouldn't come out. Dad shot him. It didn't stink less but Dad felt better. He told Mom that any dog not know-
10  ing the difference between coon and skunk ought to be killed.

"He's still back under the porch," Mom said.

"I know it," Dad answered. "I loved Tater, too. I don't reckon I could stand to bury him."

He looked at my brother and me.

"Don't you even think of putting them boys under that porch," Mom yelled, "It's your dog. You get it."

She held her nose and walked around the house. Dad looked at us again. "You boys smell anything?"

My eyes were watered up but I shook my head no.
20  "Dead things stink," said Delmer.

"So does a wife sometimes," Dad said. He handed me his rifle. "Here Junior. Put this up and fetch my rod and reel."

I ran into the house for his fishing pole and when I got outside, Dad was on his knees shining a flashlight under the porch. Back in the corner lay old Tater, dead as a mallet. Dad took the fishing pole. "Blind casting," he said. "This might turn out fun."

He spread his legs and whipped the rod, line humming under the porch. A piece of rag came reeling back. Dad threw
30  again, and hooked Tater but only pulled out a hunk of fur. On the next cast, his line got hung. Dad jerked hard on the fishing pole. The line snapped and the rod lashed over his shoulder and hit Delmer in the face. Mom came running around the house at Delmer's screams.

"What'd you do now?" she said.

"Line broke," said Dad. "Forty pound test. Lost a good split sinker, too."

"Why don't you cut a hole in the floor and fish him out like an ice pond!"

40 "Don't know where my saw's at."

"That's the worst of it! You'd have gone and done it."

She towed Delmer up the grey board steps into the house. Dad broke the fishing pole across his knee. "Never should have had no kids," he said, and threw the ruined rod over the hill. A jaybird squalled into the sky. Dad grabbed my shoulders and leaned his face to mine. "I wanted to be a horse doctor," he said, "but you know what?"

I shook my head. His fingers dug me deep.

"I quit sixth grade on account of not having nothing to
50 wear. All my kin did. Clothes was falling off us like bark."

He turned loose of me and I watched his bowed back fade into the trees. Wide leaves of poplar rustled behind him.

Seven months later Dad gave his gun away and joined the church. He got me and Delmer a pup that fell off the porch and broke its leg. Dad cried all day. I was scared, but Mom said his crying was a sign both his oars were back in the water again. She told me to be proud. That Sunday, Dad climbed on top of a church pew in the middle of service. I thought he'd felt the Lord's touch and would start talking in tongues. The
60 preacher stopped his sermon. Dad looked around the room and swore to high heaven he would heal our pup's busted leg, or die trying. Mom made him sit down and hush.

After church Dad carried the pup out the ridge to a hickory where he tried all day to fix its leg. He was still yelling at God when Mom sent us to bed. She found Dad in the morning. He'd taken off his belt and hanged himself. On the ground below him lay the pup, all its legs broken. It was still alive.

Delmer got a job and Mom got religion big time. I quit school and took to the woods hunting mushrooms, ginseng,
70 and mayapple root. I've been places a rabbit wouldn't go. Nothing but the trees knew how much crying I did out there.

Last fall Delmer pushed a trailer up a hollow and moved into it. He said the one thing I'm good for was taking care of Mom. Twice a week I walked to the old post office at the foot of the hill. It and the church was all we got and they sat side by side between the creek and the road. Most folks went to both

but me and Mom divided it up. I got more mail than her and
she took enough gospel for the whole county. I subscribed to a
whole big bunch of magazines and read everything twice, even
80  letters and household hints. Books aren't bad if they're full of
facts but I don't care much for the story kind. I've read at them
without much luck.

Some days I went to the post office early to look at
crooks the government wants. Sixty photographs were stapled
together like a feedstore calendar and the faces were just regular folks. Under each one was a list of what all the person did,
where their scars were, and if they were black or white. It
seemed odd to show a picture of a man and say what color he
was. Around here, we're mostly brown. I wouldn't mind talk-
90  ing to somebody of another color but they don't ever come
around these parts. Nobody does. This is a place folks move
away from.

One afternoon I saw a sign in the post office about a
G.E.D. Anyone could take the high school test from a VISTA
center in town. That set me to thinking on what Dad said
about quitting school. He never read anything but the King
James Bible and about a hundred maps. Dad collected maps
the way some folks keep dogs. He had big maps and little
maps, favorites and no-counts. I've seen him study maps over a
100 tree stump till way past dark. He wanted to know where the
Land of Nod was at and who all lived there. The preacher told
him it was lost in the Flood. Dad didn't think so. "Everywhere
has to be somewhere," he always said.

The G.E.D. fretted me for two days worth of walking in
the woods. I almost stepped on a blue racer sunning on a rock.
We watched each other for a spell, him shooting a little forked
tongue out and me not able to think of nothing but taking that
test. Most men ran from a snake without ever knowing if it
was poison, or just alive. The G.E.D. was the same way. Fail-
110 ing couldn't hurt me none and getting it would make everybody on the hill know I wasn't what they thought. Maybe then
they'd think about Dad different, too.

The next morning I hitchhiked to town and stood on the
sidewalk, more nervous than the time a bear saw me in the
woods. People stared from cars. My hand was on the test place
doorknob and sweat poured off me. I opened the door. The air
was cool and the walls were white. An air conditioner rattled
in the window casing. Behind a metal desk sat a lady painting

her fingernails pink, and the whole room stunk of polish. She
120 looked at me like I was a post office photograph.

"The barbershop is next door," she said.

"I don't want a haircut, ma'am. I might could use one
but that ain't what I come to town for."

"It ain't," she said like she was mocking me. She talked
fast and didn't always say her words right. I wondered what
brought her to the hills. Things must be getting awful bad if
city folks were coming here for work.

"I'll take that G.E.D." I said.

"Who sent you?"

130 "Nobody."

She stared at me a long time. Her hand moved like she
was waving away flies and when the nail polish was dry, she
opened a drawer and gave me a study book. It was magazine-
size with a black plastic binder.

"Come back when you're ready," she said. "I'm here to
help you people."

I was three hours walking home and the heat didn't
bother me a bit. By the time I got to the house, somebody had
seen me in town and told a neighbor who told Mom at the
140 prayer meeting. That's the way it is around here. A man can
cough and it'll beat him back to the porch.

"They say you're fixing to get learned up on us,"
she said.

"Might do it."

"You might read the Bible while you're at it."

"I done did. Twice."

"I ain't raised no heathen then."

After supper I hit those practice tests. My best was
reading and worst was math. A man can take a mess of
150 figures and make it equal out to something different. Maybe
some folks like math for that, but a pile of stovewood
doesn't equal a tree. It made me wonder where the sawdust
went to in a math problem. After all that ciphering, there
wasn't nothing to show for the work, nothing to clean up,
nothing to look at. A string of numbers was like an owl
pellet laying in a game path. You knew a bird had flew over,
but not the direction.

Outside, Delmer's four-wheel-drive pickup raised the
road dust. Used to, he worked on mufflers until they started
160 building a car plant in Lexington and now he drives three
hours a day to work and back. He's got a video dish and a
microwave, Delmer does.

His boots hit the porch and the front door slammed. He walked in our old room. "What do you know, Junior? All on your ownself and afraid to tell it."

I grinned and shook my head. After Dad died, Delmer went all out to make people like him. I went the other way.

"Hear you're eat up with the smart bug," he said. "And taking that school test in town."

"Thinking on it."

"You ought to let up on that and try working. Then you can wear alligator-hide boots like these."

He pulled a pantleg up.

"Where'd you get them from?" I asked.

"Down to Lex. They got a mall big as two pastures laid end to end. I bought these here boots right out of the window. Paid the man cash, too."

"He saw you coming, Delmer. They ain't made no alligator nothing in nigh ten years. Government's got them took care of."

"What makes you to know so much?"

"Read it in a magazine."

Delmer frowned. He doesn't put much store in anything but tv. Commercials are real people to him. I knew he was getting mad by a neck vein that popped up big as a nightcrawler.

"I ought to kick your butt with these boots."

"That won't make them gator."

"It won't take the new out either. And you're still wearing them goddam wishbook clodhoppers."

"Delmer!" Mom screeched from the kitchen.

She doesn't mind cussing too awful much but taking the Lord's name in vain is one thing she won't stand for. Dad used to do it just to spite her.

"You know what G.E.D. stands for?" Delmer said. "Get Even Dumber. And that's what you'll be."

He stomped to his truck and rammed it through the gears, flying low out the ridge. I went outside and watched the moon haul itself above the far ridge. Night crawled up the hollow. A long time ago I was scared of the dark until Dad told me it was the same as day, only the air was of a different color. I sat on his old map-stump and wondered if alligators knew the government watched out for them.

In a week I'd taken every practice test twice and was ready for the real one. Word got out. Everybody on the hill knew what I was doing. The preacher guaranteed Mom a sweet place in Heaven for all her burdens on earth. He said I was too hardheaded for my own good.

I got to thinking about that in the woods and decided maybe it wasn't a bad thing to be. I'm not one to pick wild-flowers and bring them inside where they'll die quicker. And I'll not cut down a summer shade tree to burn for winter firewood. Taking the G.E.D. was the first time I'd ever been hardheaded over the doing of something, instead of the not doing. Right there's where Dad and me were different. He was hardheaded over things he never had a say in.

In the morning I left the hill and walked halfway to town before getting a ride that dropped me off at the test place. The lady was surprised to see me and treated me real nice. She wrote my name on a form. Then she wanted fifteen dollars to take the test and I didn't say anything.

"Do you have the fee?" she asked.

"No."

"Do you have a job?"

"No."

"Do you live with family."

"Mom."

"Does she have a job?"

"No."

"Do you receive welfare assistance?"

"No, ma'am."

"Then how do you and your mother get along?"

"We don't talk much."

She tightened her mouth and shook her head. Her voice came slow and loud, like I was deaf.

"What do you and your mother do for money?"

"Never had a need till now."

"What about food?"

"We grow it."

The lady set her pencil down and leaned away from the desk. On the wall behind her hung a picture of the governor wearing a tie. A car horn honked outside. I looked through the window at the hardware store across the street. Dad died owing it half on a new chain saw. We got a bill after the funeral and Mom sold a quilt her great-aunt made to pay it off.

I was thinking hard and not getting far. There wasn't nothing I had to sell. Delmer would give me the money but I could never ask him. Then the thinking ran out and I started feeling. It wasn't good either. I felt sticky and sick, like I was

250 supposed to already know a man needs money. I turned to
leave.

"Junior," said the lady. "You can take the test anyway."
"I don't need the help."
"It's free when you're living in poverty."
"I'll owe you," I said. "Pay you before the first snow."
She nodded and led me through a door to a small room
with no windows. I squeezed into a school desk and she gave
me four yellow pencils and the test. When I finished, the lady
said to come back in a month and see if I passed. She told me in
260 a soft voice that I could take the test as many times as necessary. I nodded and headed out of town towards home. I
couldn't think or feel. I was doing good to walk.

Every night Mom claimed a worry that I was getting
above my raisings. Delmer wouldn't talk to me at all. I wandered the hills, thinking of what all I knew about the woods. I
can name a bird by its nest and a tree by the bark. A cucumber
smell means a copperhead's close. Yellowroot will cure the
bellyache. The sweetest blackberries are low to the ground and
locust makes the best fence post. I'm not special for knowing
270 these things. It's what it takes to live here's all. Same as city
people knowing what streets are safe and how to wait in lines.
It struck me funny that I had to take a test to learn what I
was living in. I'd say the knowing of it is what drove Dad off
his feed for good. When he died, Mom burned his maps but I
saved the one of Kentucky. Where we live wasn't on it.
I stayed in the woods three weeks straight until finally
going to the post office. The mail hadn't run yet and a bunch
of folks were waiting outside, visiting with one another. We
had a store once but the man who ran it died. Now church and
280 the post office were the main places to see people. The oldest
sat in the post office, out of the sun. The rest of us stood
in willow shade by the creek. Two Skaggs brothers took to
calling me Doctor on account of the G.E.D. They're meaner
than striped snakes, all those Skaggs are.

"Hey Doctor, you aiming to get smart and rich?"
"Yeah," said his brother. "He's going to start a whore-
house and run it by hand."
Everybody laughed, even a couple of old women with
hair buns like split pine cones. I decided to skip the mail and go
290 home. Then the one boy made me mad.

"I got a sick pup at the house, Doctor. You as good on
them as your Daddy was?"

Way it is around here, I had to do more than just fight. Sometimes a man will lay back a year before shooting somebody's dog to get its owner back, but with everyone watching, I couldn't just leave. I walked to their pickup and kicked out a headlight. The youngest Skaggs came running at me but I tripped him and he rolled in the dirt. The other one laid into me from behind, on my back, tearing at my ear with his teeth. I
300 tried to flip him but his legs were tight around me. His fist kept hitting the right side of my face. I staggered in a circle and fell backwards on the truck hood and he let go of me then. Two old men held back the other boy. I crossed the creek and climbed the steep hill home, spitting blood every step.

Mom never said a word one after she heard what the fight was over. Delmer came by the next night. His knuckles were split open and a shirt sleeve was ripped from cuff to elbow.

"I got one at the creek and the other at the head of their
310 holler," he said. "They'll not talk that way no more."

"Whip them pretty bad?"

"They knowed they was in a fight."

Delmer'd taken a lick or two in the jaw, and his neck vein was puffed out again. A railroad tie won't knock him over.

"You getting that G.E.D?" he asked.

"Friday."

"I'm getting me a tv that runs on batteries."

"What for?"
320 "To set and look at."

"Same with me, Delmer. Same with me."

He pushed his fingers at a swollen place below his cheek bone. His shoulders sagged. "I'll fight for you, Junior. And for Daddy, too. But I never could figure what a one of you ever was up to."

He walked across the front room floor and out the door, and I watched him drive away. The thinking wouldn't come. All I could do was feel. There's a lot worse brother to have than mine.

330 On Friday I walked the ridgeline above the creek all the way to town. The woods kept me calm and I ate wild grapes and fiddlehead tops. Town lay in a wide bottom between the hills. I'd never seen it from above and it looked pretty small, nothing to be afraid of. I walked down the slope, crossed the creek, and stepped onto the sidewalk. For a long time I stood

in front of the test center. I could leave now and never know if I passed or flunked. Either one scared me. I opened the door and walked in. I might be a dropout but I'm no chicken.

"Congratulations," said the lady.

340 She handed me a state certificate saying I'd achieved a high school degree. My name was written in black ink. Below it was a gold seal and the governor's signature.

"I have a job application for you," she said. "It isn't a promise of work but you qualify now. Employment is the next step out."

"All I wanted was this."

"Not a job?"

"No, ma'am."

She sighed and looked down, rubbing her eyes. She 350 leaned against the doorjamb. "Sometimes I don't know what I'm doing here," she said.

"None of us do," I grinned. "Most folks around here are just waiting to die."

"That's not funny, Junior."

"No, but what's funny is, everybody gets up awful early anyhow."

"I like to sleep late," she said.

She was still smiling when I shut the door behind me. I'd come as close as a man could get to finishing school and it 360 didn't feel half bad. At the edge of town I looked back at the row of two-story buildings. Dad used to say a smart man wouldn't bother with town but he was wrong. Anybody can go there any time. Town's just a bunch of people living together in the only wide place between the hills.

I left the road and walked through horseweed to the creek bank. It was a good way to find pop bottles and I still owed the state fifteen dollars.

## *John Updike*

·+·◄◄►◄·  ·+··+·  ◄◄►◄·  ·+·

# *Should Wizard Hit Mommy?*

1  In the evenings and for Saturday naps like today's, Jack told his daughter Jo a story out of his head. This custom, begun when she was two, was itself now nearly two years old, and his head felt empty. Each new story was a slight variation of a basic tale: a small creature, usually named Roger (Roger Fish, Roger Squirrel, Roger Chipmunk), had some problem and went with it to the wise old owl. The owl told him to go to the wizard, and the wizard performed a magic spell that solved the problem, demanding in payment a number of pennies greater
10  than the number Roger Creature had but in the same breath directing the animal to a place where the extra pennies could be found. Then Roger was so happy he played many games with other creatures, and went home to his mother just in time to hear the train whistle that brought his daddy home from Boston. Jack described their supper, and the story was over. Working his way through this scheme was especially fatiguing on Saturday, because Jo never fell asleep in naps any more, and knowing this made the rite seem futile.

The little girl (not so little any more; the bumps her feet
20  made under the covers were halfway down the bed, their big double bed that they let her be in for naps and when she was sick) had at last arranged herself, and from the way her fat face deep in the pillow shone in the sunlight sifting through the drawn shades, it did not seem fantastic that something magic would occur, and she would take her nap like an infant of two. Her brother, Bobby, was two, and already asleep with his bottle. Jack asked, "Who shall the story be about today?"

"Roger . . ." Jo squeezed her eyes shut and smiled to be thinking she was thinking. Her eyes opened, her mother's blue.
30  "Skunk," she said firmly.

A new animal; they must talk about skunks at nursery

school. Having a fresh hero momentarily stirred Jack to creative enthusiasm. "All right," he said. "Once upon a time, in the deep dark woods, there was a tiny little creature name of Roger Skunk. And he smelled very bad——"

"Yes," Jo said.

"He smelled so bad none of the other little woodland creatures would play with him." Jo looked at him solemnly; she hadn't foreseen this. "Whenever he would go out to play,"
40  Jack continued with zest, remembering certain humiliations of his own childhood, "all of the other tiny animals would cry, 'Uh-oh, here comes Roger Stinky Skunk,' and they would run away, and Roger Skunk would stand there all alone, and two little round tears would fall from his eyes." The corners of Jo's mouth drooped down and her lower lip bent forward as he traced with a forefinger along the side of her nose the course of one of Roger Skunk's tears.

"Won't he see the owl?" she asked in a high and faintly roughened voice.
50    Sitting on the bed beside her, Jack felt the covers tug as her legs switched tensely. He was pleased with this moment— he was telling her something true, something she must know —and had no wish to hurry on. But downstairs a chair scraped, and he realized he must get down to help Clare paint the living-room woodwork.

"Well, he walked along very sadly and came to a very big tree, and in the tiptop of the tree was an enormous wise old owl."

"Good."
60    "'Mr. Owl,' Roger Skunk said, 'all the other little animals run away from me because I smell so bad.' 'So you do,' the owl said. 'Very, very bad.' 'What can I do?' Roger Skunk said, and he cried very hard."

"The wizard, the wizard," Jo shouted, and sat right up, and a Little Golden Book spilled from the bed.

"Now, Jo. Daddy's telling the story. Do you want to tell Daddy the story?"

"No. You me."

"Then lie down and be sleepy."
70    Her head relapsed onto the pillow and she said, "Out of your head."

"Well. The owl thought and thought. At last he said, 'Why don't you go see the wizard?'"

"Daddy?"

"What?"

"Are magic spells *real?*" This was a new phase, just this last month, a reality phase. When he told her spiders eat bugs, she turned to her mother and asked, "Do they *really?*" and when Clare told her God was in the sky and all around them, she turned to her father and insisted, with a sly yet eager smile, "Is He *really?*"

80 "They're real in stories," Jack answered curtly. She had made him miss a beat in the narrative. "The owl said, 'Go through the dark woods, under the apple trees, into the swamp, over the crick——'"

"What's a crick?"

"A little river. 'Over the crick, and there will be the wizard's house.' And that's the way Roger Skunk went, and pretty soon he came to a little white house, and he rapped on the door." Jack rapped on the window sill, and under the covers Jo's tall figure clenched in an infantile thrill. "And then

90 a tiny little old man came out, with a long white beard and a pointed blue hat, and said, 'Eh? Whatzis? Whatcher want? You smell awful.'" The wizard's voice was one of Jack's own favorite effects; he did it by scrunching up his face and somehow whining through his eyes, which felt for the interval rheumy. He felt being an old man suited him.

"'I know it,' Roger Skunk said, 'and all the little animals run away from me. The enormous wise owl said you could help me.'"

"'Eh? Well, maybe. Come on in. Don't git too close.'

100 Now inside, Jo, there were all these magic things, all jumbled together in a big dusty heap, because the wizard did not have any cleaning lady."

"Why?"

"Why? Because he was a wizard, and a very old man."

"Will he die?"

"No. Wizards don't die. Well, he rummaged around and found an old stick called a magic wand and asked Roger Skunk what he wanted to smell like. Roger thought and thought and said, 'Roses.'"

110 "Yes. Good," Jo said smugly.

Jack fixed her with a trancelike gaze and chanted in the wizard's elderly irritable voice:

> "'Abracadabry, hocus-poo,
> Roger Skunk, how do you do,
> Roses, boses, pull an ear,
> Roger Skunk, you never fear:
> *Bingo!*'"

120       He paused as a rapt expression widened out from his-daughter's nostrils, forcing her eyebrows up and her lower lip down in a wide noiseless grin, an expression in which Jack was startled to recognize his wife feigning pleasure at cocktail parties. "And all of a sudden," he whispered, "the whole inside of the wizard's house was full of the smell of—*roses!* 'Roses!' Roger Fish cried. And the wizard said, very cranky, 'That'll be seven pennies.'"

"Daddy."

"What?"

130       "Roger *Skunk*. You said Roger Fish."

"Yes. Skunk."

"You said Roger *Fish*. Wasn't that silly?"

"Very silly of your stupid old daddy. Where was I? Well, you know about the pennies."

"Say it."

"O.K. Roger Skunk said, 'But all I have is four pennies,' and he began to cry." Jo made the crying face again, but this time without a trace of sincerity. This annoyed Jack. Downstairs some more furniture rumbled. Clare shouldn't move 140 heavy things; she was six months pregnant. It would be their third.

"So the wizard said, 'Oh, very well. Go to the end of the lane and turn around three times and look down the magic well and there you will find three pennies. Hurry up.' So Roger Skunk went to the end of the lane and turned around three times and there in the magic well were *three pennies!* So he took them back to the wizard and was very happy and ran out into the woods and all the other little animals gathered around him because he smelled so good. And they played tag, base-150 ball, football, basketball, lacrosse, hockey, soccer, and pick-up-sticks."

"What's pick-up-sticks?"

"It's a game you play with sticks."

"Like the wizard's magic wand?"

"Kind of. And they played games and laughed all afternoon and then it began to get dark and they all ran home to their mommies."

Jo was starting to fuss with her hands and look out of the window, at the crack of day that showed under the 160 shade. She thought the story was all over. Jack didn't like women when they took anything for granted; he liked them apprehensive, hanging on his words. "Now, Jo, are you listening?"

"Yes."

"Because this is very interesting. Roger Skunk's mommy said, 'What's that awful smell?'"

"Wha-at?"

"And Roger Skunk said, 'It's me, Mommy. I smell like roses.' And she said, 'Who made you smell like that?' And he
170 said, 'The wizard,' and she said, 'Well, of all the nerve. You come with me and we're going right back to that very awful wizard.'"

Jo sat up, her hands dabbling in the air with genuine fright. "But Daddy, then he said about the other little aminals run *away!*" Her hands skittered off, into the underbrush.

"All right. He said, 'But Mommy, all the other little animals run away,' and she said, 'I don't care. You smelled the way a little skunk should have and I'm going to take you right back to that wizard,' and she took an umbrella and went back
180 with Roger Skunk and hit that wizard right over the head."

"No," Jo said, and put her hand out to touch his lips, yet even in her agitation did not quite dare to stop the source of truth. Inspiration came to her. "Then the wizard hit *her* on the head and did not change that little skunk back."

"No," he said. "The wizard said 'O.K.' and Roger Skunk did not smell of roses any more. He smelled very bad again."

"But the other little amum—*oh!*—amum——"

"Joanne. It's Daddy's story. Shall Daddy not tell you any
190 more stories?" Her broad face looked at him through sifted light, astounded. "This is what happened, then. Roger Skunk and his mommy went home and they heard *Woo-oo, woooo-oo* and it was the choo-choo train bringing Daddy Skunk home from Boston. And they had lima beans, pork chops, celery, liver, mashed potatoes, and Pie-Oh-My for dessert. And when Roger Skunk was in bed Mommy Skunk came up and hugged him and said he smelled like her little baby skunk again and she loved him very much. And that's the end of the story."

200 "But Daddy."

"What?"

"Then did the other little ani-mals run away?"

"No, because eventually they got used to the way he was and did not mind it at all."

"What's evenshiladee?"

"In a little while."

"That was a stupid mommy."

"It was *not*," he said with rare emphasis, and believed, from her expression, that she realized he was defending his

210 own mother to her, or something as odd. "Now I want you to put your big heavy head in the pillow and have a good long nap." He adjusted the shade so not even a crack of day showed, and tiptoed to the door, in the pretense that she was already asleep. But when he turned, she was crouching on top of the covers and staring at him. "Hey. Get under the covers and fall faaast asleep. Bobby's asleep."

She stood up and bounced gingerly on the springs. "Daddy."

"What?"

220 "Tomorrow, I want you to tell me the story that that wizard took that magic wand and hit that mommy"—her plump arms chopped fiercely—"right over the head."

"No. That's not the story. The point is that the little skunk loved his mommy more than he loved aaalll the other little animals and she knew what was right."

"No. Tomorrow you say he hit that mommy. Do it." She kicked her legs up and sat down on the bed with a great heave and complaint of springs, as she had done hundreds of times before, except that this time she did not laugh. "Say it,
230 Daddy."

"Well, we'll see. Now at least have a rest. Stay on the bed. You're a good girl."

He closed the door and went downstairs. Clare had spread the newspapers and opened the paint can and, wearing an old shirt of his on top of her maternity smock, was stroking the chair rail with a dipped brush. Above him footsteps vibrated and he called "*Joanne*. Shall I come up there and spank you?" The footsteps hesitated.

"That was a long story," Clare said.

240 "The poor kid," he answered, and with utter weariness watched his wife labor. The woodwork, a cage of moldings and rails and baseboards all around them, was half old tan and half new ivory and he felt caught in an ugly middle position, and though he as well felt his wife's presence in the cage with him, he did not want to speak with her, work with her, touch her, anything.

# Wendy Wasserstein

# *Tender Offer*

1  *SETTING*

*A girl of around nine is alone in a dance studio. She is dressed in tradi-tional leotards and tights. She begins singing to herself, "Nothing Could be Finer Than to Be in Carolina." She maps out a dance routine, including parts for the chorus. She builds to a finale. A man, PAUL, around thirty-five, walks in. He has a sweet, though distant, demeanor. As he walks in, LISA notices him and stops.*

|  | PAUL | You don't have to stop, sweetheart. |
|---|---|---|
|  | LISA | That's okay. |
| 10 | PAUL | Looked very good. |
|  | LISA | Thanks. |
|  | PAUL | Don't I get a kiss hello? |
|  | LISA | Sure. |
|  | PAUL | *(Embraces her.)* Hi, Tiger. |
|  | LISA | Hi, Dad. |
|  | PAUL | I'm sorry I'm late. |
|  | LISA | That's okay. |
|  | PAUL | How'd it go? |
|  | LISA | Good. |
| 20 | PAUL | Just good? |
|  | LISA | Pretty good. |
|  | PAUL | "Pretty good." You mean you got a lot of applause or "pretty good" you could have done better. |
|  | LISA | Well, Courtney Palumbo's mother thought I was pretty good. But you know the part in the middle when everybody's supposed to freeze and the big girl comes out. Well, I think I moved a little bit. |
|  | PAUL | I thought what you were doing looked very good. |
| 30 | LISA | Daddy, that's not what I was doing. That was tap-dancing. I made that up. |

| | |
|---|---|
| Paul | Oh. Well it looked good. Kind of sexy. |
| Lisa | Yuch! |
| Paul | What do you mean "yuch?" |
| Lisa | Just yuch! |
| Paul | You don't want to be sexy? |
| Lisa | I don't care. |
| Paul | Let's go, Tiger. I promised your mother I'd get you home in time for dinner. |
| 40 Lisa | I can't find my leg warmers. |
| Paul | You can't find your what? |
| Lisa | Leg warmers. I can't go home till I find my leg warmers. |
| Paul | I don't see you looking for them. |
| Lisa | I was waiting for you. |
| Paul | Oh. |
| Lisa | Daddy. |
| Paul | What? |
| Lisa | Nothing. |
| 50 Paul | Where do you think you left them? |
| Lisa | Somewhere around here. I can't remember. |
| Paul | Well, try to remember, Lisa. We don't have all night. |
| Lisa | I told you. I think somewhere around here. |
| Paul | I don't see them. Let's go home now. You'll call the dancing school tomorrow. |
| Lisa | Daddy, I can't go home till I find them. Miss Judy says it's not professional to leave things. |
| Paul | Who's Miss Judy? |
| 60 Lisa | She's my ballet teacher. She once danced the lead in *Swan Lake,* and she was a June Taylor dancer. |
| Paul | Well, then, I'm sure she'll understand about the leg warmers. |
| Lisa | Daddy, Miss Judy wanted to know why you were late today. |
| Paul | Hmmmmmmmm? |
| Lisa | Why were you late? |
| Paul | I was in a meeting. Business. I'm sorry. |
| Lisa | Why did you tell Mommy you'd come instead of |
| 70 | her if you knew you had business? |
| Paul | Honey, something just came up. I thought I'd be able to be here. I was looking forward to it. |
| Lisa | I wish you wouldn't make appointments to see me. |

| | |
|---|---|
| Paul | Hmmmmmmm. |
| Lisa | You shouldn't make appointments to see me unless you know you're going to come. |
| Paul | Of course I'm going to come. |
| Lisa | No, you're not. Talia Robbins told me she's much |
| 80 | happier living without her father in the house. Her father used to come home late and go to sleep early. |
| Paul | Lisa, stop it. Let's go. |
| Lisa | I can't find my leg warmers. |
| Paul | Forget your leg warmers. |
| Lisa | Daddy. |
| Paul | What is it? |
| Lisa | I saw this show on television, I think it was WPIX Channel 11. Well, the father was crying about his |
| 90 | daughter. |
| Paul | Why was he crying? Was she sick? |
| Lisa | No. She was at school. And he was at business. And he just missed her, so he started to cry. |
| Paul | What was the name of this show? |
| Lisa | I don't know. I came in in the middle. |
| Paul | Well, Lisa, I certainly would cry if you were sick or far away, but I know that you're well and you're home. So no reason to get maudlin. |
| Lisa | What's maudlin? |
| 100 Paul | Sentimental, soppy. Frequently used by children who make things up to get attention. |
| Lisa | I am sick! I am sick! I have Hodgkin's disease and a bad itch on my leg. |
| Paul | What do you mean you have Hodgkin's disease? Don't say things like that. |
| Lisa | Swoosie Kurtz, she had Hodgkin's disease on a TV movie last year, but she got better and now she's on *Love Sidney.* |
| Paul | Who is Swoosie Kurtz? |
| 110 Lisa | She's an actress named after an airplane. I saw her on *Live at Five.* |
| Paul | You watch too much television; you should do your homework. Now, put your coat on. |
| Lisa | Daddy, I really do have a bad itch on my leg. Would you scratch it? |
| Paul | Lisa, you're procrastinating. |
| Lisa | Why do you use words I don't understand? I hate it. You're like Daria Feldman's mother. She |

|     |       |                                                                                                                    |
| --- | ----- | ------------------------------------------------------------------------------------------------------------------ |
| 120 |       | always talks in Yiddish to her husband so Daria won't understand.                                                   |
|     | PAUL  | Procrastinating is not Yiddish.                                                                                     |
|     | LISA  | Well, I don't know what it is.                                                                                      |
|     | PAUL  | Procrastinating means you don't want to go about your business.                                                     |
|     | LISA  | I don't go to business. I go to school.                                                                             |
|     | PAUL  | What I mean is you want to hang around here until you and I are late for dinner and your mother's angry and it's too late for you to do your homework. |
| 130 | LISA  | I do not.                                                                                                           |
|     | PAUL  | Well, it sure looks that way. Now put your coat on and let's go.                                                    |
|     | LISA  | Daddy.                                                                                                              |
|     | PAUL  | Honey, I'm tired. Really, later.                                                                                    |
|     | LISA  | Why don't you want to talk to me?                                                                                   |
|     | PAUL  | I do want to talk to you. I promise when we get home we'll have a nice talk.                                        |
|     | LISA  | No, we won't. You'll read the paper and fall asleep in front of the news.                                          |
| 140 | PAUL  | Honey, we'll talk on the weekend, I promise. Aren't I taking you to the theater this weekend? Let me look. *(He takes out appointment book.)* Yes. Sunday. *Joseph and the Amazing Technicolor Raincoat* with Lisa. Okay, Tiger? |
|     | LISA  | Sure. It's Dreamcoat.                                                                                               |
|     | PAUL  | What?                                                                                                               |
|     | LISA  | Nothing. I think I see my leg warmers. *(She goes to pick them up, and an odd-looking trophy.)*                     |
|     | PAUL  | What's that?                                                                                                        |
| 150 | LISA  | It's stupid. I was second best at the dance recital, so they gave me this thing. It's stupid.                       |
|     | PAUL  | Lisa.                                                                                                               |
|     | LISA  | What?                                                                                                               |
|     | PAUL  | What did you want to talk about?                                                                                    |
|     | LISA  | Nothing.                                                                                                            |
|     | PAUL  | Was it about my missing your recital? I'm really sorry, Tiger. I would have liked to have been here.               |
|     | LISA  | That's okay.                                                                                                        |
|     | PAUL  | Honest?                                                                                                             |
| 160 | LISA  | Daddy, you're prostrastinating.                                                                                     |
|     | PAUL  | I'm procrastinating. Sit down. Let's talk. So. How's school?                                                       |

| | | |
|---|---|---|
| | LISA | Fine. |
| | PAUL | You like it? |
| | LISA | Yup. |
| | PAUL | You looking forward to camp this summer? |
| | LISA | Yup. |
| | PAUL | Is Daria Feldman going back? |
| | LISA | Nope. |
| 170 | PAUL | Why not? |

LISA     I don't know. We can go home now. Honest, my foot doesn't itch anymore.

PAUL     Lisa, you know what you do in business when it seems like there's nothing left to say? That's when you really start talking. Put a bid on the table.

LISA     What's a bid?

PAUL     You tell me what you want and I'll tell you what I've got to offer. Like Monopoly. You want Boardwalk, but I'm only willing to give you the
180     Railroads. Now, because you are my daughter I'd throw in Water Works and Electricity. Understand, Tiger?

LISA     No. I don't like board games. You know, Daddy, we could get Space Invaders for our home for thirty-five dollars. In fact, we could get an Osborne System for two thousand. Daria Feldman's parents . . .

PAUL     Daria Feldman's parents refuse to talk to Daria, so they bought a computer to keep Daria busy so
190     they won't have to speak in Yiddish. Daria will probably grow up to be a homicidal maniac lesbian prostitute.

LISA     I know what that word prostitute means.

PAUL     Good. *(Pause.)* You still haven't told me about school. Do you still like your teacher?

LISA     She's okay.

PAUL     Lisa, if we're talking try to answer me.

LISA     I am answering you. Can we go home now, please?

200     PAUL     Damn it, Lisa, if you want to talk to me . . . Talk to me!

LISA     I can't wait till I'm old enough so I can make my own money and never have to see you again. Maybe I'll become a prostitute.

PAUL     Young lady, that's enough.

LISA     I hate you, Daddy! I hate you! *(She throws her trophy into the trash bin.)*

|   | PAUL | What'd you do that for? |
|---|---|---|
|   | LISA | It's stupid. |
| 210 | PAUL | Maybe I wanted it. |
|   | LISA | What for? |
|   | PAUL | Maybe I wanted to put it where I keep your dinosaur and the picture you made of Mrs. Kimbel with the chicken pox. |
|   | LISA | You got mad at me when I made that picture. You told me I had to respect Mrs. Kimbel because she was my teacher. |
|   | PAUL | That's true. But she wasn't my teacher. I liked her better with the chicken pox. *(Pause.)* Lisa, I'm |
| 220 |   | sorry. I was very wrong to miss your recital, and you don't have to become a prostitute. That's not the type of profession Miss Judy has in mind for you. |
|   | LISA | *(Mumbles.)* No. |
|   | PAUL | No. *(Pause.)* So Talia Robbins is really happy her father moved out? |
|   | LISA | Talia Robbins picks open the eighth-grade lockers during gym period. But she did that before her father moved out. |
| 230 | PAUL | You can't always judge someone by what they do or what they don't do. Sometimes you come home from dancing school and run upstairs and shut the door, and when I finally get to talk to you, everything is "okay" or "fine." Yup or nope? |
|   | LISA | Yup. |
|   | PAUL | Sometimes, a lot of times, I come home and fall asleep in front of the television. So you and I spend a lot of time being a little scared of each other. Maybe? |
| 240 | LISA | Maybe. |
|   | PAUL | Tell you what. I'll make you a tender offer. |
|   | LISA | What? |
|   | PAUL | I'll make you a tender offer. That's when one company publishes in the newspaper that they want to buy another company. And the company that publishes is called the Black Knight because they want to gobble up the poor little company. So the poor little company needs to be rescued. And then a White Knight comes along and makes |
| 250 |   | a bigger and better offer so the shareholders won't have to tender shares to the Big Black Knight. You with me? |

LISA       Sort of.

PAUL       I'll make you a tender offer like the White Knight. But I don't want to own you. I just want to make a much better offer. Okay?

LISA       *(Sort of understanding.)* Okay. *(Pause. They sit for a moment.)* Sort of, Daddy, what do you think

260       about? I mean, like when you're quiet what do you think about?

PAUL       Oh, business usually. If I think I made a mistake or if I think I'm doing okay. Sometimes I think about what I'll be doing five years from now and if it's what I hoped it would be five years ago. Sometimes I think about what your life will be like, if Mount Saint Helen's will erupt again. What you'll become if you'll study penmanship or word processing. If you speak kindly of me to your psychiatrist when you are in graduate school. And how the hell I'll pay for your graduate school. And

270       sometimes I try and think what it was I thought about when I was your age.

LISA       Do you ever look out your window at the clouds and try to see which kinds of shapes they are? Like one time, honest, I saw the head of Walter Cronkite in a flower vase. Really! Like look don't those kinda look like if you turn it upside down, two big elbows or two elephant trunks dancing?

PAUL       Actually still looks like Walter Cronkite in a

280       flower vase to me. But look up a little. See the one that's still moving? That sorta looks like a whale on a thimble.

LISA       Where?

PAUL       Look up. To your right.

LISA       I don't see it. Where?

PAUL       The other way.

LISA       Oh, yeah! There's the head and there's the stomach. Yeah! *(LISA picks up her trophy.)* Hey, Daddy.

290 PAUL       Hey, Lisa.

LISA       You can have this thing if you want it. But you have to put it like this, because if you put it like that it is gross.

PAUL       You know what I'd like? So I can tell people who come into my office why I have this gross stupid thing on my shelf, I'd like it if you could show me your dance recital.

|       |      |                                                                                              |
|-------|------|----------------------------------------------------------------------------------------------|
|       | LISA | Now?                                                                                          |
|       | PAUL | We've got time. Mother said she won't be                                                     |
| 300   |      | home till late.                                                                              |
|       | LISA | Well, Daddy, during a lot of it I freeze and the big girl in front dances.                    |
|       | PAUL | Well, how 'bout the number you were doing when I walked in?                                   |
|       | LISA | Well, see, I have parts for a lot of people in that one, too.                                 |
|       | PAUL | I'll dance the other parts.                                                                   |
|       | LISA | You can't dance.                                                                              |
|       | PAUL | Young lady, I played Yvette Mimimeux in a *Hasty*                                             |
| 310   |      | *Pudding Show.*                                                                               |
|       | LISA | Who's Yvette Mimimeux?                                                                         |
|       | PAUL | Watch more television. You'll find out. *(PAUL stands up.)* So I'm ready. *(He begins singing.)* "Nothing could be finer than to be in Carolina." |
|       | LISA | Now I go. In the morning. And now you go. Dum-da.                                             |
|       | PAUL | *(Obviously not a tap dancer.)* Da-da-dum.                                                    |
|       | LISA | *(Whines.)* Daddy!                                                                            |
|       | PAUL | *(Mimics her.)* Lisa! Nothing could be finer …                                               |
| 320   | LISA | That looks dumb.                                                                              |
|       | PAUL | Oh, yeah? You think they do this better in *The Amazing Minkcoat?* No way! Now you go—da da da dum. |
|       | LISA | Da da da dum.                                                                                 |
|       | PAUL | If I had Aladdin's lamp for only a day, I'd make a wish …                                     |
|       | LISA | Daddy, that's maudlin!                                                                        |
|       | PAUL | I know it's maudlin. And here's what I'd say:                                                 |
|       | LISA and PAUL | I'd say that "nothing could be finer than to be in                                   |
| 330   |      | Carolina in the mooooooooooornin'."                                                          |

# Nikki Giovanni

## *Poem for a Lady Whose Voice I Like*

1 so he said: you ain't got no talent
    if you didn't have a face
    you wouldn't be nobody

    and she said: god created heaven and earth
        and all that's Black within them

    so he said: you ain't really no hot stuff
        they tell me plenty sisters
        take care better business than you

    and she said: on the third day he made chitterlings
10    and all good things to eat
        and said: "that's good"

    so he said: if the white folks hadn't been under
        yo skirt and been giving you the big play
        you'd a had to come on uptown like everybody else

    and she replied: then he took a big Black greasy rib
        from adam and said we will call this woeman and her
        name will be sapphire and she will divide into four parts

that simone may sing a song

and he said: you pretty full of yourself ain't chu

20  so she replied: show me someone not full of herself
    and i'll show you a hungry person

## David Dabydeen

# Coolie Mother

1  Jasmattie live in bruk—
Down hut big like Bata shoe-box,
Beat clothes, weed yard, chop wood, feed fowl
For this body and that body and every blasted body,
Fetch water, all day fetch water like if the whole—
Whole slow-flowing Canje river God create
Just for *she* one own bucket.

Till she foot-bottom crack and she hand cut-up
And curse swarm from she mouth like red-ants
10  And she cough blood on the ground but mash it in:
Because Jasmattie heart hard, she mind set hard

To hustle save she one-one slow penny,
Because one-one dutty* make dam cross the Canje
And she son Harilall *got* to go school in Georgetown,
*Must* wear clean starch pants, or they go laugh at he,
Strap leather on he foot, and he *must* read book,
Learn talk proper, take exam, go to England university,
Not turn out like he rum-sucker chamar* dadee.

*dutty:* piece of earth
*chamar:* low-caste

*Philip Levine*

# The Sweetness of Bobby Hefka

1   What do you make of little Bobby Hefka
    in the 11th grade admitting to Mr. Jaslow
    that he was a racist and if Mr. Jaslow
    was so tolerant how come he couldn't
    tolerate Bobby? The class was stunned.
    "How do you feel about the Jews?"
    asked my brother Eddie, menacingly.
    "Oh, come on, Eddie," Bobby said,
    "I thought we were friends." Mr. Jaslow
10  banged the desk to regain control.
    "What is it about Negroes you do not like?"
    he asked in his most rational voice,
    which always failed to hide the fact
    he was crazy as a bed bug, claiming
    Capek's *RUR* was far greater than *Macbeth*.
    Bobby was silent for a long minute, thinking.
    "Negroes frighten me," he finally said,
    "they frighten my mother and father who never
    saw them in Finland, they scare my brother
20  who's much bigger than me." Then he added
    the one name, Joe Louis, who had been
    busy cutting down black and white men
    no matter what their size. Mr. Jaslow
    sighed with compassion. We knew that
    before the class ended he'd be telling us
    a great era for men and women was imminent

if only we could cross the threshold
into humanitarianism, into the ideals
of G. B. Shaw, Karel Capek, and Mr. Jaslow.
30  I looked across the room to where Bobby
sat in the back row next to the windows.
He was still awake, his blue eyes wide.
Beyond him the dark clouds of 1945
were clustering over Linwood, the smokestack
of the power plant gave its worst
to a low sky. Lacking the patience to wait
for combat, Johnny Mooradian had quit school
a year before, and Johnny was dead on an atoll
without a name. Bobby Hefka had told the truth
40  —to his own shame and pride—and the rains
came on. Nothing had changed for a roomful
of 17 year olds more scared of life than death.
The last time I saw Bobby Hefka he was driving
a milk truck for Dairy Cream, he was married,
he had a little girl, he still dreamed
of going to medical school. He listened
in sorrow to what had become of me. He handed
me an icy quart bottle of milk, a gift
we both held on to for a silent moment
50  while the great city roared around us, the trucks
honking and racing their engines to make him move.
His eyes were wide open. Bobby Hefka loved me.

*Leonard Nathan*

# Ragged Sonnets

## I.

1 "So shall I live," the poet said, "supposing
  thou art true," but he wasn't referring to you,
  who are faithful, but to another woman,
  the one whose beauty he compared to Eve's apple
  and who, I add here, must have seemed
  a cruel emblem of reality,
  the way it comes in layers—a frank face
  and what's behind that face, another creature
  thinking its own thoughts, dreaming dreams
10 that wake us with a sob. Even you
  have sat bolt upright crying your surprise.
  There's nothing for it. Apples will be eaten.
  "So shall I live, supposing thou art true."
  I do not here, of course, refer to you.

## II.

1 Esteemed Nathan, forty years ago
  I warned you beauty ist ein trick conjured
  by Natur up to fool you into love
  for Her own purpose, ja—perpetuation
5 of das kind, and I predicted so:
  one evening you would wake mit strange children
  all around. Die Goddess of Delusion
  makes Her kleine joke and you are it.
  But how could you escape? Through art? It taught you
10 hopeless craving for perfection. Und sainthood
   was for braver souls. Nein. Be content
   that, when der wolf of instinct wore you like
   ein sheepskin, awhile you felt its macht, its power.
   Your liebe freund, Arthur Schopenhauer.

## Al Young

# *The Blues Don't Change*

*Now I'll tell you about the*
*Blues. All Negroes like Blues.*
*Why? Because they was born with*
*the Blues. And now everybody*
*have the Blues. Sometimes they*
*don't know what it is.*
     —Leadbelly

1 And I was born with you, wasn't I, Blues?
  Wombed with you, wounded, reared and
       forwarded
  from address to address, stamped, stomped
  and returned to sender by nobody else but you,
  Blue Rider, writing me off every chance you
  got, you mean old grudgeful-hearted, table-
  turning demon, you, you sexy soul-sucking gem.

  Blue diamond in the rough, you *are* forever.
  You can't be outfoxed don't care how they cut
10 and smuggle and shine you on, you're like a
  shadow, too dumb and stubborn and necessary
  to let them turn you into what you ain't
  with color or theory or powder or paint.

  That's how you can stay in style without sticking
  and not getting stuck. You know how to sting

where I can't scratch, and you move from frying
pan to skillet the same way you move people
to go to wiggling their bodies, juggling their
limbs, loosening that goose, upping their voices,
20 opening their pores, rolling their hips and lips.

They can shake their boodies but they can't shake *you.*

# WRITING ASSIGNMENTS

1.  Write a story of emergence in which a young person is trying to escape from family and community problems (whether urban, suburban, or rural) to find a better life. Use the regional accent of the people in your dialogue. Try to focus on a major dramatic incident, something that changes the person's whole direction in life.

2.  Write a one-act play or short story that is mainly a dialogue between an adult and a child. Choose a situation in which there is a problem of some sort or dramatic tension. For example:
    a)  A parent and adolescent child discuss a school report about frequent absences. Where has the child been, and with whom?
    b)  A mother tells her daughter that they are going away to live in another state. She plans to divorce her husband for some reason. Who would the daughter prefer to stay with?
    c)  A detective or social worker questions a child about some terrible things he or she witnessed. Through the child's confusion and fear a story emerges.

3.  Write a one-act comedy or humorous story in which the dialogue is witty and amusing.

4.  Write a poem in which you use a regional or ethnic accent.

5.  Write the lyrics for a song.

6.  Write a poem that evokes nostalgia, perhaps about the memory of a sweet or sad, unforgettable moment.

# Chapter 9

# *Thoughts*

## Introduction

## *Fiction*

## *Poetry*

## *Writing Assignments*

An indispensable technique for rounding out characters is setting down their thoughts: their impressions of the world, their dreams, their fears, and their inner conflicts. A character's thoughts can also move the plot ahead, reveal attitudes, suggest symbols and explore themes.

The thoughts of a character can be revealed in many ways. In drama, of course, thoughts are conveyed mainly by dialogue. The same strategy is often used in fiction. If a story is written in the first person, the "I" of the story has thoughts about the events, characters, and settings (see "In Sight of Josephine," this chapter). In the third person an omniscient narrator can simply tell us what the characters are thinking.

"A Poor Unhappy Wretched Sick Miserable Little French Boy," by David Kirby, begins with an anecdote in which a boy tells his father (in dialogue) that, yes, he would mind if the father brought a woman to their room, that "it would make him feel funny." The poet/persona extends the metaphor—always in his thoughts—to identify with the embarrassed French boy (always doing something wrong), and to cast the angry father as the world. Thus, the theme deals with the awkward but appealing individual who faces stern authority—society, God, or tradition. The thoughts of the narrator have created the theme of this poem; even better, they've made us laugh.

"In Sight of Josephine" has a central character who is a pianist. The whole story is the unwinding reel of her thoughts; everything is reported through her perceptions, her selection of detail and dialogue. Sometimes her thoughts are direct ("I can be lifted on the mystical wing of beauty ... ") and sometimes indirect (" ... my stray thoughts were so often on Josephine").

As the story proceeds we realize that she is an unusually sensitive person, observing the city around her, alive to the implications of poverty and affluence. The details, however, are carefully selected, and eventually we see her quick sense of social responsibility and her desire to help focus on a rather stylish homeless woman to whom she gives the name of Josephine.

In her personal life she is preoccupied with her passion for music and her desire to give a concert of her own. Josephine—representing the need she feels to improve the miserable world she sees around her—and her music compete with each other for her time and attention. The language in which the author explores her thoughts is exquisitely precise, yet flexible:

> Some days too, for better or for worse, both my almost posh job and the ugly tragedies beyond my window fade away entirely, as I feel the smooth ivory beneath my fingers and work on an intricate phrase of Beethoven or Liszt until the music flowers as if from my nerve endings.

There is a certain ease in conveying thoughts when a story is presented in the first person. (See also "Sacred Heart," which appears in Chapter 3.)

"Takes," by Stephen Dixon, is again almost wholly composed of thoughts. In this story, Dixon takes the omniscient point of view and reveals the thoughts of eight characters as they relate to the tragedy. Because six of them are worried about Corinne, the central character, the suspense mounts. The story is written—as the title suggests—in a series of cinematic takes, each revealing the circumstances as seen from a different point of view. The aim here is not so much to deepen the character portrayals as to keep the reader interested. The would-be murderer is rapidly reviewing the physical situation in order to make his plan more foolproof. Corinne is doing the same, hoping to figure out an escape. Such thoughts generate plot by describing the conflict between two characters. The excitement surrounding the inner thoughts of all eight characters turns a banal city incident into a work of considerable appeal.

That nature may be perceived in different ways is the subject of William Matthews' poem, "Landscape with Onlooker." It is fall and the moon has risen "fat as a beachball." Sometimes these night hours are filled with dread, the author thinks, but tonight "the air's as sweet as a freshly peeled orange./ There's a moon on the lake, and another in the sky." One's thoughts, the author suggests, may create the quality of the scene.

Another nighttime poem deals with the dreams of a husband and wife. Amusingly entitled "The Long History of the Short Poem," the poem deals with subconscious thought. The narrator comments sardonically after each stanza on the meaning of the dream. Are we to understand that each dream is a poem? And that the interpretation of poems may be as arbitrary as that of dreams? At any rate, the substance of the poem lies in his, hers, and the narrator's thoughts.

Is Ulysses' wife Penelope a baited trap, the "calm center of all strife," or a martyr? In "Penelope," Mark McWatt projects the thoughts of three different characters (the schoolboy, the man, and Ulysses) as they muse on Penelope—and, by extension, on women in general.

Charles Simic's poem, "A Book Full of Pictures" begins with the description of a scene at home, seen through the eyes of the narrator, the son. The scene rapidly gives way to his thoughts about it, although that is not shown in any mechanical way. There are no quotation marks for his thoughts, no italics. The narrator begins to make connections: the father's theology, the black raincoat, the mother's black knitting needles that "made crosses." In the third stanza description and thought merge: "In the book full of pictures/A battle raged: Lances and swords/ Made a kind of wintry forest/ with my heart bleeding in its branches."

The lances and swords relate back to the mother's knitting needles, and the wintry forest to the black crosses that they form. The narrator's thoughts (the crosses, the bleeding heart) suggest religious imagery, especially in connection with the line "The soul is a bird," which seems to be spoken by the father. Here we have references to the sacred heart, the dove ascending, the Father, the Son, and the Holy Ghost. The book has pictures of dead royalty. Whose heart, then, is bleeding? That of humanity, always in battle? That of the boy? Of the boy as a Christ figure?

The poem is an organic melding of suggestive imagery referring both to Christian emblems and human frailty. All is conveyed by linkages in the boy's mind, his thoughts.

*Carol Ascher*

# *In Sight of Josephine*

1 People change, as do the times. You think you might be able to go along with it all, but you don't really know what *it all* entails. And then one day, changing becomes moot. Things have gone too far.

"The difference between you and me is that you see people first in the ways that they're oppressed or victimized," Nan, my roommate, pointedly informed me a month ago— when I was still at least amenable to entertaining such talk. Nan claims her job as city reporter on the *Newark News* has

10 given her the calming knowledge that people of all colors, no matter how poor or afflicted, have ingenious ways of giving their lives satisfaction.

"Like watermelon? Like having babies?" I asked.

No longer the one to be caught feeling guilty, Nan didn't blink. "They have more normal lives than we do," she said, and bit her lip accusingly.

But perhaps it was only my outdated guilt that made me notice the reproach in her reddened lip. Am I responsible for her being loose once again, and childless, as she inches toward

20 forty? Or for the way that, late starting her career, she now slogs out copy until all but the most ambitious have long gone, and then must sit clutching bag and papers amidst the late-night junkies also crossing the Hudson on the PATH train?

Still, I'm no reformer. Social work was never tempting, social theory only in one devout period when I doggedly devoured the Frankfurt school—Horkheimer, Adorno, Benjamin: all refugees, hiding in their bitter analyses an old-world hope for salvation that I secretly still share. Yet even with a Germanic dialectic in which to clothe my inarticulate anguish,

30 my activist fervor took hold only spasmodically in those euphoric high pressure moments, now fading into youthful romance, when I had been dragged by friends to walk hot but heroic among the thousands of marchers waving banners for freedom, justice, an end to war.

So that, nearing two decades later, when my street corner fills, as if behind my insufficiently caring back, with the outgorgings of the nearby city hospital mental ward, the Veterans Administration a block up Seventh Avenue, and the local welfare office, I know I have no legitimate case. Misery has as great a
40 right to the corner as I—to the bagged beer and grape soda sold by the Lebanese who have recently taken over the corner deli, or to the crack and recycled methadone available from less conspicuous vendors in the recessed doorway one building in. For gin and sweet wine, one has to travel all the way up Twenty-Third toward Eighth: past the xerox shop where the Hassidic owner, reddish curls wound primly around his ear, and his Dominican helper (who spent the Vietnam War wrapping corpses in plastic) trade off their raucous teasing like tightrope walkers tempting a mutually cruel pit; past the Chelsea Hotel, with its classier drug
50 supplies hidden like Rapunzel in its towers; past the theatre where Polish exiles contemptuously offer their new countrymen nudity and violence as revolutionary avant-garde.

I'm a pianist—one who, nearing her middle years, still dreams of Carnegie Hall. Though I practice several hours daily, my public appearances are generally before small audiences: to accompany a singer on a cycle of Schubert Lieder, a violinist performing nineteenth-century sonatas, or a choral group too poor to hire a full orchestra. It's over three weeks ago now that I gave a rare solo recital—but more of that later.
60 After far too many years of teaching irregular piano lessons and "saving myself for my music," I now earn a decent nine-to-five living as one of the new breed. Nan was proud of me when I wrangled the job, my Juilliard degree no longer fresh, and my "prior experience" spotty at best. "Maybe you'll stop identifying with all those nuts on the street," she said. I'm a fundraiser, for the New York City Opera Guild. I remind the corporate heads and the private rich of the tax benefits, the good exposure, and perhaps even the moral uplift that will come to them from enriching the city's cultural offerings. The
70 Opera in the Park series was my personal project, though the program gave thanks to the Avon Foundation, the McNeil Fund, the John and Mary Knoll Corporation, and the Mayor, as well as half a dozen individuals from one of our special lists.

Beyond the back window of my apartment, at my piano's edge—close enough, as the expression goes, to hear a toilet flush—is the Stanford Hotel. Except that, last year, had my ear been more attentive, I might have noted an absence of

toilets flushing—I certainly did notice the coarse shouting, the howl of a dog being tortured, and the blare of transistors set
80 inconsiderately (even aggressively?) on the open window ledges. "Two working toilets for 150 residents," read the quickly-scrolled signs of the ragged tenants who miraculously collected themselves enough one afternoon to call in the television cameras and stage a picket before the Stanford's cracked front door. Nan, of course, was also there taking her spikey notes—the readers of the *Newark News* always enjoy the pleasing sensation of trouble in Manhattan. The Stanford's owners, long in the shadows, appeared to be hiding out at an unidentifiable Florida address; and then (perhaps the building
90 was instantly sold?) rumor held that the hotel was owned by the Franciscan order.

"So much for the Church!" crowed Chris, our lanky upstairs neighbor, a Texan in the recording business, who still finds comfort in discovering that religion is as callow as everything else.

But Nan chewed her pencil tip with an indignation as rare as it once was common, and said: "I'd like to bust open those Franciscans."

Defensively, I take on the voice of a cynic. For I'm achy
100 with too recent memory. A lonely sorrow threaded with a guilt I have no wish to extract, weights my chest. Yet even now, as if in a life as secret as masturbation, I can be lifted on a mystical wing of beauty. A sonata wets my eyes—with inexplicable relief, ancient sadness on which new grief rings its chords, a hope for the reconciliation of humankind as senseless as it is urgent. In the dark of movie houses, my chest expands with exaltation, I sense my own boundless artistic potential, images of finiteness and loss send me sobbing through my drenched tissues until the lights are turned back on, and Nan, if she is
110 with me, pats my hand. Some days too, for better or worse, both my almost posh job and the ugly tragedies beyond my window fade away entirely, as I feel the smooth ivory beneath my fingers and work on an intricate phrase of Beethoven or Liszt until the music flowers as if from my nerve endings.

I think of the police horse, whose burst eardrums no longer reverberate with sudden noises, and whose blinders keep its attention focused serenely on the street ahead. I have an old school friend who, raising a two-year-old, has temporarily forsaken the news in favor of comics. Protectively, we take

120 things in in spasms. And even where our eye lingers, it reshapes.

But I am speaking of myself—of that first sight of her over a year ago—and of what has happened since. It was a glorious early spring day. I had come out for those five minutes of dazzling sun between our dusky apartment and the subway's timeless false light. Blue sky, as if painted anew, outlined the brick buildings at the corner of Twenty-Third and Seventh Avenue, where men swinging attaché cases and women carrying the vast bags that hide high-heels as well as office papers

130 rush in myopic flatfootedness to substantial jobs. And there, like a peaceful island that parted the businesslike stream, stood a tall large-boned black woman and two black men passing around their day's first bottle of bagged wine. The woman looked to be in her late thirties—an age-mate. Though she had the loose mouth of a child, her cheeks were puffy, and dark crescents lined the undersides of her large soft innocent eyes. Her old leather jacket made me take a second look, for it might have been the height of fashion hung on the lean shoulders of one of the neighborhood's gay men. Red socks offered a perky

140 snip of color below worn jeans, stylishly rolled to midcalf. As I passed, the woman veered like a ship encountering a wave to yank the bag from where it had gotten stuck.

"Listen," she imperiously directed the men who had been roughly talking, and made them, for a moment, absolutely stop. "Listen! I ain't got all day. You hear?"

And I actually wondered as I descended to catch my train, now cheerfully humming Beethoven's "Pastorale"— thought there was something in its being improbable that made the woman's press of time all the more wonderful—as if

150 she had an urgent appointment, somewhere important to go.

With Darlene, my therapist (an efficient weekly stop on my way home from work), talk that evening revolved around why the street woman had been so interesting to me.

"It was the proud way she dressed and talked. It gave me hope."

"Hope?"

"That she could take care of herself, I guess."

"Don't you feel you can take care of yourself? You've been doing so well lately—in the professional arena."

160 I have belatedly come to understand that, for Darlene, doing well professionally is making enough money to pay her annual fee increases. Also, not unlike any parent, she wants her clients' jobs to have impressive titles she can be proud

of—even a few juicy details she can relay–when she gossips with colleagues and friends. But clever Darlene is always suggesting more advanced goals for our work: ever since I provided for us both with my excellent new job, she has wanted to see me through to a nice solvent second marriage. "Why not first worry about turning me into a concert pianist," I once
170 said recalling unforgivingly how Ben, now a successful violinist with the Philharmonic, used to begrudge my practice time. Darlene's answer came in an intricate, rather old-world theory: once I'm in a satisfying relationship with a mature man (who is presumably not himself a musician), the problem of my performing will take care of itself. I must ask her if she believes that my generous prospective husband will insist that I immediately give up my job for full-time practice, or that with romantic and erotic love surrounding me, my longing to work at my piano will simply abate.
180      "Also the woman had dignity," I remember saying, with the sinking feeling of having lost my credibility. "She had enough dignity to reverse the order of the street!"

    "Imagine the street. You are standing in the middle of the sidewalk."

    Comfortably lying on the burnished leather couch, I obediently closed my eyes to create what Darlene calls a waking dream. This and similar mystical trappings have been Darlene's most recent attempts to upgrade her own skills—she's not only ambitious for me. Like the yogis, who ask one to
190 chant "peace, peace, peace" as a disarmament strategy, Darlene's "imaging" is meant not merely to give one the relieving pleasure of imagination, but actually, in my case, to instigate both pay raises and concert bookings, find an appropriate mate, as well as (when I press her with my concern) lighten the suffering of my street.

    I wouldn't have to put up with such "imaging" more than once, except that I still retained the glow of some years ago when I had just left Ben and was seriously floundering, and Darlene was greatly loving and helpful to me.
200      "It seems like practice in becoming God," I've told her, with a sarcasm she finds obstructive of healing. In any case, she insists that anyone who wants to can attain this higher state. And if everyone does, won't their omniscient plans be like grandiose bumper-cars slamming into each other?

    "You stick to worrying about *your* desires," I can hear Darlene say. It is also to Darlene that I owe the not entirely reassuring insight that I will be less moved by the deprivations of others once I *really* take care of myself.

210    It is perhaps noteworthy, then, that mornings when, in order to avoid the subways' warm weather stench I walked toward the Eighth Avenue uptown bus, I began to be on the lookout for Josephine. Sometimes she would be leaning enigmatically into the arm of a buddy—she seemed to be a favorite with the men, black or white: she made you notice that they were once good-looking, and you even wondered how she might transform them into dashing male idols, if only she went through the bins to choose their clothes.

        Then, as it grew hot, Josephine often lay curled on her
220    side, thumb in mouth, napping in front of the pizza shop or, across the street, in the doorway of a building temporarily sealed by real estate speculators. As if she had assured herself of the protection of locks and the softness of cool sheets on a well-made bed, her long body would stretch in marvelous relaxation. Did her trustful deep sleep mean she had already drunk herself into a cozy paradise? Or that, homeless and forced to stay vigilant the long night hours, she had finally succumbed to an exhaustion too great for the pettiness of discomfort and worry?

230    One morning I saw Josephine sitting against the peeling sealed building, as if under a luxuriously shading tree. This was the morning that, seeking to encompass my secretly growing affection, I decided to call her Josephine.

        While Henry lunches with the wealthy or sits in a vacant dark auditorium, swinging his gold pin in rhythm to rehearsals we have helped fund, I write proposals and take brisk phone messages from those on our special lists. On slack days, when instead of being released to run home and practice, I am tied to my desk, I entertain myself by calculating how the money it takes
240    to mount a single opera production would keep me comfortably practicing piano for several reincarnations. *Die Meistersinger,* this summer's ambitious blockbuster, requires a seventeenth-century Nürnberg street corner, complete with two-story homes and lit church spires rising on the horizon—as well as an entire citizenry dressed in three changes of authentic Hanseatic clothes.

        "Perhaps we should send the costumes to the homeless when we're through," I joked disingenuously with Henry. "Or give the mayor the little German houses to use as shelters."

        Henry was casually rocking on the back two legs of the
250    chair by my desk. Because of the air conditioning, he wore a

matching cotton lavender vest over his light lavender shirt. Giving me a worried look, he pulled a tanned hand through his blow-dried hair. Actually, his look of worry was also disingenuous, since Henry, a boy from the liberal Philadelphia suburbs, enjoys the way bantering about my outdated social conscience makes him feel like one of the new realists that New York seems in the avant-garde of breeding.

"This isn't the 1960s—or even the '70s, thank goodness," said Henry, who thinks back on that wanton period
260 with the spite of someone left out of the action.

Coming home that evening, I saw Josephine on the metal steps that lead to the upstairs tax offices of H.&R. Block from February to April 15th. In a pink T-shirt and jeans, and a thick pink ribbon around her hair, she was sharing cigarettes and booze with a pasty-faced woman whose stringy hair had been pulled into a pencil at the back of her head.

"Spare change?" said Josephine. Her hips swung forward with the flow of wine as she stood up from the metal stairs to panhandle me for the first time.

270 I dug into my pockets, wishing I had the healthy check Henry had brought back from his Tavern-on-the-Green lunch. I had a few coins and, curiosity drawing me to prolong the moment, looked warmly at the streaked yellows of Josephine's eyes.

"You look great today," I told her.

"Thanks." She steadied herself proudly as she pocketed the change.

"Take care of yourself," I said feeling that poetic surge in my chest that I now know accompanies giving spare change.

280 At home, I imagined Josephine and her friend as snug roommates. More intimate than Nan and I in these troubled days, they would whisper their stories until late at night, giggle, trade clothes. Perhaps they had found a temporary room at the Stanford, where all the toilets presumably now flushed.

Josephine's jobs, 1965–85: One day, in my own way "imaging" Josephine onto a safer plane, I invented a vita. With the impulse of sisterhood, I started with the year of my own high school graduation. Had Josephine worked, say, in the fields long before that? Was she ever a waitress? Did she clean
290 other people's thickly carpeted homes? For a time did she hold a factory job, stuffing tissue in the new-smelling leather bags? Could she have been a typist, stenographer, key puncher, Girl Friday? Perhaps she was one of the lonely women who empty

wastecans and dust off desks in those skyscrapers that stay brightly lit at night.

And then I chastised myself that my fantasy had been cast by my own prejudice; for why otherwise give Josephine such a marginal work history when I was so drawn to her? Would I have argued backwards in the same way from a white woman's drunken life on the street?

I imagine us in the first grade: Her hair is in tight, brightly ribboned braids, her knees are bony, but she can run as fast as any boy, and on the playground can she give out a shriek! As for me, a subdued barrette at the side, eye-glass level, holds a wad of my straight hair; I practice every afternoon when I get home from school and am awkward with other children. Josephine and I never speak—or even notice one another. First, I live in Kansas and she ... probably in South Carolina. Second (or is this the first?), we both go to segregated schools.

The tendency is to tell a story about Josephine that leads sadly but nobly to her life on my street—and to what has happened since. Did she have a little girl who had to be given into foster care?

I imagine, on the other hand, that Josephine earned a B.A. degree from a small local college in art or psychology. She was going to be someone—her mother expected it, as did her frail grandmother, who told of being a slave in a voice so quiet it sounded like rain. The family had done without comforts for Josephine. Then she began to drink (too much pressure?) and to hang out with dissolute men.

On the weekend, practicing Chopin and Satie until Nan, who was at her computer, cautiously asked for a break, I roamed the street looking for Josephine. I wanted to admit: "Josephine, I'm doing your vita." I longed to drop a quarter, a dollar into her hand. But of course the woman wasn't out. Perhaps (I hoped) that meant she had gotten a steady home. Or that she had gone upstate to see her family—a worried mother, the teenage daughter who had written. More likely, she had simply been picked up for loitering on the metal stairs.

Sitting in Darlene's tastefully muted office, stricken by raw grief, I hear the most fantastic new theory. Though she grants racial prejudice, she happily now believes that each of us is born in a black or white or yellow skin for a reason. Karma. Everything that happens to us in this life, including, incredible as it may seem, whom we choose as our parents and how we live and, yes, die, is our responsibility. Karma. This is because everything that happens—the word may be too passive—is our way of working through our failures last time 340 around.

"What did Josephine do wrong last time?" I belligerently ask, fumbling for my purse with the thought of making a beeline for the door. "What did the European Jews do wrong?"

"Don't be judgmental," Darlene warns, though her voice is soft and her brown eyes remain bottomless pools of comfort. "You have to think of karma in a loving way."

No less a clotheshorse than Josephine, to the degree that my sources are more elegant and varied, I'm certainly less cre-350 ative in achieving my effects. One drizzly autumn day, from a little shop on Twenty-Third Street, I bought myself a tailored woolen skirt in hope for the coming season: a visit to an old Juilliard professor, who is known for his contacts in the recital world; an inadvertent introduction to an impresario by Henry at work. As I came out, plastic bag in hand, Josephine was prying up one of her men friends from where he had drunkenly fallen on the sidewalk, while a policeman stood by tapping his nightstick.

The problem with fantasies of repair: even if I had led 360 Josephine into the shop and let her choose whatever lovely dress she pleased, there would be the implacable question of where to wear it. Or hang it up at night.

And then one frosty November afternoon, having left work early, I rounded the corner to find Josephine under the eaves of the five-and-ten cent store, shivering on a cardboard sheet. She was wearing a rust wool plaid coat with a matching rust scarf and hat. A vast black handbag from which several items spilled sat carefully protected by her side. With great concentration, she was eating a muffin half encased in a rolled 370 paper bag. (The method a peculiar adaptation from wine?) Though Josephine hadn't noticed me, I stopped and pulled a dollar from my coat.

"What time is it?" asked Josephine, pocketing the money with no further ado.

"About four, I think."

"Three-thirty or four," Josephine replied, evaluating my information with her own inner gauge.

"It's actually a little after four," I said pedantically, remembering a clock I had just passed.

380       "Well, three-thirty, four, around that time." Josephine held her ground.

"Where are you going when the sun sets?"

"Don't know." Josephine's eyes clouded, as if by the oddity of the question.

"It'll be even colder, as soon as the sun goes down."

"Well, I have this." Josephine pointed with some disdain to a pale blue satin quilt stuffed behind her handbag. "Some lady gave it to me, but I don't like its color."

      Ecstatically, Nan paraded around the house: she had
390 been assigned to cover a little story about Wall Street white-collar crime, and had actually gotten herself into the brokerage firm.

"They're just like us," she said, her eyes watery with exaltation.

"'Wow! Like everything is everything, man,'" I replied, quoting an earlier Nan, and looked up from the piano. When I first met Nan, though she had returned from an unhappy commune in Vermont, her long pale hair still hung long over her braless Indian shirts, and she still sat in the lotus, eyes
400 closed, palms up, meditating for half an hour each morning before drinking her rose hip tea. It was only later, when she had become a reporter for listener-sponsored radio, that, exhorting me to take the enemy seriously, she began dashing from picket to march or demonstration with a tape recorder slung over her shoulder, while I sat guiltily glued to my piano, hoping the new world well. Perhaps it's the short rope that links me to these ivory keys, I now thought almost regretfully, that makes my shifts of desire and belief so slight in comparison to Nan's energetic swings. And, taking advantage of a frail
410 reassurance, I went to the telephone to call Professor Markus. Would he hear the pieces I was now practicing, and if he liked them would he help me think of places to perform?

      With the illusory excitement of tinsel and holiday partying suddenly over, winter had set in with cold as raw as it was endless. Yet time moved forth, for I was finally in my old professor's Persian-carpeted home, sitting at the piano that looked out over Central Park, white with snow in the moonlight. Behind me, rows of books in German, French, and Russian filled the high walls. I played a Schubert and a Hindemith
420 sonata, then the three Gymnopedies of Satie—felt, even, as I played that the beauty of the music was such that the world must be redeemed. Turning from my stool, I saw the grateful

moisture in the corner of Professor Markus's usually disappointed eyes.

"Your work pays off," he said, with a slow wrinkled nod that transformed his pleasure into my own private redemption.

There was tea from a silver pot, cubed sugar taken with tongs, as we spoke of how I might proceed.

430      My face was still aflame with happiness as I hurried homeward along Fifth Avenue with its lit glassy buildings rising high above the wide snowy sidewalks. Above me, the night was so clear that here and there stars shone a rare blue-white despite the city lights. Pulling my scarf up over my chin, I felt elation that seemed to lift into a clarity as sharp as the night. Suddenly, I saw how the city had two kinds of places: there were the warm light quiet insides and the dark windy icy outsides, whose only illusory heat was the roar of traffic. The forbidden buildings, with their tempting windows, locks,
440 doormen, television screens; and those grates, recesses, and niches where one might or might not be allowed a slim chance at life. It was Josephine's New York, the city as Josephine must see it. Yet there was no question: I wanted to be, would be, one of those inside.

My insight would have seemed complete, sufficient for an evening, but life in its excess had still another image awaiting me. Too cold to sustain the long walk home, I had gotten onto the downtown bus and then switched to the crosstown at Twenty-Third. As I stepped down at my corner, I saw a
450 woman in a navy parka squatting over the sloshy curb. Her buttocks shone in the light of the street lamp, while a growing huddle of the street's drunks cheered and hooted her on. It was Josephine, and while all watched she was taking a shit into the dirty snow.

St. Ann's Church in Brooklyn was initiating a series of fine Sunday evening concerts in its acoustically beautiful chapel. Thanks to Professor Markus, I was to be the second performance. I had taken a trip to Brooklyn: the church's grand piano would be lovely to play. In the last tense happy
460 weeks before my concert, with afternoons off from the office, I was back at my piano six or seven hours a day. Besides writing the most dazzling public releases for me and sending them to every metropolitan paper, Nan was telling everyone at the *Newark News* about the concert and threatened to fill the church with her colleagues alone. "I'm going to have to forgive

all your crazy new opinions," I told her, and gave her a big hug. Even Henry, who had suggested the cut in hours with an effort of grace that made him almost grand, promised to be there. If, as Professor Markus had forecast, Nan's press re-
470 leases led to good notices, I could easily have my next recital back on my own dear Manhattan side of the river.

Perhaps it will seem unfitting, even perverse, that, in this period of growing nervous pleasure, my stray thoughts were so often on Josephine. Would the woman, who disappeared for days on end, last the winter? And what, more than the simple fact of not having a bathroom, had defecating before the eyes of all meant? Sometimes, as if in an argument for dignity and hope, an odd fact would apparently burst in on me: I had never seen Josephine scratching lice, or carrying paper shopping
480 bags stuffed with useless items.

Then one cold snowy late evening, from a darkened doorway near the Chelsea Hotel I heard a woman's wail: "Help! Help!" Coming closer, I glimpsed Josephine in a tai-lored grey coat.

"Help!" called out Josephine, in a voice so piteous I wondered if it were a cat.

My heart quickening, I impulsively turned toward the doorway. "Hi, you have a new coat on," I said breathlessly, wanting to be clear that the painful cry could be easily
490 assuaged.

"The lady I used to work for give it … I think she's in the hospital now," confided Josephine, whose eyes did swim more with drink than sorrow. "I want to visit her … fix up first. Can't have her … seeing … like a bum."

"I think you look great," I said, thrilling in my capacity to transform Josephine from victim to neighborly, if besotted and inarticulate, confidante, and ignoring for the moment the housekeeping connection her words implied. If only I ran into her more often, I bragged inwardly, our very conversation
500 might keep her clear! "Also, I like the way you wrapped your black scarf."

"Well, I try to do a little something … here and there." Josephine gingerly touched her frayed coat.

"I always think you have a sense of style," I confessed, though the next moment I was uncertain whether Josephine even recognized me from one time to another. And the next, I recalled the woman's rather unstylish posture at the curb. Did Josephine have a former uptown employer in an expensive apartment near Professor Markus's on whom she still relied

510 for periodic money and clothes? I pulled a dollar from my wallet, which Josephine crinkled unceremoniously into her coat pocket.

"But you can't hardly get what ... anymore." Josephine yawned ambiguously.

Was I meant to give her another dollar?

"They got that place over there, but it was all full up when we come over ... ," she was saying.

There was no excess traffic on the street, yet Josephine's lips moved in wordless play. It seemed, even, as she continued
520 (she was saying something about a hotel now), that what I heard was like a beautiful batik cloth with clear designs broken where the strings had been tied.

"I didn't see you for a while, until the other night," I broke into one of the blanks.

"Well, I do try to come back."

Like someone too busy for regular visits, I thought, and had the insane wish to invite her to my concert. "Anyway, keep warm," I uselessly told her. And, moving on, I heard the last words Josephine ever said to me:
530 "Listen, take care of yourself, you hear?"

It was the afternoon of my concert, a warm billowy spring day. My windows were open. Those of the Stanford's were too. On the third or fourth repeat, I had even gone to the window to ask someone in the shadows to turn down their heavily percussioned tape. Nan was to come home early from Newark, in a company car with a driver who would take us both to Brooklyn. I had bought a striking new black dress.

There is a quality to Beethoven's sonatas that drives one on; as if on a dangerous thruway or a tunnel with no exits, and
540 drivers starting and stopping and changing speeds on all sides, one scarcely dares a breath or a twist in one's seat. I had memorized the Sonata in E major, Opus 109, though the manuscript lay on the ledge before me one last time. Having played the surprising and romantic first movement, with its startling tempo changes, I was sailing through the *Prestissimo,* with its magical sense of freedom. Throughout the piece, from time to time I had heard the calming sounds of children playing—for children too live in the Stanford. And then, midway in the third movement, the *Andante molto cantabile ed espres-*
550 *sivo,* I heard moaning and a call for help. Skirting all distraction, I poured myself into the theme and its six variations. When the piece was over—rising in a roll of passion and

settling finally in a mood of austere quiet—I stood and, relaxing my shoulders, peered out of the window.

There on the low roof that borders the Stanford, four floors below the Stanford's own higher roof, were two bodies. While I was playing they had jumped. Or one had pushed the other. The man was lying twisted and moved slightly. The woman lay sprawled, face up. The sound of sirens announced
560 that someone had noticed the accident before I, and a moment later two men in white emergency uniforms appeared on the roof. I don't hold back to be coy: one glance told me the woman was Josephine. Always concerned for her appearance, she had on pale turquoise peddle pushers and a matching T-shirt. It was hard to be sure of the expression on her face, but from where I stood it looked inscrutable, calm.

Climbing out my window onto the fire escape, I sat, a silently horrified and grieving funeral party of one, while the emergency crew slid a blow-up stretcher under the man. For
570 Josephine, a white sheet over her entire body made the point. Crazy thoughts wound through my head. Now, even had I invited her, she wouldn't be able to attend my concert. Why had I never asked her real name? I glanced back inside at my elegant dress which now seemed to hang uselessly on its rack. Conversations with Henry, with Nan, and with Darlene ran through my head. Anger at all the words that pass these days for wisdom. At the superficial consolation for suffering that is offered as healing. Guilt at what I hadn't done and still, even now, would not do for her. An imaginary resumé. An unex-
580 tended invitation to come in out of the cold.

It took the emergency crew a good half hour to blow up the stretcher. Apparently the man had sufficient life in him to warrant such care. Would his bones be mended in the hospital only in order that he might be sent on to prison? And why—if he had—had he thrown Josephine from the roof? Or, in a boozy brawl, not really noticing the ledge, had they both simply fallen? Or had Josephine, far more desperate than I would have ever wanted to face, taken it upon herself consciously and willfully to end her life?
590 These questions are as useless as—what? As the reasons given for suffering, and for not noticing suffering.

I was glad Nan had not been at home.

When the men had taken the bodies from the roof and I could see the white van moving off along Twenty-Second Street, I climbed back inside and went to my piano.

That night I gave my concert, which went even better than I had expected.

## Stephen Dixon

# *Takes*

1   Man's waiting in the service elevator right next to the passen-
ger elevator. Someone comes—a woman, hopefully a young
one, through the front door or from one of the apartments
upstairs or on this floor—he'll step out behind her with the
knife, threaten her with it, take her in the automatic elevator
rather than this hand-operated one to the top floor, walk her
up to the roof, knife always on her throat, he always behind
her and threatening softly but with a real scary tone in his
voice, "One scream and I'll use it; make even a move from
10   this knife or to see me and I'll kill you," take her to a good
dark out-of-the-way spot on the roof—all depending what
lights from the other buildings' windows are on it—rape her.
She'll never see his face and his voice won't be his own. She
doesn't put up a fuss, he'll leave her there gagged and tied up.
He's scouted out the building. Not many tenants come in or
leave their apartments this late, but it's worth the wait. Someone will come. Lots of single women in this neighborhood, so
has to be a few in this building too. But on Saturday night,
most, he bets, will be with men friends. One won't though and
20   that's who.
   Tenant on the eighth floor. Can't sleep. Something's up.
Hasn't always been right when she thought something bad
was going to happen, but enough times she has. It's not from
any crazy imagination she's thinking this. The winos were
really loud tonight. Few more bottles and things smashed on
the street or whatever they're smashed against than usual too.
And a couple more souped-up cars and motorcycles than she's
used to racing past her building too. Why don't the police do
something? If it's because they don't know of these things
30   going on or they're too lazy to patrol or can't because of
cutbacks, then why don't people call them more? This city. She
turns the TV off. Get some sleep.
   Young woman's mother in Connecticut. Thinking about
her daughter. She went to New York to do graduate work in
painting. Took an apartment with another young woman, a

friend from college. But the building's bad. Filthy, poorly
maintained, bell system that doesn't work; a firetrap, she's
sure. Even if some of the neighborhood's okay, and some of
the river buildings even elegant, and as co-ops or rented apart-
40 ments, quite expensive, much of it's very bad. Welfare hotels.
Cheap rooming houses. Awful looking men and women on the
street day and night. Little park nearby where men drink and
some dope and urinate in the open and make vulgar remarks
to passing women and all sorts of other things. Beggars. In the
*Times* she's read of break-ins and muggings and seen a city
crime statistic chart that put her neighborhood near the top.
Worried.

Man in a cab going across town. Should have got out of
the cab and escorted her upstairs. Didn't like the looks of her
50 building and block. But then he hardly knows her. She might
have thought he was being funny in a way—forward, not
funny. And he had this cab, was in it, did only promise to take
her to the street door, or rather: just see, while he sat in the
cab, she got inside that door, and then he might not have got
another cab after he left her building or not so fast. Could have
asked the cab to wait while he saw her to her apartment door.
Now he thinks of it. But she said she'd be alright. He did ask.
And he's sure that no matter how hard he insisted on taking
her to her apartment door, she would have said no. *Still.*

60 Woman's in the lobby, presses the elevator button. Light
above the elevator door says the car's on the top floor, the
eighth. Slow elevator, takes days to get down. She doesn't like
waiting in this creepy lobby. Anyway, her friend Jean will be
upstairs and they can talk about tonight. The man she met. He
was nice. Took her home in a cab, wouldn't let her share the
fare with him. She wishes she had accepted his suggestion and
let him walk her to her door. But then she would have had to
invite him in. And offer him a coffee or a beer, when really all
she wants to do, if Jean's up—she'll be up—is talk a little with
70 her and go to sleep. Elevator's about here. It's here.

Man thinks now's the time. She's a good-looking one.
Long legs, big ass. She'll screw well. He'll screw her well. He'll
screw her till she cries for more, more. He steps out. She turns
around. Knife's out. Damn, she saw him. "Don't say a word or
I'll kill you right here." He gets behind her and puts the knife
to her neck. Opens the elevator door, knife always against her
neck. "We're going to the roof. I know this building. Don't say
a word, make a peep—nothing—don't even sneak a look at me
again or you're dead. I know how to get out of this building

80 easily so I'll be out of here before you hit the ground. Now get in."

She gets in. She doesn't believe this. What should she do? This is a dream. A nightmare. It's the worst thing that's ever happened to her. Think, think. That knife. It pricks. They go up. He pressed eight. He said "roof." Maybe someone will stop the elevator on the fourth floor, fifth. There's only one outside button for each floor. No down and up buttons—just one, and if you press that button when you want to go down and the elevator's going up, it stops. Please. Someone.

90 It's too late to call her, her mother thinks. She'd like to. She wants very much to speak to Corinne, tell her how worried she is about her. Tell her that Dad and she will give her a hundred dollars a month extra to find a better building to live in. Two hundred. It'll be a sacrifice for them, but it just shows how anxious they are about where she's living now. If she's going to live in that city, she'll tell her, then it has to be on these terms. Of course she could say no, she likes where she's living now, took months to find and then paint and set up, doesn't want to take any more money from them than she already does

100 and so on, and they really wouldn't be able to do anything about it. It's too late to call. But it's Saturday. She dials. Corinne's phone rings. If she answers it, or if Jean answers it—she hasn't once thought of Jean, for instance how she'd take to Corinne's parents' subsidizing most of their rent— she'll apologize for calling this late, but both will have to know she only has their best interests at heart. That's not enough. She slams down the receiver. She can wait till tomorrow? Has to, since Corinne will see her anxiety at this hour as bordering on mania. Just another nine or ten hours. Eleven's okay to call

110 on Sundays for women that age. Even if they're with men friends who stayed the night, which, let's face it, could well be the case. She goes upstairs to wash up for bed. Her husband says from the bedroom "What've you been doing? I heard you slamming the phone down, picking it up, then slamming it again." "I only slammed it once. I was worried about Corinne. Worked it out in my head though, so it's now all okay."

Roommate at a party downtown. Wonders if Corinne's home by now. She's sure she's expecting her to be there when she gets home. Note she left will explain it or should. Some-

120 thing like "Aaron called. Sudden invite to a big bash at a south of Soho artist's loft and wanted me to join him. I know. Swore I'd grind away at the books all weekend and maybe never see Aaron again, but what, dear, can I say?" They have a phone

here? If so, she'll call Corinne and say she doubts she'll be coming home tonight, and she should try to do that before two. She's just about never seen or heard Corinne up after two. "Excuse me," to a woman she thinks is one of the three people giving the party, "but is there by any chance a phone in this place I may use?" "As long as it's not to out of town," the
130 woman says. "Positively not." "Actually, if you're a good friend of either of the other hosts, you can make that call to as far west as Columbus, south as Washington, and as far north as Boston, let's say."

She's also a very pleasant girl, man in cab thinks. Attractive. Even pretty. He'd definitely call her pretty, even beautiful in some ways, though he doubts a couple of his friends would. Still. And she had spark. Bright, besides. Far as he could make out, bright as any woman he's met in a year. He's definitely phoning her tomorrow. Monday night, not tomorrow.
140 Doesn't want to appear too eager. Why not? She seemed like she'd like eagerness. Directed at her, but not just to score. She complained how most men she meets these days don't really care or get excited about anything but making money and getting ahead. Don't really read, don't think much about serious things, aren't interested in much art other than movies and music. She didn't say he was different but implied he was. She also gave him her phone number willingly enough. He likes her name. She seems to come from a good family: intelligent, moral, involved, well-off. He thinks she sort of took to him
150 too. Maybe that's why he should act fast: so she doesn't forget why she was attracted to him, if she was. Tomorrow night. No, Monday's soon enough. He hopes she paints well. If she doesn't, he could always say at first—later he could level with her more—"Hell, what do I know?"

Top floor. Roof stairs and door. Always trying to get a look at him to see if he means it—seemed he did. Had one of the most maniacal faces she's ever seen, when she saw him just that glimpse. Slim, young, smelly, wiry, ruthless, cagey-looking. He's crazy. He's going to kill her. If it was just robbery he
160 would have taken the bag downstairs and fled. Knife isn't on her neck anymore. Rape and possibly kill her. She has to find a way to get away. She has to scream, run, kick, maybe on the roof. Now she's thinking. Roof, where there's space. Stairs he's got her trapped. This building's attached to the corner one and unless there's barbed wire or something separating the two roofs, she can make a run for it yelling all the time. Pick up a brick if they have one on the roof and he's cornered her

against something like a wall or by a roof edge and throw it at
him. Anything: teeth, knees and fists and then down a fire
170 escape, but to escape. There's one that goes all the way past her
bedroom window to the narrow alleyway on the ground floor.
Corner building must have one too. If not, down her building's
fire escape screaming, knocking, banging, breaking all the
windows along the way if she has to till someone comes, wakes
up, shouts, whatever, but helps chase the man away.

Tenant hears footsteps on the roof right above her. Who
could be up there this hour? Trouble. Either some junkies got
in the building or corner one next door and got to the roof that
way and are shooting up. Or winos or runaways or just plain
180 bums making a home for the night up there. Why can't it rain
now or snow? Get them off. She just hopes the roof door's
locked tight so they don't start walking down the building's
stairs and making noise and throwing up in the hallways as
happened a couple of times or trying all the doors. What else
could it be up there but something awful? She hopes not someone forced to go for the worst of purposes. That's happened
on one or two other buildings around here but never hers.

"Now you know what I want," the man says. "I want to
screw you but I want it without holding the knife to your face.
190 That way it'll be better for me and easier and quicker for you.
Then if you're good to me and a good little girl all around and
give no trouble I'll let you go. You're a real piece of ass, you
know? I could tell right away you screw well and that you've
screwed around a lot. You got the face for it. Saucy. Sexy. So,
you going to do it like I say? You don't, you're dead."

"No, I don't want to do it with you." the woman says.
And then louder: "Now let me alone. Let me get by you and
downstairs. Now please—I'm asking—please!" He stabs her
in the chest. She raises her arms. He stabs her several times. She
200 goes down. She screams. She says "Help, I'm being murdered." He gets on one knee and stabs her where he thinks her
heart is.

"Stop that, stop that," the tenant shouts out her window. "Whoever it is, leave that girl alone. Help police, someone's killing someone upstairs! On the roof. Stop that, you
butcher, stop that, stop!" "Help me, I'm dying," the woman
says. "Stupid bitch," the man says. He jumps up. Lights have
gone on in some of the apartment windows in buildings that
overlook the roof. "Shit," he says. "Hey you there," a man
210 says from one window. "What is it, what's going on?" a man
says from a window right next to that one. "I've called the

police," a woman shouts from what seems like the building
he's on. "They're coming. They're on their way. Everybody
call to make sure they come. Girl, don't be afraid. They're
coming. People from this building will be up there for you
too." "Shit," he says and leaps over the low wall to get to the
next building's fire escape.

Her mother thinks about the dream she just had. All the
apartment buildings around hers were falling down, one after
220 the other. She lives in a suburban townhouse and has never
lived in anything but a private home, but in the dream she was
in an apartment in a tall old apartment building in a large city
that looked more European than American. The buildings
collapsed straight down as if heavy explosives had been set off
under them. For a while it seemed the window was a TV screen
and she was watching the buildings fall in slow motion in a
documentary. She was with her three daughters, all about four
to eight years younger than they are now, and her husband
and mother, who's dead. Then her building was falling. She
230 held out her arms to her family and said "Here, come into
me." Her arms became progressively longer as each person
came into her. She kissed their heads in a row—they were all as
small as little children now—and started crying. Then they
were at her family's gravesite behind her grandparents' farmhouse, burying her mother. "This proves life can go on," she
said to her husband, daughters and grandmother. She doesn't
know what the last part of the dream means. There is no
farmhouse or family gravesite. Her parents and grandparents
are buried in three different enormous cemeteries. Where was
240 her son in the dream? She gets out of bed, goes to the kitchen,
writes down the dream and what she thinks the end of it
means. "That everything will be OK with C (living in her city
hovel)? That I really needn't be anxious about any of my kids
or really about anything in life (how'd I come to that last
conclusion?)? That if people stay in mind & memory (just
about the same thing; I realize that) they're never really dead?
That living, dying, illness, frailty, tragedy, mayhem, mishaps,
madness, revolutions, terrorism (from inside & out) and the
rest of it are all quite normal? (Was that all you were going to
250 say?) That we're all basically entwined &—now stop all that;
it was never in it. Then what? Time for God? Not at any price
& why'd that idea pop in? (To interpret it theologically, that's
all.) An important dream though, start to end, no matter what
I don't make of it. Read all this back tomorrow. Underscore
that: read, read! Maybe then."

Her father can't sleep. He feels for his wife in bed. She left it before but is there now. "Hilda, you up? I can't sleep; want to talk." No answer or movement. Why'd she have to worry him so? Not that he can't handle it, but— He gets up, 260 goes to the bathroom, drinks a glass of water. That was stupid. Meant to take two aspirins first. He gets the aspirins out of the medicine cabinet, puts them in his mouth and washes them down with another glass of water. Now he'll feel better. In about fifteen minutes. And his dreams are usually more vivid and peaceful in theme when he takes aspirins. His doctor thinks he should take an aspirin a night to reduce the fat or plaque on his blood vessel walls. He doesn't mind, especially for the side benefits of a more peaceful sleep and dreams, but usually forgets to.

270     The woman's being treated by paramedics. She gives a description of her attacker and details of what happened. "Honestly, try not to talk," one of the paramedics says. "Yes, you probably shouldn't," a policeman says. She says "No, I want you to know what happened. If I go over it enough times, you'll get everything. I came into the building. We're still on my building?" "Yes, of course," the policeman says. "I meant, he didn't drag me over the parapet to the next building?" "If he did, he brought you back or you got back here on your own." "No, what am I talking about?" she says. "I came into 280 the building. I'll proceed chronologically, no digressions. I came into the building." "I really don't want her talking," the paramedic says. "You heard him, Miss. Don't talk." "I came into the building. He was waiting for me in the service elevator. That elevator ought to be locked at night, not left open. People can hide there. I'm digressing, but so what? The lobby door should have a better lock. Anyone, with a little force, can push the door open when it's locked. The building should have better lights. Look at the lights when you leave in the lobby and hallways. Thirty watts, maybe. One to a hallway if you're 290 lucky. There's a city law. My roommate's checked. She's studying to be a lawyer. Where is she?" "If you mean Miss Kantor," the policeman says, "she's not home. We've been inside your apartment. To look for your attacker. I hope you don't mind." "There's a city law saying the wattage should be higher, Jean said. Minimum of two lights too. In case one goes out. He had a long knife. Said he'd kill me unless. Well, he nearly did. Maybe he will have. No he won't. I should say that. No he won't." "You shouldn't say anything," the paramedic says. "This officer and I say *don't*." "But I wouldn't have sex

300  with him. Why would I? It would have been worse than anything. He was filthy. A beast. A jungle. I thought I could escape
on the roof. I should have tried to break away sooner. In the
lobby. That way I would have had a chance. But I was so
scared. I couldn't think. I got my wits about me going up the
elevator. His knife seemed shined. Maybe he shines it with
polish. He was sick enough. Maybe I should have let him do it.
Screw me, he said. Maybe it would have been worth it, filth
and all. When you can't do anything." "Now that's enough.
Absolutely no more talk." "This has all been very valuable,
310  Corinne," the policeman says, "but this man is right. Save
your strength. I insist. For your own sake." "All right."

He's in a bar about ten blocks away having a beer and
scotch. He got about twenty dollars from her bag. He's standing a man he just met to a drink. He says "Oh boy, did I have a
good one tonight. Met a chickie on Broadway. She hadn't been
laid for months. She just looked at me and said 'I'll give you a
twenty if you lay me in a basement I know of—it's the only
place we can go. If you don't want to, just say so and I won't
say another word about it.' No bullshit. Under a bus shelter.
320  We were both waiting for the number four and she turns to me
and says this. 'My husband's home,' she says. 'He never lays
me. He likes men only now. You don't like men,' she says, 'do
you? I hope not.' That's what she said. I told her I like women
only. All parts of them, not just the ones that count. And I can
do it all night. This is what I tell her. 'Or at least I used to. Now
only half the night which is fine for most ladies, okay?' So we
went to this basement. I was so hot by now I could have done it
to her right on the street. She gave me the twenty. It was cozy
down there. Even had a mattress and nice little table lamp on
330  the floor. She took me into an alleyway and made me shut my
eyes the last minute of walking so I wouldn't ever find the
place alone. Even turned me all the way around a few times so
I'd be all mixed up in my directions. I bet she did it with lots of
guys down there. But twenty. For laying her. She was great.
Clean. Wet. Smelled good. A Mother Earth, no Miss Twiggy.
Big hips. Big tits. Big everything. I felt I was swimming in her. I
would've paid her if I had a twenty and she asked. If I'd known
how good she was, is what I meant, for I don't pay anyone for
sex. Things are free now, free now, you don't have to pay.
340  Women walking around without panties and bras, kids doing
it before your eyes in cars—man, it's all over the place. But to
get paid for it? Hey, I'll take it! But that was it. Twice. That
was all she could take and to lay it on the line to you, me too.

She was too much. She nearly killed me. Then we got dressed and left together and she made me shut my eyes again till we got into the street. She never gave me her name or phone number or address, but I bet she lives in that same building but higher up. You think she had a husband?" Other man raises his shoulders. "I don't. I think that's just her line so you don't think of going to her apartment right after to rob her. You know, some guys could just get her address from her bag while they're even balling her. 'If we meet, we meet,' she said when I said what about us doing this again sometime? 'You were the best,' was the last thing she said to me. Even if I wasn't, what do I care? All I know is she gave me a great time and made me twenty bills heavier."

The other man says "That's a fantastic story—unbeatable—I only wish it was me," and thinks if ever a guy was full of it, this one's it. He downs his drink, says "Got enough for a refill?—I'm a little low." "I think I can make it." "Thanks. I'm going to hit the pisser. Tell Rich for me to put a soda in back of mine this time," and goes to the men's room.

Her parents' phone rings. He looks at the clock. "Who can be calling so late? Probably a wrong number. You answer it, please, or just let it ring. I can't even move off the bed." Which one of her children? she thinks, going to the phone. It can't be anything but bad. It's rung too many times.

Her sister's sitting in a movie theater in Seattle. The phone's ringing in her apartment. Another sister's working in the sun on an archaeological dig in Egypt. This work is harder than she ever thought it would be, she thinks, and no fun. She wishes she was back home. Face it: she's homesick. She never would have believed it but she is. Her brother's sleeping in his college fraternity house. The person calling the house gets a recorded message that the phone's been temporarily disconnected.

The tenant leaves the building very early, says good morning to the policeman guarding the front door, asks how the girl is. "I haven't heard." "Do you know if they caught the man who did it yet?" "I don't think so." She goes to church, kneels, prays for the girl's life and that the man is caught and that the whole city becomes more peaceful again, at least as peaceful as it was about twenty years ago, but if only one prayer's answered then that the girl lives. She sits, covers her eyes with her hands, just let things come into her. It's quiet in here, she thinks. For now, this is the only place.

The man who took her home the night before gets up
around nine, has coffee, goes out for the *Times* and a quart of
390   milk and two bagels, dumps half the newspaper sections into a
trash can, reads the front page of the news section as he walks
home, reads the sports and book sections while having a
toasted bagel and coffee at home, looks at his watch, 9:42, still
much too early, slips in a tape cassette, does warm-up exer-
cises, goes out for a six-mile or one-hour run, whichever comes
first, comes back, did good time—must have been all the alco-
hol last night that gave him so much sugar—showers, shaves,
checks the time, 11:38, no, not yet; twelve, on Sunday, is really
the earliest he can call someone he just met. If she worked as
400   hard as she said she did this week—studying, painting, her
waitress job every other weekday afternoon and all-day Saturday—she'll need a good ten-hour sleep. But once she gets up
she'll probably need an hour just to get started. One. Call her
at one.

*Paul Hoover*

# Long History of the Short Poem

1  She dreamed they lived in Africa,
on a beautiful green savannah,
where they raised speckled apples
and owned a bright blue ladder.
Life was good and they were happy.
The following day, she knew,
they had to go on a trip
to buy some beautiful dirt,
the most beautiful dirt in the world!

10  This was a dream about money

He dreamed he was lost in space,
floating around in a silver capsule,
and the name on his suit was Geezer.
Maybe he was old, the Geezer in Space or
    something.
He couldn't tell, since there wasn't a mirror,
just lots of fuzzy chrome.
All he could see was the tip of his nose,
which looked about the same.

20  The odd thing was, this music kept playing,
a black polka band or a white reggae group—
he couldn't tell the difference.
He also remembered thinking,
as he looked toward Saturn,

"If only I had a sister,
there would be nothing to fear."

This was a dream about courage.

She dreamed they owned an aquarium,
but in order to make it work
30 they had to put quarters in it,
like a Vibra-bed or TV set.
After they put one in,
the fish started moving again,
the water lights came on,
and the little mill in the corner,
with its plastic man in the doorway,
began to turn its wheel.

It was then, of course, they knew she was pregnant.

## David Kirby

# *A Poor Unhappy Wretched Sick Miserable Little French Boy*

1  A little French schoolboy
is traveling across America with his father,
and when they get to Reno,
the dad asks his son
if the boy would mind
his bringing a woman
to their room
and the boy, who has a bad cold
from all of the air conditioning in America,
10  says yes,
he would mind,
that it would make him feel funny,
and when the father says,
what do you mean, feel funny,
the little wretch says
he doesn't know what he means
and crosses and uncrosses his skinny white legs
and blows his nose into a big French handkerchief.
I feel sorry for the schoolboy,
20  for I too have felt funny without knowing why,
as when my boss says,
Could you step into my office a moment,
I'd like to have a word with you,
and I want to say I'd rather not,
it would make me feel funny,
or when my wife tells me she wants to have

a serious talk with me
this evening after I get home from work,
and I want to say, Oh, darling, let's not talk!
30 I'd feel funny if we were to talk!
At times like this,
I am the one in Reno with the orphanage haircut,
the one wearing the blazer and short pants,
my books in a strap the priests will take
to my nervous matchstick legs
when I mumble my *verbes irregulières*.
For I am turning into
a poor unhappy wretched sick miserable little
    French boy,
40 and the world is my angry, faithless father.

## William Matthews

# *Landscape with Onlooker*

1 One night shy of full, fat as a beachball, the moon
  looks not lonesome shining through the trees but replete

  with the thoughtless sensuality of well-being.
  A chill in the air? No, it's under the air, like water

  under a swimmer. The unsteadfast leaves grow crisp
  and brittle, the better to fall away. Some nights

  fear fills these hours like rising water in a well—
  the dead of night, as the phrase goes, when you quicken

  and the dank metallic sweat beads like a vile dew.
10 But tonight you stand at your window, framed and calm,

  and the air's as sweet as a freshly peeled orange.
  There's a moon on the lake, and another in the sky.

## Mark McWatt

# *Penelope*

1   As a young schoolboy
   I always thought
   of Penelope as a spider:
   all that business of making
   and unmaking the 'web'
   which—I also thought—
   was a sticky trap for the suitors.

   Now I know differently:
   Penelope threatens whenever I journey;
10  she becomes as real as any wife
   left at home, working the loom
   that woofs the filaments of my life
   with her warped duties
   —mother, stern preserver,
   calm centre of all strife.

   And now I know the web
   is spun for me—a net
   (baited with imaginary suitors)
   to haul me home,
20  full of presents and regret
   for having left Telemachus,
   Penelope.... And yet,
   sometimes I think it's all a trick
   to wish me away again,

to emphasize my wrong
so that each minor dereliction
might live forever
in her immortal web of song.

## Charles Simic

# A Book Full of Pictures

1 Father studied theology through the mail
And this was exam time.
Mother knitted. I sat with a book
Full of pictures. Night fell.
My hands trembled touching the faces
Of dead kings and queens.

There was a black raincoat in the upstairs bedroom
Hanging from the ceiling,
But what was it doing there?
10 Mother's long needle made crosses.
They were black
Like the inside of my head just then.

The pages I turned sounded like wings.
"The soul is a bird," he said.
In the book full of pictures
A battle raged: Lances and swords
Made a kind of wintry forest
With my heart bleeding its branches.

# WRITING ASSIGNMENTS

1. Write a story about an encounter between a conventionally successful person and a homeless person. Capture the thoughts of both characters either as the story is told or by telling the same story first through the eyes of one character and then the other. Make something happen that might be perceived differently by each of the characters.

2. Write an *internal monologue* of a person who has just been given six months to live. Stay within the free-association thoughts of the character.

3. Write a one-act, one-set play in which several suspects are privately questioned in the office of the police inspector. Afterwards, the inspector paces the floor of his office and thinks out loud about the case. Finally, he thinks he knows who has committed the murder. (This can either be revealed or the audience or reader can be allowed to imagine which one is the murderer.)

4. Write a love scene in which the *inner thoughts* of both characters are revealed as they express their *outer thoughts* in dialogue.

5. Write a poem about the thoughts of the poet (or persona) in one of the following situations:
   a) looking through an old photo album
   b) attending a funeral
   c) revisiting a battlefield long after the war is over
   d) revisiting the scene of an early love affair
   e) revisiting an early childhood location
   f) looking at the ruins of an ancient structure, such as the Colosseum in Rome or the Acropolis in Greece.

# Chapter 10

# *Time*

## *Introduction*

## *Fiction*

## *Poetry*

## *Writing Assignments*

All action happens in time. When time stops, action freezes, as in a single frame of film or the scene on the Grecian urn described by Keats. It is the writer's job to tell the reader not only what happened and to whom and where, but *when* it happened and *how long* it lasted.

The period of time is the first thing a writer must establish. In literature an action can occur in any imaginable period of time from the most remote past to the most distant future. In *The Time-Machine* by H.G. Wells we follow the Time-Traveler to both extremes. There are stories set in prehistoric times and in specific historical periods. Science fiction is often set in the future. Most literature, however, is set in what we broadly consider the present, since it deals, for the most part, with familiar experiences. By contemporary we usually mean within the living memory of most people now alive. Naturally, this will vary from person to person, and even what is contemporary can be subdivided into more precise segments of time, such as the sixties, seventies, eighties, or nineties.

When stories are set in the immediate present (the same time period, that is, in which the writing takes place) not much is required to establish the period. In historical works a great deal of detail is often required, especially if the period itself has an important bearing on the plot. One cannot assume that the average reader is a scholar of history. Visions of the future also require a lot of description, since they are the personal speculations of the author and often involve social and political commentaries.

In every story, no matter what its period, a time frame must be established. To avoid confusion, the writer should distinguish between *present action* and *past action* (and even, at times, *future action*). If a story, for instance, is told in the third person, past tense, and the events took place in New York in 1984, it is perfectly possible that one of the characters will think back to earlier events, perhaps a childhood experience that took place in 1974. There are often incidental references to the past within a present-action time frame. For instance, "John got into his limousine and watched the landscape slide away through tinted glass. How incredible, he thought. His parents had come to America as penniless immigrants." The *flashback* is a formal way of reaching back into the past. A transition of some sort is required and then a past event is dramatized as though it were present action. Flashbacks are frequently used in movies, where they are easy to arrange and follow.

Until recently, most stories were told in the past tense. Nowadays, the present tense has become so popular that one might look through a new anthology and find that about half the stories take place in the present. It is probably the influence of film and television that has brought about this change. The effect of the present tense is to give immediacy to the action, as though it were happening on a stage or screen. For instance, "I hear footsteps behind me. I walk faster. The street is very dark. I turn a corner and see nothing but brick walls and wire fences." Plot summaries and scenarios are written in the present tense. We say that the ghost of Hamlet's father *appears* to him and *demands* revenge. We use the present tense in such cases because we are describing a play or story that has a continuing existence. We might describe a painting in the same way. "Picasso's *Guernica* captures the horror and agony of war." The present tense has proven itself effective in many contemporary stories, but it must be used with caution. For one thing, it can flirt with absurdity, as in the following: "I am hanging here from this cliff by my fingernails. The ground gives way and I fall to my death." This is an exaggeration, but the reader has the ridiculous image, for a moment, of someone actually writing down the experience as it occurs. There is also some occasional awkwardness involved in moving back and forth between a present time frame and certain past events. Some writers switch tenses frequently, which can be annoying if not done skillfully. And some writers try to put both past and present action in the present tense (see "In Starkville" by Nicole Cooley, one of the selections in this chapter).

Indicating *duration* is another problem the writer must deal with. Significant action can take place in a few moments or over a period of many years. In "An Occurrence at Owl Creek Bridge," by Ambrose Bierce, a man is hanged. Everything that *seems* to happen in the story actually happens only in his mind in that last flash of terror and desperation. Only a few seconds of real time pass. In other stories of the same length ten or twenty years might pass.

In a one-act play there is rarely a problem with duration, since a single event takes place and moves along at about the same pace as real time. On stage and screen the passage of time can be indicated in certain traditional ways—fadeouts and curtains, prop clocks, and program notes that say, "One year later." Dialogue is also very useful in establishing duration in a play or movie. In fiction, certain obvious *transitions* can be used to make things clear: "He woke up the next morning feeling as though he had been drugged."

In some works, time doesn't much matter, but in most cases the reader would like to know *when* things happen and *how long* they last.

In "What She's Saying Now," by Lee K. Abbott, the narrator, who has heard the story from Trudy, the main character, tells us exactly what is going to happen and how long a period of time is involved: "Briefly, the plot was this: a woman named Trudy Louise Weaver of Deming, New Mexico, marries a wild youth named Bobby "Cooter" Brown of Lordsburg, Texas. Childless, they live together for nearly nine years, blissful as fairy tale couples, and then—this is one suffering part—they split up."

Nicole Cooley's "In Starkville" is another story that takes place over a long period of time. The time frame is made clear on the second page: "Janice and I break into houses. This starts ten years ago. She is thirteen. I am ten." Simple arithmetic will tell us that the narrator must be twenty years old. We have already learned in the first paragraph that "Janice disappeared last June. She has been gone three months." What we have, then, is a story about the strange relationship between a boy and his older sister. Every scene is described in the present tense no matter when it occurred in that ten-year period. The narrator says, for instance, "I am thinking of the hot days when we are little and Mama takes the fan for her room and Janice brings me into her bedroom to lie on her bed with her and drink Orange Crush." The technique is interesting, suggesting a series of cinematic scenes. As soon as the reader adjusts to the treatment of time the whole story becomes clear, vivid, and dramatic. Furthermore, the consistent merging of past and present as a technical device charges the narration with an obsessive quality. The incestuous relationship, the dead child, have taken over the boy's consciousness, it would seem, forever. For him, time stands still.

Since most poems are brief and focus on a specific experience, feeling, or idea, there is usually no problem with time. In

Robert Kelly's "The Venus of Mount Rutsen" we know that a snow-woman has been melting for a week: "The snow-woman we've seen all week,/ big-breasted, big-hipped, small/ headed, is much melted now/ by the side of Mount Rutsen Road." This event provokes an interesting description and meditation.

In "The Speed of Light" Judith Kroll deals with the passage of time, or, rather, its dissolution, so that we "move in life/ into the past and the future." What is, has been, and will be. A mystical sense of time is beautifully captured in this poem.

In "Leaves" Lloyd Schwartz starts with the annual turning of the leaves in October, the blaze of color, and sees how the death of the year is linked with one's own death. But in that moment of fire and intensity the whole world comes alive—though, he repeats over and over, it won't last.

"Falling Asleep in a Darkening Room" by Al Young is a poem about what happens to time as you doze pleasantly on a beautiful afternoon. Time melts away. One is released. "Alone, you wake up yesterday or maybe last week...."

*Lee K. Abbott*

━•━━•━━ ━•━━ ━•━━ ━•━

# What She's Saying Now

1   The whole story, as Trudy told it, was supposedly about the common themes of this age: love and the hurt of it. She liked to point out that love was life itself—fearsome and double-edged, like a fillet knife. Briefly, the plot was this: a woman named Trudy Louise Weaver of Deming, New Mexico, marries a wild youth named Bobby "Cooter" Brown of Lordsburg, Texas. Childless, they live together for nearly nine years, blissful as fairy tale couples, and then—this is one suffering part—they split up. There are other parts, too, some fetching as youth
10  itself; but, in the main, she wants you to know, hers was a story with the smell and shape of a rotted fruit.

      Like many folks who were getting divorced a few years ago, Trudy was born in that big explosion of fertility after WW II. Her parents, Earl and Mildred, had a fair-sized cotton farm south of town and from it, as Trudy grew up, the world looked to her like miracle and romance—big enough to delight, small enough to manage. She was an A student, gifted in algebra and plane geometry, a pom-pom girl for the Wildcats, a candy striper at the Mimbres Valley Hospital, and, though
20  she never made much of it, the kind of Protestant open-minded enough to read, say, D.H. Lawrence and not get slack-witted about it. She had a dark side as well—moments of fluster and mood such as, she believed, you found among otherwise stable monarchs. "I am not a—what?—a Tartar," she would say to herself when overcome by gloom. "I am aloft and beautiful as a princess but, alas, depressed." In 1966, the story goes, she won a drama scholarship to SMU where, at an October Deke mixer, she met a sophomore named Cooter. He liked to snort Buckhorn beer through his nose and in Composition class the
30  year before had carved himself a tattoo on his forearm. It was supposed to be a complete sentence—"about the crazed and genuinely goofy," he said—but she could only make out a few words, namely, Time and Fear.

As seems now inevitable—in such love and story as this—they became a pair, inseparable as bird and song. Yes, Trudy tried to explain to her roommate, Cooter was creepy—no more attractive than hair on a woman's lip. His nails were dirty, he liked to chew Redman tobacco, but—and here she'd get misty-eyed—he was, well, exciting. A force, she said. A spirit which might lead to rampage or eternal laughter. In addition, he could play guitar and sing as well as any you heard on KDFW. She particularly liked the song he made up in her honor, "A Woman at Her Window," which had in it, by virtue of its lilt and flutter, something she thought of as melty and fine as the sort of beauty she was keen for.

On the night they became engaged (she was a sopho-more now), Cooter tried to feel her up. They were parked in his Ford pick-up at Lake Dallas and for an instant, beguiled by the twinkling stars and blossom-heavy April breeze, she had no idea Cooter's hand was up her skirt.

"Hey," she said, "what do you think you're doing?"

Cooter had the expression of a slow-footed night beast caught in the glare of a headlamp. "Aw, c'mon, Trudy, we're almost—you know."

They were nothing, she said. And they would be nothing until the I do's were uttered. This was a point of pride, she said. Like another's belief in the hereafter.

"Well, I'll be damned." Cooter sounded wounded as a duck. "What can it hurt?"

Whereupon, if you believe the version most oft-told, she slugged him near the earhole and pitched herself out of his truck, saying "We're finished, Robert Brown. Say goodbye to me!"

There now pass several months—through summer and almost to Thanksgiving—during which Trudy tries to forget about that old peckerwood. There is some talk that she saw, at least twice, a French major named Eliot and that she went to a Cowboys game once with a graduate assistant in that branch of physics you need heavy, thick glasses to know; but, for the most part, these months, as she recalls now, were lived in books and the library and her room. She was taking a new curriculum now, Accounting, and she set herself to it as she imagined Hercules had set himself to the stable-clearing parts of the Seven Labors. Yet, she had to admit, she was heartbro-ken. Something had gone out of her. Something that brought to mind such language as "tingle" and "tremor." She had felt her heart, she believed, sink, shrink and harden.

And then one day by accident, she bumped into Cooter

in the bookstore. He was buying a sweatshirt which said "Be
80  Free, Die Young." His face was ruined and loose.
 "You can take me now," she said. "Let's go to your
place and be frolicsome."
 All the versions of what happened next are contrary and
troubled as dark waters, a few nearly obscene with joy; but all
agree that in May, after Cooter's graduation, they were
married, honeymooned in New Orleans, and then, because of
his father's connection with Sinclair Oil, they took up residence in Midland where Cooter worked as a petroleum geolo-
gist. It was a time, Trudy says, which seemed to have the
90  density and texture of oil itself—slow and not lovely.

Not much evidence from this period in their lives exists—a
period, Trudy believes, tense as that between earthquakes; all
that survives are two letters.
 In the first, this to her roommate, Trudy writes of ragged
wings and an epic thirst for wonderland. "Cooter has a beard
now," she said, "which brings out the Rasputin in him. Plus he
has a gang of buddies with names like Poot and Billy Boy. They
smoke that red-dirt marijuana and go off, Cooter says, into the
hinterlands. I am happy, mostly, though swamped sometimes by
100  heartpangs and the urge to be elsewhere—including the moon."
In the next paragraph, she says that Cooter thinks her too tender
for this world, that he's tired of her weep-bouts and related
downwardness, but what does he know? Men are an irksome
breed, led about largely by their glands and ancient brains. "P.S.,
we shall be here awhile as Cooter's heart murmur and flat feet
will keep him from the jungle troubles pursued by Mr. Nixon."
 The second letter, discovered only recently, was written
around the time of Cooter's twenty-sixth birthday party,
which was held at the Hitching Post and brought the sheriff to
110  end it. "Dear Mr. Brown," it began, "you don't know me as I
am the underhalf of that female you live with. I am more fire
than ice and am spoken to by wondrous spirits—who say we
are bored, our finer reaches dry as ditch weeds. There is trouble here, and inside your Trudy where I live is only dust and
smoke and such blazes as you will find when the world ends."
 Then, in 1974, Cooter Brown was fired.
 And Trudy bought a Toronado demonstrator with their
savings.
 And Cooter, except for one tune about mirth and omens,
120  stopped playing the guitar.
 And Trudy began an affair.

There's not much to know about this last event, Trudy says, except that in the context of her dismay something like sex with a stranger seemed itself golden, a pleasure for the A student still in her. O.T. LeDuc wasn't so much nicer as he was different; for he, too, as she imagines it now, was equally tragic and thrown about by life. They used to take her car into the desert and flop naked into the back seat. He was an English teacher, skinny as a pencil, and seemed full of mastery and

130 order. He used to beat his chest and holler about the bombs in his head—those that went Boom-Boom when she, herself sweaty and thrashful, cast light on the dim places his species had crawled from. "I am touching your stingy heart," she'd whisper and there, in the desert twilight, his howl sounded as lonesome and perfect as the music she imagined made by this planet spinning in space.

"Robert Brown," she said one night to her husband, "do you know what love is?"

He was collapsed by the TV and had the eyeballs of a

140 fish. She had told him about O.T. and for a time, his face mashed as any she'd ever seen, he'd tried choking her.

"I think love's a mystery," she said, "devastating as death—but meant for few."

Which produced in him an outcry such as you find today in violent comic books—bold, big enough to be read across the room: "Aaarrrggghhh!"

To be true, Trudy says, a reconciliation of sorts followed and after they moved to El Paso—Cooter's father had put in a good word with Texaco—the subject of her infidelity became

150 the first thing they mentioned to their new friends. One night, at the Cavern of Music in Juarez, Cooter made her tell the whole story again.

"Ain't that a bitch?" Cooter said.

"I was much pleased," Trudy said. "I made this noise—Ya-Ya-Ya-Ya—and flew the same flight my lover was on."

"Listen to that," Cooter said. "Doesn't that bring out the shithead in you?"

And then, one day, she knew the marriage was over. Her

160 hands were wet and everything—furniture to flatware—seemed impersonal as age. It was an insight, she remembers, which struck her with the same force Cooter had, years before, when he'd told her he had no higher ambition than to be rich or mildly famous. She was standing in the bathroom and it seemed to her that the creature in the mirror was not she at all,

but a joke of a woman dragged into the present moment by want and dashed expectation.

"Cooter," she said, "you are not the tempest I deserve."

He was in the garage, a piece of his car in his greasy 170 hands.

"You know what's in here?" She was pointing at her breast.

She tried telling him about the girl she'd been—that one who'd seen life as a pleasant march from one achievement to the next. She wanted to go home, she said, climb on that old bed of hers and sleep for ten thousand years. She wanted to stand on her daddy's porch again and watch the sun go down without the noise it was making now. "I believe in the yonder worlds, don't you?"

180 "Who was it?" Cooter said. "I bet I know the sumbitch. It's Worm Foody, ain't it?"

There was no one, she said. This was not a man-woman thing. This was another relation being addressed: her to herself.

"You give me fifteen minutes," she said. "I'll be out of here."

It is always here that she mentions her abiding fondness for Cooter. She likes to point to his virtues, such as no concern for money. That she was leaving, she insists, was not really his 190 fault; he'd just been, it appeared, the vehicle which conveyed her through this vale of tears and brought her to a crossroads where the future opened wide as the horizon and said to her, in a voice wise and breathless, "Let's dream now, little darling. We are grown now and hope to live forever."

On her last trip to that dusty, well-dinged Toronado, he grabbed her by the shoulders, shook her some.

"I could get me someone too," he said. "I got my eye right now on a lady named Brenda."

Yes, she said. Her heart, once hard as stone, seemed soft 200 now and able to soar.

And then, as she always is in this part, she is driving away, unburdened as God, certain that what lurks out here in the big world has a name and substance and gives reward to those who believe in passionate, wistful dreams.

*Nicole Cooley*

# *In Starkville*

1 THE CEMETERY

At the back beside the wire fence, a marker a little bigger
than a popsicle stick with "Baby Ramona" on it and nothing
buried underneath. Mama doesn't know it, but I drive out to
this cemetery every afternoon. I sit on the grass in front of
Ramona's grave. Every day at three, the caretaker drives by in
his red truck and waves. I lift my hat, wave back. He must
think I am in mourning, keeping a vigil after all the other
relatives have left. I don't come here to pray or talk to the dead
10 but I am waiting. Janice disappeared last June. She has been
gone three months. When she comes home, my sister will find
me here, watching over her family.

MRS. KOGER

The only person in Starkville who still asks me about my
sister.

Each Sunday, I pick her up after church. Sitting in the car
with the windows rolled down to keep the inside from filling
up with heat, I listen to the strains of music coming from the
church. "Shall We Gather at the River" ends each service. A
20 moment of silence—the air is heavy and still. Then the acolytes
push open the double oak doors. Voices rise into chatter, as
the congregation streams out of the church, ladies stopping to
admire each others' dresses, their new hats, men offering stiff
smiles as they shake hands. I have always hated shaking hands.
Mrs. Koger walks out last. She says she likes a moment of her
own with Reverend Pike. Whispering, she presses her fingers
into his hand. Reverend Pike was once Johnny Pike, in Janice's
ninth-grade class. For a whole year, he called her every night.
She refused his dates. He never acknowledges me now, though
30 he always glances across the church lawn to see the car, shading his eyes from the sun.

Mrs. Koger is seventy, but she doesn't have the old lady
smell I remember from my own grandmother—talcum powder

and crushed lavender. Instead, she smells sexy. She sprays too much perfume on. Maybe like Janice she tucks a piece of perfume-soaked tissue between her breasts. I try to imagine it—the piece of kleenex against her wrinkled skin. I remember my mother misting perfume through her hair, along the back of her neck, when she got dressed to go to parties. This was a
40 long time ago, when Janice and I were little. Maybe I invented this memory—I always see my father buttoning up the back of her dress and that cannot be true.

"What do you hear from your sister, Will?" Mrs. Koger asks, straightening the silk rose she wears pinned to the collar of her dress. She asks this question every week, as if she has forgotten that she asked me the Sunday before.

I shake my head. "I don't know."

I want to say, "Janice jumped in the river" or "She set herself on fire." Fire is the best thing I can think of to start
50 people thinking about my sister again. To make them remember that she exists. I would never have to finish telling the story because everyone would decide the ending for themselves—Janice died or was sent away to the state hospital in Vicksburg.

CHILDHOOD

Janice and I break into houses. This starts ten years ago. She is thirteen. I am ten.

The first time, we don't talk about it. There is no plan. One night, we are walking back from the park where there was a game of Hide and Seek. I sat on the gravel path while Janice
60 played with the older boys, the ones who are old enough to smoke and drive. When one of them was "it," and she got caught, she'd scream as he slapped her on the thigh or lifted up the skirt of her dress.

Janice stops in front of Mr. and Mrs. Cranes' house. She touches her finger to her lips. "Listen," she says. "What do you hear?"

Cicadas buzz. Wind ruffles the branches of the trees. "Nothing," I say.

"That's right." She tugs on my jacket sleeve. "I want us
70 to have a secret," she whispers. "Something we won't ever tell." I look up at my sister. Her face is pale in the moonlight, but her eyes glow. Round and wide, a circle of yellow around the iris. "Come with me, Will."

She leads me around to the Cranes' back fence. She crouches on the ground and clasps her hands together to make a foothold. "Go first."

"Why can't we open the gate?" I ask.

"Because. We have to do it like this."

I climb over the chain link fence, tearing my jacket on the
80  way down. Mama will be mad. My heart beats fast. What is
the secret?

The house is dark. We go through the kitchen window,
which is left unlocked. We slide over the sink. She grabs my
hand in hers and leads me down the hall, as if she knows the
way. Photographs of the family in gilt frames line the walls.
Mr. and Mrs. Crane with their arms around each other. Andrew Crane in his baseball uniform posed with a bat. I draw a
sharp breath—Andrew is in my class at school. This is dangerous. The carpet is soft and thick; I can feel it through my
90  sneakers.

We enter the first room at the end of the hall, the parents'
bedroom. In the middle of the room is a large, heart-shaped
bed. "Look," I say.

Janice gives me a stern, warning look. "Shh." Her face is
serious. "Let's lie down," she whispers. "Do this with me."

The mattress sinks underneath my weight as I lower
myself down. Janice stretches out beside me, spreading her
arms out at her sides like she is making a snow angel. Her
fingers brush my side. "Let's sleep for a little while."

100      Now I am terrified. Janice rests her hand on my arm,
below my jacket sleeve, and closes her eyes. I stare at the
ceiling fan. I figure I'll count to two hundred—One Mississippi, Two Mississippi—then wake her up. I imagine all the
bad things that could happen as we lie there—the Cranes will
arrive home, find us sleeping in their bed, call our mother, call
the police. From next door, I can hear the neighbors talking in
the yard. A man laughs. I become more and more scared until
my legs start to tremble. Janice breathes slow and even. Her
fingers cool against my skin.

110      "Janice," I whisper. "Let's go."

"Mmmmm." She turns towards me, her eyes still closed.
"Not yet. I'm not ready. I'm in the middle of a dream."

I count again this time to three hundred and back down.
A long time seems to go by. I try again, "Janice?"

Her eyes snap open. "Oh, for God's sake, you're such a
baby, Will."

We leave the same way we come in. I close the window
behind us. All the way home, as we walk in silence along the
dark street, I can't think of anything but how she says it, that
120  word, *baby*.

When we reach our house, she stops and turns to face me. Light from the streetlamps gleams in her dark hair. She says, "Mama can't find out about this." I nod to show her that I understand. She moves her hand up to my face and pushes the hair out of my eyes with a quick, light touch.

NIGHTMARES

"The bad dreams come from her father's side," Mama says. It's five-thirty, and I've just woken her up to give her the first dose of the medicine she takes since the doctors discov-
130 ered her heart murmur. She doesn't need the medicine, but after Janice left she told the doctors they had to prescribe something for her or she'd check herself into the hospital to die. Every morning, I empty two blue capsules into a cup of hot lemon water. Janice told me once this cleans out your system after a night asleep.

I tuck the quilt over my mother's knees. She sits on the couch all day and insists she is always cold. The doctors have taken me aside, have told me there is no reason my mother can't get up, walk, go to work again. She is scared. She is only
140 fifty, but she believes that if she stands up alone, her heart will start to beat too fast. Nothing I can say will make her change her mind.

"I don't have bad dreams," I tell her. Because I have never dreamed at all. I will myself to fall into a deep, unbroken sleep every night, a sleep like blank white paper.

She acts as if she doesn't hear. "Janice left us because she couldn't sleep in this house. That's what she said. She expected me to believe that. I'm her mother, so I'd believe anything."

"She did have trouble sleeping," I say. Like the time after
150 Ramona. Janice would get up from the couch and go to her room at three o'clock every day. I can imagine her lying down on the oak frame trundle bed, and spreading her fingers flat across her stomach to feel where the baby had been. What did she do after that? Did she ever cry or hit herself in the ribs with a fist or get up to look in the big cracked mirror over the dresser? She told me she was afraid to sleep because the baby appeared to her in dreams.

"Just like her father." Mama never calls him "my hus-band" or "your father," but "her father," as if he belongs only
160 to my sister.

"Drink the medicine," I tell her. "Then we can go for a drive around the river."

"I'm too sick to go anywhere. Leave me alone." She hunches down into the embroidered pillows on the couch. "My life is over and your sister has ruined hers."

Mama often tells me that. I've learned to ignore it, but, still, each time, I wait for her to tell me that I am the family's hope, the good son, the one she can count on. I want her to tell me that it matters if I stay or disappear.

170 THE BANK
The afternoons, when I sit in the cemetery, Mama thinks I still work at Am South Bank.

THE MAP
Starkville is three miles wide. You can drive the length of it in ten minutes, in a straight line from the Whitney Bank to the Dairy Queen. A row of houses, small white boxes, built for the riverboat workers fifty years ago, each one exactly the same—three front steps, a bell-shaped door, a window like an eye on either side of the entrance. A square of grass for a front
180 yard. Once in a while, you can hear a steamboat whistle or the calliope from the ferry on its way to New Orleans as you drive by. Sometimes, I count off the houses we broke into: the Hamiltons, the Bookers, the Baldwins, the Stamps. I can't remember all of the houses we have been in.

You drive the length of Starkville and there is nowhere to go and you turn back.

I find the map in my mother's bureau drawer, after she decides she is sick and makes me dress her. I don't want to dress her; I don't want to see my mother's body. I am looking
190 for her underwear that day, searching nervously through the drawers, and I pull it out, underneath the garters and silk peignoirs she never wears, a yellowed paper, folded up in squares. Why does she keep a map of the city hidden as if it were a secret?

I sit down on the edge of my mother's bed, tracing the blue lines on the paper with my finger, following the empty roads, charting the route of my escape.

THE FORTUNE TELLER
I find her on the way home from the cemetery. I have
200 driven by the sign for years—TEA ROOM   LADY PALM READER FIVE DOLLARS TO PREDICT THE HISTORY OF YOUR LIFE. A wooden placard in the front window of a house.

I've driven by so many times, but all of a sudden I know that if I were Janice, I'd stop and go inside.

I am thinking of the hot days when we are little and Mama takes the fan for her room and Janice brings me into her bedroom to lie on her bed with her and drink Orange Crush. Janice watches the ceiling like it is the sky, looking for the outline of the face of the man she'll marry. She says that if she closes her eyes then opens them very fast she can see a shadow in the air sometimes, a faint, blurred oval. There are water marks on the ceiling of her room. She tells me that the rain can come up that high in the house, like the red rises in a barometer.

The lady palm reader wears a housedress and a single gold hoop earring. I don't know if she lost one earring or if the absence is intentional. Her dress is low-cut and light—I can see the outline of her breasts through the cloth. She grabs my wrist in the doorway and stares at the lines on my palm, then takes the money and leads me by the hand to a red-curtained room in the back. It smells like she has a lot of cats. There are candles stuck in coffee saucers and a plastic incense burner. She lights a cigarette and starts talking.

"First off," she says. "I can see that you have an extraordinary power over others."

I interrupt to ask, "What does that mean?"

She looks at me, her eyes blue and level, her lips parted in a little smile. "It means your advice will never fail."

I am disappointed. "Can I ask about something specific?"

"Go ahead." She draws on her cigarette, tapping the long ash on the edge of the table.

"Can you find out where someone is? I'm looking for my sister." I realize I am talking fast, as if I'm nervous, and I am. "Her name is Janice and her middle name is—"

The fortune teller raises her hand in the air to stop me. "I've got something," she says. "I was just about to tell you that people who have names that begin with J are very important in your life." She pauses, lowering her eyes. "Especially *women.*"

I can't think of any Js except my sister and my mother, whose name is Jacqueline, but I have never once heard her called that.

"I don't want to find out about women," I say. "It's my sister—"

"Oh, of course you do," the fortune teller says. "Everyone who comes in here wants to find out about women." She leans forward and I can see down her dress. "What's the real reason you wanted to talk to me, honey? Janice isn't really your sister, now is she?"

250 CHILDHOOD

We break into the houses for years. We never once steal anything. We walk around the houses in the dark and lie down in other people's beds.

Janice often warns me about what will happen if I tell anyone about our "visits" as she calls them. "Not even your wife," she says. "Not your own children." "I'll hurt you," she tells me once. "I could kill you, do you know that?" She says, "When you least expect it, expect it. I'd track you down if you ever ran away." I don't really believe all of these threats, but I
260 am scared enough to keep quiet.

One night, I feel a little pinch, a prick, in my finger, and I jerk awake. Janice is standing over my bed. One of Mama's darning needles in her hand.

"We're going to become bloodbrothers," she says. She climbs into my bed.

My finger stings. I squeeze my eyes shut. I put my finger in my mouth to stop the bleeding. I hear Janice's sharp intake of breath and know that she's done hers. "Repeat after me," she says. "I swear—"
270 "I swear—" I keep my eyes shut.

"That I will never tell another living soul—"

"That I will never tell another living soul—"

"About the secrets I have with my sister, Janice Ann Marie." She pauses. "I will carry these secrets with me till I die, to the grave."

I repeat her words. She presses her finger to mine. I open my eyes and she is smiling at me. "We mixed our blood," she says, curling up closer to me in bed. "Now we're linked up forever."

280 FATHER

I hear Mama tell Mrs. Koger she's a widow. "He died before Will was born," she says, then, in a lower voice, almost a whisper, "He drowned." Mrs. Koger nods, her blue hat bobbing on her head. She holds her purse tightly in her lap; there are damp stains from her fingers on the leather. She is the only visitor who comes to see my mother now, comes every other week and brings macaroons in a round gold tin. Mama won't eat them—"sugar goes straight to the heart"—so I smile

politely, thank her and stack the tins on the top shelf of the
290 kitchen cupboard.

"Janice never got over her father's death," Mama says
shaking her head.

I don't contradict my mother. To the world outside our
family, she can't admit that she was left. To Janice and me, she
says once that our father is a gypsy who ran away to New
Orleans and sometimes she tells us that he goes there because
he is a Cuban refugee and can't wait to take the boat back out
of the Gulf of Mexico away from us. She tells it several different ways. What is the real story?

300 NIGHTMARES
Does my mother dream about my father?
Does Janice, wherever she is, ever dream about me?
Who is dreaming my dreams?

THE OTHER CITY
When I am ten and Janice is thirteen, Mama gets a letter
from our father. A thin blue envelope with a postmark she
won't let us see. She stands in the kitchen, leaning against a
table, turning the envelope over and over in her hands and
then slits it open with a bread knife. We watch her read, her
310 eyes scanning the lines, with no expression. She crumples it up
into a ball and leaves the room; Janice digs it out of the kitchen
trash can. The envelope is stamped Tampa, Florida, with no
return address.

He says he is married and has a son. He works on a
shrimp boat and doesn't make enough money to support two
families. He hopes she understands. He is sorry he has never
written before. He doesn't mention me or Janice.

"That bastard," Janice says, startling me. I have never
heard the word spoken out loud but I know what it means. She
320 rips the letter up into little pieces, dropping them into the drain
of the sink. She looks as if she might cry.

"It doesn't matter," I tell her. "We don't need him." But
she doesn't seem to hear me; she has turned on the cold water
faucet to force the pieces down.

We are all quiet for the rest of the afternoon. I want to
talk to Janice, but she goes up to her room and shuts the door.
I sit on the couch, picking at loose threads in the pillows,
waiting. Mama comes downstairs in her good blue coat and
hat, takes the car keys off the hall table, and leaves without
330 speaking to me.

At first, that makes me scared. My mother is going to leave us too. I start to think how Janice and I will have to live alone till we grow up, cook for ourselves, tuck each other into bed at night. The more I think about it, the more I can imagine it, the better our new life alone together seems. We won't have to go to school anymore or do chores around the house. We won't have to break into houses anymore because we will have our own house to be alone in.

Then the front door bangs open. Mama is back. "I
340 brought you all a present," she says, dropping a bag into my lap. "Call your sister down."

It is a paper doll book with pages of pieces to construct a village out of paper. Tabs of paper fit together and you can make a city. I don't want to build the city—it's wrong for boys to play with paper doll books. Mama spreads the pages on the living room floor.

"I'll help you," she says, kneeling on the rug beside me.

It gets dark outside. We don't talk. My eyes ache and my fingers stiffen and no one mentions dinner. I want to go to
350 sleep. My stomach begins to hurt. I yawn.

"We can't go to sleep till we've glued every piece in place," Mama says. Her hair falls in wisps around her face, damp with sweat.

She and Janice do most of the work. I fall asleep on the floor, resting my head on a couch cushion.

In the morning, I open my eyes and my mother and sister are gone. The village looks like something that has been rained on: all the paper has folded in on itself. I crawl across the floor and try to stick the pieces back together, but I just make it fall
360 apart even more.

Mama comes down in her blue robe. When she sees the village, she starts crying.

"I'm sorry," I say helplessly.

Later, I know it must be the humidity that keeps the glue from sticking, but still she takes it as a sign.

THE DESPERATE HOURS

At night, when Mama lets me help her out to the screen porch to watch TV, she grips my arm, leaning heavily against me. I arrange her blankets in a wicker chair and give her the
370 night medicine in a cup of tea.

One night, we watch *The Desperate Hours,* a movie that used to make Janice scared, about a family held hostage in their own home by three criminals. Trapped inside.

"That wouldn't happen," Mama says. "Those people could leave." Midway through the movie, she falls asleep, and I watch the rest alone, leaning forward in my chair to follow every word and action. Mama's head falls back against the pillow, her mouth open. Her hair is matted, her skin sags around her chin, saliva dampens her cheek. She is ugly now,
380    changed into an old woman.

Will my sister look like this someday?

MRS. KOGER

One Sunday, she turns to me in the car and asks, "Do you expect your sister will come back?"

THE RADIO

A big black box with square dials that used to be my mother's when she was a girl. The old-fashioned kind you find in junk shops now.

I imagine my mother listening to Billie Holiday as she
390    dresses for a date. She is eighteen. The music swirls in cigarette smoke; dusting powder settles in the air. My mother hums along with the music, "Am I Blue?" She sits on the edge of her bed to slip on her silk stockings, rolls them up past her knees and clips them to the garters, at the tops of her thighs.

She wraps her long hair into a twist at the back of her neck. Her hair is dark and heavy like my sister's. Leaning close to the dresser mirror, she lines her eyes. She pats powder on her face to make it pale, presses some between her breasts. Finally, she slips on her dress, a pink cloud, over the curve of
400    her hips, falling just below her knees.

Sometimes, when I imagine this scene, my mother becomes Janice. I have to stop myself.

It is too hard to stop remembering. Remembering how I used to pick her up after work at the fabric store in our red Plymouth with the broken front seat door, how she'd lay her head in my lap as I drove home. How at night, after we were sure Mama was asleep, we'd push the oak dresser up against her bedroom door and turn the radio on low to jazz or static. How she'd raise her arms like a little girl as I lifted up her
410    nightgown.

THE CEMETERY

I study the alignment of the graves. The bodies are buried on an East-West axis. Heads facing west, feet towards the east.

I learn this in Sunday School when I am eleven. We sit in a circle around a low wooden table in the parish hall. Mrs. Bender reads from a black bound book as we fidget, hands clasped in our laps. "Sit like penitents," is one of her favorite things to say. Janice and I have broken into Mrs. Bender's
420  house. We know that even though she wears a straight brown dress falling nearly to her ankles, there are lace stockings drying on the shower rod in her bathroom. There is a copy of *Lady Chatterly's Lover* on her bedside table. Her bedsheets are stiff though, like the pallets she tells us the saints slept on, itchy and hard.

Janice sits beside me in a pink dress Mama made, swinging her legs, dragging her new shoes across the floor till Mrs. Bender looks up from her reading, raises her eyebrows and goes on. "The faithful will rise to face Christ on Judgment
430  Day," she reads. "Jerusalem lies to the East." Janice kicks me lightly in the shin.

"Stop it," I whisper, bending down to rub my leg.

"Do you have something to share with the class, Will?" Mrs. Bender snaps the black book shut.

"Yes, he does," my sister says, leaning forward across the table "He wants to know what happens if some dead person gets buried backwards."

Mrs. Bender's face tightens. Her mouth set in a thin, hard line.

440  Janice repeats the question. Several children laugh.

Mrs. Bender recovers her composure. "Doesn't Will know how to speak for himself?"

"No, don't you know? He's deaf. I was sure you knew that. He can't talk at all, except to make sounds like this—" Janice opens and shuts her mouth, grunting, to demonstrate. "See?"

Laughter spreads through the room. "Out, both of you," Mrs. Bender yells. "I know your mother and I know the kind of family you come from. You ought to be ashamed."

450  Janice rises from the table, pulling me after her. "What *kind* of family?" she asks, crossing her arms over her chest. "Everybody knows we don't have a father."

Mrs. Bender slams the book down on the table. "You are not welcome in this class again."

Now, years later, I sit on the grass and stare at the graves. Since it's still summer, everyone brings flowers in coffee cans and fruit jars wrapped with tin foil. In the poor section of the cemetery, I have noticed, there are small flat headstones

460 covered with possessions—eyeglasses, broken dishes, medicine bottles, mussel shells. More relatives come to sit beside those graves.

East and West. Ramona can't rise up. Her grave an empty space.

CHILDHOOD

The first time it happens is when we break into Mrs. Koger's house. I am seventeen.

Janice is working at Hancock's Fabrics, and she hates the job. She says she is bored all day, helping ladies match thread to different colored cloth and showing them the best 470 kind of buttons to buy. When she comes home, she is restless. She sits at the kitchen table, tapping her foot against the rungs of her chair, smoking and flipping through Mama's old copies of *Harper's Bazaar,* waiting for Mama to go to bed so we can leave the house together. Janice wants to break into houses nearly every night.

That night, we leave at midnight. Janice walks fast, her high heels clicking on the pavement. She walks purposefully, taking long strides. I try to catch up and keep falling behind.

She stops in front of Mrs. Koger's house.

480 "No," I say.

"Why?" She crosses her arms beneath her breasts.

"I don't want to." Her husband died the week before. Mrs. Koger has gone to stay with her sister in Jackson.

"I'm going in." Janice starts across the lawn. "I don't care whether or not you come."

For a minute, anger rises up in me, but I can't let my sister make the visit alone. She is already inside when I run across the grass.

When I find her standing in the kitchen, she touches my 490 wrist and smiles. "I knew you'd come."

Foil-wrapped dishes stacked on the kitchen counter, brought over by the neighbor ladies. One of Mama's cookie tins in the pile. The table scrubbed clean and shining. The two chairs pulled in.

All the mirrors are covered with sheets. The blinds are drawn. Janice and I walk down the hall to Mrs. Koger's bedroom.

Next to the bed, boxes of Mr. Koger's clothes, wrapped in brown paper and labelled with his name. The blankets 500 drawn tight across the bed as if no one ever sleeps there.

"This is wrong," I say. "We should leave." My face burns. I can't look at Janice.

She pulls me down to the bed. "A dead person slept here," she says. "Let's lie down."

I am shaking. When she reaches for my hand, she laces her fingers into mine. She turns to face me. It is too dark in he room to see. She moves closer. Rises up a little. The ends of her long hair brushing against my face.

510 She touches me. I lie straight and still, then I begin to kiss her back.

"Have you ever done this before?" she whispers. "You haven't, have you?"

I shake my head. I don't want her to see that I'm scared. She fingers the buttons on my shirt.

RAMONA

If anyone knew, they would say it is a good thing she dies.

She dies two months before she is born. The doctors say she is too small to bury. The Mississippi State laws say she has 520 to have a grave. The man at the cemetery unfolds a map and shows Janice the space on the blue grid marked "Infants and Children." Janice pays for one small space, gives it a name.

Why has she never visited the grave?

FATHER

I have decided on the real story: he never knows that I am born. He never knows Mama is going to have a second child. Otherwise, he would not leave.

How does he leave? Does he take his hat from the hall table one day, open the front door, and simply disappear? Is 530 there a scene, an argument, a fight between my parents that my sister sees?

I have decided: one day he is just gone. He takes nothing with him for his next life. He leaves when no one is looking. No one expecting him to go.

CHILDHOOD

Dark houses. Windows left open. Janice loosening her dress. The shadow of her leg falling across mine.

THE MAP

Janice leaves in the middle of the night. I wake up and 540 hear her heels clicking on her bedroom floor as she walks back and forth across the room. I hear dresser drawers opening. The zipper on her suitcase pulling closed—the sound of something tearing.

I lie in bed and listen before I go to her. Have I been waiting for this to happen? For days, weeks, since Ramona, Janice will not talk to me, except to tell me about her dreams. Dreams where Ramona comes to her at different ages, as a baby, as a young child, as an old woman. Maybe Ramona gives my sister a sign. Ramona could be telling Janice it is time
550 to leave me.

I enter her room without knocking. She stands over the bed, her back to me, putting things into her purse. She wears Mama's old blue robe.

"What are you doing?" I say though we both know.

She doesn't answer, but she turns around. Her face is pale. Her hair brushed smooth to her shoulders. She tightens the belt of the robe around her waist, pulling it flat across her chest.

"Where are you going?" I step closer and she backs
560 towards the wall.

"I have to get dressed now," she says. Her voice is low, almost a whisper. "Go away."

I am still. She stares at me with no expression. She loosens the robe and drops it to the floor. For a second, she stands there, naked, in her high-heeled shoes, then, quickly, she pulls on her underwear, a thin blue dress.

"Janice," I say.

When she looks at me, her face is old. There are tiny lines at the corners of her eyes. "I'm tired," she says. "I'm tired."
570 I carry the suitcase down the stairs, walking behind her. In front of the house, she takes the suitcase from my hand. "Go back inside."

"Janice," I say.

My sister has already turned away from me. She starts slowly down the sidewalk, then stops, bends down to remove her shoes. She walks along the street, holding her shoes in her hand.

Should I have told her to take me with her? She wants to leave me. I am watching her leave me. She walks past the rows
580 of dark houses. I am watching. It takes a long time for her to disappear.

## Robert Kelly

# *The Venus of Mount Rutsen*

1 The snow-woman we've seen all week,
  big-breasted, big-hipped, small
  headed, is much melted now
  by the side of Mount Rutsen Road.

  It has come to her by day
  and the warm diminishing
  is registered each cold night
  and held there one more day.

  Today her breasts are gone
10 almost and her head's
  a little prong. But the enormous
  shapeless hips are where

  the upper body's gone.
  She is palaeolithic now, cave mother,
  naked opportunist of pure womb

  as if this road and this town too
  were fecund, and spring would come
  here fantastically and soon

  and we would beat the world at mating,
20 the snow in sunshine glinting
  like the eyes of young wives.

## *Judith Kroll*

# *The Speed of Light*

1 sometime, someone is writing of this

her hair good brown, she looks out a train window
and notices again how it frames an etching

the innocent greens of the fields
and the dark farmer
in his eye-white headcloth and loincloth, under
 the sky

and what becomes of our friends?
they blow by us like leaves

as we move in life
10 into the past and the future

we decide where to send our parents to school
we wake up younger than our children

# *Lloyd Schwartz*

# *Leaves*

### 1.

1  Every October it becomes important, no, *necessary*
to see the leaves turning, to be surrounded
by leaves turning; it's not just the symbolism,
to confront in the death of the year your death,
one blazing farewell appearance, though the irony
isn't lost on you that nature is most seductive
when it's about to die, flaunting the dazzle of its
incipient exit, an ending that at least so far
the effects of human progress (pollution, acid rain)
10  have not yet frightened you enough to make you believe
is real; that is, you know this ending is a deception
because of course nature is always renewing itself—
        the trees don't *die*, they just pretend,
        go out in style, and return in style: a new style.

### 2.

Is it deliberate how far they make you go
especially if you live in the city to get far
enough away from home to see not just trees
but only trees? The boring highways, roadsigns, high
speeds, 10-axle trucks passing you as if they were
20  in an even greater hurry than you to look at leaves:
so you drive in terror for literal hours and it looks
like rain, or *snow*, but it's probably just clouds
(too cloudy to see any color?) and you wonder,
given the poverty of your memory, which road had the
most color last year, but it doesn't matter since
you're probably too late anyway, or too early—
        whichever road you take will be the wrong one
        and you've probably come all this way for nothing.

3.

You'll be driving along depressed when suddenly
30  a cloud will move and the sun will muscle through
and ignite the hills. It may not last. Probably
won't last. But for a moment the whole world
comes to. Wakes up. Proves it lives. It lives—
*red, yellow, orange, brown, russet, ocher, vermillion,*
*gold.* Flame and rust. Flame and rust, the permutations
of burning. You're on fire. Your eyes are on fire.
It won't last, you don't want it to last. You
can't stand any more. But you don't want it to stop.
It's what you've come for. It's what you'll
40  come back for. It won't stay with you, but you'll
      remember that it felt like nothing else you've felt
      or something you've felt that also didn't last.

## *Al Young*

# *Falling Asleep in a Darkening Room*

1 Blue, the most beautiful of afternoons
　is to lie transfixed with pressure brought
　to bear on your dozing zone, and then to
　feel air being let out of the giant world,
　a balloon big enough to live on but not live in
　except perhaps to sleepers dreaming they're awake.

To lay you down to sleep with winter blowing
　through rooms where you've been worrying too much,
　run your engine's battery down to barely audible
10 palm-held miniature radio level ... *Shhhhh* ...

Now you can let laughter bubble out of silence
　like kindergarten blobs of color flung against
　emptiness, and let every unhurried passerby
　become a painted shadow remembered in a slow dream
　you always wanted to have, but haven't had yet,
　not until now when, nodding, fading, you let go.

Everything you ever thought you were leaves you.
　Alone, you wake up yesterday or maybe last week
　or, fortunate, you fade back in, expanded again,
20 feeling virginal, refreshed—a new you not so blue.

# WRITING ASSIGNMENTS

1. Write a story that takes place over a long period of time. Perhaps a long series of events leads to a dramatic scene.

2. Write a story in which flashbacks are used along with current action. For instance:
   a) Someone waits in a dreary railway station for a lover who is very late.
   b) Someone in a courtroom awaits the outcome of a trial.
   c) A wounded soldier struggles through enemy territory in search of friendly troops.

3. Write a play or story that takes place entirely in a lifeboat in which five or six people discuss their desperate plight. How can you indicate the passage of time in a play of this sort?

4. Write a poem about time that uses the following material:
   a) the four seasons
   b) youth and old age
   c) eternal love
   d) the family
   e) ancient ruins or historical places
   f) an old cemetery

# Chapter 11

# Images and Sounds

## Introduction

## Fiction

## Poetry   (Images)

## *Poetry*   (Sounds and Patterns)

Albert Goldbarth     *Lullabye*
Thom Gunn     *From the wave*
John Hollander     *Coordinating Conjunction*
Richard Kenney     *March Orrery*
Howard Nemerov     *The Air Force Museum at Dayton*
Ishmael Reed     *Bitter Chocolate*
Charles Wright     *California Spring*
                 *Laguna Blues*

## *Additional Poems*

Jonathan Aaron     *The Foreigner*
A.R. Ammons     *Revelers, Revealers*
Rosa Maria Arenas     *Mother of Shrines*
Tom Clark     *Reading the Technical Journals*
             *Looking for Work in Teaching*
Nikki Giovanni     *Revolutionary Dreams*
Eamon Grennan     *Hieroglyphic*
Marilyn Hacker     *Her Ring*
Twyla Hansen     *Garbage*
Mary Kinzie     *Sun and Moon*
Grace Morton     *What Howard Moss Has Just Mailed You*
Lisel Mueller     *Insomnia*
Sharon Olds     *Sex Without Love*
Mary Swander     *The Tattooed Man Comes for a Massage*

## *Writing Assignments*

Language, skillfully used, can create significant *images* and aesthetically pleasing *sounds*. These ingredients exist in all the literary genres; in poetry they are essential.

Images are pictures in the mind, the visual dimension of literature. They are created either by literal description or by the use of metaphors, similes, allusions, and symbols. Figures of speech involve nonliteral comparisons: "Now is the winter of our discontent/ Made glorious summer by this sun of York ..." (Shakespeare, *Richard III*). The seasons are used here *metaphorically*. If we say that "Our discontent was like a bleak winter," we have a *simile,* which involves the use of *like* or *as* (a metaphor does not).

*Allusions* make nonliteral reference to whatever is being described, using some thing or person well-known in a given culture: "When he took the government to court he was David confronting Goliath." In "Killing the Bees" (Chapter 1) the whole framework of the story depends on the reader's recognizing allusions to the Holocaust.

A *symbol* is something specific that stands for something else that is general or abstract. The cross stands not only for the Crucifixion but for all the ideals and beliefs of Christianity. In *Moby Dick* the white whale stands for something complex, some God-like knowledge, possibly, that must not be pursued by man. Hawthorne's *The Scarlet Letter* is full of symbolism, beginning with the letter "A" itself, which stands for Hester's sin—adultery.

In some works there is a pattern of images. In others, especially in poetry, there is a single dominant image. Literature can never be entirely abstract. It is rooted in concrete things, in actions and characters. In his poem about the migrations of geese (in this chapter), Galway Kinnell refers to "the streamers of their formation," each body "flashing white ... when the wings lift ... the invisible continuously perforating the visible." An image often works in that way: The unseen (emotions, abstractions) is implied by the actual (the geese). Hester's guilt is implied by the "A." Captain Ahab's overreaching ambition is implied by the whale. The abstract is found in the particular. The manipulation of images is a fundamental part of the writer's craft.

Michael Martone, in "It's Time," weaves a close pattern of recurring images which intensify the significance and impact of his story. The period is the 1940s, just after World War II. The central character, the narrator of the story—the wife—has been doing war work, painting clock faces in a factory. Everything depends on the allusion to the radium in the paint (at that time a new material for making the numbers glow in the dark), and on the reader's superior 1990s understanding of the properties of radium. The story works like a Greek tragedy, painfully moving its characters forward to their inescapable doom.

Initially everything is fresh and sparkling. Raspberry bushes bud, shooting up overnight. The baby daughter makes raspberry sounds in her crib, which is decorated with radium paint, a "dew of pulsing light." The wife's hair is paint-flecked: "He'd kiss me through a cloud of stars." Her fingertips light up, stained with radium. Time, seen on the luminous dial of a watch, is a "constellation" in the dark. It tells them there is time for love, before they have to get the baby up.

But is there time? Even here, early in the story, there are hints of doom. When the baby makes a raspberry her tongue melts "into slobber." And the wife, when she kisses the husband, leaves "welts of throbbing light." A welt is raised by a wound or blow to the body. In the factory, the narrator has sable brushes which she rolls on her tongue "to hone the point sharp enough to jewel each second." She is _licking_ radium, a radioactive metallic element. _Now_ the reader knows, though the narrator as yet does not, that the starry glittering images of radium are ironic, that their glamour conceals disaster.

Raspberries, radium, time, tongues, stars, and even fingertips are images that dominate this story and carry its emotional thrust. Finally, even the things that represent life appear to be eroded. The raspberries, white milk coating "the scoring between the tiny globes" which make up each berry remind us of the x-ray of the wife's hand, "the brittle black fingernails... etched with bone white." The raspberries are "squashed and ruptured." "So little [holds] the berry in place" is a clear image of our own fragile hold on life and the possibility that dazzling inventions may lessen that hold. By setting the story some forty-five years ago, the author is able to imply that what seems like progress may turn out to be fatal.

Many poems consist of an extended metaphor. The poet starts with a simple figure of speech and goes on to explore it in a series of variations. One such poem is Nikki Giovanni's "Kidnap Poem," in which kidnap imagery is blended with that of poetic seduction. Another, Lorna Goodison's "On Becoming a Tiger," explores the future of women once the tiger in them is liberated.

Sharon Olds contributes a comic example of the extended metaphor in "Topography." Two lovers apparently fly across the country. Afterwards in bed they make love, but it is all described in geographical terms: "my/ San Francisco against your New York, your/ Fire Island sucking my Sonoma, my/ New Orleans deep in your Texas, your Idaho/ bright on my great Lakes, my Kansas/ burning against your Kansas . . . " and so on until they become "one nation, indivisible."

There is a good example of personification in Ursula Le-Guin's "Silence." She imagines a new idea of hers as though it is a baby to whom she gives birth: "I had a little naked thought/slipped out between my thighs. . . ." She follows the metaphor through the whole poem. The idea grows. She sews words together to clothe it, ". . . and so it grows and walks and talks and dies."

Poets tend to be preoccupied with fundamentals—art, life, love, death, to name a few—and it is extraordinary that so many thousands of poems on the same basic subjects should be so varied. In Chapter I, Alan Dugan, David Ignatow, A.R. Ammons, and Mary B. Campbell write about art (or poetry), yet the images chosen by these poets to express their themes differ widely.

In "Winn's Blackbird," Eamon Grennan takes up a similar subject. Here a dead blackbird is the central image, a symbol of death, and it is the imagination of the artist that regenerates the bird in a series of sketches. Grennan addresses the artist: "Death/ is what you're giving life to," he says, and in the end: "your bird . . . takes flight."

Death is well represented in poetry. We have already discussed Atwood's "Last Day" (Chapter 7) which deals with death as well as rebirth ("This is the last day of the last week"). The image for death is "nothing, which is oval/ and full." This *nothing* becomes an egg, and then the sun, and the last day becomes the new day.

In "The Shroud," Galway Kinnell explores a similar theme. He describes a milkweed seed that "dips-and-soars," a goldfinch whose undulating flight suggests a needle going through cloth, and asks what whole-earth shroud they may be stitching. An organic death-in-life, or life-in-death, is imaged here, and the poet asks, "When will it ever be finished?"

Charles Simic, in "Obscure Beginnings," chooses a series of somewhat medieval images to suggest that death is omnipresent and life merely an interlude. To be a fly in a house of spiders is to be doomed. "Queen Insomnia" and her henchmen imply man's condition, brought on by dread of death and judgment. A glimpse of pastoral beauty—life itself—can only pain the doomed person (everyone, that is). Death notices ("posted everywhere") can only remind us of our fate. The sky is vast and empty (is there a heaven?) and similarly the ceiling (referred to three times) is "pale as the flowers." Ashen, one might say. The child being dressed for religious instruction is being dressed "for slaughter." Is there life, even? Yes: "the red parrot screaming in the parrot house." His time, too, is limited. Or is it that he suggests the very blood in one's veins? A chilling but effective image, one of many in this poem.

In "The Toes," Raymond Carver explores the life of the body through the toes, which "used to strain/ with anticipation/ simply/ curl with pleasure/ at the least provocation." Finally the toes, those "terminal digits," come to represent the very center of being as it regrets life, faces death.

Crows, in "The Thing About Crows," by Josephine Jacobsen, represent death. They are hoarse, they croak about approaching winter in their "autumnal voices" on a spring day when the "buds on roses puff out."

A variety of poets, then, have embodied—or at least suggested—the idea of death in a multiplicity of concrete images: spiders, death notices, crows, a shroud, a blackbird, and "terminal digits." Life, as opposed to death, has been evoked by such detail as toes "curling with pleasure," milkweed seed, sheep nibbling wild flowers, a red parrot, budding roses. It is noteworthy, however, that birds figure largely as favored images.

In "Pajamas," Sharon Olds has written a lyric in a happier mode. Through the image of a daughter's pajamas, which she likens to the skin of a peeled peach, the poet evokes the whole living, youthful downy person. By means of a second image, that of a caterpillar's shed skin, she further implies the daughter's emergence from the larva stage into full life. Reverting to the first image, the poet suggests again the excitement of the newly released life through a smell, a "sharp fragrance like peach brandy."

In "The Woods," Josephine Jacobsen compares the dangers of "real" woods—those difficult adventures found in the outside world—to the dangers of "invisible woods" or confusions of the mind. "Fewer are lost," she says, continuing the metaphor, "in the visible wood."

The manipulation of sounds is also part of the writer's craft. Language itself evolved as an organization of sounds for human communication, entirely oral. It was years before it became a written form of communication. It is impossible to say when language first had any aesthetic value. Perhaps from the very beginning. Some kind of narration seems to have existed since prehistoric times. With the advent of writing came the experience of reading to oneself, but the sounds of language are still there in the reader's mind.

Drama and fiction may rely heavily on plot and character, but sounds and rhythms are as fundamental there as they are in poetry. Gustave Flaubert, perhaps the first modern novelist and the author of *Madame Bovary,* spent hours and hours rewriting his work as he searched for "*le mot juste,*" the right word. It must convey precisely what it is meant to convey; it must suggest what the writer wants it to suggest; it must sound right.

The very language and cadence of some prose is such that one can actually visualize the work as poetry. "In the Night," a short story by Jamaica Kincaid (not included in this book) is a good example. It opens as follows: "In the night, way into the middle of the night, when the night isn't divided like a sweet drink into little sips, when there is no just before midnight, midnight, or just after midnight, when the night is round in some places, flat in some places, and in some places like a deep hole, blue at the edge, black inside, the night-soil men come." How naturally this passage arranges itself into verse:

In the night,
Way into the middle of the night,
When the night isn't divided

Like a sweet drink into little sips,
When there is no just before midnight,
Midnight,
Or just after midnight,
When the night is round in some places,
Flat in some places,
And in some places like a deep hole,
Blue at the edges,
Black inside,
The night-soil men come.

When we discuss the sound of poetry we usually talk about *rhyme, rhythm,* and *form.*

Rhyme refers to the similarity of sounds in a poem (*hair, fair*). It can involve accented or unaccented syllables and can be polysyllabic (*beauty, duty; compel, dispel*). It can be *end-rhyme* or *internal rhyme.* The sounds can be identical or just close, as in *off-rhyme* (*good, blood*). The repetition of sounds can involve consonants or vowels: "I wake and feel the fell of dark, not day" (Gerard Manley Hopkins).

*Rhythm* refers to the regular beat in the measuring out of sounds. It is linked with the broader rhythms of the body and nature, such as the heartbeat and the regularity of waves. There is considerable variety in pause, pitch, and the periodicity of stress. When we say that Shakespeare uses *iambic pentameter,* we mean that he stresses every other syllable in a line of five beats: "Whĕn Í dŏ coúnt thĕ clóck thăt télls thĕ tíme." To understand all the complexities of rhythm and rhyme one must consult a handbook, such as *The Princeton Handbook of Poetic Terms,* edited by Alex Preminger et al. (Princeton University Press, 1986). Also useful are Lewis Turco's *New Book of Forms* (University Press of New England, 1986), Babette Deutsch's *Poetry Handbook* (HarperCollins, 1982), and *Strong Measures,* edited by Philip Dacey and David Jauss (HarperCollege, 1989).

In poetry, *form* usually refers to structure, the arrangement of elements within the poem, the patterns of rhythm and rhyme. All sonnets have fourteen lines, but the Shakespearean sonnet, for instance, consists of one stanza containing three quatrains of alternating end-rhymes—*abab cdcd efef*—and a rhyming (or "heroic") couplet at the end. The dominant rhythm is *iambic pentameter.*

There are many traditional forms, including the ballad, limerick, sestina, and villanelle, and there are literally thousands of possible patterns that a poet can use.

*Form* can also be found in poems that do not have a rigid structure. A distinction is made these days between *closed form,* which refers to a precise pattern, and *open form,* which refers to what some people call *free verse,* poetry without severe regularities of rhyme and rhythm. Such poetry may not *scan* (conform to metrical rules). The concept of *organic form* suggests that it is an internal force that makes the work cohere and that content and container cannot be separated. Obviously, an unscannable poem that sounds good must have its own cadence, its own music, something driven by a total vision that includes sound.

Jamaica Kincaid's story in this chapter, "What I Have Been Doing Lately," has that same quality, though it is clearly fiction. The images crowd in, all seen with the immediacy of a child's perception—each object complete in itself, pure, unaffected by cliché or any traditional way of seeing things. "I saw a monkey in a tree." Such images seem to arrive directly from some subconscious wellspring, like the material of dreams, each one a vivid example of what we mean when we say *concrete detail.* The sentences are short and have a simple structure, creating their own rhythm and impetus. The repetition of words has a poetic and musical effect, and the repetition of actions gives the sense of closure that a poem offers, as well as underlining the themes. The narrator wakes, has various adventures, and wakes again to the same dreamscape with variations. In the end she prepares to wake again. Which is the inner life and which the outer?

The extraordinary freshness and individuality of the way the narrator sees things in this story are opposed to her perceptions of what is expected of her. The title itself refers to her response to the kind of question polite grownups ask children, expecting a polite response couched in "government school ink." The story reveals what is really going on in the child's mind. In her conversation with the mother figure she says: "I have been listening carefully to my mother's words, so as to make a good imitation of a dutiful daughter." Each time she wakes it is because the doorbell rings, demanding her attention. She goes to answer, but no one is there. Nothing is expected of her; she is released to go back to being herself. But her feelings are mixed. Later, she hopes that she might find her mother or "anyone else that I loved" making a custard for her.

All the selections in this chapter can be examined in terms of the manipulation of sounds, but we can mention a few that are clear examples of the multiple options that are open to the poet.

Albert Goldbarth's "Lullabye" is, indeed, a lullaby. It has one of the patterns commonly used in such "songs."

John Hollander's "Coordinating Conjunction" uses the rhyme scheme of the *terza rima*. In each three-line stanza, or *tercet,* the first and third lines rhyme, and the second line rhymes with the first and third lines of the next tercet: *aba, bcb, cdc,* and so on. Hollander's lines, however, are briefer than the usual eleven syllables of *terza rima*. He creates a syllabic pattern of 5-7-5 in each tercet.

"From the wave" by Thom Gunn is a nicely structured poem with lines of four beats alternating with lines of two beats and *abab* end-rhymes. How appropriate for the "timed procession" of the waves.

Howard Nemerov's structured quatrains in "The Air Force Museum at Dayton" are written in a roughly iambic pentameter and form a rhyme scheme of *abab, cdcd,* and so forth. The structure is appropriate to the elegiac quality of the poem, which comments on the worship of death-dealing inventions "enshrined in glass."

Any poem that appears on paper has a visual dimension. In some cases that aspect of the poem is routine; in others it is extremely important. Words can be used to create a picture, not only through their meaning, but physically and literally. "March Orrery" by Richard Kenney is about "pale beech leaves" and is shaped in the form of a curled leaf.

Some poems sound as though they were written to be sung. One can almost hear the music for which the words are the lyrics. In Ishmael Reed's "Bitter Chocolate," the cadence suggests rap, the rhyme and refrains suggest the blues. Behind both, the pronounced beat of jazz is somehow translated into poetry.

The three-line stanza is used a lot in contemporary poetry, with or without end-rhyme and regular rhythm. "California Spring," by Charles Wright, has some structured elements, but, ultimately, it is fairly free. Notice, however, the sonorous quality introduced by the stressed words in the first and second lines, ("At dawn the dove croons"), and by alliteration, or the repetition of initial sounds (dawn, dove, croon, hawk, hang, -ambar, hundred, hands). There are a lot of long vowel sounds that have a similar melancholy ring and there is an alliteration of *d*'s and *h*'s. It is these sounds that create the music in this stanza and make an ironic comment on the title (surely we expect spring to be better than this!). The introductory lines of the last three verses echo the sounds of the first, binding the whole poem together. "Laguna Blues," by the same poet, is almost a song. Repetition, as we have seen in "Bitter Chocolate," is an effective poetic device.

Other good examples of open form can be found in the section called ADDITIONAL POETRY. Tom Clark's poems are freer in form than any mentioned so far. Eamon Grennan's "Hieroglyphic" and Marilyn Hacker's "Her Ring" are metered, while Nikki Giovanni's "Revolutionary Dreams," Sharon Olds' "Sex Without Love," and Jonathon Aaron's "The Foreigner" are unstructured in the formal sense.

Jamaica Kincaid

# What I Have Been Doing Lately

1 What I have been doing lately: I was lying in bed and the
doorbell rang. I ran downstairs. Quick. I opened the door.
There was no one there. I stepped outside. Either it was drizzling or there was a lot of dust in the air and the dust was
damp. I stuck out my tongue and the drizzle or the damp dust
tasted like government school ink. I looked north. I looked
south. I decided to start walking north. While walking north, I
noticed that I was barefoot. While walking north, I looked up
and saw the planet Venus. I said, "It must be almost morning."
10 I saw a monkey in a tree. The tree had no leaves. I said, "Ah, a
monkey. Just look at that. A monkey." I walked for I don't
know how long before I came up to a big body of water. I
wanted to get across it but I couldn't swim. I wanted to get
across it but it would take me years to build a boat. I wanted to
get across it but it would take me I didn't know how long to
build a bridge. Years passed and then one day, feeling like it, I
got into my boat and rowed across. When I got to the other
side, it was noon and my shadow was small and fell beneath
me. I set out on a path that stretched out straight ahead. I
20 passed a house, and a dog was sitting on the verandah but it
looked the other way when it saw me coming. I passed a boy
tossing a ball in the air but the boy looked the other way when
he saw me coming. I walked and I walked but I couldn't tell if I
walked a long time because my feet didn't feel as if they would
drop off. I turned around to see what I had left behind me but
nothing was familiar. Instead of the straight path, I saw hills.
Instead of the boy with his ball, I saw tall flowering trees. I
looked up and the sky was without clouds and seemed near, as
if it were the ceiling in my house and, if I stood on a chair, I
30 could touch it with the tips of my fingers. I turned around and
looked ahead of me again. A deep hole had opened up before
me. I looked in. The hole was deep and dark and I couldn't see
the bottom. I thought, What's down there?, so on purpose I

fell in. I fell and I fell, over and over, as if I were an old suitcase. On the sides of the deep hole I could see things written, but perhaps it was in a foreign language because I couldn't read them. Still I fell, for I don't know how long. As I fell I began to see that I didn't like the way falling made me feel. Falling made me feel sick and I missed all the people I had loved. I said, I
40　don't want to fall anymore, and I reversed myself. I was standing again on the edge of the deep hole. I looked at the deep hole and I said, You can close up now, and it did. I walked some more without knowing distance. I only knew that I passed through days and nights, I only knew that I passed through rain and shine, light and darkness. I was never thirsty and I felt no pain. Looking at the horizon, I made a joke for myself: I said, "The earth has thin lips," and I laughed.

Looking at the horizon again, I saw a lone figure coming toward me, but I wasn't frightened because I was sure it was
50　my mother. As I got closer to the figure, I could see that it wasn't my mother, but still I wasn't frightened because I could see that it was a woman.

When this woman got closer to me, she looked at me hard and then she threw up her hands. She must have seen me somewhere before because she said, "It's you. Just look at that. It's you. And just what have you been doing lately?"

I could have said, "I have been praying not to grow any taller."

I could have said, "I have been listening carefully to my
60　mother's words, so as to make a good imitation of a dutiful daughter."

I could have said, "A pack of dogs, tired from chasing each other all over town, slept in the moonlight."

Instead, I said, What I have been doing lately: I was lying in bed on my back, my hands drawn up, my fingers interlaced lightly at the nape of my neck. Someone rang the doorbell. I went downstairs and opened the door but there was no one there. I stepped outside. Either it was drizzling or there was a lot of dust in the air and the dust was damp. I stuck out my
70　tongue and the drizzle or the damp dust tasted like government school ink. I looked north and I looked south. I started walking north. While walking north, I wanted to move fast, so I removed the shoes from my feet. While walking north, I looked up and saw the planet Venus and I said, "If the sun went out, it would be eight minutes before I would know it." I saw a monkey sitting in a tree that had no leaves and I said, "A monkey. Just look at that. A monkey." I picked up a stone and I threw it at the monkey. The monkey, seeing the stone,

quickly moved out of its way. Three times I threw a stone at
80  the monkey and three times it moved away. The fourth time I
threw the stone, the monkey caught it and threw it back at me.
The stone struck me on the forehead over my right eye, making
a deep gash. The gash healed immediately but now the skin on
my forehead felt false to me. I walked for I don't know how
long before I came to a big body of water. I wanted to get
across, so when the boat came I paid my fare. When I got to the
other side, I saw a lot of people sitting on the beach and they
were having a picnic. They were the most beautiful people I
had ever seen. Everything about them was black and shiny.
90  Their skin was black and shiny. Their shoes were black and
shiny. Their hair was black and shiny. The clothes they wore
were black and shiny. I could hear them laughing and chatting
and I said, I would like to be with these people, so I started to
walk toward them, but when I got up close to them I saw that
they weren't at a picnic and they weren't beautiful and they
weren't chatting and laughing. All around me was black mud
and the people all looked as if they had been made up out of
the black mud. I looked up and saw that the sky seemed far
away and nothing I could stand on would make me able to
100  touch it with my fingertips. I thought, If only I could get out of
this, so I started to walk. I must have walked for a long time
because my feet hurt and felt as if they would drop off. I
thought, If only just around the bend I would see my house
and inside my house I would find my bed, freshly made at that,
and in the kitchen I would find my mother or anyone else that I
loved making me a custard. I thought, If only it was a Sunday
and I was sitting in a church and I had just heard someone sing
a psalm. I felt very sad so I sat down. I felt so sad that I rested
my head on my own knees and smoothed my own head. I felt
110  so sad I couldn't imagine feeling any other way again. I said, I
don't like this. I don't want to do this anymore. And I went
back to lying in bed, just before the doorbell rang.

## Michael Martone

# *It's Time*

1 I remember the time each year when my husband cut back the raspberry bushes. I always thought he took too much, afterward a row of whittled spikes where once a tangled mass of brambles boiled along the fence. He ripped out the dead canes altogether, brittle straws, pruned the branches down to nothing. He dug up the newly rooted tips where last year's growth had bowed over to the ground and took hold, the first long stride into the garden. Every spring, I believed they would never grow back, but in a few weeks, with the days lengthen-
10 ing, the stubby canes streaked with red, budded, shot up overnight.

Does it count as a first word? The other raspberry, the sound my daughter made, her tongue melting into slobber between her lips, stirring before dawn in the tiny bedroom down the hall. It was dark, and the wet blasts helped me navigate, the floors covered with her blocks and toys. Her room was pitch, the only light the daubs of radium I swiped from the factory outlining the rails and bars of her crib. At night it looked like a bridge lit up, suspended over the var-
20 nished surface of a wide, still river. The paint had dripped on the floor, formed a tiny drifting phosphorescent slick. My daughter tottered about. I could see only her shadow, her shape blotting out the dew of pulsing light behind her. She sprayed her one note greeting. When I picked her up, her tongue rasped next to my ear. I felt her whole body going into the sound, her breath dying down, her spit a mist on my cheek.

"Don't go," my husband had said. "Stay in bed. She's not crying. Ten minutes more. Let her go."

I could see he was looking at the time. I watched the
30 luminous dial of his watch float up off the nightstand. The little wedge the hands made rotated as he fumbled to right the face. From eleven o'clock the time spun to a little past six-thirty. "She's up early," I heard him say. The little constellation spiraled back to the table.

Often there were flecks of paint in my hair. He said he

could always find me in the dark. He'd kiss me through a
cloud of stars. I'd shake my head and the sparks spilled down
onto the pillow, sprinkling his face. My fingertips too lit up,
stained where I held the brush and the tiny pot. I became
40  distracted with my own caresses, streaks of light tracing his
back, neck, hips. Flakes of light caught in the hairs on his chest
and eyebrows, blinked on and off as he opened and closed his
eyes. Where I kissed him I left welts of throbbing light. His lips
grew brighter. It seemed like the fire should die out but it
didn't, would only disappear with the dawn in the windows.
We could see everything then and still hear our daughter down
the hall cooing to herself, inventing a language to call me to
her.

        This was in Orange right after the war. They used
50  women at the factory there to paint the clocks. Our hands
were steady. We were patient, perfect for the delicate trim-
ming, outlining the numerals with the radium, down to the
marks on the sweep face, sketching hairlines on the minute
hand. I had sable brushes I rolled on my tongue to hone a point
sharp enough to jewel each second. The paint was sweet and
thick, like a frosting laced with a fruity essence. We'd thin it
with our spit. Rich and heavy like the loam in the garden. It
was piecework. At the long tables we'd race through the piles
of parts, my hands brushing the other hands, reaching in for
60  the next face or stem. The room was noisy. Alvina sang to
herself. Blanche reeled off recipes. Marcella clucked. We
talked with our eyes crossed over our work, "She had to get
married. They went to Havre de Grace by train and were back
by noon the next day." We paused between each sentence or
verse as we dabbed the brushes to our lips. It was as if our
voices came from somewhere else. I'd look away, out the huge
windows to the brilliant sky. I can still hear the buzz above the
table as something separate from the people there, another
kind of radiation in the room that never seemed to burn out.
70  The stories and the songs blend into one ache.

        What more is there to tell? Our bones began to break
under the slightest pressure—getting out of bed, climbing
stairs. Our hair rinsed out of our scalps. Our fingertips turned
black and the black spread along the fingers by the first
knuckle while the skin held a wet sheen. Our hands were
negatives of hands. The brittle black fingernails were etched
with bone white.

        But this was after so many of those afternoons at the
plant with its steady northern light. I remember cursing an
80  eyelash that fluttered onto a face and smeared my work, how I

damned my body for the few pennies I had lost, the several wasted minutes of work. "I'll race you, Myrna!" There were many factories in Orange, and their quitting whistles at the end of the day were all pitched differently. The white tables emptied, the heaps of silver parts, like ashes, at each place. Another shift, the night one, would collect the glowing work and ship it somewhere else to be assembled. We ran to the gates, to the streetcars waiting, to the movies that never stopped running. It was all about time, this life, and we 90 couldn't see it.

At the trial, not one of us would speak, and the newspapers said how happy we were, considering the sentences already imposed. We sat there with our smiles painted over our lips to hide our teeth. During recess in the ladies, we powdered over the bruises again. We couldn't blot the lipstick, since our skin was so tender. Four clowns in the mirror, mouths like targets, stared back at us. We couldn't cry. It would ruin our work. In court, we listened to the evidence and covered our faces when we laughed at what was being said. I watched the 100 clerk who recorded everything, his pencil stirring down the page. Sometimes he would be called upon to read testimony back, and I was taken by the accuracy of his words. I remembered the speeches that way. It seemed right, right down to some of the sounds he noted, pausing to insert *laughter* or *unintelligible*. I liked these moments best, when the words were the only solid things left in court. The lawyers, the witnesses, the gallery, the jury, were all poised, listening to the clerk. They might have been an audience from another time. The only thing left of us was that string of knots on paper, the 110 one sound in the room.

My daughter loved the fresh raspberries in milk. The white milk coated the scoring between the tiny globes on each berry in the bowl. It looked like the milk drying on her tongue. The berries as they steeped turned the milk pink. She grabbed at the fruit, crushing it into her fist and then sliding the pulp into her mouth.

I haven't been able to speak since soon after the trial, and eating now, even the raspberries so ripe they liquified when I picked them, is painful. The berries have seeds that shouldn't hurt the way they do. I can't explain this to my husband, who 120 sits reading the newspaper on the other side of the table, his fingers smudged with ink. I make the same sounds now the baby made, little whines and grunts. He's already used to it. I feel I am being whittled away like the nub of the pencil I write this with then sharpen with the paring knife. Why do people lick the lead point? Perhaps it is just a gesture of thought, a habit, hoping that the sound of a voice will rub off.

    I'm not afraid. I know this now. It happened this morning when I was picking the berries. The bees were in the late
130  blossoms on the canes above me. The canes trembled, about ready to bow over. Sweat scalded the skin of my arms and neck. The berries hung in clusters everywhere among the thorns and sharp leaves. I have no feeling left in the tips of my fingers, and as I watched my black hand close on each berry, the fruit seemed to leap from the stem into the numb folds of my palm. So little had held the berry in place, a shriveled ball and socket. The berry, a dusty matte red that soaked up the light, bled a little, a pool in my palm. I thought about sucking the raspberry into my mouth, straining it through what was
140  left of my teeth. I thought of my daughter. Instead, I reached out for another berry and then another, dumped them into the pint baskets squashed and ruptured, and rushed them into the house. I found a pencil and a piece of paper to write this down. Each word fell on the page, a burning tongue.

## Nikki Giovanni

# *Kidnap Poem*

1 ever been kidnapped
 by a poet
 if i were a poet
 i'd kidnap you
 put you in my phrases and meter
 you to jones beach
 or maybe coney island
 or maybe just to my house
 lyric you in lilacs
10 dash you in the rain
 blend into the beach
 to complement my see
 play the lyre for you
 ode you with my love song
 anything to win you
 wrap you in the red Black green
 show you off to mama
 yeah if i were a poet i'd kid
 nap you

*Lorna Goodison*

# On Becoming a Tiger

1 The day that they stole her tiger's eye ring,
was the day that she became a tiger.
She was inspired by advice received from Rilke

Who recommended that if the business of drinking
should become too bitter,
one should change oneself into wine.

The tiger was actually always asleep
inside her, she had seen it
stretched out, drowsing and inert

10 When she lay upon her side and stared
for seven consecutive days into a tall mirror
that she had turned on its side.

Her focus had penetrated all exterior
till at last she could see within her
a red glowing landscape of memory and poems,

A heart within her heart
and lying there big, bright and golden
was the tiger, wildly, darkly striped.

At night she dreams that her mother
20 undresses her and discovers that under
her outerwear, her bare limbs are marked

With the broad and urgent striations
of the huge and fierce cat of Asia
with the stunning golden quartz eyes.

She has taken to wearing long dresses,
to cover the rounded tail coiling behind her.
She has filled her vases with tiger lilies

And replaced her domestic cat
with a smaller relative of hers, the Ocelot
30  At four in the morning she practices stalking

Up and down the long expanse of the hall.
What are the ingredients in tiger's milk?
Do tigers ever mate for life?

Can she rewrite the story of little Black Sambo?
Can a non-tiger take a tiger for a wife?
To these and other questions,

She is seeking urgent answers
now that she is living an openly
tigerly life.

## Eamon Grennan

# Winn's Blackbird

for Winn and Larry Smith

1 Drawn out of the oven's dark,
He's laid to rest on the kitchen table.
Every feather dry as a leaf;
He's nested with death all winter.

You take the shutters down. Summer
Beats white wings in every corner:
The big light broods on familiar objects;
The house hatches round his final silence.

For you, he's the dead you live with:
10 Your friends, your blood, your buried women.
You welcome him to your painter's eye and
Day by day make him articulate again.

Each sketch an act of faith: death
Is what you're giving life to. In your favorite
He seems almost buoyant—charcoal neck
Stretched with a sense of purpose.

At dinner, remembering the dead we share,
We five fall silent, letting them enter. You say
*There's a life in things outgrows our knowing.*
20 The drenched grapes, the strawberries, glitter

Like stars. Out in the studio (dark as an oven),
Adjusting to the status of all caught things,
The finished sketches sleep. But
Your bird, imagine, takes flight.

*Josephine Jacobsen*

# *The Thing About Crows*

1                                                    is, they are hoarse.
When you are hoarse, and shout,
you sound either desperate or ominous.
The crows are not desperate.

I say they are not desperate, but one flapped
desperately, dive-bombed this side, that,
by something tiny, with blue murder
and fury on its side.

It's a gentle day. Foliage shifts
10 gently in the air, and the buds on roses
puff out, and clouds maneuver and part
and meld in a gentle silence.
Now a crow goes heavily by, pounding
the air. Crows gather, gather, to shout
in their autumnal voices, hoarsely,
at the vulnerable spring.

*Josephine Jacobsen*

# The Woods

1  In this summer month, two separate men were lost
in the local woods. Can woods be local?
Is there more than one wood? It is unlikely.
Though there are two kinds of woods, visible, and not.

The first man was feeble-minded. Left
his goodwill party, saw something, heard
something, went to it. They found his body
later, after something found it first.

Fright, or starvation; or exposure. Woods
10  which are close and secret, practice exposure.
If he heard the cries, the dogs, the cries,
why didn't he answer? Why didn't they hear him?

Anyway, the second man was strong-
minded as another; knew woods, went in alone.
They say: Never go in alone. But even in visible
woods, is that persuasive? They are interesting.

Even in high sun they offer such levels
of shade—the tops of their tallest trees just stir
in the biggest wind. They are dark green to black
20  according to whether the light is sun or moon.

The second man was never found at all.
Never. So people began to say he came out
elsewhere, into sunlight or moonlight, for his own
purposes. But could the woods make him vanish?

The difference is, the visible wood stays put,
though it stirs and acts within itself. It is bounded.
The invisible wood stretches, arrives, and is there.
Going in alone is inevitable, unfortunately.

Also, dogs are forbidden, and silence enforced.
30  There is supposed to be a treasure, or witch, at the center.
But which, cannot be known, short of encounter.
And those lost who return—and there are some—

cannot find the dictionary word to tell
how it went. If it's the treasure, they usually stay;
and if it's the witch, they can stay too,
and she will send out a Doppelgänger instead.

Another difference is that fewer are lost,
even temporarily, in the visible wood.
And another yet, that those broken or careless few
40  who are, are usually found; and found in time.

## Raymond Carver

# *The Toes*

1 This foot's giving me nothing
but trouble. The ball,
the arch, the ankle—I'm saying
it hurts to walk. But
mainly it's these toes
I worry about. Those
"terminal digits" as they're
otherwise called. How true!
For them no more delight
10 in going headfirst
into a hot bath, or
a cashmere sock. Cashmere socks,
no socks, slippers, shoes, Ace
bandage—it's all one and the same
to these dumb toes.
They even looked zonked out
and depressed, as if
somebody'd pumped them full
of Thorazine. They hunch there
20 stunned and mute—drab, lifeless
things. What in hell is going on?
What kind of toes are these
that nothing matters any longer?
Are these really *my* toes?
Have they forgotten
the old days, what it was like

being alive then? Always first
on line, first onto the dance floor
when the music started.
30  First to kick up their heels.
Look at them. No, don't.
You don't want to see them,
those slugs. It's only with pain
and difficulty they can recall
the other times, the good times.
Maybe what they really want
is to sever all connection
with the old life, start over,
go underground, live alone
40  in a retirement manor
somewhere in the Yakima Valley.
But there was a time
they used to strain
with anticipation
simply
curl with pleasure
at the least provocation,
the smallest thing.
The feel of a silk dress
50  against the fingers, say.
A becoming voice, a touch
behind the neck, even
a passing glance. Any of it!
The sound of hooks being
unfastened, stays coming
undone, garments letting go
onto a cool, hardwood floor.

*Galway Kinnell*

# *The Geese*

1  As soon as they come over the mountain
into the Connecticut valley and see the river
they will follow until nightfall,
bodies, or cells, begin to tumble
between the streamers of their formation,
thinning the left, thickening the right,
until like a snowplowing skier the flock shifts weight
and shaking with its inner noises
turns, and yahonks and spirit-cries
10  toward that flow of light spelled into its windings
endlessly ago—each body flashing white
against the white sky when the wings lift,
and black when they fall, the invisible
continuously perforating the visible—
and trembles away, to vanish, but before that
to semi-vanish, as a mirage
or deepest desire does when it gets
the right distance from us and becomes rhythmic.

## Galway Kinnell

# The Shroud

1   Lifted by its tuft
of angel hairs, a milkweed
seed dips-and-soars
across a meadow, chalking
in outline the rhythm
that waits in air all along,
like the bottom hem of nowhere.
*Spinus tristis,* who spends
his days turning gold
10   back into sod, rises-and-falls
along the same line the seed
just waved through the sunlight.
What sheet or shroud large enough
to hold the whole earth
are these seamstresses' chalks
and golden needles
stitching at so restlessly?
When will it ever be finished?

*Charles Simic*

# Obscure Beginnings

1  I was a winter fly on the ceiling
   In the house of arachnids.
   Silence reigned. Queen Insomnia
   Sipped tea in the parlor,
   Death and Judgment by her side.

   The ceiling like a polar expedition.
   The window like a theater of cruelty
   With its view of the fields:
   Sheep nibbling wild flowers,
10 And the sky beyond them, vast and empty.

   Death notices posted in every room.
   The old woman dressing a small child for slaughter
   In a convent's school uniform.
   The ceiling pale as the flowers.
   The red parrot screaming in the parrot house.

## Ursula LeGuin

# *Silence*

1 I had a little naked thought
  slipped out between my thighs
  and ran before it could be caught
  and flew without having been taught,
  O see how quick it flies!
  My baby thought, my little bird
  all rosy naked goes.
  I must sew word to word to word
  and button up its clothes
10 and so it grows and walks and talks and dies.
  When I am dead look for the rose
  that grows between my eyes.
  Birds will perch on leaf and thorn,
  silent birds to silence born.

## Sharon Olds

# *Topography*

1  After we flew across the country we
got in bed, laid our bodies
delicately together, like maps laid
face to face, East to West, my
San Francisco against your New York, your
Fire Island sucking my Sonoma, my
New Orleans deep in your Texas, your Idaho
bright on my Great Lakes, my Kansas
burning against your Kansas, your Kansas
10  burning against my Kansas, your Eastern
Standard Time pressing into my
Pacific Time, my Mountain Time
beating against your Central Time, your
sun rising swiftly from the right my
sun rising swiftly from the left your
moon rising slowly from the left my
moon rising slowly from the right until
all four bodies of the sky
burn above us, sealing us together,
20  all our cities twin cities,
all our States United, one
nation, indivisible, with liberty and justice for all.

## Sharon Olds

⋯◀▶⋯ ⋯◀▶⋯

# *Pajamas*

1 My daughter's pajamas lie on the floor
inside out, thin and wrinkled as
peeled skins of peaches when you ease the
whole skin off at once.
You can see where her waist emerged, and her legs,
her arms, and head, the fine material
gathered in rumples like skin the caterpillar
ramped out of and left to shrivel.
You can see, there at the center of the bottoms,
10 the raised cotton seam like the line
down the center of fruit, where the skin first splits
and curls back. You can almost see the hard
halves of her young buttocks, the precise
stem-mark of her sex. Her shed
skin shines at my feet, and in the air there is a
sharp fragrance like peach brandy—
the birth-room pungence of her released life.

*Albert Goldbarth*

# *Lullabye*

1  sleep, little beansprout
  don't be scared
  the night is simply the true sky
  bared

  sleep, little dillseed
  don't be afraid
  the moon is the sunlight
  ricocheted

# *Thom Gunn*

# *From the wave*

1  It mounts at sea, a concave wall
      Down-ribbed with shine,
And pushes forward, building tall
      Its steep incline.
Then from their hiding rise to sight
      Black shapes on boards
Bearing before the fringe of white
      It mottles towards.

      Their pale feet curl, they poise their weight
10      With a learned skill.
It is the wave they imitate
      Keeps them so still.

The marbling bodies have become
      Half wave, half men,
Grafted it seems by feet of foam
      Some seconds, then,

Late as they can, they slice the face
      In timed procession:
Balance is triumph in this place,
20      Triumph possession.

The mindless heave of which they rode
      A fluid shelf
Breaks as they leave it, falls and, slowed,
      Loses itself.

Clear, the sheathed bodies slick as seals
    Loosen and tingle;
And by the board the bare foot feels
    The suck of shingle.

They paddle in the shallows still;
30    Two splash each other;
Then all swim out to wait until
    The right waves gather.

## *John Hollander*

# *Coordinating Conjunction*

1    And ... and so it goes:
As the thread outlasts the spool
     So the thorn, the rose.

     Time observes its rule:
Each instant leaps back into
     The dark lilied pool

     It sprang from. Each blue
Tile along the garden wall
     Ends where it has to

10   End, in a thin scrawl
Of grout that marks out its grave.
     Summer comes to fall.

     Though breathing and brave,
The sentence stops, that must burn
     The air in its cave.

     Thus our great concern—
Feeling shut in by the wall
     Of our own pattern—

     Seems quite natural:
20   Even with some makeshift plan,
     How to keep it all

Going, how to fan
The embers of aftermath
Up now into an

Even flame—not wrath
Nor sudden lust yielded to—
But light on a path

That would continue
Until some kind of an end
30      Crept up into view

From around some bend
Or straight toward us from the dark.
Who but would extend

That path, keep the spark
Still left glowing, nursed along
A last walk through stark

Finality? (Strong
Last words will count more than fond
Scraps of sometime song.)

40      Reaching out beyond
A last bit, we understand,
Breaks some kind of bond:

Desperate, a hand
Trembling adds yet one more *and*
And *and*, and *and*, and

## Richard Kenney

# *March Orrery*

1    Listen:
    pale beech leaves
      branch-clung all winter long,
      their tissues frail as paper lanterns,
    lucent, ornamental, touch the pane.
    Diminutive ribcages, curled and weightless,
    slant along the axis of the rain,
    touch *click,* click loose at random underneath
    the eaves, and turn a brief descent, and skitter
10  one by one in wind, and gone, as quick
      as shell-ice down an onion dome,
        or unshared memory,
          or old rice paper,
            blown.

## Howard Nemerov

# *The Air Force Museum at Dayton*

1 Under the barrel roof in solemn gloom
The weapons, instruments, and winged shapes,
The pictured dead in period costumes,
Illustrate as in summary time-lapse

Photography the planetary race
That in the span of old men still around
Arose from Kitty Hawk to sky to space,
Cooped up as if it never left the ground.

After the pterodactyl and the Wright
10 Brothers every kite carries a gun
As it was meant to do, for right and might
Are properly understood by everyone.

Destructive powers, and speeds still unforeseen
But half a life ago, stand passive here,
Contraptions that have landed on the Moon
Or cancelled cities in a single flare.

When anything's over, it turns into art,
Religion, history; what's come to pass
Bows down the mind and presses upon the heart:
20 The ancient bombsight here enshrined in glass

Is the relic left us of a robot saint
With a passion for accuracy, who long ago
Saw towns as targets miniature and quaint,
Townsfolk invisible that far below.

## Ishmael Reed

# *Bitter Chocolate*

### *I*

1 Only the red-skins know what
I know, and they ain't talkin
So I keep good friends with
turkey whiskey
Or try to do some walkin
Don't want no lovin
Ain't anxious to play
And you want to know how
I got that way
10 Bitter Chocolate
Bitter Chocolate
Blood like ice water
Kisses taste like snuff
Why are all of my women
so jive and full of stuff

They call me a runaway father
But they won't give me no job
They say I'm a thief
when I'm the one gettin
20 robbed
Most of me was missing when
They brought me back from
Nam
My mama and my sister

cried for me
But my government didn't give
a damn
Bitter Chocolate
Bitter Chocolate
30  Sullied and sullen black
man

## II

1  When they come to lynch somebody
Always breaking down my door
When they lay somebody off
I'm the first one off the floor
Bitter Chocolate
Bitter Chocolate
Veins full of brine
Skin sweatin turpentine
Cold and unfriendly
10  Got ways like a lizard

## III

1  Well, it's winter in Chicago on
a February day
O'Hare airport is empty and
I call you on the line
It's 9:00 a.m. where you are
and the phone rings seven times
Hello, who is this? you say
in a sleeping heaving sigh
Your woman in the background yells
10  Who in the hell is that guy
Bitter Chocolate
Bitter Chocolate
I'm standing in the rain
All my love is all squeezed
out
All that I can give is pain
All that I can give is pain

## Charles Wright

# *California Spring*

1 At dawn the dove croons.
A hawk hangs over the field.
The liquidambar rinses its hundred hands.

And the light comes on in the pepper trees.
Under its flat surfaces horns and noises are starting up.
The dew drops begin to shrink.

How sad the morning is.
There is a tree which rains down in the field.
There is a spider that swings back and forth on his thin strings
   in the heart.

10 How cold the wind is.
And the sun is, caught like a kite in the drooped limbs of the tree.
The apricot blossoms scatter across the ice plant.

One angel dangles his wing.
The grass edges creak and the tide pools begin to shine.
Nothing forgives.

## Charles Wright

# *Laguna Blues*

1   It's Saturday afternoon at the edge of the world.
White pages lift in the wind and fall.
Dust threads, cut loose from the heart, float up and fall.
Something's off-key in my mind.
Whatever it is, it bothers me all the time.

It's hot, and the wind blows on what I have had to say.
I'm dancing a little dance.
The crows pick up a thermal that angles away from the sea.
I'm singing a little song.
10   Whatever it is, it bothers me all the time.

It's Saturday afternoon and the crows glide down,
Black pages that lift and fall.
The castor beans and the pepper plant trundle their weary heads.
Something's off-key and unkind.
Whatever it is, it bothers me all the time.

## Jonathan Aaron

# *The Foreigner*

1 When I wake up, the game is already over.
The dusky city is full of people out of their minds
with disappointment, fat people eating pizza,
thin people whose only remaining ambition
is to gain weight or die. Inside the stadium
fans are still attacking the goal posts
like antibodies. The restaurant I enter is crowded
with the sound of quiet weeping, for now
that the season is over and the championship settled
10 forever, all that's left is the sweet sorrow
of eating. The new mayor himself is a dietitian.
Moments after his inauguration, I hear him
explain why his first official act will be to move
his family into a house carved from a gigantic
   onion.
I've never felt better in my life! he announces
from his half-peeled doorstep, his face shining
with tears. Everyone keeps quiet, expecting the
   words
20 *Health* and *Victory* to appear in black ink
above the neighboring woods. But soon my eyes
   start watering
when the wind shifts. My fingers itch for something
   more
to hold on to than a vegetable. The next thing
   I know

I'm standing on a promontory overlooking the
   harbor.
From here I can see the entire city,
30  hear its traffic like someone's breath
in a dark room. I figure I can reach the water
in less than ten minutes by running fast enough.

## A. R. Ammons

# Revelers, Revealers

1 Prose is for explicit, poetry for
   implicit dealings: I'm not a prose
   person: I'm not coming straight out

   with the truth: the tiny truth would
   remove the work of massive
   implication: I can tell over and

   over clever (engaging, metaphorical,
   metonymic?) near misses around the truth,
   honing the curves like an ice skater

10 and so good at it it hurts; the lies
   hurt with beauty: the truth, though, told,
   haunted untold, would just stop

   dead in an expended center, nowhere
   to go, nothing to say, no weaves to sweep,
   veils to dangle: except, of course,

   it may not be that way: the bead of
   the truth may burn at a blistering high
   and knife-edged men may arrive to see

   what the light is, and it
20 could be a lasting wonder to them or
   trouble their dreams a bit too much.

## Rosa Maria Arenas

# Mother of Shrines

1 Mother has paid tribute to her dead relatives
with shrines—candles, plastic flowers, plastic saints,
set on altars draped with lace doilies and satin—
since time immemorial. The real motives
for this hobby? Could it be genetic:
some ancient impulse to preserve the remains
of loved ones against decay, against Satan?
In return the dead are empathic,
and can be called upon in times of need.
10 After all, some of the dead were real brains;
they're flattered you seek their superior reason.
And they're bored—can't read, can't feed, can't breed.
So, it's a racket. What isn't these days?
Light a candle, close your eyes. Call out a name.

## Tom Clark

# *Reading the Technical Journals*

1  The linguistic skil
  saw of the contemporary
  academic manual,
  a drone of interact
  and interface
  somehow more faceless
  and inactive
  than Death itself,
  threatens nothing
10  more than whatever's
  left of Sense.
  A yellowjacket at least
  deposits its stinger in
  its victim, then goes off to die
  expressing a justice in nature
  that no longer applies:
  for having injected you with
  their toxic load, *these*
  drones shuffle off to get promoted.

*Tom Clark*

# *Looking for Work in Teaching*

1   I swallowed my pride
    filed my heart away in the bottom
    of the drawer
    put my imagination
    on the back burner
    and covered all the openings
    of my soul with spackle,
    plaster and electrical tape

    Then I sat down with
10  The MLA and AWP
    job guides and found out
    that unless I could quickly develop
    a strong background in the
    instruction of remedial English
    composition to lefthanded
    Icelandic women with green eyes
    I might as well forget it

## Nikki Giovanni

# Revolutionary Dreams

1  i used to dream militant
  dreams of taking
  over america to show
  these white folks how it should be
  done
  i used to dream radical dreams
  of blowing everyone away with my perceptive
    powers
  of correct analysis
  i even used to think i'd be the one
10  to stop the riot and negotiate the peace
  then i awoke and dug
  that if i dreamed natural
  dreams of being a natural
  woman doing what a woman
  does when she's natural
  i would have a revolution

*Eamon Grennan*

# *Hieroglyphic*

1 Mid-February. Our first redwing blackbird
wheezes high up in the locust tree and I
call you out in your bathrobe to look,
listen. Your cup of coffee in the cold air
sends up propitiatory curls of steam, an
offering to the frost to soften its heart
and hurry home to mother; an offering
to the last sad carcasses of filthy snow
sprawled on any spot of all-day shade,
10 that they may take the heat and run,
praising in their own cold bodies
light, fluency and light, those
shape-shifters from way back. Your eyes
follow my finger to the bunched small blackness
in a crosshatch of twigs that haven't yet
begun to swell with a sense of things
to come. The redwing wheezes and briefly
clacks. Safe after riding storms and starlight
north from God knows where, he scans the brush
20 for a likely site, a soft spot near water,
where he'll flash his fiery epaulettes
and declare himself all spring and summer—
balancing a cattail while his mate broods
in hiding. I imagine a seedy, head-high field
brimming with their din and business, till
your shiver brings me back to where we stand

looking up at this solitary orator over our
skeletal world, this harbinger ahead of his
time. Cold, we go indoors again, satisfied

30 with this one sign for now—like archaeologists
who unearth a clay-caked single shard and
see in cracked turquoise a scallop-wing come
clear, and know a whole civilization lies
sleeping beneath their feet.

## Marilyn Hacker

# *Her Ring*

1 Her ring is in a safe-deposit box
with hundred-dollar bills and wills and deeds.
You used to hide my letters with the stock
certificates, unlock a room to read
those night thoughts in a vault under the bank
where we descend this noon: a painless loan
of cash from you to me, for which I thank
you, but tremble. Half as a joke, we sign
a promissory note on a loose-leaf
10 page: odd, to see your name written with mine.
You fold that, file it in a plastic sleeve,
then rummage in the artifacts to find
and show me what you've just inherited:
your mother's knuckle-duster diamond ring,
a fossil prism in a satin bed.
You model it. I see your hand shaking.
You ask me if I want to try it on
but I won't put that diamond on my hand.
Once, I gave you a ring. You loaned me one.
20 What I borrowed that day has been returned.

## *Twyla Hansen*

# *Garbage*

1  Riding the rails like a tired bum,
      garbage

  makes its way from the East Coast,
      hits the Midwest

  on its runaway boxcar,
      crop prices

  so low we resort to almost anything
      to make a buck,

  these clay-loam ravines filling now
10      with imports

  from New York: household throwaways—
      kosher wrap,

  fruit no longer fresh from the
      corner stand,

  disposables of all shapes and sizes,
      bits and pieces

  of lives a thousand miles away,
      sent here

to these wide-open spaces, spaces
20  vast

and about as hard to imagine as,
  say, an angus,

we small-town entrepreneurs
  welcoming all

that is unwanted, unloved, the homeless,
  our hayseed grins

wide as the broadside of a barn,
  our retort

like the odor of manure: "Smells
30  like money."

## *Mary Kinzie*

# *Sun and Moon*

1  Complements. Like figures in statuary
Gardens, his a cabled athletic pose, hers
A mermaid's slithering beyond the pool's lip,
    They employ difference

To define, play out such exaggerations
As *Water Floods Rock*. Each the other's private
Lightness tries to ground, or black weight help lighten,
    Acting the obverse.

Struggling to take shape, he contrives a drama
10  *(Rock Displacing Water)* of will, his *Too-Calm*
Brought to simmering by her permitted *Fire*.
    Fighting indifference,

Meticulous his study, its blazing page
Neat and thoughtful. Hers a rough centrifuge of
Clutter thrown out from the abject crescent where,
    Leaning on elbows,

Head in hand, she worries about his future
while he suffers old indignation. Thus they
Stiffen into orbit, for all their future
20     Equal in exile.

What can have put them on this track where turning
Off is met by turning toward exactly?
Instability, which could not have fused them
    But at a distance?

Much more likely sentiment—hall umbrellas
Touching with a hesitant air, their questions
Nervous, soft and forced—even their deference
    Coarsened by sadness

And remorse. The flesh at this hint more shrouded
30  Glimpses down the vista of itself stiff arms
Like three limbs in rites so redundant they are
    Thought to lack magic.

Lurid as if scarred by a fire, their garden
Shines with punishment, while the simple planets
Crank about the sky manifesting signs of
    Knowledge and justice.

## Grace Morton

# *What Howard Moss Has Just Mailed You*

1  Yes! We are happy to accept   Yes! This is why
I became an editor!   I came to work   listless,
  depressed
then   A miracle on my desk!
Our next *New Yorker*   will be blank except for
  your eight-line poem
The first two lines
revolutionize the English language
The last line   integrates all of recorded literature
Do you have any more?   We will buy them!
We will buy your letters and your postcards!
10  We will buy your used typewriter ribbons!
We are closing our offices for a month   to arrange
a Reception at the White House   a Banquet at
  Versailles
a World Poetry-Reading tour   We hope
you will accept!   We hope   you will accept
the enclosed lifetime acceptance slip   And the
  Blank Check
and Yes!   We completely agree
misery and poverty are not required for
  poetry   And You,
the Writer, deserve to be   Happy!

*Lisel Mueller*

# Insomnia

1  The prayers of people who do not pray
keep me awake, the prayers of people
like me who do not believe in God.
Of course they pray; everyone does,
but their prayers have nowhere to go.
On nights when the moon is merciless
in its clarity, like a surgical lamp,
I hear them through the bedsprings,
garbled, their voices disguised for protection.

*Sharon Olds*

# Sex Without Love

1  How do they do it, the ones who make love
  without love? Beautiful as dancers,
  gliding over each other like ice-skaters
  over the ice, fingers hooked
  inside each other's bodies, faces
  red as steak, wine, wet as the
  children at birth whose mothers are going to
  give them away. How do they come to the
  come to the   come to the   God   come to the
10  still waters, and not love
  the one who came there with them, light
  rising slowly as steam off their joined
  skin? These are the true religious,
  the purists, the pros, the ones who will not
  accept a false Messiah, love the
  priest instead of the God. They do not
  mistake the lover for their own pleasure,
  they are like great runners: they know they are
     alone
  with the road surface, the cold, the wind,
20  the fit of their shoes, their over-all cardio-
  vascular health—just factors, like the partner
  in the bed, and not the truth, which is the
  single body alone in the universe
  against its own best time.

## Mary Swander

# *The Tattooed Man Comes for a Massage*

1 A few drops of oil, then the long effleurage,
scales gleaming, my hands gliding higher
toward his shoulder where the tail
of the rattler wiggles with each flex of the biceps.
Then digging down into the skin, and I'm lifting
his whole arm, elbow bent, hand resting near my
    neck.

And I'm moving with the slow, sure steps
of the believer, fangs sinking no deeper than his
    palms.
The mermaid swims from clavicle to cervical,
10 and over the right pectoral, the dragon's breath
blossoms into a rose. Now, Sharon, and Susan
and Becky and Bett, who was to say that

one day I would find us all here together?
Petrissage the thigh, rotate the ankle, stretch
the calf and shin. For don't we have faith
in the earth and its final loss? Then let me
press my fingers into this side, and squeeze,
slide, and lift these folds that draw us in.

# WRITING ASSIGNMENTS

1. Write a story or play dominated by a central image, such as:
   a) a lighthouse
   b) smog and heavy industry
   c) mysterious caves
   d) a beehive or anthill
   e) windmills
   f) a smoldering volcano

2. Write a poem with animal imagery.

3. Write a poem about crows and the feelings and ideas that they evoke.

4. Write a poem with a fabric of images drawn from one of the following areas:
   a) the Holocaust
   b) war
   c) celestial bodies
   d) academic life
   e) agriculture or food
   f) athletics
   g) human physiology

5. Write a Shakespearian sonnet.

6. Write a ballad using the traditional rhyme and rhythm.

7. Write several limericks.

8. Write a triolet or sestina or villanelle: For examples, look up Thomas Hardy, "Birds at Winter Nightfall" (triolet); Rudyard Kipling, "Sestina of the Tramp-Royal"; Dylan Thomas, "Do Not Go Gentle into That Good Night" (villanelle).

9. Write a poem that sounds like some form of music, such as jazz, country and western, rock, rap.

10. Write a poem that relies heavily on sounds, but has no regular rhyme or rhythm.

# BIOGRAPHICAL NOTES

**Jonathan Aaron** was born in Northampton, Massachusetts, in 1941 and lives in Cambridge. He teaches writing at Emerson College. His poetry has appeared in such publications as *The New Yorker, Ploughshares,* and *The Yale Review.* His books include *Second Sight* and *Corridor.*

**Lee K. Abbott** was the winner of an O. Henry Award in 1984. His work has appeared in such magazines as *Harper's* and *The Atlantic.* His books include *Strangers in Paradise, Dreams of Distant Lives,* and *Living After Midnight.*

**Ai** was born in 1947 and has been awarded Guggenheim and N.E.A. fellowships. Her recent books include *Fate, Sin, Killing Floor,* and *Cruelty.*

**A. R. Ammons** was born in Whiteville, North Carolina, and is presently Goldwin Smith Professor of Poetry at Cornell University. He has received a Guggenheim Fellowship, an American Academy of Arts and Letters Fellowship, the Levinson Prize, the National Book Award, the Bollingen Prize, and a MacArthur Prize Fellow Award. His recent books include *The Really Short Poems of A. R. Ammons* and *Sumerian Vistas.*

**Max Apple** teaches at Rice University in Houston, Texas. He is the author of *Arranging America, Zip, Free Agents,* and *Propheteers. Trotsky's Bar Mitzvah* is his first play.

**Philip Appleman** lives on Long Island, New York. His books include *Let There Be Light, Apes and Angels, Darwin's Ark,* and *Darwin's Bestiary.*

**Rosa Maria Arenas** lives in East St. Louis, Missouri. Her poetry has appeared in *The Kenyon Review* and other quarterlies.

**Carol Ascher**   is the author of nonfiction as well as fiction. Her books include *Simone de Beauvoir: A Life of Freedom, Between Women,* and *The Flood.*

**Susan Astor**   lives on Long Island, New York. Her work has appeared in *West Hills Review, Partisan Review, Paris Review, North Atlantic Review, Black Warrior Review.* Among her books of poems is *Dame.*

**Margaret Atwood**   was born in Ottawa, Canada, in 1939. She is the author of considerable fiction and nine books of poetry. Her recent titles are *Cat's Eye, Dancing Girls, Bluebeard's Egg,* and *Selected Poems 1965–1984.*

**Kate Barnes**   lives in Union, Maine. Her recent work has appeared in *Country Journal, Beloit Poetry Journal, Harvard Magazine, The New Yorker,* and *Harper's.* Her most recent book is *Talking in Your Sleep.*

**Amy Bloom**   was brought up in the suburbs of New York City and now lives in a small town in Connecticut. Her work has appeared in *Room of One's Own, Story, River City,* and other magazines. She has had stories in the annual collection *Best American Short Stories* (for both 1991 and 1992), and her collection, *Come to Me,* will be published by HarperCollins in 1993.

**Bruce Bond**   was born in Pasadena, California, in 1954 and now lives in Pennsylvania. He has degrees in music and English. His work has appeared in *The Kenyon Review, Poetry (Chicago), The New Republic, Ploughshares, The Georgia Review,* and other quarterlies. His three collections of poetry are *The Ivory Hours, Independence Days,* and *The Anteroom of Paradise.*

**Paul Bowles**   was born in New York in 1910. He studied musical composition with Aaron Copland and was a music critic for the *New York Herald Tribune.* He has lived in Tangier, Morocco, since 1947, and is the author of many books, most recently *Days* and *Points in Time.*

**Mary B. Campbell**   teaches at Brandeis University. Her poetry has appeared in *The Atlantic, The Paris Review, Partisan Review,* and *Agni.* Her books include *The World, the Flesh, and Angels.*

**Raymond Carver** (1938–1988)   was born in Clatskanie, Oregon. He lectured at many colleges and universities before becoming a professor of English at Syracuse University. He received many awards for his writing. His poems are collected in *Near Klamath* (1968), *Winter Insomnia* (1970), and *At Night the Salmon Move* (1976). His story collections include *What We Talk About When We Talk About Love* (1981) and *Where I'm Calling From* (1988).

**Maxine Chernoff**   lives in Chicago. She won the Carl Sandburg Award for *New Faces of 1952.* Her most recent books are *Plain Grief* and *Leap Year Day: New and Selected Poems. Bop* is a collection of her stories.

**Tom Clark**   was born in Chicago in 1941. He was a Fulbright scholar at Cambridge University and has received Rockefeller and Guggenheim grants. He lives in Berkeley, California. His recent books include *Fractured Karma* and *Disordered Ideas.* He has written biographies of Damon Runyon, Jack Kerouac, and Ted Berrigan.

**Nicole Cooley**   won the 1991 Academy of American Poets Award at Emory University, where she is a Ph.D. candidate in English and Comparative Literature. Her work has appeared in *Epoch, The North American Review, Antioch Review, Iowa Review* and *Mississippi Review.*

**Robert Cooperman**   lives in Pikesville, Maryland. His most recent books include *In the Household of Percy Bysshe Shelley, The Trial of Mary McCormick,* and *Seeing the Elephant.*

**David Dabydeen**   was born in Guyana in 1957. He is a lecturer at Warwick University in England and at the University of Virginia. He is a novelist, cultural historian, and poet.

**Stephen Dixon** teaches writing at Johns Hopkins University. His books include *Time to Go, Fall and Rise, Love and Will, All Gone.*

**Mark Doty** lives in Provincetown, Massachusetts. His most recent book is *Bethlehem in Broad Daylight.*

**Alan Dugan** is the winner of the 1962 Pulitzer Prize for Poetry. His most recent volume of poetry is *Poems 6.*

**Stuart Dybek** teaches at Western Michigan University in Kalamazoo. His books include *The Coast of Chicago, Childhood and Other Neighborhoods,* and *Brass Knuckles.*

**Jennifer Egan** lives in New York. Her short stories have appeared in *The New Yorker, The North American Review, Gentlemen's Quarterly, Mademoiselle,* and other magazines.

**Horton Foote** was born in Wharton, Texas, in 1916. He studied at the Pasadena Playhouse and worked as an actor in New York and in summer stock theaters. A prolific writer for stage, television, and films, he has won Academy Awards for his adaptation of Harper Lee's *To Kill a Mockingbird* and for his original screenplay *Tender Mercies.*

**Nikki Giovanni** was born in Tennessee and raised in Ohio. She now lives in New York. Her books include *The Women and the Men, Black Feelings, Black Talk/Black Judgment,* and *My House.*

**Albert Goldbarth** was born in Chicago in 1948. He is Distinguished Professor of Humanities at Wichita State University. One of his many books of poetry, *Jan 31,* was nominated for the National Book Award. He has had Guggenheim and N.E.A. awards. His recent books include *Arts and Sciences, Original Light, Heaven and Earth,* and *A Symphony of Souls.*

**Lorna Goodison** is a Jamaican writer and artist. She is the author of three books of poetry, most recently *Heartease,* and one book of short stories.

**Nadine Gordimer** was born in Springs, South Africa. Recipient of the 1991 Nobel Prize for Literature, she is the author of many novels and collections of short stories; among them are *Face to Face, The Soft Voice of the Serpent, Friday's Footprint, Not for Publication, Livingston's Companions, A Soldier's Embrace, Something Out There, July People,* and *My Son's Story.*

**Eamon Grennan** was born in Ireland and teaches at Vassar College. His poems have appeared in such publications as *The New Yorker, The Kenyon Review,* and *New England Review.* His most recent books include *Twelve Poems, What Light There Is and Other Poems,* and *As If It Matters.*

**Thom Gunn** was born in England in 1929 and has lived in California since 1954. He teaches at the University of California at Berkeley. His recent books include *The Passages of Joy, Selected Poems, Occasions of Poetry,* and *The Man with Night Sweats.*

**A. R. Gurney** is the author of many plays, the most recent of which are *Later Life, The Old Boy,* and *The Fourth Wall.* He has also written three novels. He won a Drama Desk Award in 1971, a Rockefeller Award in 1977, and a Lucille Lortel Award in 1989. In 1987, he received the Award of Merit from the American Academy and Institute of Arts and Letters. He is on the Artistic Board of Playwrights Horizons, and on leave from the faculty of M.I.T., where he taught literature for over twenty years.

**Marilyn Hacker** was born in New York in 1942 and is currently the editor of *The Kenyon Review.* Her book *Presentation Piece* won the National Book Award in 1975. Her other books include *Separations, Taking Notice, Assumptions,* and *Going Back to the River.*

**Twyla Hansen** was raised on a farm in northeast Nebraska and now teaches at Nebraska Wesleyan University. Her poetry has appeared in such quarterlies as *Cimarron Review, Prairie Schooner, Laurel Review,* and *Swamp Root.*

**John Hollander** was born in New York in 1929. In 1958 he was chosen by W.H. Auden for the Yale Younger Poets Series. In 1983 he was awarded the Bollingen Prize. He is currently a professor of English at Yale University. His books include *Harp Lake, Melodius Guile, Blue Wine, Powers of Thirteen*, and *In Time and Place*.

**Paul Hoover** was born in Harrisonburg, Virginia, in 1946. He is a poet-in-residence at Columbia College (Chicago) and co-editor of *New American Writing*. Hoover's book *The Novel* (1990) is a book-length poem. Other books include *Idea, Nervous Songs*, and *Saigon, Illinois* (a novel).

**David Ignatow** lives in East Hampton, Long Island, New York. His recent books include *If We Knew, Shadowing the Ground, Despite the Plainness of the Day: Love Poems*, and *The One in the Many: Memoirs*.

**Josephine Jacobsen** was born in Coburg, Canada, in 1908. She has served as consultant to the Library of Congress and on the literature panel of the N.E.A. She received the Lenore Marshall Award for her book *The Sisters* (1987). Her work has appeared frequently in the *O. Henry Prize Stories* anthologies. Other recent works include *A Walk with Raschid and Other Stories* and *The Chinese Insomniacs*.

**Alice Jones** is a psychiatrist in the San Francisco Bay area. A recent book by her is *The Knot*. In addition, her work has appeared in such magazines as *Poetry (Chicago)*, ZYZZYVA, and *The Cream City Review*.

**Brigit Pegeen Kelly** was born in Palo Alto, California, in 1951. *To the Place of Trumpets* was the winning volume in the 1987 Yale Younger Poets Series.

**Robert Kelly** was born in New York in 1935. He is Asher B. Edelman Professor of Literature at Bard College and director of the writing program at the Avery Graduate School of the Arts. His recent books include *Doctor of Silence, Not This Island Music, Flowers of Unceasing Coincidence, Cat Scratch Fever*, and *Strange Market*.

**Richard Kenney** was born in Glens Falls, New York, in 1948. He teaches at the University of Washington. *The Evolution of Flightless Bird* won the 1983 Yale Younger Poets Series competition. His most recent book is *Orrery*.

**Jamaica Kincaid**   lives in North Bennington, Vermont. Her work has appeared in many publications, including *The New Yorker* and *The Paris Review*. Her most recent titles are *Lucy, Annie John, A Small Press,* and *At the Bottom of the River.*

**Galway Kinnell**   was born in Providence, Rhode Island, in 1927 and now lives in Vermont and New York. He teaches at New York University. His *Selected Poems* won the Pulitzer Prize for Poetry in 1983.

**Mary Kinzie**   teaches creative writing at Northwestern University. She is the author of four volumes of poetry, most recently *Autumn Eros.*

**David Kirby**   is McKenzie Professor of English at Florida State University. His most recent works include *Mark Strand and the Poet's Place in Contemporary Culture* and *Writing Poetry: Where Poems Come From and How to Write Them.*

**Judith Kroll**   was born in Brooklyn, New York. She has taught at Vassar College, and for ten years lived in India with her Indian husband. Since 1989 she has taught at the University of Texas at Austin. Her books include *In the Temperate Zone: Poems* and *Chapters in a Mythology: The Poetry of Sylvia Plath.*

**Ursula LeGuin**   was born in Berkeley, California, in 1929. She has won many science-fiction awards. Her books include *The Last Book of Earthsea, Wild Oats & Firewood, The Wind's Twelve Quarters, Orsinian Tales, The Beginning Place,* and *Hard Words and Other Poems.*

**Philip Levine**   was born in Detroit in 1928 and now teaches at California State University in Fresno, California. He has twice received the National Book Critics Circle Award for his poetry. His recent books include *What Work Is* and *New Selected Poems.*

**Robert J. Levy**   won an N.E.A. fellowship in 1988. His work has appeared in *Poetry (Chicago), The Georgia Review, Boulevard, Pequod,* the *Quarterly,* and elsewhere. He has published three collections: *The Glitter Bait, Whistle Maker,* and *Partly Green Till the Day We Die.*

**Leo Litwak** was raised in Detroit and now teaches in the Creative Writing Program at San Francisco State University. His works include *Waiting for the News,* a novel, and *Nobody's Baby and Other Stories.*

**Michael Martone** teaches at Syracuse University. He is the author of three collections of short stories: *Alive and Dead in Indiana, Safety Patrol,* and *Fort Wayne Is Seventh on Hitler's List.*

**William Matthews** was born in Cincinnati, Ohio, in 1942. He is a professor of English at City College in the City University of New York. His recent books of poems include *A Happy Childhood, Foreseeable Futures, Blues If You Want,* and *Selected Poems and Translations 1969–91. Curiosities* is a collection of his essays.

**Tim McCarthy** lives in Kansas City, Missouri. His books include *Hispanics in the U.S.* His fiction has appeared in *The Carolina Quarterly, Arizona Literary Magazine, The Colorado Review,* and other quarterlies. "The Windmill Man" was included in *The Best American Stories of 1978.*

**James McKinley** is director of the Professional Writing Program at the University of Missouri/Kansas City. His work has appeared in such publications as *Playboy* and *The Missouri Review. Acts of Love* is a collection of his short stories, and he is currently at work on another collection.

**Mark McWatt** was born in Guyana in 1947. He is a senior lecturer in English at the University of the West Indies in Barbados and the author of *Interiors* (poems, 1988).

**Daniel Meltzer** lives in New York. His work has appeared in such publications as *The Gettysburg Review* and many other magazines. He received an "Outstanding Writer" citation in the *Pushcart Prize Anthology* for his story "People," which also appeared in *Prize Stories 1992: The O. Henry Awards.*

**W. S. Merwin** was born in New York in 1927 and has lived in Europe and Hawaii. He received the 1971 Pulitzer Prize for

Poetry for *The Carrier of Ladders*. His recent books include *Opening the Hand, Rain in the Trees,* and *The Lost Upland.*

**Grace Morton**  lives in Cambridge, Massachusetts. Her poetry has appeared in *Open Places* and other quarterlies.

**Lisel Mueller**  lives in Lake Forest, Illinois. Her work has appeared in *The Paris Review, Poetry (Chicago), Georgia Review, Poetry East,* and other quarterlies. Her books include *Learning to Play by Ear, Waving from Shore, Second Language,* and *Need to Hold Still.*

**Leonard Nathan**  teaches at the University of California at Berkeley. His work has appeared in such magazines as *The New Yorker, The Atlantic,* and *Salmagundi.* His books include *Carrying On: New and Selected Poems* and *With the Skin.*

**Howard Nemerov** (1920–1992)  was a distinguished poet who won the National Book Award, the Pulitzer Prize for Poetry, and the Bollingen Prize for Poetry. He was a member of the National Institute of Arts and Letters and the American Academy of Arts and Letters. He was the nation's third poet laureate. His books include *Inside the Onion, Sentences,* and *Figures of Thought.*

**Jean Nordhaus**  was born in Baltimore, Maryland. She ran the poetry programs at the Folger Shakespeare Library, 1980–83, and was the winner of a PEN/Faulkner Award for fiction. Her books include *A Language of Hands* and *A Bracelet of Lies.*

**Joyce Carol Oates**  was born in Lockport, New York, in 1938. She is Roger S. Berlind Distinguished Professor in the Humanities at Princeton University. She is the author of over a dozen novels, including *Black Water* (1992) and *them;* for the latter she received the National Book Award. Her short story collections include *By the North Gate, The Wheel of Love, Marriage and Infidelities, Nightside, A Sentimental Education,* and *Last Days.* Among her books of poetry is *The Time Traveler.* Her plays appear in *Twelve Plays.*

**Tim O'Brien** was born in Austin, Minnesota, in 1946. His stories have appeared in such magazines as *Esquire, Atlantic Monthly, Redbook, Shenandoah, The Massachusetts Review,* and *Ploughshares.* His novels include *Northern Lights, If I Die in a Combat Zone, Going After Cacciato,* and *The Nuclear Age.* A recent collection of his stories is *The Things They Carried.*

**Chris Offutt** was born and raised in Kentucky. His stories have appeared in *Ploughshares, Willowsprings, Quarterly West,* and *High Plains Literary Review.*

**Sharon Olds** was born in San Francisco in 1942 and lives in New York. Her work has appeared in such publications as *The New Yorker, The Atlantic Monthly, The Paris Review,* and *The Nation.* Her books include *Satan Says, The Gold Cell,* and *The Dead and the Living.*

**Jay Parini** was born in 1948. He holds a Ph.D. from the University of St. Andrews, Scotland, and teaches at Middlebury College in Vermont. His books include *Singing in Time, Anthracite Country, The Love Run,* and *Town Life.*

**Ishmael Reed** grew up in Buffalo, New York. He is a poet, novelist, playwright, and songwriter. He teaches at the University of California at Berkeley. His books include *Reckless Eyeballing, Japanese By Spring, The Terrible Twos,* and *Writin' Is Fightin': Thirty-Seven Years of Boxing on Paper.*

**Kit Reed** is the author of *Mastering Fiction Writing* (1991). Her work has appeared in a number of magazines and anthologies. Her most recent books include *Gone, Thief of Life and Other Stories,* and *Catholic Girls.*

**Alberto Alvaro Ríos** was born in Nogales, Arizona, in 1952. He teaches at Arizona State University. He has won the Walt Whitman Award, the Western States Book Award for Fiction, and three Pushcart Prizes. His books include *The Lime Orchard Woman, Teodoro Luna's Two Kisses, The Iguana Killer: Twelve Stories of the Heart,* and several collections of poetry.

**Lloyd Schwartz** was born in Brooklyn, New York, in 1941. He is one of the directors of the Creative Writing Program at the

University of Massachusetts in Boston. He has been a music critic for *The Boston Phoenix* and National Public Radio. His books include *These People* and *Goodnight, Gracie.*

**Lynne Sharon Schwartz** lives in New York. Her stories have appeared in such magazines as *Redbook, Ploughshares, Transatlantic Review,* and *The Chicago Review.* Her books include *Disturbances in the Field, Rough Strife, Balancing Acts, Leaving Brooklyn,* and *The Melting Pot and Other Subversive Stories.*

**Charles Simic** was born in Yugoslavia in 1938. He came to the United States in 1949 and lives in New Hampshire. He has received a MacArthur Fellowship (1984) and a Pulitzer Prize for Poetry (1990). He teaches at the University of New Hampshire. The most recent of his many books are *Selected Poems, The Book of Gods and Devils, Hotel Insomnia,* and *The World Doesn't End.*

**William Stafford** was born in Hutchinson, Kansas, in 1914. He is Professor Emeritus at Lewis and Clark College. His many awards include N.E.A. and Guggenheim grants and the National Book Award. He has been named the poet laureate of Oregon. His recent books include *An Oregon Message, You and Some Other Characters, Brother Wind,* and *Wyoming.*

**Mary Swander** has received numerous grants and awards. Her work has appeared in such publications as *The Nation, The New Yorker,* and *Poetry (Chicago).* Her books of poetry include *Succession* and *Driving the Body Back.*

**James Tate** was born in Kansas City, Missouri, in 1943. He teaches at the University of Massachusetts. His first book, *The Lost Pilot,* won the Yale Series of Younger Poets Award in 1966. His other books include *Riven Doggeries, Constant Defender, Reckoner,* and *Distance from Loved Ones.*

**John Updike** was born in Shillington, Pennsylvania, in 1932. He has studied art and worked for *The New Yorker.* His *Rabbit at Rest,* the concluding novel of a biographical quartet, received the 1991 Pulitzer Prize for Fiction. *Rabbit Is Rich* (1981) was awarded both the National Book Award and the 1982 Pulitzer Prize. He received an earlier National Book Award for *The Centaur* (1963). His recent novels include *Memories of the Ford Administration, Roger's Version,* and *The Witches of Eastwick.* Updike has been highly praised for his short stories (*Too Far to Go* and *Pigeon Feathers,* among other collections) and nonfiction (including *Self-Consciousness, Odd Jobs,* and *Hugging the Shore*). He is also the author of several volumes of poetry, including *Facing Nature* (1985).

**Wendy Wasserstein** won the 1989 Pulitzer Prize and a Tony Award for Best Play for *The Heidi Chronicles.* Her plays include *The Sisters Rosensweig, Any Woman Can't, Montpelier Pa-Zazz, Isn't It Romantic,* and *When Dinah Shore Ruled the Earth* (co-authored with Christopher Durang). She has also written for magazines, television, and film.

**Claire Nicolas White** lives in St. James, Long Island, New York. Her work has appeared in many quarterlies, including *The Partisan Review, Anais, Primavera, Confrontation,* and *Footwork.* Her recent books include *Fragments of Stained Glass* and *River Boy.*

**Charles Wright** was born in Tennessee in 1935. He is a poet-in-residence at the University of Virginia. He won a PEN translation prize for his translation of Eugenio Montale's *The Storm and Other Poems* and was co-recipient of the National Book Award in 1983 for *Country Music: Selected Early Poems.* His recent books include *The World of the 10,000 Things, Zone Journals,* and *Half Life.*

**Al Young** is a novelist and poet who has taught at Stanford University, the University of California, and the University of Washington and has been Andrew Mellon Professor of Humanities at Rice University. His recent books include *Kinds of Blue, Bodies and Soul, Heaven: Collected Poems 1956–1990,* and *Seduction by Light.*

# Permissions
# and
# Acknowledgments

# Permissions and Acknowledgments

**Aaron, Jonathan.** "The Foreigner" from *Second Sight* by Jonathan Aaron. Copyright © 1982 by HarperCollins Publishers. Reprinted by permission of HarperCollins Publishers.

**Abbot, Lee K.** "What She's Saying Now" by Lee K. Abbott. From *Witness*, Volumes 1 and 2, Summer 1987. Reprinted with the permission of the author.

**Ai.** "The Mortician's Twelve-Year-Old Son" from *The Killing Floor* by Ai. Copyright © 1979 by Ai. Reprinted by permission of Houghton Mifflin Company. All rights reserved.

**Alvaro Rios, Alberto.** "Waltz of the Fat Man" by Alberto Alvaro Rios. From *Kenyon Review*, Vol. 13, No. 3, Summer 1991. Reprinted by permission of the author.

**Apple, Max.** *Trotsky's Bar Mitzvah*, by Max Apple. From *Antaeus 67*, Fall 1991. Reprinted by permission of the author.

**Appleman, Philip.** "Gathering at the River" from *Let There Be Light* by Philip Appleman. Copyright © 1991 by HarperCollins Publishers. Reprinted by permission of the author.

**Arenas, Rosa Maria.** "Mother of Shrines" by Rosa Maria Arenas. From *Kenyon Review*, Vol. 13, No. 4, Fall 1991. Reprinted by permission of the author.

**Ascher, Carol.** "In Sight of Josephine" by Carol Ascher. From *Witness*, Vol. 1, No. 4, 1987. Reprinted by permission of the author.

**Atwood, Margaret.** "Happy Endings" from *Murder in the Dark* by Margaret Atwood. Copyright © 1983 Coach House Press. Reprinted by permission of the author.
"Variations on the Word *Sleep*" and "Last Day" from *True Stories* by Margaret Atwood. Copyright © 1981 by Margaret Atwood. Reprinted by permission of the author.

**Barnes, Kate.** "The Old Lady's Story" by Kate Barnes. From *Beloit Poetry Journal*, Fall 1991. Reprinted by permission of the author.

**Bloom, Amy.** "Love is Not a Pie" from *A Room of One's Own* by Amy Bloom. Copyright © 1990 by Amy Bloom. Originally published in A Room of One's Own and *The Best American Short Stories 1991*, edited by Alice Adams. "Love is Not a Pie" is included in her collection of short stories *Come to Me*, published by HarperCollins Publishers in May of 1993.

**Bond, Bruce.** "Gallery of Rivers" by Bruce Bond. Reprinted by permission of the author. First appeared in *Quarterly Review of Literature.*

**Bowles, Paul.** "The Eye" from *A Distant Episode* by Paul Bowles. Copyright © 1988 by Paul Bowles. Reprinted by permission of the author.

**Campbell, Mary B.** "Money," "Sexual Terrorist," and "Warning: Nuclear Waste Dump" from *The World, the Flesh, and the Angels* by Mary B. Campbell. Copyright © 1989 by Beacon Press. Reprinted by permission of the author.

**Carver, Raymond.** "The Toes" by Raymond Carver. From *Poetry*, Vol. CLI, Nos. 1-2, 1987. Reprinted by permission of Tess Gallagher.

**Chernoff, Maxine.** "The New Money," copyright © Maxine Chernoff, is reprinted from her book *Leap Year Day: New and Selected Poems* (Another Chicago Press, Box 11223, Chicago, Illinois 60611; 1990), and is used by permission.

**Clark, Tom.** "Reading the Technical Journals" and "Looking for Work in Teaching" Copyright © 1987 by Tom Clark. Reprinted from *Disordered Ideas* with the permission of the Black Sparrow Press.

**Cooley, Nicole Ruth.** "In Starkville" by Nicole Ruth Cooley. From *Iowa Review*, Vol. 21, No. 2, 1991. Reprinted by permission of the author.

**Cooperman, Robert.** "Isabella Bird Rides in a Round-Up, Colorado Territory, 1873" by Robert Cooperman. From *Webster Review*, Fall 1988. Reprinted by permission of the author.

**Dabydeen, David.** "Coolie Mother" by David Dabydeen. From *Graham House Review*, No. 14, Spring 1991, Hansib Publications. Reprinted by permission of the author.

**Dixon, Stephen.** "Takes" from *Love and Will* by Stephen Dixon. Copyright © 1989 by British American Publishing. Reprinted by permission of the author.

**Doty, Mark.** "Noir" by Mark Doty. From *Mississippi Review*, Vol. 17, No. 3, 1989. Reprinted by permission of the author.

**Dugan, Alan.** "Against the Text 'Art is Immortal' " by Alan Dugan. Originally from *Agni*, 1990. Reprinted by permission of the author.

**Dybek, Stuart.** "Pet Milk" from *The Coast of Chicago* by Stuart Dybek. Copyright © 1990 by Alfred Knopf, Inc., New York. Reprinted by permission of the author.

**Egan, Jennifer.** "Sacred Heart" copyright © 1991 by Jennifer Egan. Reprinted by arrangement with Virginia Barber Literary Agency, Inc. All rights reserved.

**Giovanni, Nikki.** "Kidnap Poem," "Revolutionary Dreams," and "Poem for a Lady Whose Voice I Like" from *The Women and the Men* by Nikki Giovanni. Copyright © 1975 William Morrow and Co., New York. Reprinted by permission of the author.

**Goldbarth, Albert.** "Lullabye" by Albert Goldbarth. From *Beloit Poetry Journal*, Winter 1991-1992. Reprinted by permission of the author.

**Goodison, Lorna.** "On Becoming a Tiger" by Lorna Goodison. From *Michigan Quarterly Review*, Fall 1991. Reprinted by permission of the author.

**Gordimer, Nadine.** "A Find" by Nadine Gordimer. From *Salmagundi*, Fall/Winter 1990-1991, No. 88-89. Reprinted by permission of the author.

**Grennan, Eamon.** "Winn's Blackbird" and "Hieroglyphic" from *What Light There Is* by Eamon Grennan. Copyright © 1989 North Point Press. Reprinted by permission of the author.

**Gunn, Thom.** "From the wave" from *Moly and My Sad Captains* by Thom Gunn. Copyright © 1973 by Thom Gunn. Reprinted by permission Farrar, Straus & Giroux, Inc.

**Gurney, A. R., Jr.** *The Problem* copyright © 1968 by A. R. Gurney, Jr. ALL RIGHTS RESERVED.

CAUTION: Professionals and amateurs are hereby warned that *The Problem* is subject to a royalty. It is fully protected under the copyright laws of the United States of America, the British Commonwealth, including Canada, and all the countries of the Copyright Union. All rights, including professional, amateur, motion pictures, recitation, lecturing, public reading, radio broadcasting, television, and the rights of translation into foreign languages, are strictly reserved. In its present form the play is dedicated to the reading public only.

*The Problem* may be given stage presentation by amateurs in theatres seating less than 500 upon payment of a royalty of fifteen dollars for the first performance, and ten dollars for each additional performance. PLEASE NOTE: For amateur productions in theatres seating over 500, write for special royalty quotation, giving details as to ticket price, number of performances, and exact number of seats in your theatre. Royalties are payable one week before the opening performance of the play, to Samuel French, Inc., at 45 W. 25th St., New York, N.Y. 10010;

or at 7623 Sunset Blvd., Hollywood, California 90046; or to Samuel French (Canada), Ltd. 80 Richmond St. East, Toronto, Ontario, Canada M5C 1P1.
Royalty of the required amount must be paid whether the play is presented for charity or gain and whether or not admission is charged. French, Inc.
Stock royalty quoted on application to Samuel French, Inc.
For all other rights than those stipulated above, apply to Samuel Particular emphasis is laid on the question of amateur or professional readings, permission and terms or which must be secured in writing from Samuel French, Inc. Copying from this book in whole or in part is strictly forbidden by law, and the right of performance is not transferable.
Whenever the play is produced the following notice must appear on all programs, printing and advertising for the play: "Produced by special arrangement with Samuel French, Inc."
Due authorship credit must be given on all programs, printing, and advertising for the play.

**Hacker, Marilyn.** "Her Ring" by Marilyn Hacker. From *Kenyon Review*, Vol. 13, No. 2, Spring 1991. Reprinted by permission of the author.

**Hansen, Twyla.** "Garbage" from *How to Live in the Heartland* by Twyla Hansen. Copyright © 1992 by Twyla Hansen; originally appeared in West Branch.

**Hollander, John.** "Coordinating Conjunction" from *Harp Lake* by John Hollander. Copyright © 1988 by John Hollander. Reprinted by permission of Alfred A. Knopf, Inc.

**Hoover, Paul.** "Long History of the Short Poem" by Paul Hoover. From *Idea*, copyright © The Figures Publishing Company. Reprinted by permission of the author.

**Ignatow, David.** "Witness" by David Ignatow. From *Poetry*, Vol. CLI, Nos. 1-2, 1987. Reprinted by permission of the author.

**Jacobsen, Josephine.** "The Thing About Crows" by Josephine Jacobsen. From *Kenyon Review*, Vol. 13, No. 2, Spring 1991. Reprinted by permission of the author.
"The Woods" by Josephine Jacobsen. From *Ploughshares*, 1991. Reprinted by permission of the author.

**Jones, Alice.** "Anorexia" is reprinted from *The Knot* by permission of the author and Alicejamesbooks. Copyright © 1992 Alice Jones. Originally published in The Cream City Review, 1991.

**Kelly, Brigit Pegeen.** "Young Wife's Lament" from *To the Place of Trumpets* by Brigit Pegeen Kelly. Copyright © 1988 Yale University Press. Reprinted by permission of the author and Yale University Press.

**Kelly, Robert.** "The Venus of Mount Rutsen" and "Farewell Letter" copyright © 1987 by Robert Kelly. Reprinted from *Not This Island Music* with the permission of Black Sparrow Press.

**Kenney, Richard.** "March Orrery" and "Aubade" from *Orrery* by Richard Kenney. Copyright © 1985 by Atheneum, Inc. Reprinted by permission of the author.

**Kincaid, Jamaica.** "What I Have Been Doing Lately" from *At the Bottom of the River* by Jamaica Kincaid. Copyright © 1981, 1983 by Jamaica Kincaid. Reprinted by permission of Farrar, Straus & Giroux, Inc.

**Kinnell, Galway.** "The Geese" and "The Shroud" from *The Past* by Galway Kinnell. Copyright © 1985 by Galway Kinnell. Reprinted by permission of Houghton Mifflin Company. All rights reserved.

**Kinzie, Mary.** "Sun and Moon" from *Autumn Eros and Other Poems* by Mary Kinzie. Copyright © 1991 Alfred A. Knopf, New York.

**Kirby, David.** "A Poor Unhappy Wretched Sick Miserable Little French Boy" by David Kirby. From *Chattahoochee Review*, Vol. XI, No. 2, Winter 1991. Reprinted by permission of the author.

**Kroll, Judith.** "The Speed of Light" by Judith Kroll. From *Quarterly Review of Literature*, Poetry Series X, Vol. XXX, 1991. Reprinted by permission of the author.

**Le Guin, Ursula K.** "The Maenads" copyright © 1988 by Ursula K. Le Guin; first appeared in *Wild Oats and Fireweed*; reprinted by permission of the author and the author's agent, Virginia Kidd.
"Silence" copyright © 1986 by Ursula K. Le Guin; first appeared in *Calapooya Collage 10*; reprinted by permission of the author and the author's agent, Virginia Kidd.

**Levine, Philip.** "Keats in California" by Philip Levine. From *Poetry*, Vol. CLI, Nos. 1-2, 1987. Reprinted by permission of the author.
"The Sweetness of Bobby Hefka" from *What Work* Is by Philip Levine. Copyright © 1991 by Philip Levine. Reprinted by permission of Alfred A. Knopf, Inc.

**Levy, Robert J.** "Paradise Fish" by Robert J. Levy. Originally printed in *Southwest Review*, Spring 1991. Reprinted by permission of the author.

**Litwak, Leo.** "Mouth to Mouth" by Leo Litwak. From *Witness*, Vol. 1, No. 2, Summer 1987. Reprinted by permission of the author.

**Martone, Michael.** "It's Time" by Michael Martone. From *Voices Louder than Words and North American Review* 1991. Reprinted by permission of the author.

**Matthews, William.** "Landscape with Onlooker" by William Matthews. Reprinted by permission of the author. Originally published in *The New Yorker*, copyright © 1991.

**McCarthy, Tim.** "The Windmill Man" by Tim McCarthy. From *Colorado Quarterly*, 1978. Reprinted by permission of the author.

**McKinley, James.** "Ozark Episode" from *Acts of Love* by James McKinley. Copyright © 1987 Breitenbush Books, Portland, Oregon. Reprinted by permission of the author. James McKinley is editor of *New Letters*, a literary quarterly, and director of the Professional Writing Program at the University of Missouri-Kansas City.

**McWatt, Mark.** "Penelope" by Mark McWatt. From *Graham House Review*, No. 14, Spring 1991, Colgate University Press, Hamilton, N.Y. Reprinted by permission of the author.

**Meltzer, Daniel.** "People" by Daniel Meltzer. "People" was first published in the Fall 1990 edition of *Gettysburg Review*. It was the winner of an O. Henry Prize and appears in Prize Stories 1990: *The O. Henry Awards*, published by Anchor Publishing, a division of Doubleday Publishing, New York. "People" also received an "Outstanding Writer" citation in the *Pushcart Prize Anthology*, by Pushcart Press.

**Merwin, W. S.** "At Home" from *Finding the Islands* by W. S. Merwin. Copyright © 1982 by W. S. Merwin.

**Mueller, Lisel.** "Insomnia" and "Statues" by Lisel Mueller. From *Willow Springs 28*, Summer 1991. Reprinted by permission of the author.

**Nathan, Leonard.** "Ragged Sonnets" by Leonard Nathan. From *Salmagundi 90-91*, Spring 1991. Reprinted by permission of the author.

**Nemerov, Howard.** "The Air Force Museum at Dayton" from *Inside the Onion* by Howard Nemerov. Copyright © 1984, University of Chicago Press. Reprinted by permission of the Howard Nemerov Trust.

**Nordhaus, Jean.** "My Life in Hiding" by Jean Nordhaus. From *Quarterly Review of Literature*, Poetry Series X, Vol. XXX, 1991. Reprinted by permission of the author.

**Oates, Joyce Carol.** "Nairobi" by Joyce Carol Oates. From *Paris Review*, 1984. Copyright © 1984 by Joyce Carol Oates. Reprinted by permission of John Hawkins & Associates, Inc.
*Under/Ground*, from *Twelve Plays*, by Joyce Carol Oates. Copyright © 1991 by The Ontario Review, Inc. Used by permission of New American Library, a division of Penguin Books USA Inc.

**O'Brien, Tim.** "The Things They Carried" from *The Things They Carried* by Tim O'Brien. Copyright © 1990 by Tim O'Brien. Reprinted by permission of Houghton Mifflin Company/Seymour Lawrence. All rights reserved.

**Offutt, Chris.** "Sawdust" by Chris Offutt. From *Northwest Review*, Vol. 20, No. 2, 1991. Reprinted by arrangement with the Virginia Barber Literary Agency, Inc. All rights reserved.

**Olds, Sharon.** "Topography" from *The Gold Cell* by Sharon Olds. Copyright © 1987 Alfred A. Knopf, Inc. "Sex Without Love" and "Pajamas" from *The Dead and the Living* by Sharon Olds. Copyright © 1984 Alfred A. Knopf, Inc. Reprinted by permission of the author.

**Parini, Jay.** "Coal Train" and "Working the Face" from *Anthracite Country* by Jay Parini. Copyright © 1982 by Random House, New York. Reprinted by permission of the author.

**Reed, Ishmael.** "Bitter Chocolate" and "Grizzly" from *New and Collected Poems of Ishmael Reed* by Ishmael Reed. Copyright © 1988 Atheneum, a division of Macmillan, New York. Reprinted by permission of the author.

**Reed, Kit.** "Winter" by Kit Reed. Copyright © 1969. Reprinted by permission of Kit Reed and Macmillan, London.

**Schwartz, Lloyd.** "Leaves" by Lloyd Schwartz. From *Goodnight, Gracie*. Copyright © 1992 University of Chicago Press. Originally published in *The New Republic*, 1991.

**Schwartz, Lynne Sharon.** "Killing the Bees" from *The Melting Pot* by Lynne Sharon Schwartz. Copyright © 1987 by Lynne Sharon Schwartz. Reprinted by permission of HarperCollins Publishers.

**Stafford, William.** "A Proposition" by William Stafford. From *Willow Springs* 27, Winter 1991. Reprinted by permission of the author.

**Swander, Mary.** "The Tattooed Man Comes for a Massage" by Mary Swander. From *Southwest Review*, Summer 1991. Reprinted by permission of the author.

**Tate, James.** "I Am A Finn" and "I Am Still A Finn" by James Tate. From *Iowa Review*, 1991. Reprinted by permission of the author.

**Updike, John.** "Should Wizard Hit Mommy?" from *Pigeon Feathers and Other Stories* by John Updike. Copyright © 1959 by John Updike. Reprinted by permission of Alfred A. Knopf, Inc. Originally appeared in The New Yorker.

**Wasserstein, Wendy.** *Tender Offer* by Wendy Wasserstein. From *Antaeus*, Spring 1991. Reprinted by permission of the author.

**White, Claire Nicolas.** "Home-Coming" by Claire Nicolas White. From *Primavera*, Vol. 14-15, 1991. Reprinted by permission of the author.

**Wright, Charles.** "California Spring," "Dog Yoga," and "Laguna Blues," by Charles Wright. From *The Southern Cross*. Copyright © 1981, Random House, Inc., New York. Reprinted by permission of the author.

**Young, Al.** "The Blues Don't Change," "New Autumn, New York," and "Falling Asleep in a Darkening Room" reprinted by permission of Louisiana State University Press from *The Blues Don't Change: New and Selected Poems* by Al Young. Copyright © 1982 by Al Young.

# Indices

# Index

The names of contributing writers appear in CAPITAL LETTERS; the titles of plays, novels, and poems in *italic type;* and the titles of short stories within quotation marks.

## Index of First Lines of Poems

# About the Authors

Robert DeMaria is professor of English and director of the writing program at Dowling College in Oakdale, New York. He has published more than a dozen novels, beginning with *A Carnival of Angels* in 1961. In praising the "extravagant comic virtuousity" of his *Decline and Fall of America*, the *Antioch Review* hailed Mr. DeMaria as "one of the ablest satirists writing today." His short fiction and poetry have appeared in *Antæus, Southwest Review, California Quarterly*, and *New Letters*, among other journals. A onetime editor with Macmillan, Mr. DeMaria is a member of the Authors Guild and of PEN, an international poets', writers', and editors' organization.

Ellen Hope Meyer is a freelance writer and adjunct associate professor of English at Dowling College. Before turning to writing and teaching, she was a theatrical designer in London and New York, where her experience included work with the Metropolitan Opera. She was also co-editor of *The Mediterranean Review*, an international quarterly. Her works include the novel *Extreme Remedies*, published by Dell; she is now writing a second.